# Enriching the Sociological Imagination

# Studies in Critical Social Sciences

*Series Editor*

DAVID FASENFEST
College of Urban, Labor and Metropolitan Affairs
Wayne State University

*Editorial Board*

JOAN ACKER, Department of Sociology, University of Oregon
ROSE BREWER, Afro-American and African Studies, University of Minnesota
VAL BURRIS, Department of Sociology, University of Oregon
CHRIS CHASE-DUNN, Department of Sociology, University of California-Riverside
G. WILLIAM DOMHOFF, Department of Sociology, University of California-Santa Cruz
COLLETTE FAGAN, Department of Sociology, Manchester University
MARTHA GIMENEZ, Department of Sociology, University of Colorado, Boulder
HEIDI GOTTFRIED, CULMA, Wayne State University
KARIN GOTTSCHALL, Zentrum für Sozialpolitik, University of Bremen
BOB JESSOP, Department of Sociology, Lancaster University
RHONDA LEVINE, Department of Sociology, Colgate University
JACKIE O'REILLY, WZB, Berlin
MARY ROMERO, School of Justice Studies, Arizona State University
CHIZUKO UENO, Department of Sociology, University of Tokyo

# Enriching the Sociological Imagination

## How Radical Sociology Changed the Discipline

*Edited by*

Rhonda F. Levine

ENRICHING THE SOCIOLOGICAL IMAGINATION
*Edited by* Rhonda F. Levine

© Koninklijke Brill NV 2004
© Aakar Books for South Asia 2016

First Published in India 2016

ISBN 978-93-5002-436-2

Published in agreement with Koninklijke Brill NV, Leiden, The Ņeatherlands for publication and sale only in the Indian Subcontinent (India, Pakistan, Bangladesh, Nepal, Maldives, Bhutan and Sri Lanka)

All rights reserved. No part of this book may be reproduced or transmitted, in any form or by any means, without the prior permission of the publisher.

*Published by*
**AAKAR BOOKS**
28 E Pocket IV, Mayur Vihar Phase I, Delhi 110 091
Phones : 011 2279 5505, 2279 5641
aakarbooks@gmail.com; www.aakarbooks.com

*Printed at*
Sapra Brothers, Delhi 110 092

## Contents

# Preface

The 21st Century began with a very different political and social environment when compared with most of the last century: Capitalism as a system evolved from national and rapacious, to international and imperial, to global and invasive. The revolutionary workers' movements at the start of the last century, with its hopes for international solidarity in the struggle against capitalism begun at the end the 19th Century, culminating in the Russian Revolution of Workers and Peasants in 1917 and the Chinese Revolution in 1949, faded by the end of the 20th Century with the dissolution of the Soviet Union and with China experimenting with a "people's capitalism". The social welfare gains won in industrial Europe and to some extent the United States have been eroded in the name of liberal deregulation, international competition, and global rationalization. The Third World is much worse off both relatively and in most cases even absolutely as developed countries, that had promised spreading of the wealth, have turn their backs – or perhaps have never made a full effort to improve these countries economically.

For the last 35 years scholars associated with the *Insurgent Sociologist*, and more recently *Critical Sociology*, have sought to both understand and change the social, political and economic climate of this society (and by extension how our society impacts on the rest of the world). As Rhonda Levine's Introduction to this volume chronicles, the journal charts a journey that brings radical and critical thinking into the mainstream of sociology. In 1999 a decision was made to celebrate 25 years of articles in the journal that helped shape the academic landscape and created a whole generation of scholars by publishing a retrospective issue with updated commentary by the original authors. The response was very positive and many people asked how this issue could be made more widely available. After discussions with Joed Elich at Brill Academic Press, and with the recognition that the time is right to provide an outlet for new critical writings, this series was created. It is dedicated to publishing expanded versions of recent special issues of *Critical Sociology* as well as new books and collections of essays.

We launch the series with this volume, a update of *Critical Sociology* 25:2/3 to reflect on 30 years of critical scholarship, because we believe we can look forward by looking back. In addition, this first volume ends with a challenge that critical sociologists – who have managed to bring radical thinking into the mainstream – should now bring their analysis of contemporary society into the mainstream of public discussion. This volume helps us see what we have accomplished and what still needs to be done.

Future volumes we will be guided by two general conceptual frameworks. First, that Marx was a thinker and writer who provided us with perhaps the most comprehensive analysis of capitalism as a system of production unlike no other that came before. Many have prematurely heralded the end of Marxism because of the end of the European experiment with some version of socialism. However, so long as we live in a capitalist society Marx still provides us with best tools and concepts to help us understand how that society works so that we can continue to struggle for positive social change.

Second, Marx and Marxism is not a complete system of thought in response to our complex society. As the scholarship of the past 50 years by critical scholars of race and gender should make clear, there are serious gaps that continue to demand our attention. The second volume of this series, *Race and Ethnicity – Across Time, Space and Discipline* edited by Rodney Coates, takes up the question of how must be understood as part of the very fabric of society and cannot be analyzed as a thing on its own. There are concerns of culture, history, sexuality, ethnicity, and many others that are not addressed by the central writings of Marx. Furthermore, capitalism today is not the capitalism of 150 years ago; globalization and new information technologies have introduced new problems and presented old relationship in new ways.

The coming century offers us many new challenges. As the events in Chiapas, Mexico, the farmers' movements against the McDonald Corporation in France, efforts by workers to organize internationally, and the rising awareness of local communities everywhere as they struggle with and resist the consequences of globalization all make clear, we live in a time with new and old forms of resistance and opposition to the course of modern capitalism. Future volumes in this series will endeavor to address the challenges posted by this new century, will offer new insights and recast old theories, and will promote critical social science research.

David Fasenfest, series editor
Detroit, Michigan

Rhonda F. Levine

# Introduction: Legacies of *The Insurgent Sociologist*

"Don't trust anyone over 30." I suspect that many people over 50 (and maybe some a little younger) are like me in remembering how often we said that as we protested various social injustices and made our way as aspiring sociologists. In our efforts, we had the aid and encouragement of a radical publication that was way under 30 itself, and therefore much to be trusted. I refer of course to *The Insurgent Sociologist*, which helped many of us chart the course of our careers as radical and critical sociologists. But now, *The Insurgent*, as we affectionately called it, is well over 30, just like many of us, and it is has been renamed *Critical Sociology* to mark its success and adulthood. Looking back over its history, and thinking about how it helped us reshape sociology, we now know we can trust people and journals over 30.

In this book, some of the classic articles from *The Insurgent Sociologist* return as a springboard for carrying forth the project of radical sociology into the 21st century, hopefully rejuvenating former insurgents and appealing to a new generation of critical sociologists – a new generation that should at least trust us veterans of earlier decades a little bit.[1] This

[1] This book is an outgrowth of a special issue of *Critical Sociology* edited by Beth Mintz and me. *Critical Sociology* 25:2/3 celebrated the 15 years when the journal was called *The Insurgent Sociologist* by presenting edited versions of influential articles that appeared in it and became the basis for many books and extended articles. Some of these articles and additional ones are reprinted in this volume.

book therefore serves as both a reminder of how *The Insurgent Sociologist* helped transform sociology and as a basis for renewing a critical and relevant sociology, this time as both a public and scientific sociology. It celebrates the past by reprinting – in compacted ways that highlight the key points – the kinds of articles that made *The Insurgent* so essential to the effort to develop a radical sociology that would provide the critical lens to expose an unjust social structure and provide a framework for its restructuring.

However, this book also points to the future by including the current thoughts and reflections of the original authors, based on their later research and new developments in the discipline. They often state frankly where they think they went a little wrong on some points, and then suggest how we and they can do better in the future. Some of these authors may have changed their minds in interesting ways on some points, but they certainly have not given up on a critical sociology. They are still trying both to further transform the discipline and to provide frameworks for a more egalitarian, just, and open society. It is this dialogue between the past and the present that gives this book the spontaneity and spark that characterized *The Insurgent Sociologist* in its most exciting days.

*The Insurgent Sociologist* first appeared in 1969 as a newspaper put out by the now-defunct Sociology Liberation Movement/Union of Radical Sociology, and in 1971 it began publishing as a quarterly journal, headquartered at the University of Oregon with an editorial collective guided by the late Al Szymanski. The journal was clearly a product of the political and intellectual ferment of the time. The student movements of the 1960s and early 1970s supplied a vision of a different world and we thought sociology offered the tools for implementation.[2] *The Insurgent Sociologist* was the outlet for the developing critical and radical scholarship, at the time largely unwelcome in traditional sociology departments and professional journals.

The journal played a central role in furthering the growth and development of a radical sociology in the 1970s that oftentimes took Marxism as a point of departure, but also included debates about the usefulness of Marxism and on how it might need to be modified. *The Insurgent Sociologist* indeed viewed itself as "insurgent," differentiating itself from a mainstream sociology

---

[2] For a wider discussion on the Sociology Liberation Movement see Oppenheimer, Murray, and Levine (1991).

that too often legitimated a system of inequality and domination. In its newspaper days, it printed the call for a counter-convention to the 1969 American Sociological Association convention, listing radical sessions and radical activities that challenged the mainstream sessions and activities. It also printed important statements on what the role of radical sociology ought to be, which argued about whether it should be outside of academia aiding various social movements, orienting research to aid social movements, exposing biases in research that served to reproduce the status quo, changing the ASA, and/or protecting radicals in teaching positions.

*The Insurgent* was one of the few publications that covered the politically motivated firings of radical sociologists. It also printed important initiatives like the 1969 statement and resolutions to the general business meeting of the ASA by the Women's Caucus (soon to be Sociologists for Women in Society). In its newspaper form, *The Insurgent* also published responses to Reinhard Bendix's 1970 ASA presidential address after the association refused to publish these responses in any ASA-sponsored journal. In its early journal phase, *The Insurgent* published discussions on what organizational form, if any, radical sociologists should take within the professional association. Many of those early dialogues found their way into the by-laws of the Marxist Sociology Section of the ASA. *The Insurgent* also played a major role in compiling and publicizing the alternate slate of candidates for elective ASA offices in 1974, with the hope of opening up the association to a wider spectrum of sociological perspectives. Then, rightfully ignoring its usual suspicion of those well over 30, the journal campaigned wholeheartedly for the election of one of the few radical sociologists who had stayed the course since the 1930s, Alfred McClung Lee, who thereby became the first insurgent president of ASA in 1976.

By the mid-1970s, then, the ASA began to open up the professional gates, as also demonstrated by the acceptance of the Marxist Sociology Section as an official part of the ASA. With professional battles largely won, *The Insurgent* was soon transformed into a journal for insightful and path breaking articles that sought to understand the complexities of continued social inequality, the ways that power and resources were distributed, and how we could begin to build a better society. These articles discussed and debated the significance of capitalism as a system of exploitation, the changing nature of the class system across time and space, the role of power and ideology, and steps to overcome systems of injustice. Articles tended to focus primarily on the United

States, and issues of race, gender, and culture tended to take a back seat to social class concerns, at least in the early years.

The journal was more, though, than merely an alternative academic voice. It served also as a socializing agent for an entire generation of young sociologists. When I decided to go to graduate school, for example, I remember going through *The Insurgent*, looking at the institutional affiliations of its authors to help me decide which sociology programs to apply to. It must be a good program, I thought, if faculty are publishing in this radical journal, one that I began subscribing to in 1973. So, naturally, the highlight of my first participation in an annual ASA meeting (1976) was going to *The Insurgent* table and meeting Al Szymanski. Al and the others who had table duty when I happened by were not only actively selling issues of the journal, including copies of back issues at bargain prices, but they would talk to anyone and everyone about anything at all to convince them to read the journal and use it in the classroom. For several years thereafter, *The Insurgent* table was not only *the* place where the most intellectually exciting discussions were happening as far as I was concerned, but also the most politically relevant. It was there that we could find out about the activities and sessions of the Marxist Sociology Section and other radical groups, and feel part of a progressive sociological community. The journal provided a place, both figuratively and concretely, for many of us who felt marginalized by the sociological mainstream, as represented by those who were in leadership positions of the ASA and most of its sections.

As Richard Flacks and Michael Burawoy both state in their reflections on the discipline for this book, mainstream sociology turned out to be far more responsive to a critical approach than most of us ever would have imagined. It was able to incorporate much of radical sociology into a revised model that transformed the mainstream from a monolithic whole based on the one right method into the heterogeneous and vibrant discipline it is today. By the mid-1980s, radical sociology was no longer "insurgent" because issues of class, race, gender, and even Marxist theory had found their place at annual meetings and in academically respected journals. The discipline and profession were becoming more open to alternative perspectives, so much so that when gay, lesbian, and transgendered sociologists demanded a place at the table, hardly an eyebrow was raised. So, in 1987, in a very different political context, *The Insurgent* left behind its youthful past and changed its name to *Critical Sociology*. Then in 1999, *Critical Sociology* took another big step by leaving the collective management at the University of Oregon that had been its home for so long to begin a new life with a commercial publisher. Like radical sociology itself, *Critical Sociology* has come a long way from its modest beginnings.

Not only has radical sociology impacted the discipline, but radical sociologists became leaders in the profession. This has long been evident in state and regional associations, where many important discussions of teaching and methodology take place, and where graduate students are socialized into the discipline. Now it is reflected in the increasing representation of insurgent and feminist sociologists on the Council of the ASA, and in the growing list of prominent critical sociologists who have held an elected office and followed Alfred McClung Lee into the presidency of the association.

The articles included in this book reflect radical sociology's continuing interest in capitalist development and in questions of class, of race and gender, and of the structure of power. Both theoretical considerations and empirical studies are included here to illustrate the breadth of the historical contributions of radical sociology. To capture a sense of the ambitious goals that radical sociologists originally set for themselves, the first section reprints Flacks' 1972 "Towards a Socialist Sociology: Some Proposals for Work in the Coming Period," which he wrote "so that radical sociology could move beyond criticism of the discipline and become helpful in providing an intellectual basis for the movements for change in the U.S." In his reactions to what he wrote back then, "The Trajectory of a Radical Sociology: Reflections," Flacks succinctly summarizes the key assumptions of radical sociologists and compares the world we live in now with the one envisioned over 30 years ago. Flacks notes that sociology has changed a great deal since the 1970s because of the influence of radical sociologists, but at the same time he argues that professional advancement, not social mobilization, has largely shaped the work of many leftist academics. Undaunted by the many unexpected directions taken by American society since the 1970s, Flacks thinks it remains a worthy agenda for radical sociology to help develop "frameworks of action that can promote genuinely democratic restructuring." Readers may want to compare what he says with what is proposed by Burawoy in the final chapter, "The Critical Turn to Pubic Sociology," as a way to go beyond what radical sociology has accomplished up to this point.

With the article and reflection by Flacks providing a context, the second section on power and class captures a dominant theme of *The Insurgent Sociologist*. Goran Therborn's "What Does The Ruling Class Do When It Rules?", reprinted numerous times, looks at the different ways that power can be conceptualized, rooting his analysis in classical Marxist thought. In his reflection, he wonders whether the framing of his initial question in terms of class struggle has merit today when the ruling class appears to be all powerful and there seems to be little class struggle. He now believes that future challenges to the rulers of the world will come from other sources than industrial labor. But even though today's questions about power may be less specific than they were thirty years ago, he still sees a great need for both insurgent sociologists and a critical sociology.

G. William Domhoff's "State and Ruling Class in Corporate America," is one of several articles he published in the journal over the years. He describes it in his refection as his "most gratifying" *Insurgent* publication because its contents were the culmination of the cumulative effort by power structure researchers to answer the claims of the reigning orthodoxy of the time, the pluralists. His article reminds us of the vibrancy and passion that animated the debates around power structure research in the 1970s and 1980s. His reflections on that heady time give him the opportunity to correct what he sees as empirical mistakes, but most of all he focuses on how changes in the power structure triggered by the Civil Rights Movement have made it possible for the left to consider new political strategies in the 21st century.

Harvey Molotch and Marilyn Lester's "Accidents, Scandals, and Routines: Resources for Unsurgent Methodology" explores the ways through which the powerful work to construct and interpret the experiences of general publics, but the article also turns the tables and shows how sociologists can take advantage of accidents and scandals that the ruling class cannot anticipate or control in order to learn more about how the power structure operates. It advocates a methodology that is an example of insurgent sociology at its best. Looking back on this effort, Molotch reaffirms our continuing need for methods and tools that can provide concrete ways of investigating the power-knowledge process.

The third section includes a series of articles that are unified by their attention to class and inequality. Samuel Bowles, Herbert Gintis, and Peter Meyer argue in "The Long Shadow of Work: Education, the Family, and the Reproduction of the Social Division of Labor" that we can better understand the social relations of the American educational system by exploring the capitalist economy in which it is rooted. The article presents many of the ideas developed more fully in the award-winning *Schooling in Capitalist Society.*

Bowles and Gintis now believe they did not pay enough attention to what schools should be, but they still hold that schools continue to be "the testing grounds and battlegrounds for building a more just and freer society." Val Burris' "Class Structure and Political Ideology" is part of the very important project of understanding intermediate class positions, arguing that Marxist debates on class structure have not resolved the ambiguity of boundaries between proletarian and non – proletarian class positions and its implication for political strategy. His current thoughts on that debate suggest there has been a fruitful dialogue between Marxist and Weberian perspectives on class. However, Burris notes that just when class analysis has made inroads into mainstream sociology, it has declined in importance among those on the left because concepts of race and gender have come to dominate much research on social inequality. For Burris, the future of class analysis, in terms of theory and research, is filled with both opportunity and challenge.

Martha Gimenez's "The Feminization of Poverty: Myth or Reality?" had an impact when it first appeared in 1987 as a timely and much needed critique of the "feminization of poverty" literature. Drawing on her Marxist framework, she convincingly argues that relying on broad categories of this sort obscures the larger processes of social transformation, which are generating declining standards of living for the entire working class. As she notes in her reflection, this point is still lost on much sociological research on poverty because the dominant way of thinking about poverty separates it from the class structure. Gimenez argues that we need to think of the poor as the most vulnerable layer of the working class, and then investigate the ways other forms of exclusion and oppression, based on age, gender, race, and ethnicity, cause differential poverty.

The fourth section, on race and gender, includes articles by Edna Bonacich and Zillah Eisenstein that turned out to be starting points for later work that had a great impact. In Bonacich's "Class Approaches to Ethnicity and Race" we see the emphasis on the relationship between race, ethnicity, and class that she has developed so effectively over the years. She was one of the first to provide a powerful critique of the then – common notion that race and ethnicity are primordial. In her work she has succeeded in integrating a wide variety of class-based approaches to the study of race and ethnicity by arguing that an adequate class analysis of ethnicity and race must take into account all of the possible class relations between ethnic and racial groups that happen as a result of imperialism. In other words, it is not only class relations within nations that structure race and ethnicity, but also class relations between nations. In her reflective comments, Bonacich notes that it is now widely accepted that race and ethnicity are socially constructed, and not primordial, but like Burris, she thinks that the concept of class has suffered a decline in its centrality. She still maintains that we need to understand how capitalism works in order to understand race and ethnicity, but this by no means suggests that race is secondary to class in importance.

In Eisenstein's "Constructing a Theory of Capitalist Patriarchy and Socialist Feminism" we see the basis for her superb discussion of the socialist feminist position in her 1979 book, *Capitalist Patriarchy and the Case for Socialist Feminism*. The article reprinted here is one of the earliest statements of how a Marxist class analysis can combine with a feminist analysis of patriarchy to produce a theory of how gender and class intersect as systems of inequality. In her reflection, Eisenstein acknowledges that early socialist feminist analysis paid scant attention to the racial aspects of gender inequality, but thinks we are now beginning to theorize capitalist patriarchy more completely by paying attention to its racial and global contexts.

The fifth section includes two classic pieces by controversial Marxist sociologists of the 1970s who went on to professional prominence a decade later. Erik Olin Wright's 1975 article on "Alternative Perspectives in Marxist Theory of Accumulation and Crisis" considers traditional Marxist categories and illustrates the importance of a solid theoretical foundation in the development of radical thought. Fred Block's "Contradictions of Capitalism as a World System" explores the role of U.S. interests in maintaining global inflation, providing an effective backdrop for thinking about the current globalization process.

Even more, however, their current reflections demonstrate the ongoing dialogue about Marxism in the discipline. Wright has made it his project over the past 30 years to deepen and extend Marxist analysis, while abandoning those parts of it – the labor theory of value, the inherent tendency towards crises, and the inevitability of socialism – that he does not think are any longer useful. Block, on the other hand, has jettisoned Marxism altogether, making him more critical of his earlier work. But he remains a person of the Left in his reflections on his earlier work, providing an interesting and timely comparison between the American wars in Vietnam and Iraq in terms of the relationship between capitalism and military intervention.

The final section looks at the past with an eye to shaping the future thanks to an original and highly spirited argument in "The Critical Turn to Public Sociology" by Burawoy, who by a happy coincidence is serving as president of the ASA in the year that this book first appears. Burawoy uses his reading of everything that has gone before in this book, including the recent reflections by all of the authors, as a way to advance the idea of a critical "public sociology," which he has been developing over the past several years. Burawoy not only assesses the impact of radical sociology, but provides an agenda for how the next version of critical sociology should relate to and strengthen the heterogeneous world of civil society.

The concluding chapter by Burawoy, when read as a dialogue with the other contributions, especially when they touch on issues of how to bring about progressive social change, captures the spirit and purpose of this volume. Hopefully, then, the book will provide progressive sociologists with not only an understanding of how radical sociology developed out of the movements of the 1960s and 1970s, and then went on to change the discipline, but also with some ideas about how they might re-enter the public arena and be of use in present-day social struggles. As the articles and reflections in this volume show, we have come a long a way from where we started, but we still have a long way to go.

# I. Conceptualizing Sociology for Radicals

Richard Flacks

# The Trajectory of a Radical Sociology: Reflections

"Toward a socialist sociology" – the very title is quaint. Indeed, one might assume at first glance that this was some kind of manifesto from the 1930s. But, in fact, it captures, for me at least, that particular moment when the sixties were turning into the seventies. The potential for social transformation that was so palpable in the late 60s was still very much alive, but the expectation of apocalyptic social upheaval was passing. New Left "veterans" (the oldest turning 30) were talking about settling in for the "long march". That settling in demanded serious attention to "theory", to "strategy", to "program" and "vision": the "system" was not going to collapse, after all, and mass uprising was not after all impending. Instead, the American Left was going to have to figure out how to communicate with an American majority, to organize in the American mainstream, and to work for reformation at many levels and in diverse locations. This essay expressed – and tried to advance – that moment's fusion of optimism and perplexity.

The paper, though written by me, was an effort to summarize several months of discussion among the group of sociologists who happened to be together in Santa Barbara for the previous year. It has some of the flavor of having been written by a "committee", most particularly the fact that it is essentially an inventory of questions and debate topics rather than an effort to state a definite position. Even though the group was homogeneously white male, our disagreements were considerable and sometimes fierce. Indeed, all the participants were enormously voluble; there was no shortage of ego in the room when we were together.

We did share certain assumptions in 1971 that energized our discussions and our decision to put out a sort of intellectual manifesto for the discipline. Here are some of the key ones:

1. *Sociology in particular (and maybe academia in general) was in a moment of transformation.* Established paradigms and modes of operation were disintegrating in the face of global social change. There was a rising new generation of intellectuals, schooled in the sixties movement, that would demand a critical sociology, create a radical sociology.
2. *A new model of academic social relations was needed that would be consciously democratic, egalitarian and collectivist in spirit.* Our all white male group certainly lacked feminist consciousness, but most of us gave some lip service to the idea that hierarchical, authoritarian academic practices needed to be overcome.
3. *A new national left organizational structure was emerging.* The protest and resistance of the sixties era had shaken the established order. The struggle would continue but it had to be expressed in a more organized, structured, strategic way. Maybe a new party would come into being, but whatever organizational format might emerge, it would be crucial, we thought, to try to envision and name its social trajectory.
4. *The emerging Left would seek to transcend the welfare state and the two party system.* We thought that a shared agenda of democratic social transformation would help unify the movements across the class, racial and gender lines that tended to divide them, and that such a unified force could, over time, compete electorally with established political leaderships. We were meeting while Vietnam still raged, before McGovern, and before the "new" social movements (including feminism and environmentalism) had clearly gathered force. It was the "new left" that defined our shared political identity, and it was that identity we were trying to build upon and advance.
5. *We shared the view (widespread in the beginning of the seventies) that the New Left needed to engage with Marx and Marxism.* Not in the doctrinaire fashion of the old left, of course, nor in the cult-like fashion of the so-called new communist parties that were sprouting at the time. We shared the assumption that the Sixties new left lacked a "class analysis" and that the

first theoretical priority was to revitalize class and class struggle as the key to strategies of social change. We assumed that race and racial conflict were being subsumed by class and, at the same time, that the so-called "generation conflict" and "youth revolt" of the sixties needed to be recast in "class" terms. Clearly "gender" was not on our agenda!

6. *Mainstream sociology, to the extent that its practitioners had any policy interest, was driven by the knowledge needs of the welfare state, its many institutional expressions, and the political forces that sustained it. We took for granted that this structure was the status quo; therefore, a radical sociology would direct its critique at this structure, and that the alternative political and social formation would come from the Left.*

I list these assumptions as a way to compare the world we inhabit with the one we envisioned 35 years ago. And that comparison is worth doing because it will tell us something about the trajectory of the American Left in these years. Let's take a look then at each of these:

1. *Sociology's moment of transformation*. Sociology changed a great deal in the Seventies under the influence of the new generation. Indeed, some of those in the Santa Barbara group had a hand in making that change. Macro level theorizing and analysis focusing on social change came to the foreground. A neo-Marxian political economy, led by Jim O'Connor, Gabriel Kolko and many others was articulated on the left fringe of economics and strongly taken up in sociology that creatively re-opened the examination of capitalism's contradictions and crises, and incorporated an emphasis on the state (Both Zeitlin and Mankoff published major readers in this vein in the following years). A Marxian influenced return to historical analysis, led by Barrington Moore, Immanuel Wallerstein, and Chuck Tilly led on to world systems and comparative historical theorizing that came to dominate the discipline. A focus on the nature of class domination in American society led by Bill Domhoff and joined by Harvey Molotch (both members of the group) reshaped political sociology. American sociology became less provincial, opening up to European critical theory (some of which had been re-shaped by US empirical sociology). All of these kinds of developments are anticipated in the "socialist sociology" essay. Other transformative developments were not anticipated, particularly the rise of feminist sociologies.

Academic sociology turned out to be far more responsive to the critical turn than we had expected. It wasn't long before departments wanted to hire "radical sociologists" of various stripes, and the departments like ours at

UCSB that pioneered in incorporating unconventional paradigms and welcoming unconventional graduate students found that our PhD's did surprisingly well on the job market. By the mid seventies, a cohort of new sociology PhD's who had come out of the student movement were entering the field and it seemed likely that the vision of a new sociology in a new university might be plausible.

2. *A radical academy?* Social relations in the university also changed in these decades, especially with respect to the inclusion of women and minorities in the academic profession. One of affirmative action's significant impacts was to change the process by which academic appointments are made: forcing a degree of open competition and transparency to replace the old boy's networks. The proportion of white males has obviously declined in the last 30 years, but the academy remains far from a multi-racial haven. The institutionalization of ethnic, feminist and gay studies, struggles over sexual harassment, "hate speech" and "political correctness" – all of these are hot button topics in mainstream media depiction of the post-sixties academy. Those depictions do reflect a changed (and improved) reality with respect to race and gender relations in the university. But rather than radicals dominating the academy, the reverse is more nearly true. To a great extent the competitive individualism of academic life is as characteristic of post-sixties universities as it ever was. And the hope that university based intellectuals would link their work to the building of a transformative political force has only fitfully been realized. In the early seventies networks of university based radicalism – especially radical caucuses in the disciplines – sprouted. These had considerable effects on some disciplinary organizations: electing left figures to leading offices, changing the content of annual meetings, creating new subdisciplines. But over time these formations have tended to fold back into the mainstream. Meanwhile the individualizing logic of professional advancement rather than the logic of social mobilization has tended to shape the work of self-identified academic leftists.

3. *The party's over.* No national left emerged out of the sixties in the form of a national party-like organization. There are many ways to account for this, and I have myself written quite a bit on this theme (See Flacks 1988; Flacks 1995). Instead, the Left is constituted by a host of movements, campaigns, projects, national lobbies and locally based organizations that are sporadically coordinated by voluntaristic effort and shared threat rather than systematic interconnection. This fragmentation is often bemoaned, and often

"identity politics" is blamed. A case can be made, however, for the practical and moral virtue of a decentered, movement based, non-bureaucratized left. But the result of this situation is that it is hard for left intellectuals to find ways to address their work to programmatic and strategic needs of activists (except at local levels and in particular moments). There has been no coherent 'socialist sociology' primarily because there is no coherent left.

4. *The implausibility of radical alternatives*. Thirty years ago we didn't anticipate the rise of a new Right that would attack the foundations of welfare state liberalism and social democracy. We assumed then that "liberalism" had become the universal language of mainstream politics, and the framework of the capitalist state, and that social democracy as practiced in western Europe and reflected in the New Deal coalition was an insufficient framework for achieving democracy and justice.

Through much of the seventies these assumptions seemed warranted. Remember that Nixon did not materially roll back the New Deal and the Great Society, and indeed in his years, a host of reforms were adopted: including key environmental laws, affirmative action, and freedom of information. By the mid-seventies a new electorally oriented Left was emerging, with intensive programmatic work on "economic democracy", sustainable environmentalism, Naderite consumerism, and other structural reforms on the agenda.[1] Tom Hayden, in 1976, ran in the Democratic Primary for US senate in California on a detailed program (drafted in large part by new left academics) aimed at "economic democracy", while in localities across the country similar electoral projects were launched. At the same time, citizen action organizations formed in a number of states with populist/progressive agendas.

Meanwhile, in Europe much ferment in the organized left led to the enunciation of "Eurosocialist" and "Eurocommunist" politics aimed at overcoming cold war rivalries and incorporating the energies of sixties movements into established Left politics. It certainly seemed plausible that out of all of this experimentation and new thinking a new, post-social democratic movement was emerging.

These developments had much to do with the economic crises experienced by US and European capitalist states in that period – crises indicating that

---

[1] See Carnoy and D. Shearer (1980) for a detailed compendium of such thinking in the 1970s. A recent effort to lay out feasible, community based policy alternatives is Williamson, Imbroscio, and Alperovitz (2003).

the Keynesian formulas of the post war period were no longer effective. But the political vacuum that was opening up as a result turned out to be filled more by the right than the left. The achievement of a strong popular base for neo-conservatism, Reaganism, Thatcherism, new right fundamentalism and libertarianism – and the installation of rightwing regimes on the basis of these – forced everyone on the left toward a defense of the welfare state and into defensive coalition with centrist politicians rather than allow rightwing takeovers.

I think the demise of the Soviet Union and communism was the final nail in the coffin of 1970s Left revival. Most Left intellectuals assumed that the dynamic in Eastern Europe was toward a democratic reform of the communist party states and that the dissident intellectuals and activists in those countries were going to work for democratic socialist alternatives. It was a big shock when free marketeering turned out to be hegemonic in Poland, Czechoslovakia, Hungary and the former USSR. The promise of "euro-socialism/communism" came crashing down.

Today the global justice movements proclaim that "another world is possible". That phrase captures one of the core themes of "Toward a Socialist Sociology". The hunger for alternative vision remains, after a whole generation has passed in which the idea that "there is no alternative" (as Maggie Thatcher declared) has prevailed. And so a new opportunity for sociologists to effectively contribute to processes of radical envisioning is now upon us.

We who were talking together 30 years ago in Santa Barbara thought that a new era was opening. That sense was right; those years did mark the passing of what we now see as the "post war period". But the social world we are now in is not the one we were counting on. We were certainly not alone in our failure to anticipate the shape of the future. Consider for example the whole construct of "post-industrial society" that seemed so compelling at that time. The US we have actually experienced is hardly one in which corporations and financial institutions have lost power to the university and other centers of knowledge creation, nor have knowledge workers (or other versions of the "new class") become the dominant political force. But we certainly did enter a new era. It is a time when "socialism" as a framework of thought and action seems to have been invalidated. But so has "neo-liberalism" (or whatever other label we might want to use for corporate dominated society). Another world is necessary. Whether it is possible depends on finding frameworks of action that can promote genuinely democratic restructuring. Helping that quest seems like a worthy agenda for a radical sociology of this time.

Richard Flacks

# Towards a Socialist Sociology: Some Proposals for Work in the Coming Period[1]

Anyone who works as a radical in academic life, experiences extreme intellectual isolation. This fact is probably important in explaining why radical intellectuals in America have been relatively effective at criticism and markedly deficient in working out coherent alternatives to established intellectual structures in the academic disciplines.

During the spring of 1971 in Santa Barbara, a few self-defined radical sociologists had the opportunity to break down some of that isolation since we all happened to be living or visiting in Santa Barbara. As a result of being together, we decided that we might fruitfully try to develop a program of intellectual work for radical sociologists in the hope of stimulating those who shared our perspective to orient toward a common set of problems – so that radical sociology could move beyond criticism of the discipline and become helpful in providing an intellectual basis for the movements for change in the U.S.

The members of our group included: William Domhoff, Milton Mankoff, Harvey Molotch, John Seeley and Maurice Zeitlin. A radical economist, Andrew Winnick, participated in a number of our sessions. The following paper was written by me in an effort

---

[1] The original version of this article appeared in *The Insurgent Sociologist*, 2:2 (Spring, 1972), pp. 18–27.

to summarize our sessions. It represents my own perspective on what was discussed; the others should not be held responsible for its many weaknesses, although it is infused with their ideas. A version of this paper was presented and discussed at the meetings of the American Sociological Association in Denver, August, 1971.

This paper is intended to be part of a continuing discussion – not a finished product. I am therefore eager to have any thoughts it might stimulate, and suggestions about how this discussion can be institutionalized so that all who wish to can take part in it.

If there is a "crisis in Western Sociology" reflected in its increasing incoherence and its failure to apprehend central features of contemporary reality, those of us who claim to be radicals in sociology must nevertheless recognize our own failure to create alternative models of work for ourselves and for those who are attracted to our perspective. In fact, the "radical sociology" which emerged in the past decade appears to have completed its limited role. If we were mainly seeking to legitimate a socially critical, "anti-establishment," stance within the discipline, we have largely succeeded.

There can be little doubt that sociologists now are increasingly sensitive to the over commitment of the discipline to established power and the status quo; that social criticism of considerable range and depth is now more possible within the official forums of the discipline; that there has been a general loosening of theoretical and methodological inhibitions so that critical problems concerning conflict, change, power and exploitation can more freely be addressed; that the Marxian tradition has a new acceptability within the discipline; and, that texts and other curricular materials embodying radical or critical perspectives are increasingly published and gaining use in undergraduate education. If it is not "safe" to be a radical in sociology, especially if one tries to act as a political radical, it is nevertheless increasingly intellectually respectable to work in the radical tradition.

The legitimation of "radical sociology" is part of the wider fact that the "adversary culture" has been reborn among American intellectuals generally. And, the impact of this rebirth has been very substantial. As exposure, dissent, and fundamental political criticism have become increasingly legitimate and practiced by intellectuals, there has been a corresponding delegitimation of established elites, prevailing values and institutions.

Radical criticism contributes to widespread public disaffection, the articulation of discontent and the declining self-confidence of the powerful. But, by itself, it has so far been unable to do two kinds of work which ought to be integral features of the role of radical intellectuals: first, to provide theoretical tools and empirical materials which would enable the forces of insurgency to map a strategy of social transformation; second, to formulate programs and visions which might make a social alternative credible.

Those of us who have participated in preparing these notes have been working as radical social scientists for a number of years. Each of us has worked in his own special area; the group as a whole represented a surprisingly diverse range of "specialties." Yet, if there is a common thread in our work, it has involved the effort to be critical – to expose the myths embodied in the ruling ideologies of advanced capitalism, and to interpret the historical meaning of new forces of opposition, domestic and international, to advanced capitalism. The fact that we have been in the same town and able to come together frequently during the past few months has helped us understand the need now to begin to clarify and change some of our intellectual priorities: to see that beyond criticism lies the work of positive formulation.

There are, no doubt, some important political differences among us; nevertheless, we agreed that we shared a commitment to what would best be called a "socialist" America (though several of us are uncomfortable with some of the historical connotations which that word conveys to Americans). That is, we agreed that the collective aspirations of Americans could have a chance of realization only if the capitalist system of privately controlled economic decisions made in terms of profit-maximization were to be replaced by a system in which such decisions were made by public bodies whose goals involved the maximization of social, economic and political equality, the abolition of alienated labor, and the use of technology to promote public happiness. We also tended to agree that many of the material conditions for such a social transformation were coming into existence. Finally, we agreed that it was necessary to free socialism of its authoritarian, bureaucratic and technocratic implications, by opposing such tendencies within the socialist tradition, and by trying to work out concrete visions of a socialized economy which fostered decentralization, diversity, democracy, individuality, civil liberties and personal initiative.

Finally, we agreed that virtually none of the necessary intellectual work needed for a socialist transformation was being done, but that the possibilities for doing such work had perhaps never been better. We decided that one way to promote such work was to try to lay out in some concreteness an inventory of the types of tasks which were needed. One way to phrase our objective was this: Let us imagine that an organized socialist movement or party existed in the US, what kinds of things would sociologists do who were allied to it?

In certain respects, we failed to fulfill our initial aspirations. We had hoped, initially, to produce a document which would not only sketch a few programmatic ideas, but would be a rather detailed review of the work being done by radical intellectuals, in an effort to summarize major contributions, highlight important controversies and gaps in knowledge, call attention to work which provides models. We hoped, too, to formulate some new perspectives on method. But to do such an exhaustive and systematic analysis required more commitment from each of us to the collective enterprise than any of us was willing to give. So, it turned out that none of us was ready to work in a collective way: in part, because each of us was highly involved in ongoing work of our own, but also, more fundamentally, because of the deeply ingrained individualism which is characteristic of each of us. The competitiveness and self-importance which each of us possessed was often a barrier to systematic discussion and cooperative work. In any case, this draft is considerably less, at this point, than what needs to be done. What we hope for, at least, is that it will stimulate those who share its perspective, including ourselves, to intensify the process of defining and fulfilling the role of the socialist intellectual in these times.

## Some Central Theoretical Issues

One of the marks of the radical intellectuals is that they are blessed (and cursed) by a drive to make theory – theory which will comprehend the operation of society in its totality, link the present with the past organically, and reveal the necessary contradictions and unravellings of the established order. As Marx demonstrated, theory can have enormous power – to enable people to transcend the pressures of their particular existence, to guide the practice of movements, to provide people with the courage derived from seeing their struggles as historically meaningful, to offer a vision of a social alternative – an alternative made credible because it seems to flow out of the potentialities of the present. A theory can help people decide how to allocate their energies, justify their sacrifices, undermine the confidence of the enemy, and, above all, learn from experience.

Radical sociologists have always criticized American sociology for its theoretical barrenness and naiveté. However, since its inception, the American left has exhibited its own share of theoretical weakness. There are, however, signs that this situation is changing. The international revival of creativity within Marxism has begun to have a substantial impact even in the U.S. The rise of the New Left within the U.S., combined with the emergence of neo-Marxian theorists internationally, has greatly improved the chances that a new critical theory, relevant to the situation of advanced capitalism, will be realized. In any case, we think the creation of such a theory is rightfully a central preoccupation of radical intellectuals.

## The Problem of Agency

Perhaps the major achievement of the past decade, on the part of American radical social scientists, has been to attempt to apply Marxian theory to the analysis of the structure of power in America. The effort to demonstrate the existence of a power elite, acting in the interest of a capitalist class, is critical in a society whose political structure depends for its legitimacy so fundamentally on an ideology of democracy, and in which the leading social scientists have been so committed to the reality of the pluralist model. The effort to demonstrate that American foreign policy is rooted in imperialist drives is critical in a society in which both intellectuals and masses have believed that America's world role was limited to the defense of democratic principles. The effort to demonstrate that domestic social reform has largely been either limited by, or in the interest of, monopoly corporate power is critical in a society in which both workers and intellectuals have believed that the welfare state was an alternative to business domination and that welfare reformism was made possible by the operation of the established political system. If American radicals, then, have devoted most of their energy to the exposure of the myths of power, it is because, perhaps unlike other peoples, Americans are unusually illusioned by such myths, and more likely to be radicalized when such illusions are broken.

In any case, although our understanding of the structure of the society has been clarified during the past decade, there has been little theoretical development with respect to what might be called the dynamics of American society.

A key question for radicals – perhaps the key one – with respect to dynamics is the question of "agency." If there is a ruling class, then what is its "negation"? Is there a definable social grouping which has the potential consciousness, and the potential means, to lead a struggle for the overthrow of established power?

Marx, of course, had a clear answer – the industrial proletariat is the agency for the overthrow of capitalism, just as the bourgeoisie had been the agency for the overthrow of feudalism. The empirical failure of that prediction in industrial capitalist countries has, of course, created Marxism's central theoretical problem. More importantly, the difficulties involved in defining the "agency" have posed the gravest strategic problems for the new left and other radical movements in the advanced capitalist countries, and have been the source of bitter factional dispute within these movements.

Two broad hypotheses have emerged in contemporary Marxism which propose new agencies.

First, there is the view that the class struggle has been internationalized, and has become a struggle between the imperialist mother countries and the peoples of the colonized Third World. This view tends to argue that the standard of living of white Americans, and the viability of the capitalist system as a whole, depends on the maintenance and expansion of imperialist domination of the Third World. It thus tends to predict, on the one hand, continuing conservatism of the white industrial working class (as well as other strata within the mother country), but the eventual overthrow of their imperialist system through the combined and separate liberation struggles occurring in Third World Countries and among Third World minorities within the U.S.

Second, there is the more recent and rather less well-known proposal which emanates from those who have tried to theoretically comprehend the student uprisings of the Sixties. This view argues that the student movements of the advanced capitalist countries are harbingers of a new class-consciousness and class struggle internal to those countries – a situation resulting from the necessary creation of a "new" working class of educated workers in order to meet the needs of advanced technology and sophisticated system management. This view argues that the "new working class" is as crucial for advanced capitalism as the traditional proletariat was for an earlier stage, and that it can play a vanguard revolutionary role, not because of its material deprivation, but because of its openness to anti-capitalist ideology.

These notions are not mutually exclusive, but neither are they entirely compatible with each other. Moreover, in practice. they have led to rather severe differences in strategy within the left. What is important, for our purposes here, is that, although these ideas form the basis for much debate and action within the left, there has been little effort to study them systematically.

In a real sense, "Third World" and "mother country" liberation movements are interconnected. A powerful socialist movement within the U.S. is critical for the success of revolutionary movements in the Third World, just as successful resistance to imperialism internationally helps us to build support for fundamental change in America.

Although our group differed on the relative weight of emphasis to be given to these two sources of agency, my own bias is to stress the necessity for American radicals to comprehend the possibilities for change internal to the U.S., and particularly within the white population. The "new working class" notions require a deep scrutiny and are open to questions of many kinds. It would seem, therefore, that this is a very good time to launch a program of systematic research and theoretical analysis bearing on this question.

Among the relevant issues are these:

- The question of definition. Just what are the boundaries of the stratum? What theoretical principles, if any, permit the establishment of boundaries? What internal differentiation exists within this stratum, and what political consequences are predicted as a result?
- The question of consciousness. Is there any evidence, aside from the radicalization of students, that a new working class consciousness exists, and that it has or could have, a socialist content? How is the consciousness of educated workers affected by considerations of status, career, income, working conditions? What features of educated work are "alienating"? To what extent do workers in this category identify themselves as workers? As members of an elite?
- Linkages to the economic system. Just how central is the "knowledge industry"? What are the implications of the current contraction of job opportunities for the educated, and the cutbacks in investment in education, science and military technology which underlie this contraction?
- Class Struggles of the Educated. What is the fate of efforts to organize educated workers? Of radical caucuses and other political expressions?

The problem of "agency" would not, however, be settled simply by obtaining data which might support the socialist potential of the "new" working class. For that stratum contains within its very definition a limitation on its potential as agency. First, it does not constitute the majority in itself. Even if it were politically united, it would have to ally itself with other strata to achieve revolutionary aims. Second, its relative material well-being generates a crucial ambiguity – the educated are likely to profess a universalistic concern for the freedom and well-being of those more oppressed, but they surely cannot be trusted to speak and act for the more oppressed and less articulate masses. In theoretical terms, the issue is the extent to which the interests of "educated labor" coincide and conflict with other strata that are in motion. Is there any theoretical way to link, for instance, the radicalization of white students with the black revolt in the U.S. and with revolution in Third World countries? Clearly the revolts of the hungry have catalyzed and inspired the revolt of students and educated workers. But in practice the conflicts between the two are deep and glaring. What common interest do these groups share?

Meanwhile, in the background is the "white working class," the traditional proletariat, who exist for contemporary radical intellectuals as stereotypes, and whose articulate spokespeople are evidently opposed to both student and Third World revolutionaries. Is there, in theory, a basis for a unified working class?

Finally, there is the fact that much of the conflict in American society is not easily reduced to class struggle. It has become possible to analyze the student revolt in class terms, but what of the broader youth consciousness, which has certainly played a role in stimulating rebellion within the military and in prisons? What of the women's liberation movement? And what of the fact that serious revolutionaries, despite their Marxism, have typically found it necessary to recognize the revolutionary potentialities of nationalist and other "non-class" bases of solidarity?

All of these questions imply the need for deep conceptual clarification and systematic research. The problem of agency and the concept of class have always been, we suspect, more ambiguous in Marxism than many Marxists have recognized. These issues are not academic; for the answers to these questions determine very concretely how energies are used by political movements. Nor can the answers be arrived at through academic means alone. It may well be that by its very nature sociology as an academic enterprise cannot comprehend the social bases of rebellion in American society. It seems likely that without political practice intellectuals are largely incapable of anticipating possibilities for political motion. I shall return, briefly, to this issue below.

## The Problem of Limits

Marx did not rest with the question of agency (although a sociologist might). His theoretical purpose was deeper: to uncover the main laws of motion of capitalist society – the inner contradictions and tendencies upon which predictions of future development might be based. The ultimate aim was to discover the limits of the system, the points at which it could develop no further without breaking apart.

The history of theoretical Marxism is in large part the history of efforts to elaborate and eventually revise the economic model which Marx began to develop in pursuit of these aims. Those efforts continue. Contemporary analysis of this question focuses on such issues as: the degree to which imperialism is a necessary component of American economic growth; the consequences for domestic growth of rising international trade competition; the degree to which the state can effectively manage problems of unemployment and inflation; the fiscal problems of the public sector, etc. The analysis of political economy has at least two purposes: to demonstrate the underlying irrationality of capitalism – the fact that it *must* perpetuate one or another barbarity (imperialism, war, unemployment, poverty, urban squalor, militarism, etc.) to preserve its stability; secondly, such analysis helps solve the problem of agency, by suggesting likely sources of discontent. Ultimately, there is the hope of demonstrating a contradiction so overwhelming that the defeat of the system will be inescapable (but this hope is perhaps quixotic).

Sociologists *qua* sociologists have relatively little to offer such analytic work – a fact which illustrates the incompatibility between academic specialization and the task of theory construction. But lately, there has begun to emerge a theoretical perspective within the Marxian framework which is more directly sociological (rather than economic) – a perspective which sees the limits of capitalism not primarily in economic terms but rather in terms which are broadly social, cultural and psychological. Briefly, it is proposed that capitalism reaches its limit when it creates the material-technological basis for abolishing or greatly reducing alienated labor, but cannot implement that possibility.

Marx himself was aware of this as a theoretical possibility, but apparently believed that the socialist revolution would occur before this point was reached.

The idea that we are on the verge of a new historical stage, in which, for example, the production of goods will be secondary to other activity, in which the power of those who manage production will be subordinated to considerations of comprehensive planning, in which people will be freed from economic priorities – this idea in a variety of forms is being proposed by people of various persuasions. There is a technocratic version of "post-industrial" society and a variety of socialist versions. One can see how the notion of a "new working class" as a revolutionary agency is derivable from such a perspective. That a "post-industrial" society is now (or shortly to be) materially possible fits with the yearnings of alienated youth and gives such yearnings historical meaning. It also fits with certain tendencies of the environmentalist movement and the quest for a limit on the exploitation of natural resources.

There is an idea here, and if intellectual convergence means anything, it is an idea whose time has come. So far, as far as we are aware, it is little more than a speculation – and not very well worked out at that.

Here are some basic issues raised by the "post-industrial" perspective:

- To what extent is it true that existing technology can liquidate routinized human labor?
- What are the political, economic, cultural and social barriers to such a development under capitalism?
- To what extent is the technocratic vision of decisive power in the hands of expertsand a system of comprehensive planning a plausible one? How can it be criticized?
- Is post-industrialism possible within one country? Can "post-scarcity" be achieved without imperialism?
- Is the goal of reduced economic growth and labor time compatible with the goal of abolishing poverty and inequality of living standards?
- Does post-industrialism imply a reduction in the production of consumer commodities and a reallocation of resources to the creation of better public services, environmental values and collectively shared goods? If so, to what extent are Americans prepared to trade certain kinds of possessions and commodities for reduced labor, improved natural and urban environments, a richer community life, education, health and other social services? Which Americans are most and least resistant to such a trade? Why?

These are some of the researchable questions which have occurred to us in trying to formulate our thoughts on the "post-industrial" notion. If this notion is at all plausible, it is decidedly appealing, not only as a conceptual lever for comprehending important trends in advanced capitalism, but as the keystone for the construction of a socialist vision with direct relevance to such a society. But it is crucial that, at this point, serious analysts not accept the concept as given, but attempt to work out its underlying assumptions and implications, and the means to test empirically the major assertions which flow from it. It is also important for radicals to pay serious attention to the elitist and technocratic versions of the post-industrial image of the future, and to sharply distinguish these from socialist and humanist images.

## Culture, Character and Consciousness

An important development of the past decade in critical theory has been the revival and development of work on the ways in which processes of socialization, mass communication and other means of control operate to undermine (and facilitate) revolutionary forms of consciousness. The efforts to link Marx and Freud, to study the consciousness effects of schooling, mass media, and other institutions represent the theoretical side of this work, while an enormous range of practical efforts have been made to deal with the same issues in the real world. (We are referring here, of course, to many of the efforts to create forms of communal living, to develop alternate media, to attack consumerism and sexism, to develop new forms of education and child-rearing, to develop new forms of therapy.) Many of these experiments are justified precisely as part of an effort to free individuals from cultural and psychological constraints, not only because that is held to be intrinsically desirable, but because of the political consequences of eradicating some of the bases of "false consciousness."

The theoretical and practical importance of studying consciousness cannot be overemphasized. It is clear that one of the deficiencies of classical Marxism was its failure to develop this theme. But the question has never been more pressing, given the steady elaboration of the means of control and the many ways in which the existence of material abundance can serve to deplete social solidarity.

For a socialist movement in this country at this time there is a critical need to develop modes of activity which can link the personal, the cultural, the social and the political. In part, such modes must arise from practice. But, in part, we suspect that clues to some answers will be derivable from theory. American social scientists have much to learn on this topic from recent

European work, but radicals in sociology, social psychology ethnomethodology and related fields could make an important contribution by, for instance, reinterpreting much of the "micro" and abstractedly empiricist work in this area in terms of the "macro," the "critical" and the political.

## The Need for Radical Research

One suspects that radical intellectuals do not need much encouragement to engage in theorizing. A primary intent of this paper is to encourage much more systematic engagement in empirical-practical work by radical sociologists; to urge that we go beyond the endless elaboration of polemical criticism of sociology, to produce systematic inquiry that has real use for movements for social change. We keep asking – what would a hypothetical socialist movement in America demand of its members who had been trained in sociology? In our discussions we did not get as far as we would have liked in formulating concrete answers to such a question, but here are some:

1. The development of a process of mapping the structure of power in the United States. Such a process involves, on the one hand, the continuous collection of data on the membership of the "power elite," and on the other hand, the use of sophisticated methods of data analysis to depict patterns of interlock, the structure of corporate interest groups, linkages between corporate and political elites, possible sources of cleavage and connection, etc., as well as efforts to define the relationships between specific corporate interests and specific policies and issues. This is already the most typical kind of research in which radicals are engaged, and has been the basis for a considerable amount of effective anti-corporate activity. In addition to expanding and deepening the "databank" concerning corporate-political structure, however, there is a need to attempt more systematic efforts at broad mapping – in which case we may find some radicals seeking to acquire skills which they previously disdained – e.g., computer programming, advanced methods of data reduction and statistical analysis.

2. The study of constituencies for socialism. Despite the enormous elaboration of opinion and attitude research in America, there is precious little systematic study which provides detailed knowledge about which sectors of the population are likely to support various kinds of social change. Furthermore, it is likely that whatever conclusions can be drawn from the extant body of

such research are likely to be wrong. There is no doubt that survey research contains inherent limitations as a tool for predicting changes in consciousness; nevertheless, we are convinced that its potentialities have not been fully tested by any means. There is, at best, only a handful of radicals who have used survey methodology as a way into research on class consciousness, and, although fruitful and suggestive, even their work is relatively primitive.

The practice on the movements of the Sixties has taught us far more about the potentialities for consciousness-raising in America than all the academic research on public opinion and political behavior. And yet, we feel that it ought to be possible to combine techniques of survey, depth interviewing and political organization to increase our comprehension.

How do various potential constituencies react to proposals for fundamental structural reform? To visions of alternative social organization? To anti-capitalist sentiments and slogans? What are the sources of support for, and resistance to existing movements for change? What latent and explicit hostilities exist to established elites, authorities and institutions? Under what conditions do people see their private discontents as rooted in social conditions and political processes? Under what conditions would people undertake what kinds of political action themselves?

This is just a sample of the kinds of questions which a socialist movement needs to answer, and which sociologists are supposed to have the skill to answer, concerning political consciousness and behavior. In the absence of "professional" assistance, a movement will attempt to supply answers using its own methodologies. One of the critical questions for sociology is to comprehend the process by which social movements do in fact formulate and test hypotheses about the social environment in which they must operate, about political behavior of potential constituents, about social control, about the political psychology of potential recruits, and about their own successes and failures. Not only is that process intrinsically interesting, it seems crucial for sociological method – since movements are often more "correct" than academic sociologists in predicting certain events and outcomes. We did not in our discussions go deeply into this question, but I believe it is crucial. To wed the practical understanding of movement activists to the systematizing skills of the sociologist would represent a major breakthrough in the struggle to understand the conditions which give rise to collective revolt in a society like ours.

## Making Socialism Credible

But the main problem far a socialist movement – the reason that none exists – is not the problem of defining its agencies or constituencies. Rather, it is the fact that all existing ideas of what socialism means are discredited or irrelevant for Americans (including American radicals). In our time, socialism has come to mean either an authoritarian system applicable to the situation of pre-industrial society, a welfare state which seems ineffective in coping with the deepest problems of advanced industrial society, or a system to increase and even totalize the control apparatus of the modern state.

Nevertheless, we centered our discussion around the need for a commitment to socialism. We did so because we knew of no other word which encompasses the vision of a society organized so that production is carried on for use rather than profit, class-based privilege and inequality is abolished, and people have equality of access to power and to the fruits of human labor.

The question is – how to make such a vision relevant to the conditions, problems and discontents of our time? How to demonstrate to ourselves and to people generally that the abolition of capitalism is possible, and that an alternative to it can be constructed which provides the means to solve the problems presented by capitalism?

An element of an answer lies in the development of concrete models. Such models are not proposals for reform of the existing system, but hypotheses about how activities would be organized assuming the abolition of the private corporate system. For example, can we imagine concretely how any of the following might "work" in "advanced industrial society?"

- The allocation of resources at the national, regional and local level is determined through a process of public debate and popular decision-making.
- Self-determination and personal initiative are maximized within a system in which resource allocation is centrally planned and coordinated.
- Civil liberties are guaranteed within a system of collective ownership.
- Access to the full benefits of advanced technology is provided while routinized human labor is abolished, reduced and shared.
- Americans are not deprived of material well-being despite massive redistribution of control over resources internationally.
- The distinctions between "town and country" are abolished without destroying the positive values of either.
- All people have maximum and equal opportunity to work creatively, fulfill their intellectual, aesthetic and sensual potentialities, and govern themselves.

Marxists have always, with good reason, opposed the effort to create blueprints. The substance of socialist society will be a product of practical struggles, not speculation by an intellectual elite. What is here being proposed is not the elaboration of blueprints, in the sense that one is trying to manufacture panaceas for society's ills. Instead, what we are suggesting is a kind of work which might be called mental experimentation – the development of hypothetical models of reconstructed social relations in order to stimulate debate and analysis, in order to catalyze practical experiment – all for the purpose of making alternatives to the status quo credible. The creation of credible theoretical alternatives is an important aspect of criticism; in fact, after a period in which increasing numbers of people have learned to oppose or mistrust the existing order, criticism, as such, can lead to despair unless it is coupled with reasons for hope. We sense that the new left has reached a dead end, precisely because it has been effective at criticism and negation, but simultaneously unable to provide grounds for hope. It is not so much that the constituencies in favor of basic change are lacking, it is that they have no idea what change might mean. Sociologists and other intellectuals cannot provide *the* answer but we can help to provide the concrete ideas from which answers can be constructed.

Another function of such models is that they provide material for the development of programs for fundamental structural reform. By "structural reform" we refer to popular demands for institutional change which cannot in fact be met under capitalism. Socialist movements search for such demands because popular movements around them tend experience radicalization as their aspirations are frustrated. It is not up to us as sociologists to formulate such programs (although popular movements may find our efforts useful), but the effort to concretize the meaning of socialism can help movement activists figure out the kinds of programs which will be both relevant to the felt needs of people and fundamentally challenging to the system.

Finally, utopian thinking is relevant to the effort to build "counter-institutions." For the latter makes sense politically to the extent that it is defined as a conscious struggle to establish a piece of the future in the present. Such practice – the building of communes, the counter-institutional movements in education, health, childcare, the movements for self-determination in the black and youth ghettoes, etc. – provides an important ground for learning about the problems and potentialities of recreating social relations. The efforts to build counter-institutions are then a major source of "data" for "model-building" – while at the same time these efforts can be stimulated and influenced by the theoretical models which are devised.

In general, both the source and the test of the ideas of radical intellectuals lies with the movements for social change. As sociologists, what we bring to such movements is this: some knowledge of the "literature" which might be relevant to political work; a certain degree of training to generalize from particular experience, to synthesize diverse experiences, to confront discomforting data, to examine underlying assumptions, to entertain alternative explanations for events; possibly some factual knowledge which might be of use. One of the critical questions which we, as a group, evaded was just this – how to integrate a socialist sociology with the movements for change. This question is not simply an "organizational" problem – it strikes to the heart of sociology's conception of itself as a discipline. The fact that it is evaded here does not mean that we thought that a socialist sociology would be organized and conducted in the ways which have been characteristic of academic sociology. On the contrary, our failure to confront this question was partly due to our feeling that we, as a group, could never achieve consensus on the issue; partly because the question cannot really be decided by a small group of relatively established types – but only through a continuous effort at practical redefinition on the part of all those who seek to build a socialist movement.

If such a movement already existed, the task of self-definition would be greatly simplified. Perhaps radicals in sociology and other disciplines will have the chance to take part in building such a movement. But, in the meantime, to *imagine that one exists* seems a good way to begin to give form and direction to our collective work. Such an act of imagination might turn out to be a self-fulfilling fantasy.

# II. Power and Class

Göran Therborn

# The Ruling Class Thirty Years Later

My *Insurgent* article of 1976 was first written in 1975 as a paper for the annual British Sociological Association Conference. Some of its basic "structuralist" premises go back to a 1972 book in Swedish on conceptions of economic systems and of classes. Its argument was elaborated in a book appearing in London in 1978, *What Does the Ruling Class Do When It Rules?* (NLB/Verso). Twenty years later it was still used as a textbook (in Spanish translation) in several parts of Latin America.

It is a serious paper, I still think, one of my children, and I am not going to repudiate it. But I would not be able to write this paper today. There are the two points I would like to argue here, without going into detail.

The fundamental questions raised by the paper are neither wrong nor trivial, they are important. I am less sure today about their relative merits, but I think the distinction between three very different perspectives on power remains valid, Who has power? How much power is there? What is power used for? The paper suggests how to deal with the third question, in an empirically manageable way.

This task is carried out in two ways, in critical polemics and in a typological construction. The former may or may not have dotted all the I's. But its polemical style is something I still stand by, and try to teach. It is directed at the best representatives of the then most pertinent alternatives; it is concrete, specific, and referenced. The original section III of the paper that presents my view of Weber, Giddens, and Runciman is omitted here for space considerations.

Typologies have a controversial odor, more now than then perhaps. They fall short of explanatory accounts, an important criterion of theorizing I have always recognized. However, social scientists and philosophers are currently, rather more than previously, prepared to accept that the way phenomena are named, labelled, characterized, and grouped together are enormously powerful tools of narration and persuasion. In other words, typologies *are* important, *are* powerful. They are ways of sniffing out reality. Furthermore, typologies differ from naming or labelling in their drive to systematicity, to laying out the field of alternatives. They are meant to be eye-openers, rather than fixtures of praise or condemnation.

The limitations of the article are not more than the limitation of everything profane and of everything after thirty years of learning – in its questions, its approach to answering them, its form of polemics, or its form of theoretical construction. The limitation in the current context is the style of the construction. To make sense, its style of construction presupposed two things, neither valid for the time being. Firstly, that at least some people cared whether there was a ruling class or not. In othe words, that capitalism in a political democracy operated with a popular, civic legitimation. That shareholder value was not everything to a market society.

Second, and most importantly, that there was class struggle, i.e., two or more classes fighting, not just one ruling and exploiting. If there are fighting classes, class movements in combat, or preparing for battle in ways not readily visible, then gauging the class power configurations of locales of class struggle makes sense, indeed may be decisive. Now, there is certainly class power of capital, but little of class struggle, even on the horizon. When a ruling class is all powerful, analyses of it lose their sex appeal.

Many social theories and analyses are deeply enmeshed in the contexts of meaning and in the discursive formations of their times that it is both a strength and a weakness. It is a strength for possible intervention in your time and society. It is a weakness when looked upon from very different circumstances thirty years later.

Looking back, I would cite Edith Piaf, "je ne regrette rien" (I don't regret anything). Those were years of hope, in the end unfulfilled, but of intellectually inspiring hope, of international friendship and comradeship, at a time many years before most student exchanges and international research groups, not to speak of internet chats. This thing about friendship and comradeship is meant sociologically more than personally. Marxism of the late 1960s and 1970s was an international brother- and sisterhood, not too dissimilar from the travelling monks or students and (less frequently) nuns of the European Middle Ages, for whom there was almost always some hospitality of strangers in foreign lands.

Now what? I think we have passed the century of working class challenge, of modern class struggle at its strongest, which had its global centre in one particular continent, Europe. The future challenges to the rulers of the world will come from other sources than industrial labor. The social dynamic has changed axis. Today's question is less specific: What do the rulers do when they rule? But then the three questions will have to be answered, all of them: Who rules? What is the rule used for? How much rule is there?

There is certainly still a great need for insurgent sociologists, as well as for critical sociology.

Göran Therborn

# What Does the Ruling Class Do When It Rules? Some Reflections on Different Approaches to the Study of Power in Society

What is the place of power in society? What is the relationship between class and power? Answers differ, as is to be expected, given the obvious significance of class and power to the evaluation of a given society. The question itself, however, appears simple and straightforward enough. Ideological biases apart, what seems to be at issue is the famous question of scientific method, of what is the most adequate method to answer the question.[1] But is the question really so clear and simple? From what we know about "paradigms" (Kuhn) and "problematics" (Althusser) of science is it very likely that, for example, a proletarian revolutionary and critic of political economy (Marx), a German academic historian and sociological follower of Austrian marginalism (Weber), a descendant of Jeffersonian democracy (Mills), an admirer of

The original version of this article appeared in *The Insurgent Sociologist* 6:3 (Spring, 1976), pp. 3–16.

[1] See, e.g., R. Dahl, "A Critique of the Ruling Elite Model", *American Political Science Review (APSR)* 52 (1958), pp. 463–69; N. Polsby, "How to Study Community Power: The Pluralist Alternative", *Journal of Politics* 22 (1960), pp. 474–84: P. Bachrach – M. Baratz, "The Two Faces of Power", *APSR* 56 (1962), pp. 947–52; P. Bachrach – M. Baratz, "Decisions and Nondecisions: An Analytical Framework", *APSR* 57 (1963), pp. 641–51; R. Merelman, "On the Neo-Elitist Critique of Community Power", *APSR* 62 (1968), pp. 451–60; *APSR* 65 (1971), pp. 1063–80; F. Frey, "Comment: On Issues and Nonissues in the Study of Power", *APSR* 65 (1971), pp. 1081–1101; R. Wolfinger, "Rejoinder to Frey's 'Comment', *APSR* 65 (1971), pp. 1102–04. An overview can be gained from the reader edited by R. Bell, D. Edwards, and H. Wagner, *Political Power* (New York: Free Press, 1969).

contemporary liberal economics (Buchanan-Tullock, Parsons), or an adherent of some of the ruling political ideas of present-day U.S.A. (Dahl, Giddens[2]), would be concerned with the same problem and ask the same question – even when they use the same words?

Leaving subtler points and distinctions aside we can distinguish at least three different major approaches to the study of power in society. The first and most common one we might call the *subjectivist approach*. With Robert Dahl it asks: Who governs?,[3] or with William Domhoff: Who rules America?,[4] or in the words of a British theorist of stratification, W.G. Runciman: "who rules and who is ruled?",[5] or in the militant pluralist variant of Nelson Polsby: "Does anyone at all run this community?"[6]

This is a subjectivist approach to the problem of power in society not in the same sense as "subjective" in the so-called subjective conceptions of stratification, which refer to stratification in terms of subjective evaluation and esteem, in contrast to stratification in terms of, say, income or education. It is a subjectivist approach in the sense that it is looking for the *subject of power*. It is looking, above all, for an answer to the question, *Who* has power? A few, many, a unified class of families, an institutional elite of top decision-makers, competing groups, everyone, or no one really? The focus of the subjectivists is on the power-holding and power-exercising subject.[7]

The common subjectivist question can then be studied and answered in various ways. This has in fact given rise to a very lively methodological as well as substantial debate in the United States in the fifties and sixties, which still has not been superseded, between the "pluralists" and the elite and the ruling class theorists.[8] Essentially, it has been a debate within the framework

---

[2] According to Giddens the U.S.A. is the most democratic advanced society in the world: A. Giddens, *The Class Structure of the Advanced Societies* (London: Hutchinson, 1973), p. 175. For a comment on the issue, see below. Dahl's conception of the prevailing regime in U.S.A. is expounded in, among other places, R. Dahl, *Pluralist Democracy in the United States: Conflict and Consent* (Chicago: Rand McNally, 1967).

[3] R. Dahl, *Who Governs? Democracy and Power in an American City* (New Haven: Yale Univ. Press, 1961).

[4] W. Domhoff, *Who Rules America?* (Englewood Cliffs, N.J.: Prentice-Hall, 1967).

[5] W.G. Runciman, "Towards a Theory of Social Stratification", in F. Parkin, ed., *The Social Analysis of Class Sructure* (London: Tavistock, 1974), p. 58.

[6] Polsby, *op. cit.*, p. 476.

[7] In the egalitarian orientation of Bachrach-Baratz this focus is coupled with a lookout for who, if any, gain and who, it any, are handicapped by the existing "mobilization of bias". Besides their above-mentioned articles see their *Power and Poverty* (New York; Oxford University Press, 1970).

[8] The substantial debate includes, from the elitist side, F. Hunter, *Community Power Structure* (Chapel Hill: Univ. of North Carolina Press, 1953): C.W. Mills, *The Power*

of liberal political ideology and liberal political theory, accepting the liberal conception of democracy as a starting-point and then investigating whether the contemporary manifestations of liberal democracy, in the present-day United States or in other Western countries, correspond or not to that conception. But it has also included important contributions from Marxist authors, who have basically confined themselves within this framework, accepting battle on the terrain chosen by the enemy.[9] The latter case, by the way, highlights the far-reaching effects of prevailing ideology, shaping even the form of opposition to itself.

Outside the subjectivist fold and its internal polemics about different methods and answers, another type of question is raised by some authors who base themselves on liberal economic ideology and liberal economic theory. We might label it the *economic approach*. In the businessman's manner, the question here is not who, but *how much*. Power is regarded above all as a capacity to get things done. The primary emphasis is on "power to" rather than "power over" and the crucial question is not the distribution but the accumulation of power. As a theory of power the economic approach features two main variants, a sociological and a utilitarian. The main proponent of the former is Talcott Parsons. Parsons conceives power "as a circulating medium, analogous to money"[10] and defines it as "generalized capacity to secure the performance of binding obligations by units in a system of collective organization when the obligations are legitimized with reference to

---

*Elite* (New York: Oxford Univ. Press, 1956); W. Domhoff, *op. cit.*, Bachrach-Baratz, *op. cit.*: M. Parenti, "Power and Pluralism: A View From the Bottom", in M. Surkin – A. Wolfe, eds., *An End to Political Science* (New York: Basic Books, 1970), pp. 111–43; M. Creson, *The Un-Politics of Air Pollution* (Baltimore: The John Hopkins Press, 1971). Among the contributions of the pluralists are S.D. Riesman, *et al.*, *The Lonely Crowd* (New York: Doubleday Anchor, 1953); R. Dahl, *Who Governs?*; E. Banfield, *Political Influence* (New York: Free Press, 1961). For references to the methodological discussion see above note 1.

[9] The most important example is R. Miliband, *The State in Capitalist Society* (London: Weidenfeld & Nicolson, 1969). The polar opposite kind of Marxist stance is exemplified by N. Poulantzas, *Political Power and Social Class* (London: NLB, 1973). In a well-argued article the latter has been criticized for not coming to grips with, and thus not really revealing the weaknesses of, the problematic of his opponents: E. Laclau, "The Specificity of the Political: The Poulantzas-Miliband Debate", *Economy and Society*" (1975), pp. 87–110. Although mainly restricted to a distinction between different approaches to the problem of power, the present article tries to take account of the criticisms of both Poulantzas and Miliband. At the same time I am indebted to them both for their very valuable contributions.

[10] T. Parsons, "On the Concept of Political Power", *in idem*, *Sociological Theory and Modern Society* (New York: Free Press, 1967), p. 306.

their bearing on collective goals and where in case of recalcitrance there is a presumption of enforcement by negative situational sanctions – whatever the actual agency of that enforcement."[11]

In the utilitarian "economic theories of democracy," little attention and consideration is allotted the phenomenon of power and its conceptualization. Politics is seen from the perspective of an "individualist theory of collective choice" and the meaning of power is then derived from the assumed blessings of market exchange. "This approach", write Buchanan and Tullock, "incorporates political activity as a particular form of *exchange*; and, as in the market relation, mutual gains to all parties are ideally expected to result from the collective relation. In a very real sense, therefore, political action is viewed essentially as a means through which the power of all the participants may be increased, if we define power as the ability to command things that are desired by men."[12]

Although they can be said to share a common approach to power, inspired by liberal economics, concentrating as they do on non-conflictual "power to", the two main variants of the economic approach also show differences that are by no means insignificant. In the sociological variant, power is generated and operates in social relationships, whereas in the utilitarian conception it is basically a non-relational asset. In both the problem of class and power by and large disappears.

With little of the elaborate theoretical imagination of the above-mentioned authors, the economic approach to power has also been applied to the problems of political development and "modernization", above all by Samuel P. Huntington. Huntington starkly emphasizes the importance of the "accumulation of power" over the question of its distribution. He opens his book *Political Order in Changing Societies* by proclaiming, "The most important political distinction among countries concerns not their form of government but their degree of government. The differences between democracy and dictatorship are less than the differences between those countries whose politics embodies consensus, community, legitimacy, organization, effectiveness,

---

[11] *Ibid.*, p. 308.

[12] J. Buchanan – G. Tullock, *The Calculus of Consent* (Ann Arbor: Univ. of Michigan Press, 1962), p. 23. Anthony Downs' somewhat less sanguine view of power does not refer to "power over" either, but to unequal "power to", because of inequalities of information and income. A. Downs, *An Economic Theory of Democracy* (New York: Harper & Row, 1957), pp. 257–58.

stability, and those countries whose politics is deficient in these qualities."[13] "Modern political systems differ in the amount of power in the system, not in its distribution."[14] To Huntington it is the general liberal ideas about economic development, rather than liberal economic theory, which provides the model.

The third approach might be named a structural-processual approach. But with its focus on society as an objective structured totality and on contradiction, motion, and change, we had perhaps better call it the *dialectical-materialist approach,* embodied in the new scientific study of history and society founded by Marx, historical materialism. Here the primary focus is on the historical social contexts and modalities of power, and the first question is: *What kind of society is it*? Then: *What are the effects of the state upon this society,* upon its reproduction and change?

The central task of *Capital* was not to identify those who have the wealth and those who are poor, nor those who rule and those who are ruled, but, as the author pointed out in his preface, to lay bare "the economic law of motion of modern society." That is, Marx was above all interested in how wealth and poverty, domination and subjugation are being (re)produced and how this can be changed. The basic focus of study is on neither property nor the property owners but on capital, that is, on (particular historical) relations of production and their relationship to the productive forces and to the state and the system of ideas.

## II

This third approach to the problem of power in society owes its more roundabout character to the fact that it seriously and systematically tries to tackle two fundamental problems largely neglected by the other approaches. One concerns "power to", the other relates to "power over".

One question which should be seriously faced is: Power to do what? What is a particular amount of power used for? The utilitarian answer – to maximize one's utility – is hardly very satisfactory in view of the enormous variety of historical social forms, and thereby systems, of power. For the same reason we do not learn very much from Parsons' discussion of power in terms

13 S. Huntington, *Political Order in Changing Societies* (New Haven: Yale Univ. Press, 1968), p. 1.

14 *Ibid.*, p. 144.

of realization of "collective goals."[15] Nor should it be assumed *a priori*, or made a part of the definition, that, as Parsons contends, power is exercised "in the interest of the effectiveness of the collective operation as a whole",[16] rather than in the interest of the exploitation of one class by another.

What "power to" means depends on the kind of society in which it operates. A Marxist analysis of a given society first of all focuses on its mode(s) of production, its system(s) of relations and forces of production.

By determining the relations of production the Marxist analyst at the same time determines *if* there are classes in the given society and *what* classes there are, because classes in the Marxist sense are people who occupy certain positions in society as basically defined by the relations of production. If immediate production – in husbandry, agriculture, industry, transport, etc. – and the appropriation and control of the surplus produced are separated among different role incumbents, and are not united in an individual or in a collective, there are classes. And the different modes of separation (slavery, feudalism, capitalism, etc.) mean different classes.[17]

Determining the relations of production does not pertain only to the *context* of political power. It is also directly related to the question of power, since the separation between the immediate producers and the appropriators of the surplus product entails specific relations of domination and subordination.[18] Exploitative relations of production directly involve relations of domination, and in what may be called the key passage of Marx's materialist interpretation of history he says, "The specific economic form in which unpaid surplus labour is pumped out of the direct producers, determines the rela-

---

[15] Parsons, *op. cit.*, p. 308.

[16] *Ibid.*, p. 318.

[17] I have developed an analysis of the Marxist concept of class in my *Klasser och okonomiska system* (Staffanstorp: Cavefors, 1971). Cf. the first part of my 'Classes in Sweden 1930–70', in R. Scase, ed., *Readings in the Swedish Class Structure* (London: Hutchinson, forthcoming).

[18] Power in a society should of course be studied not only in terms of the non-specific, extra-organizational power of organizational elites, but also in terms of the mode of organization itself, particularly the mode of organization of people's working lives, which differ both in the kind and the amount of domination and independence. However, the Marxist focus on exploitation and class is related to the discussion of power only in the broad sense of the latter, in the sense of A significantly affecting B in a situation of possible negative sanctions against B's non-compliance. The specification of power in terms of responsibility, choice, and agreement, and distinctions between fate, coercion, authority, manipulation, and power, are internal to a subjectivist discourse and as such are outside the Marxist analysis proper. The latter does not start from "the point of view of the actor" but from ongoing social processes.

tion of domination and servitude, as it emerges directly out of production itself and in turn reacts upon production." Marx then continues and makes his basic proposition about the relationship between the economy and the polity (the meaning, truth and fruitfulness of which proposition is under debate): "Upon this basis, however, is founded the entire structure of the economic community, which grows up out of the conditions of production itself, and consequently its specific political form. It is always the direct relation between the masters of the conditions of production and the direct producers which reveals the innermost secret, the hidden foundation of the entire social edifice and therefore also of the political form of the relation between sovereignty and dependence, in short of the particular form of the state."[19]

For the adherents of the subjectivist approach, in both its pluralist and elitist variants, to raise the problem of "power to do what?" means to ask: *What do rulers do when they rule? Where do the leaders lead the led?* To say or imply that what rulers do when they rule is to maintain their ruling position is at best trivial – and not infrequently wrong. Intentionally and unintentionally what rulers do and do not do affects the ruled, and the same sort of power subjects – in terms of personal background and present interpersonal relations – may affect the ruled in very different ways. There are different effects under pluralism or elitism, different effects under, say, military governments and centralized "oligarchical" organizations.[20] And there are many ways for a ruling class to exercise and maintain its rule, other than by supplying, from its own ranks, the political personnel. It may therefore be argued that rulers and ruling classes would be better identified not by their names and numbers, their social background and power career – although all this is of course not without importance – but by their actions, that is by the objective effects of their actions. From this perspective, the Marxist interjects into the subjectivist discussion, polarized around democracy and dictatorship or, in its contemporary, somewhat lower-pitched versions, pluralism and elitism: democracy of what class, dictatorship of what class?

There is a second aspect to what rulers do when they rule. Talcott Parsons once made a famous critique of utilitarianism for its inability to account for

---

[19] K. Marx, *Das Kapital* (Otto Meissner, 1921), III:2, p. 324; T. Bottomore – M. Rubel, eds., *Karl Marx. Selected Writings in Sociology & Social Philosophy* (London: Watts & Co., 1956), p. 99.

[20] Consider, for instance, the sterility of the Michels type of organizational theory when faced with the completely different behavior of Social Democratic and Communist parties in August 1914 and September 1939, respectively.

social order.[21] What all kinds of subjectivist elite and ruling class theorists are unable to do is to account for *social change.* Characteristically enough, the classical elite theorists, who really thought out the consequences of their theories, all basically held that society did not change. Instead they drew a picture of an eternal cycle of rising, ruling, degenerating, and falling elites. This goes for all of them, Gumplowicz, Mosca, Pareto, and Michels.[22] Ultimately they tended to reduce people and human society to biology.[23] Now, though men certainly are biological organisms, it is an obvious fact that human society has changed over the ages of its existence and has taken a number of forms. The task of a social science must necessarily be to analyse these different historical forms and their change. This cannot be done by taking the subjects of power, their psyche, their will, as the starting point, but only by taking the social context in which they rule.

The society in which the rulers rule contains certain possibilities and tendencies of change. The rulers rule in a certain stage of development of a certain social structure, and their rule both affects and is affected by the tendencies and contradictions inherent therein. The subjectivists stop before analysing these tendencies and contradictions and typically conclude: Look, only a few have power, that is bad! Or: Look many have power, that is good! It should be noted that the important thing in this context of power and change is the effect of the rule – not directly upon individuals, nor upon the gains and handicaps it means for persons and groups[24] – but upon the social structure and social relationships in which the individuals live, because it is the latter, rather than the sheer fact of being handicapped or exploited, which determine the possibilities of change and revolt.

Besides the problem of "power to", there is also a very important neglected problem involved in "power over". Are the different moments of the exercise of somebody's power over somebody else related to each other? If we assume neither that social life is completely random and unpatterned, nor

---

[21] T. Parsons, *The Structure of Social Action* (New York: McGraw-Hill, 1937).

[22] See G. Therborn, *Class, Science and Society* (Goteborg: Revopress, 1974), ch. 4.2; English edition, London: NLB, 1976 forthcoming (American distributor: Humanities Press).

[23] Pareto "extended" the theory of class struggle into the thesis that "The struggle for life and welfare is a general phenomenon for living beings." V. Pareto, *Les Systemes Socialistes* (Paris, 1902–03), 11, p. 455. Michels referred to the struggle between organized workers and strikebreakers in terms of "struggle for feeding-ground." R. Michels, *Political Parties* (Glencoe: Free Press, 1958), p. 307.

[24] This is in contrast to the approach of Bachrach-Baratz, *op. cit.*

that it is a unified, consensual, collective operation, then how should the relationships be studied and how can they be grasped?

At first sight it might appear gratuitous to call this a neglected problem, as it is precisely what the substantial polemics between pluralists and elitists have been about. True to their common subjectivist core, however, the pluralists and the elitists have concentrated on a secondary aspect of the problem. What they have been debating is whether there is an *interpersonal* relation between the different moments of power in society: Is there a cohesive elite which unites the different exercises of power by making the decisions in different areas? Or is there a fragmentation of decision-making between different little or not-connected groups? What this formulation of the issue does not take into serious account is that an interpersonal fragmentation of decision-making does not necessarily mean that the different power events are random and unpatterned. On the contrary, it is a basic, and it seems, warranted, assumption of social science that the events in human society are in some ways always patterned, and therefore possible to grasp by scientific analysis. What the elitism-pluralism theorists have been doing, then, is to concentrate on the existence or non-existence of one possible form of the patterning of power in society and, it should be added, on a form which hardly seems to be the most important one in modern complex societies.

Little is gained in answering this kind of objection by referring to another kind of interpersonal identity than that ensured by overlapping membership in cohesive power groups – by referring, that is, to a common identity of ideas, to a consensus of values.[25] How is a particular kind of consensus and its maintenance to be explained,[26] and how does it actually operate, so general

---

[25] Dahl has written, "... democratic politics is merely the chaff. It is the surface manifestation, representing superficial conflicts. Prior to politics, beneath it, enveloping it, restricting it, conditioning it, is the underlying consensus ... among a predominant portion of the politically active members." R. Dahl, *A Preface to Democratic Theory* (Chicago: Univ. of Chicago Press, 1956), p. 132. But what if "consensus" is the surface manifestation of something else, "enveloping, restricting and conditioning" electoral politics?

[26] This is a weak spot in the otherwise well-substantiated critique of pluralist these by Miliband (*op. cit.*). Miliband basically shrinks from really analysing governments whose personnel is not recruited from the economic elite, and where the higher echelons of the administration may also be recruited otherwise. In such cases he merely refers to the ideology of the political leaders as part of a bourgeois consensus (see ch. 4, part IV). He does provide some empirical material and suggestions for a study of the problem, but it is fundamentally outside his model of control. For the analysis of advanced bourgeois democracies, of reformism fascism, and military governments, a more complex model seems crucial. Similarly, the important works of William

and abstract as it tends to be in modern societies? What objective social structures and social relationships are brought about and/or maintained, how are people's lives patterned by the different exercises of supposedly consensual power?

Important methodological critiques of pluralism have been developed by Bachrach and Baratz,[27] and most recently by Lukes,[28] with their inclusion of institutional "mobilization of bias" and of "non-decision-making,[29] and in the case of Lukes, of latent conflicts and of the effects of inaction.[30] But they do not deal with the present problem, of "power over." In fact, the subjectivist orientation of these authors seems to preclude a way out for the elitists in this respect. What their refined methods can do is to detect more hidden manifestations of elite rule, but they can hardly find social patternings of exercise of power other than those of a unified power subject. With Bachrach-Baratz this is strongly implied by their conception of power, and its related concepts, as an interpersonal relation between A and B.[31] With Lukes it follows from the author's moralistic concern with responsibility. For this reason Lukes is uninterested in impersonal forms of domination and wants to concentrate on cases where it can be assumed that the exerciser(s) of power could have acted differently from how they did. And in this context he throws in a distinction between power and fate![32] To Lukes too, then, power should be analysed

---

Domhoff, on the *haute-bourgeois* backgrounds and connections of American politicians and administrators, and on the cohesiveness of the top-most stratum of the U.S. bourgeoisie, would benefit from being located in a much more elaborate conceptualization and analysis of the U.S. power structure and of the contradictory development of U.S. society.

[27] Bachrach-Baratz, *op. cit.* (1962, 1963, 1970).

[28] S. Lukes, *Power: A Radical View* (London: Macmillan, 1974).

[29] A nondecision means "a decision that results in suppression or thwarting of a latent or manifest challenge to the values or interests of the decision-maker," Bachrach-Baratz, *op. cit.* (1970), p. 44.

[30] Lukes, *op. cit.*, chs. 4, 7. Lukes draws upon the work of Crenson, *op. cit.*

[31] Bachrach-Baratz, *op. cit.* (1970), ch. 2.

[32] Lukes, *op. cit.*, pp. 55–56. Cf. Marx: "I paint the capitalist and the landlord in no sense *coleur de rose*. But here individuals are dealt with only in so far as they are the personifications of economic categories, embodiments of particular class-relations and class interests. My standpoint, from which the evolution of the economic formation is viewed as a process of natural history, can less than any other make the individual responsible for relations whose creature he socially remains, however much he may subjectively raise himself above them." *Das Kapital*, I, p. viii; *Capital* (London: Lawrence & Wishart, 1970), vol. 1, p. 10. Marx's view certainly did not mean that the power of the capitalist was a fate to submit to, but something that could be combatted and abolished. It does mean, however, that it is rather pointless to accuse the capitalists of not behaving like non-capitalists. The Marxian standpoint implies, of

primarily with a view to finding subjects of power, identifiable, free, and responsible originators of acts (and nonacts). He seems to remain stuck within the pluralist-elitist framework, of either a unified elite or various elites or leadership groups (whose interrelationship as a relation of power over others remains obscure, unless they themselves are aware of their relationship).

Marx opened up a path out of the pluralist-elitist impasse, one which seems to have remained almost completely unnoticed among sociologists and political scientists, including writers who have explicitly referred to Marx, more or less critically. The radical novelty and dissimilarity to others of the Marxian approach seems to have been drowned in subjectivist receptions and reinterpretations. The way out indicated by Marx is that the study of a given society should be not just a study of its subjects nor of its structure only, but also and at the same time should be an inquiry into its process of *reproduction*. Significantly, it is in the study of the process of reproduction that Marx analyses the class relationships of exploitation and domination.

Capitalist production, therefore, under its aspect of a continuous connected process, of a process of reproduction, produces not only commodities, not only surplus-value, but it also produces and reproduces the capital relation; on the one side the capitalist, on the other the wage-labourer."[33] In a critique of the subjectivist conceptions of market exchange in 18th- and 19th-century economics Marx provided a critique in advance of 20th-century sociologists as well: "To be sure, the matter looks quite different if we consider capitalist production in the uninterrupted flow of its renewal, and if, in place of the individual capitalist and the individual worker, we view them in their totality, the capitalist class and the working-class confronting each other. But in so doing we should be applying standards entirely foreign to commodity production."[34]

For the study of power in society the perspective of reproduction means that the commanding question of all the variants of the subjectivist approach – Who rules, a unified elite or competing leadership groups? Is the economic elite identical with or in control of the political elite? – is displaced by the question: What kind of society, what fundamental relations of production, are being reproduced? By what mechanisms? What role do the structure and

---

course, that the arm of criticism is replaced by the criticism of arms (i.e., the class struggle in all its forms).

[33] Marx, *op. cit.*, I. p. 541; Lawrence & Wishart editions, I. p. 578.

[34] *Ibid.*, p. 549 and p. 586, respectively.

actions and nonactions of the state (or of local government) play in this process of reproduction, furthering it, merely allowing it, or opposing it?

The analysis of reproduction makes possible an answer to the question of how the different moments of the exercise of power in society are interrelated, even if there is no conscious, interpersonal interrelation. They are interrelated by their reproductive effects. A given kind of relations of production may be reproduced without the exploiting (dominant) class defined by them being in "control" of the government in any usual and reasonable sense of the word, even though the interventions of the state further and/or allow these relations of production to be reproduced. And yet the fact that a specific form of exploitation and domination is being reproduced, *is* an example of class rule and is an important aspect of power in society.

## III

The limited aim of this paper is to distinguish between different approaches to the problem of class and power, particularly between the dialectical-materialist (Marxist) approach and the variants of the subjectivist approach. Such a distinction seems important in order to open up possibilities for the application of the specific Marxist approach, given the fatal flaws of the prevailing subjectivist one. The distinction is particularly important at the present juncture in the social sciences, where, in spite of a renewed interest in and acknowledgement of Marx, an evaluation of the truth and fertility of Marxist theory tends to be made impossible by the amalgams currently fashionable in post-1968 sociology. In such eclectic constructions – which appear to be made according to a recipe like, one part Marx, two parts Weber, and two parts more recent sociology (including ingredients supplied by the cook himself), seasoned with differing amounts of hot (radical) and mild (liberal) spices – the distinctly Marxist analysis is drowned.

With such an aim, the present paper is not a direct contribution to the study of class and power. But within this limitation I will finally try to indicate a few guiding threads for a Marxist type of empirical investigation of the problem of class and power. That only rather general and tentative guiding threads will be offered reflects, I think, not only the limitations of the present paper and of its author, but also the fact that Marx opened up a radically new scientific path, to be constantly cleared of the lush vegetation of dominant ideologies, and on which only the very first steps in the direction of systematic theory have been taken.

The primary object of empirical study, for a grasp of the relations of class, state, and power, should be neither interpersonal relations between different elites (for instance, the government and the business elites), nor their social backgrounds, nor issues and decisions and non-decisions – although all this is important. The primary object should be the effects of the state on the (re)production of a given (whether found or hypothesized) mode (or modes) of production. The relations of domination entailed by the relations of production are concentrated in the state. Through the state the rule of the ruling class is exercised. The character of this rule has to be grasped from the effects of the state. There are two aspects to these effects: *what* is done (and not done) through the state, and *how* things are done that are done through the state. We need a *typology of state interventions* and a *typology of state structures*.

The typology of state structures should distinguish among the differential effects (of legislative, administrative, and judiciary arrangements and procedures, of mechanisms of governmental designation, of organization of army and police, etc.) upon the extent to which the state can be used by different classes – that is, their effects on whether and to what extent the rule of a given class of people (with certain characteristics and qualifications as defined by their position in society) can operate through the state structure under investigation.[35] In this way broad types of state structures can be identified and distinguished in terms of their class character, for example feudal states, bourgeois states and proletarian states (in which the principle of "politics in command", as realized in soviets, workers' parties, mass movements of cultural revolution, etc., seems to be a central characteristic). Various specific state apparatuses, such as legislative bodies, the judiciary, or the army, could also be studied from this point of view. It should of course not be assumed that a concrete state at a specific point in time necessarily has a homogeneous class character in all its institutions – which raises the problem then of how to establish its dominant class character.

To study the process by which the state actually operates we also have to have a typology of state interventions (including non-interventions significant

[35] This seems to indicate a way out of the dilemma posed by Claus Offe in his very penetrating essay, 'Klassenherrschaft und politisches System. Zur Selektivitat politischer Institutionen', in his *Strukturprobleme des kapitalistischen Staates* (Frankfurt: Suhrkamp, 1972). This is an "objectivist" approach to the problem of the selectivity of the state, but it is not based on any definitions of the objective interests of the revolutionary class, which Offe rejects (p. 86). Neither does it mean that an empirical inquiry into the class character of the state only can be made *post festum*, as Offe concludes (p. 90), when the class struggle has developed to the point where the limits of a given state appear.

| Effect upon given relations of political domination (Structure of administration and repression) | Effect upon given relations of production | | |
|---|---|---|---|
| | Further | Allow | Go against/ Break |
| Increase | 1 | 2 | 3 |
| Maintain | 4 | 5 | 6 |
| Go against/ Break | 7 | 8 | 9 |

to the (re)production of given relations of production). Such a typology could be almost endlessly refined. Basically, however, it should comprise two dimensions. One concerns what is done, and the other how it is done. In other words, one refers to the external effects of state intervention on other structures of society, above all on the relations of production, (but also on the ideological system), and the other refers to the internal effects upon the state itself. State intervention can either further, merely allow, or go against, and at the limit break, given relations of production.

And they can either increase, maintain, or go against, and at the limit break, given relations of political domination as embodied in the character of apparatuses of administration (and government) and repression. (The possibilities of successfully breaking given relations of production are fundamentally determined by the particular stage of the relations and forces of production, and the stage of the relations of force between classes which this implies.) The following table illustrates the types of state intervention possible along these two dimensions.

This typology can be applied both to a given political measure, such as a social security program, nationalization, a land reform, a school reform, etc., and to the sum of actions undertaken by a given government over a given period. It is in this way that the class character, in the Marxist sense, of a regime or a policy is to be ascertained. For example, a nationalization act or a land reform can allow and even further capitalist relations of production if it is carried out through the rules of the capitalist game, involving compensation more or less at market value, implementation through the established legislative and administrative procedure, and the creation of enterprises run by new owners using wage labor for profit (or for subsidizing other enterprises run for profit). But such measures can also be put into effect in the opposite manner, without necessarily meaning the complete abolition of capitalism in the society. A regional policy can be carried out with the help of various kinds of subsidies, such as tax rebates, to capitalist enterprises, thus following the logic of capitalist relations of production but making a certain localization of plants more profitable. But the same measure can also go against that logic, through mandatory planning. The class character is determined on the basis of the identity of the dominant (exploiting) class (i.e., the dominant class of the particular relations of production furthered or allowed by the interventions). If there is a discrepancy in the effects upon the relations of production and the structure of the state, this indicates a contradictory and unstable situation. For instance, in the case of the last period of Czarist Russia, the state furthered the developing capitalist relations of production while at the same time basically maintaining a largely pre-capitalist form of state; Soviet Russia in the 1920's allowed capitalist relations of production to develop while maintaining a proletarian dictatorship; and the Allende regime in Chile partly allowed, partly went against, capitalist relations of production while maintaining the existing state structure (its administration, judiciary, and army).

It should be underlined that, as a rule, there are a number of ways in which given relations of production can be furthered in a given situation. Opinions therefore usually differ over which is the best one. Consequently, a given state intervention may very well go against the current opinion of business organizations, but still further capitalist relations of production. The bourgeoisie as a class, and its interests, are not identical with the identity or ideas of a particular group of business leaders at a particular point in time. From this perspective we can understand the pattern that frequently appears in capitalist politics, wherein policies, when first introduced, are opposed by business groups and conservative parties, but once carried out, are accepted by them, with longer or shorter delay (e.g. collective bargaining, social security programs, Keynesian economics). This phenomenon is hidden by the issues-and-decisions approach of the pluralist methodologists.

*The ruling class* of a given society is the exploiting class of that exploitative system of relations of production furthered (above others, if there are other relations of production in the society) by the content and form of the totality of state interventions during a given period. The ruling class need not necessarily be the economically dominant class, in the sense of the exploiting class of the dominant mode of production in a society where there are several modes of production (e.g., self-subsistence farming, feudalism, petty commodity production, capitalism).

One possible refinement of the typology is to distinguish among their effects on the two different classes (exploiting and exploited) that bear the exploitative relations of production that the interventions in question further, allow, or go against. For instance reformist governments usually are to be found in squares 4 and 5 in the table above although certain of their measures will be found in 1 and 2, as for example anti-strike measures – but a more refined typology would direct the study to their possible effects on the *relations of distribution within the given relations of production*. Another refinement, as regards the effects on the state, would be to differentiate between the class effects on the *administrative* and on the *repressive* apparatuses of the state. Fascist regimes, analyzed in terms of their effect on capitalist relations of production, belong in square 1, but they are more closely characterized within that type by their increase in the repressive apparatus of the bourgeois state.[36] A third elaboration would be to distinguish between effects of the state on different fractions of capital, e.g., industrial versus banking (or commercial or agrarian) capital, domestic versus foreign capital, big (monopoly) versus small capital. In this way different hegemonic fractions of the bourgeoisie can be identified.

What the ruling class does when it rules, in the Marxist sense, then, is not to make, as a compact unit, all important decisions in society. The rule of the ruling class is exercised by a set of objectively interrelated but not necessarily interpersonally unified mechanisms of reproduction, through which the given mode of exploitation is reproduced. The ruling class, in this sense, is not a unified power subject. The rule of the ruling class is not necessarily, and is usually not, expressed in conscious collective decisions and actions by the class as a whole. What the ruling class does when it rules is not primarily a matter of subjective intentions and actions. Its rule is embodied in an objective social process, through which a certain mode of production is maintained

[36] Fascism is also distinguished by its furthering of monopoly capitalist relations of production, which points to still another distinction in terms of fractions of classes furthered or disadvantaged by the state interventions. Cf. N. Poulantzas, *Fascism and Dictatorship* (London: NLB, 1974).

and expanded, guaranteed and furthered by the state. This means that the pluralist-elitist debate does not pertain to the existence of a ruling class in the radically different Marxist sense. What that debate is concerned with are certain aspects of the mode of organization of the ruling class, such as its cohesion.

It should be noticed that neither the existence of a ruling class, nor what class is the ruling class, nor the amount of its power, are defined here *a priori*. What classes there are has to be uncovered by an analysis of the relations of production in a given society. The ruling class has to be identified and the amount of its political power, the range of its rule, has to be ascertained by a study of the structure and the interventions of the state. The dialectical-materialist approach to power in society is an empirical approach, although of a quite different kind. Having located the ruling class, another task is then to lay bare the mechanisms of its rule, which includes finding an answer to why the actual interventions of the state function – as such mechanisms.

The state power of the ruling class is part of the total reproduction process of society. As Poulantzas[37] has pointed out, there are two aspects of reproduction (and it should be added of revolution as well): the reproduction of the positions of the given social structure, and the reproduction of individuals who can occupy them. For example, capital, wage labor, and capitalist enterprise have to be reproduced, as does the state apparatus. The reproduction of position also involves, at least in the long run, the production and reproduction of a compatibility between the different levels of the social structure. The reproduction of capitalism requires not only the reproduction of capitalist enterprise but in the long run the reproduction of a compatible capitalist state as well.

But also, new generations of individuals – and the given individuals year in and year out – have to be trained to occupy the given positions, to be qualified or subjected to fulfill adequately the tasks provided by the social structure. Out of the new-born infants a given proportion have to be reared to become owners and managers of capital, other portions to become workers, white collar employees, and administrative and repressive personnel, or petty-bourgeois farmers, shop-keepers, and artisans.

What broad types of mechanisms of reproduction – within which we can seek and find the concrete mechanisms in concrete societies – can be identified?

[37] N. Poulantzas, 'On Social Classes', *New Left Review* 78 (1973), p. 49.

One of primary importance is, of course, economic constraint. Economic constraint functions, in ways laid bare by specific economic analysis, in and through the stage of the productive forces, the inherent dynamics of the relations of production, and the interdependence of the forces and relations of production. It operates on various levels and decisively affects both the reproduction of positions and of the agents to occupy them. A given level of the development of the productive forces excludes certain relations of production, makes them untenable or obsolete and non-competitive; and the necessity for some kind of material reproduction then favors certain other relations of production, and determines the range of political options, such as for the Bolshevik government after the civil war. On a lower level, economic constraint imposes certain limits upon what a capitalist corporation or a feudal manor can do to stay in business, limits for instance on the extent to which one corporation or manor can tamper with the capitalist and feudal relations of production governing other corporations or manors. Economic constraint operates in a constant process to reproduce a certain structure of economic positions, by sanctions of bankruptcies, unemployment, poverty, and sometimes outright starvation. Economic constraint is an important mechanism for keeping even revolutionarily-conscious peasants and workers in line and harnessing them for the reproduction of the society they would like to overthrow.

Another important type of mechanism of reproduction is political, and includes two basic subtypes, administration and repression, which in modern societies are both regularly concentrated in a distinct state apparatus (or, rather, system of state apparatuses). Through administrative interventions – taxation, regulations, subsidies, countercyclical policies, etc. – the reproduction of a certain mode (or modes) of production is favored or hindered. Administration also functions in the reproduction of agents for the positions of the given modes of production, through such things as manpower policies (from binding peasants to their landlords to stimulating labor market mobility) and social security policies (from providing dreaded workhouses to supplying social security benefits, which function both to alleviate dangerous discontent and to stimulate business). Administrative interventions operate to ensure the overall compatibility of the substructures of society. The mechanism of administration also includes mechanisms for the reproduction of the state apparatus itself, embodied in constitutional provisions, procedures for the due handling of issues, or legal conceptions. These can hinder a government which may intend on far-reaching social change, or can restrict the accessibility to the state of certain classes or sections of classes.

Repression is the other important political mechanism of reproduction. The development or maintenance of certain modes of production can be repressed by the army, the police, prisons, or the executioner. Movements of opposition can be repressed in various ways and degrees. (One interesting and neglected object of study in this respect concerns to what extent the development of the labor movement in the United States has been stopped by repression, especially after World War I and World War II.) Individuals who refuse to accept any of the given positions can be taken care of, for instance in prisons or in mental hospitals.

Mechanisms of reproduction, then, are not only, nor even mainly, ideological, as sociologists are prone to assume.[38] But ideological mechanisms are of course important too. Their primary role is not in legitimating the prevailing system,[39] but rather in a differential shaping of aspirations and self-confidence

---

[38] Parsons treats the problem of reproduction or "pattern-maintenance" solely in terms of transmission of values. For a relatively recent formulation see T. Parsons. *The System of Modern Societies* (Englewood Cliffs, N.J.: Prentice-Hall, 1971), pp. 10–15. Similarly all "social sources of stability" singled out by Parkin (*op. cit.*, 1971, ch. 2) refer to ideological mechanisms: mobility, the educational system, religion, gambling, and the fostering of beliefs in luck. A noteworthy exception is H.F. Moorhouse's interesting account of the political and economic constraints imposed upon the British working class up to 1918 and their role in shaping later working class "deference", in his "The Political Incorporation of the British Working Class: An Interpretation," *Sociology* 7 (1973), pp. 341–59. See also the discussion by R. Gray, "The Political Incorporation of the Working Class," *Sociology* 9 (1975), pp. 101–04; H.F. Moorhouse, "On the Political Incorporation of the Working Class: Reply to Gray." *Ibid.*, pp. 105–10. See footnote 72, on the concentration (in the discussion of social reproduction) on legitimation, a preoccupation coming out of the Weberian tradition.

[39] To identify the ideological mechanisms of reproduction with the processes of legitimation would imply that people do not revolt against the given rule under which they live because they regard it as legitimate. This seems hardly warranted. People may not revolt, political and economic constraints aside, because they do not know the kind of domination they are subjected to. That is, they may be hold ignorant not only of its negative features but of its positive claims and achievements as well. They may be ignorant of alternatives, or they may feel themselves incapable of doing anything about it, even if they know of other possible types of societies. But this ignorance, disinterest, and lack of confidence are not simply there, as characteristics of certain individuals and groups, they are produced by definite social processes. See the important distinction between pragmatic and normative acceptance made by Michael Mann, "The Social Cohesion of Liberal Democracy." *American Sociological Review* 35 (1970), pp. 423–39. The one-eyed concentration on legitimation is often related to a normative conception: that every rule should be based on the true and knowing consensus of the ruled, thereby holding it legitimate. See, for instance, J. Habermas, *Legitimationsprobleme im Spatkapitallismus* (Frankfurt: Suhrkapm, 1973), esp. pp. 162ff. But that is another question. Interestingly enough, Habermas and Offe

and in a differential provision of skills and knowledge. This process of qualification and subjection, in which little human animals are formed into members of different classes, takes place in a number of ideological apparatuses: the family, the educational system, the church, the mass media, on-the-job training, and the workplace (where so much of the inculcation of hierarchy and discipline takes place).[40] These apparatuses and the dominant ideological formation which takes place in them, are not necessarily congruent with each other. One particularly problematic relationship is that between the family and other apparatuses, such as the church and (above all in modern capitalism) the educational system. On the one hand, the family is an important mechanism of reproduction; but on the other, a certain amount of individual mobility is crucial to the reproduction of the system. For individual mobility implies that the commanding positions are occupied by more competent persons, as well as offering an obvious channel of discontent. As Marx pointed out, referring both to capitalist enterprise and to the Catholic Church of the Middle Ages: "The more a ruling class is able to assimilate the most prominent men of the dominated classes the more stable and dangerous is its rule."[41] The Marxist perspective notes that rigidly differentiated access to the educational system tends to make exploitation *less* stable. In the Marxist perspective, what is most important to the reproduction of exploitation is not differential access to the educational system, but the differential educational system itself. Mobility, then, is essentially an ideological mechanism of reproduction. So also is another phenomenon dear to all subjectivists, interpersonal intercourse, which contributes to a common outlook among the representatives of different constituencies.

---

both accept Weber's ideal type of competitive capitalism, against which they contrast modern capitalism with its enormously increased amount of state interventions, supposedly making more ideological legitimation necessary (Habermas, *op. cit.*, Ch. II.; Offe, "Tauschverhaltnis und politische Steuerung. Zur Aktualitat des Legitimationsproblems," in Offe, *op. cit.*, pp. 27–63). This view tends to veil the important role of ideology in the era of competitive capitalism – the era of human rights declarations, of the ascendance of bourgeois nationalism, and of still-strong established and dissenting religions – and to veil as well the economic and Political mechanisms of crisis and revolution in the present period, a period which has witnessed the shattering of the economic foundations of the British Empire and is witnessing the shaking of the supremacy of the United States.

[40] See the very important essay by Louis Althusser, "Ideology and Ideological State Apparatuses (Notes towards an Investigation)," in his *Lenin and Philosophy and Other Essays* (London: NLB, 1971), pp. 121–273. For unconvincing reasons, however, Althusser talks of ideological state apparatuses.

[41] Marx, *Das Kapital*, III: 2, p. 140; Bottomore-Rubel, *op. cit.*, p. 190.

Through these mechanisms of reproduction the ruling class can exercise its rule and keep state power without necessarily having to supply the political and administrative personnel. The economic laws of motion of a given society set a very high threshold for their possible trespass by politicians. The structural arrangements of the state (its class character) circumscribe the state interventions decided upon by the government. The ideological mechanisms of reproduction shape both the politicians – even labor politicians with no personal intercourse with the bourgeois cream – and the population at large, including the exploited classes.

All these mechanisms operate in and through the conflict and struggle of classes. Class struggle then does not mean, even mainly, battles between unified, self-conscious entities. It means conflict and struggles between people who occupy different positions in exploitative modes of production.

Reproduction and revolution, consequently, are not to be understood in terms of mechanisms of reproduction versus class struggle. The reproductive mechanisms also produce, at the same time, mechanisms of revolution. To realize this is, of course, a basic feature of a dialectical approach. Marx analyzed, for instance, how the expanded reproduction of capital also meant the development of contradictions between the relations and the forces of production. That analysis might be extended to the political and ideological processes of reproduction. For example, the strengthening of the state – and with it the strengthening of administrative and repressive operations of the state – which characterizes the modern, imperialistic state of capitalism, has been accompanied by more devastating contradictions among capitalist states. The two world wars of the 20th century gave rise to non-capitalist regimes among a third of humanity. Similarly, at the ideological level, the role of the intelligentsia, both in old Russia and China and recently in the advanced capitalist societies, testifies to the fact that the mechanism of qualification and subjection might also take on the character of a revolutionary mechanism, developing a contradiction between qualification and subjection. There are also mechanisms of revolution which operate in and through the class struggle. And, looked at from the other side of the same coin, the class struggle is fought in and through mechanisms of reproduction and revolution. But all that is another part of the story, and, maybe, part of another paper.

G. William Domhoff

# State and Ruling Class in Corporate America: Reflections, Corrections, and New Directions

The paper reprinted here from a 1974 issue of *The Insurgent Sociologist* is one of the most gratifying I ever wrote because it marks the culmination of the efforts by power structure researchers, starting with C. Wright Mills (1956) and Floyd Hunter (1959), to show critics of class-dominance theories exactly how the corporate rich dominate the federal government. Building on the work of many social scientists and historians who came of age in academe within the spaces created by the new social movements of the 1960s, the four-process model I present in the paper later gained widespread acceptance when it was fleshed out in *The Powers That Be* (Domhoff, 1979), a book that went on to be one of the top 50 best sellers in sociology since World War II according to a study by Gans (1997). I think the theory is as accurate and relevant now as it was when I wrote it.

Drawing on a detailed tracing of linkages among individuals, institutions, money flows, and policy issues that anticipated the later mainstream interest in network analysis, the model suggests there are four relatively distinct, but overlapping processes through which the tightly knit corporate community controls the public agenda and then wins on most issues that are taken up by the federal government:

1. The *special-interest process* deals with the narrow policy concerns of specific corporations and business

sectors. It operates through lobbyists, company lawyers, and trade associations, with a focus on congressional committees, departments of the executive branch, and regulatory agencies.

2. The *policy-planning process* formulates the general interests of the corporate community. It operates through a policy-planning network of foundations, think tanks, and policy-discussion groups, with a focus on the White House, relevant Congressional committees, and the high-status newspapers and opinion magazines published in New York and Washington. It has "moderate-conservative" and "ultra-conservative" tendencies within it.

3. The *candidate-selection process* is concerned with the election of candidates who are sympathetic to the agenda put forth in the special-interest and policy-planning processes. It operates through large campaign donations and hired political consultants, with a focus on the presidential campaigns of both major political parties and the Congressional campaigns of the Republican Party.

4. The *opinion-shaping process* attempts to influence public opinion and keep some issues off the public agenda. Often drawing on rationales and statements developed within the policy-planning process, it operates through the public relations departments of large corporations, general public relations firms, and many small opinion-shaping organizations, with a focus on middle-class voluntary organizations, educational institutions, and the mass media.

The model in this paper originally was aimed at the pluralists, the then-ascendant theory group within the social sciences, which went into decline in the late 1970s and 1980s. Happily, the model proved to be just as useful in the arguments that later arose with the state autonomy theorists. For example, building on original research by historian Laurence Shoup (1975; 1977) on the role of the Council on Foreign Relations in shaping post-World War II foreign policy, I was able to refute through new archival research the claims by Stephen Krasner (1978) concerning the alleged role of autonomous state elites in making the postwar foreign policy decisions that eventually led to the Vietnam War (Domhoff, 1990, chapter 5). Today there are few social scientists who would deny that a foreign policy "establishment," rooted in the policy-planning network discussed in this paper, shapes American foreign policy.

Even more satisfying, the four-process model made it possible to do original archival research on the origins of the Agricultural Adjustment Act (1933) and Social Security Act (1935), which shows just how wrong Theda Skocpol

(1980) and her students (Amenta, 1998; Finegold & Skocpol, 1995; Orloff, 1993) are about the New Deal because they rely exclusively on secondary sources that miss all the important issues (Domhoff, 1996, chapters 3 and 5). The model also proved robust in refuting the claims of Gregory Hooks (1991) on the industrial mobilization for World War II, which did not lead to an autonomous Pentagon, as he claims, but to the incorporation of the generals and admirals into the corporate-based leadership group (Domhoff, 1996, chapter 6), just as Mills (1956) had said 40 years earlier. In the mid-1990s, most of these state autonomy theorists began to call themselves "historical institutionalists." They expressed satisfaction that they supposedly established for the first time how "the logics of state-building and the international states system are not reducible to an economic or class logic" (Orloff, 1993, p. 85). Actually, this idea was news to very few people. Meanwhile, these theorists still discuss the "potential" autonomy of the state, about which there never was very much dispute, but they no longer claim autonomy for the American state.

However, just at the time when the state autonomy theorists were in effect abandoning the debate over state power to engage in other pursuits, the pluralists within political science began a revival through claims about "liberal" victories in the late 1960s and 1970s. They were able to do so because they overlooked the determinative role of the moderate conservatives within the policy-planning process. Although there were indeed some genuine victories for liberalism through the civil rights movement, the feminist movement, and other movements for group and individual rights and freedoms, the victories in relation to issues concerning corporate and class power have been few and far between.

The most detailed statement of this neo-pluralist view (Berry, 1999) suggests a "new liberalism" has arisen in the form of citizen's lobbies. For example, all environmental groups are counted as part of this new liberalism, but the key groups as far as policy formulation are still funded by large foundations and are part of the moderate-conservative wing of the policy-planning network (Domhoff, 2002, chapter 4). True enough, liberal and left environmentalists have sensitized public opinion on environmental issues, created watchdog groups whose reports receive attention in the mass media, and developed new ideas and technologies for controlling pollution that have been grudgingly accepted by the corporate community. But since 1975 they have not been able to pass any legislation that is opposed by the Business

Roundtable. The environmental movement as a whole, and the liberal wing in particular, is more marginal in a power sense than its public reputation would suggest. It is also true that the consumer movement that developed out of the movements of the 1960s was able to pass many new consumer protection laws between 1967 and 1974 (Vogel, 1989). However, there is less evidence of liberal power in this story than meets the eye, because the relevant business groups either agreed with the legislation or forced modifications to make it acceptable.

Contrary to the claims by the neo-pluralists, the only significant defeat for a united corporate community since the 1960s is the establishment of the Occupational Safety and Health Administration in 1970, which was strongly opposed by corporate leaders as both a possible precedent for enlarging government regulation and as a potential stronghold for unions. Even here, the ensuing history of this new agency is instructive in terms of corporate power through lobbying and legislative in-fighting: By the 1980s, as detailed studies show, the corporate community had turned the agency into a "political prisoner" through delays in providing information, legislative amendments limiting its power, legal victories that further reduce its power, and budget cuts that make inspections fewer and more superficial. As if to make this case even more difficult for pluralists, these changes occurred despite strong public sentiment in favor of enforcing workplace safety laws (Noble, 1986; Szasz, 1984).

As these comments on the state autonomy theorists and neo-pluralists suggest, I strongly believe the four-process model has stood the test of time and fended off its rivals. Its regular appearance in mainstream political sociology textbooks also attests to its success. However, I also think I made three mistakes in the paper that don't have to do with the model itself. My first mistake is an overemphasis on "ideological hegemony" in explaining the acceptance of the current socioeconomic system. I still think that the "ideology process" is an important part of the overall governance process, but merely as an "opinion-shaping network" that "attempts" to influence public opinion. Despite what I now would see as a lack of complete success, the opinion-shaping process is still useful because public acceptance of corporate policies allows the system to run much more smoothly than it otherwise would. I also continue to doubt that public opinion is influential even when it is opposed to the policy preferences of the corporate community, except in setting broad limits. I have made this argument in detail in an edited book on public opinion featuring rival viewpoints (Domhoff, 2002a). The concluding chapter of that book, by one of the co-editors (Page, 2002), largely sides with my view rather than the claims by sophisticated quantitative modelers of a pluralist persuasion within political science.

Soon after my 1974 paper was written, I came to emphasize even more than I had before that people go along with the system for many reasons, not just ideological ones, starting with the fact they like their everyday lives, but also including the fact that they don't see any good alternatives or any structural openings that would make any risks worth the trouble (Flacks, 1988; Mann, 1975; Molotch, 1976). I agree with Flacks (1988) that we should start with the assumption that people's lives are as sensible as they can be under the circumstances they face. The people are not bamboozled. They hold many opinions that are contrary to what the corporate elite tries to market through the opinion-shaping process, especially on economic issues (Page & Shapiro, 1992).

My second mistake appeared in a sentence where I say that the executive branch of the federal government is now "the most important." Here I was following Mills (1956) and the general overemphasis on the executive branch in the 1960s, which was due to the government's many overseas involvements. Even while making this claim, I was at the same time reading in daily newspapers and weekly magazines about the myriad ways that liberal legislation was bottled up and mangled in Congress. Today I would make the point that the interactions among the branches of the federal government do not allow for such generalizations about "most important." They all matter.

The section of the paper containing the sentence about "most important" has been removed for purposes of this reprinting because it merely repeats my previous attempts to satisfy pluralist criticisms, and would be of little interest to 21st century readers. However, it is important to acknowledge this mistake because the power of the corporate elite in the executive branch is based in good part on the fact that conservatives always have been a majority in both houses of Congress. In the past, this conservative majority functioned as a conservative voting bloc made up of Southern Democrats and Northern Republicans. Since the 1990s, as everyone knows, the Northern and Southern rich have been united in the Republican Party. What has changed is that the southern conservative Republicans may be even more conservative on many issues, such as social spending, than the old Southern Democrats. As representatives of plantation capitalists, the Southern Democrats of yore had a little different agenda, and as members of the Democratic Party they had to compromise on some issues with Northern liberals and machine Democrats (Domhoff, 1990, chapter 9).

My third mistake is closely related to the second in that I thought the Southern rich and their politicians would stay in the Democratic Party, making any liberal or progressive change through the two-party system extremely difficult, to say the least. Although it is true that Southern Democrats, and the conservative voting bloc, did remain powerful in Congress much longer than the pundits said they would, as later research showed (Alston & Ferrie, 1999; Domhoff, 1990; Shelley, 1983), my claim was wrong because it did not take seriously two major structural changes of the previous decades, one in the Southern economy, the other in the Southern polity. First, the economy in the South was changing, partly due to the mechanization of Southern plantations in the aftermath of the Agricultural Adjustment Act, but also due to the gradual industrialization of the South hastened by World War II defense contracts and the movement of industrialists to the low-wage, anti-union South to escape unionization in the North. Second, the Civil Rights Movement changed the structure of Southern politics through the Voting Rights Act of 1965. The change in the economy meant that the Southern capitalists had less reason to remain Democrats, and the change in the polity meant that African-Americans had the ability to force the worst racists out of the Democratic Party through their votes in both primaries and regular elections. The end result was that most of the Southern rich were on their way to the Republican Party, taking the majority of average-income whites with them on the basis of appeals to racism and religious fundamentalism.

I did not have a full appreciation of how these changes in the South would play out for three reasons. First, I had done interviews with white Southerners for *Fat Cats and Democrats* (1972) that convinced me it made both economic and political sense for conservative rich whites to remain Democrats. Second, I was fooled by the gradualness of the change due to the fact that few elected Southern legislators were willing to give up the power they enjoyed by virtue of being Democrats with long seniority. Third, I underestimated the power potential of the African-American vote in reshaping the Democratic Party.

Since the late 1980s I have seen the situation very differently. I now say that the massive social movement called the Civil Rights Movement changed the power structure in the Democratic Party and made possible a nationwide liberal-labor-left coalition within the two-party system for the first time in

American history. It is a major structural opening created by the kind of movements that all varieties of insurgent sociologists extol as the key to history. This movement made normal politics possible, and it made taking over the Democratic Party sensible and feasible.

Most political sociologists and social movement theorists agree that power needs an organizational base. Putting aside arguments among Marxists, Weberians, cultural theorists, and military theorists about what Mann (1986) calls "ultimate primacy," perhaps we can all agree that the major organizational bases are few: the economic system, the political system (the state), the military, and religion. For example, social classes rooted in capitalist economic relations give rise to business organizations on the one hand and trade unions on the other. The political system gives rise to political parties (as structured in number and form by the nature of electoral rules), elected officials, and state-based administrative/bureaucratic elites. The means of violence give rise to armies (regular and guerilla), and religion gives rise to faith-based places of worship that can be a base for power, which in the United States means everything from synagogues and Southern black churches on the liberal side to evangelical Protestant churches on the right.

In addition, there is probably widespread agreement among sociologists that the slave/Jim Crow political economy in the South made unions and a liberal political party impossible in that region, which in turn warped all of American politics. Perhaps there is also agreement that the American presidential/winner-take-all/single-member-district system is not conducive to third parties of the left or right. In the case of left-wing third parties, for example, they can hurt the short-run interests of low-income workers, feminists, environmentalists, and religious liberals if Republicans win the election due to their efforts, and thereby make liberals and leftists into bitter rivals rather than potential coalition partners. Within that context, we can see why the Civil Rights Movement and Voting Rights Act are so important over and beyond what they did for African-Americans. They gave liberals, leftists, and union members their first potential nationwide organizational base, an argument I have made in detail in a book on how to bring about progressive social change in the United States (Domhoff, 2003. Chapters 1 and 2).

I stress the word "potential" in the previous sentence because a coalition of social movements and progressive trade unionists is by no means close to controlling the Democratic Party. There still aren't enough liberals to matter in Congress. Nor is such a coalition likely to come into being without the moral energy and organizational skills provided by the kinds of activists who created the social movements of the 1960s and the global justice movement of the 1990s. If such activists currently have any focus on the political arena at all, it is usually through one or another third party, as demonstrated by the continuing efforts of the Green Party despite the disastrous outcome of the 2000 presidential elections for the programs its members believe in. Moreover, even if these activists did decide to redirect their energies into transforming the Democratic Party through the creation of "clubs" (their own organizations) inside of it, and then challenging on progressive platforms in its primaries, they still would have to overcome the many barriers to liberal black/white voting coalitions in the Southern states. That is, they could not concede nearly one-third of the Congress to the Republicans, which is what the states of the Old South now represent, and have any hope of defeating the corporate-conservative coalition that currently rules America (Domhoff, 2002b).

Structurally speaking, then, I believe that it is now feasible to use primaries to agitate for alternative economic arrangements thanks to the Civil Rights Movement. Voters who care deeply about Social Security, government support for fuller employment, civil rights, or abortion rights – which includes a majority of women, a majority of African-Americans, Asian-Americans, Jews, and Latinos, and many low-income and/or liberal white Protestants and Catholics – may come to prefer any Democrat to any Republican all other things being equal. The problem, of course, is that "all other things" are never equal. Liberals and leftists need a complete program on everything from the economy to foreign policy to be competitive.

In closing, let me add that there is one anachronism in the paper in addition to the three mistakes. The paper starts with the assumption, based on polls of the 1960s, that few people agree there is a ruling class in America. Since the 1980s, however, a large majority of people have concluded that big corporations and the wealthy few run everything, and that the federal government does not care about the average person. The radical sociologists who did research on the power structure in America from the 1950s through 1990s can take no credit for this large change in viewpoint. Many different wars, political scandals, and corporate scams since the 1960s caused it.

However, radical sociologists can take satisfaction in the fact that their once-marginal views on the power structure have been incorporated into mainstream sociology. Their findings, concepts, and models did make sense once scholars had the motivation to look at them seriously thanks to the upheavals of the 1960s and 1970s. Today there are very few sociologists who question the idea of corporate dominance in the United States. The idea of a "power structure" is taken for granted in introductory sociology textbooks, for example, with most disagreements focusing on just how dominant the corporate rich are and exactly how they operate.

But this success does not mean the work of power structure researchers is complete. There is much more to be learned, and the power structure is constantly shifting to some degree besides. Even more, new power structure researchers within sociology have to figure out where there are cracks and openings in the American power structure, such as the one created within the Democratic Party by the Civil Rights Movement. I hope this reflection and the article reprinted here contribute to this effort.

G. William Domhoff

# State and Ruling Class in Corporate America*

On top of the gradually-merging social layers of blue and white collar workers in the United States, there is, a very small social upper class which comprises at most 1% of the population and has a very different life style from the rest of us. Members of this privileged class, according to sociological studies, live in secluded neighborhoods and well-guarded apartment complexes, send their children to private schools, announce their teenage daughters to the world by means of debutante teas and debutante balls, collect expensive art and antiques, play backgammon and dominoes at their exclusive clubs, and travel all around the world on their numerous vacations and junkets.

There is also in America, an extremely distorted distribution of wealth and income. Throughout the twentieth century, the top 1% or so of wealth-holders have owned 25–30% of all wealth and 55–65% of the wealth that really counts, corporate stock in major businesses and banks. But even that is not the whole story, for a mere .1% have at least 19% of all the wealth in the country – 190 times as much as they would have if everyone had an equal share. As for income, well, the maldistribution is not quite as bad. But one recent study argues that if income from capital gains is included, the top 1.5% of wealthholders

---

* This original version of this article appeared in *The Insurgent Sociologist* 4:3 (Spring, 1974), pp. 3–16.

receive 24% of yearly national income. And, as all studies on matters of wealth and income are quick to point out, these estimates are conservative.

It is not hard for most of us to imagine that the social upper class uncovered in sociological research is made up of the top wealthholders revealed in wealth and income studies. However, it is not necessary to rely on our imaginations, for it is possible to do empirical studies linking the one group to the other. The first systematic studies along this line were reported by sociologist E. Digby Baltzell, but there have been others since.

In most countries, and in most times past in our own country, it would be taken for granted that an upper class with a highly disproportionate amount of wealth and income is a ruling class with domination over the government. How else, it would have been argued, could a tiny group possess so much if it didn't have its hooks into government? But not so in the United States of today. This nation is different, we are assured. It has no social classes, at least not in the traditional European sense, and anyhow there is social mobility – new millionaires are created daily. Besides, many different groups, including organized labor, organized farmers, consumers, and experts, have a hand in political decisions – at least since the New Deal. There is no such thing as a ruling class in America.[1]

In this paper I am going to suggest that in fact a ruling class does dominate this country, a suggestion which not only flies in the face of prevailing academic wisdom, but raises problems for political activists as well. To support this suggestion, I will describe four processes through which the wealthy few who are the ruling class dominate government. Let me begin by defining two terms, "ruling class" and "power elite." By a ruling class, I mean a clearly demarcated social upper class which

a. has a disproportionate amount of wealth and income:

b. generally fares better than other social groups on a variety of well-being statistics ranging from infant mortality rates to educational attainments to feelings of happiness to health and longevity;

c. controls the major economic institutions of the country; and

d. dominates the governmental processes of the country.

---

[1] For typical expressions of this view, consult sociologist Arnold Rose, *The Power Structure* (Oxford University Press, 1967), political scientist Robert Dahl, *Pluralist Democracy in the United States* (Rand McNally, 1967), or political scientist Grand McConnell, *Private Power and American Democracy* (Alfred A. Knopf, 1966).

By a power elite I mean the "operating arm" or "leadership group" or "establishment" of the ruling class. This power elite is made up of active, working members of the upper class and high-level employees in institutions controlled by members of the upper class.

Both of these concepts, I contend, are important in a careful conceptualization of how America is ruled. The distinction between ruling class and power elite allows us to deal with the everyday observation, which is also the first objection raised by critics of ruling-class theory, that some members of the ruling class are not involved in ruling, and that some rulers are not members of upper class. Which is no problem at all, in reality. There always have been many members of ruling classes who spent most of their time playing polo, riding hounds, or leading a world-wide social life. And there always have been carefully-groomed and carefully-selected employees who have been placed in positions of importance in government.

The most important criticism of class-dominance theory is championed by political scientists, who say proponents of ruling class theory do not spell out the mechanisms by which the ruling class supposedly dominates government. Not content to infer power from such indicators as wealth and well-being statistics, they want the case for governmental domination by a ruling class demonstrated in its own right, without appeal to statistics on wealth, income, health, and happiness.

Despite the generally negative response I have received from political scientists, I would like to take another stab at satisfying their major criticism of ruling-class theory. Perhaps it is masochism that motivates this near-hopeless task, but I have a new way of thinking about the problem of ruling class and government that may put things in a new light. Simply put, I think there are four general processes through which economically and politically active members of the ruling class, operating as the leaders of the power elite, involve themselves in government at all levels. I call these four processes:

1. the special-interest process, which has to do with the various means utilized by wealthy individuals, specific corporations, and specific sectors of the economy to satisfy their narrow, short-run needs;

2. the policy-planning process, which has to do with the development and implementation of general policies that are important to the interests of the ruling class as a whole;

3. the candidate-selection process, which has to do with the ways in which members of the ruling class insure that they have "access" to the politicians who are elected to office; and

4. the ideology-process, which has to do with the formation, dissemination, and enforcement of attitudes and assumptions which permit the continued existence of policies and politicians favorable to the wealth, income, status, and privileges of members of the ruling class.

Let me now turn to each of these processes to show their role in ruling class domination of the government. Although my focus will be on the federal government in Washington, I believe the general schema can be applied, with slight modifications, to state and local governments.

The special-interest process, as noted, comprises the several means by which specific individuals, corporations, or business sectors get the tax breaks, favors, subsidies, and procedural rulings which are beneficial to their short-run interests. This is the world of lobbyists, Washington super-lawyers, trade associations, and advisory committees to governmental departments and agencies. This is the process most often described by journalists and social scientists in their exposés and case studies concerning Congressional committees, regulatory agencies, and governmental departments.

I do not think I need spend any time giving examples of how this process works. Indeed, each reader will have his or her favorite studies for demonstration purposes. There are many fine studies of this process, and more are appearing all the time.

The information in these studies might seem on its face to be impressive evidence for ruling-class theory. After all, it shows that members of the ruling class are able to realize their will on innumerable issues of concern to them. They can gain tax breaks, receive subsidies, subvert safety laws, and dominate regulatory agencies, among other things. However, in the eyes of most political scientists this is not adequate evidence, for it does not show that the various "interests" are "coordinated" in their efforts. Moreover, it does not show directly that they dominate policy on "big issues," or that they control either of the political parties. This typical view is even expressed by Grand McConnell, the political scientist most sensitive to the many ways in which various private interests have taken over the piece of government of greatest concern to them. After concluding that "a substantial part of government in the United States has come under the influence or control of narrowly based and largely autonomous elites," he then asserts there is no need to talk of a power elite because

> These elites do not act cohesively with each other on many issues. They do not rule in the sense of commanding the entire nation. Quite the contrary,

> they tend to pursue a policy of noninvolvement in the large issues of statemanship, save where such issues touch their own particular concerns.[2]

Moreover, the big interests do not dominate the government as a whole. The political parties and the Presidency seem to be beyond their reach:

> Fortunately, not all of American politics is based upon this array of small constituencies. The party system, the Presidency and the national government as a whole represent opposing tendencies. To a very great degree, policies serving the values of liberty and equality are the achievements of these institutions. Public values generally must depend upon the creation of a national constituency.[3]

In order to deal with the kind of argument presented by McConnell, it is necessary to consider next the policy-formation process, the process by which policy on "large issues" is formulated, for it is in the policy process that the various special interests join together to forge general policies which will benefit them as a whole. The central units in the policy network are such organizations as the Council on Foreign Relations, the Committee for Economic Development, the Business Council, the American Assembly, and the National Municipal League, which are best categorized as policy-planning and consensus-seeking organizations of the power elite. I will not repeat here the information on the financing and leadership of these organizations which shows beyond doubt that they are under-written and directed by the same upper-class men who control the major corporations, banks, foundations, and law firms.[4] More important for our purpose is what goes on in the off-the-record meetings of these organizations.

The policy-planning organizations bring together, in groups large and small, members of the power elite from all over the country to discuss general problems – e.g., overseas aid, the use of nuclear weapons, tax problems, or the population question. They provide a setting in which differences on various issues can be thrashed out and the opinions of various experts can be heard. In addition to the group settings, these organizations also encourage general dialogue within the power elite by means of luncheon and dinner speeches, special written reports, and position statement in journals and books.

---

[2] McConnell, *op. cit.*, p. 339.
[3] *Ibid.*, p. 8.
[4] Domhoff, *The Higher Circles.*

Let me be content to summarize the policy-planning network by means of a diagram, and list some of the most important functions of this process:

1. They provide a setting wherein members of the power elite can familiarize themselves with general issues.

2. They provide a setting where conflicts within the power elite can be discussed and compromised.

3. They provide a setting wherein members of the power elite can hear the ideas and findings of their hired experts.

4. They provide a "training ground" for new leadership within the ruling class. It is in these organizations that big businessmen can determine which of their peers are best suited for service in the government.

5. They provide a framework for commissioned studies by experts on important issues.

6. Through such avenues as books, journals, policy statements, press releases and speakers, they can greatly influence the "climate of opinion" both in Washington and the country at large.

There are several points for political scientists and other critics of ruling-class theory to consider in contemplating the policy-planning network. First, it provides evidence that businessmen, bankers, and lawyers concern themselves with more than their specific business interests. Second, it shows that leaders from various sectors of the economy do get together to discuss the problems of the system as a whole. Third, it suggests that members of the power elite who are appointed to government are equipped with a general issue-orientation gained from power-elite organizations that are explicitly policy oriented. Fourth, it reveals that the upper-middle-class experts thought by some to be our real rulers are in fact busily dispensing their advice to those who hire them.

In short, if political scientists were to take the idea of a policy-planning process seriously, they would not be able to agree with Grant McConnell when he downgrades the importance of the Business Council by saying "the really effective participants in business politics are those [organizations] which direct their energies almost wholly to hard, specific matters of immediate economic concern to business firms."[5] Instead, they would say that trade associations are among the most important influences in the special-interest process and that the Business Council is one of the Archimedean points of the policy process.

---

[5] McConnell, *op. cit.*, pp. 292–293.

If I am right that members of the ruling class gain their narrow interests through the well-known devices of the special-interest process and their general interests through the little-studied policy-planning process, then the question immediately arises: how is all this possible when we have a government elected by the people? Shouldn't we expect elected officials to have policy views of their own that generally reflect the wishes of the voters who sent them to office? These is certainly one group of political scientists who believe this to be the case – they have developed a detailed argument to suggest that the deep-seated political ambitions of individuals and parties lead them to take the policy stands which will get them a majority of the vote, thereby insuring that the policy views of politicians will reflect more or less the views of the people.

To answer questions about our elected officials, we must examine the political parties and the candidates they nominate. When it comes to the parties, political scientists have suggested that a fully developed political party fulfills four functions: (1) integrating conflicting regional, ethnic, and class identifications; (2) selecting candidates to fill offices; (3) political education; and (4) policy making. In the United States, however, the parties have little or nothing to do with political education or policy making: "Particularly in our own century," writes political scientist Walter Dean Burnham, "American political parties have been largely restricted in functional scope to the realm of the constituent [integrative function] and to the tasks of filling political offices."[6]

It is because American politics is restricted largely to office-filling functions that I prefer to talk about the candidate-selection process rather than the political process. The term political process gives the impression that more is going on in our electoral system than is really the case. And it is precisely because the candidate-selection process is so individualistic and issue-less that it can be in good part dominated by means of campaign contributions from members of the ruling class. In the guise of fat cats, the same men who direct corporations and take part in the policy groups play a central role in the careers of most politicians who advance beyond the local or state legislature level in states of any size and consequence.

The fat cats, of course, are by and large hard to distinguish in their socioeconomic outlook whatever their political party. Indeed, most corporations,

---

[6] Walter Dean Burnham, "Party Systems and the Political Process," p. 279. In *The American Party Systems*, William Chambers and Walter Dean Burnham, eds. (Oxford University Press, 1967).

banks, and law firms try to have personnel who are important donors to both parties. Then too, many of the fattest cats of the opposing parties join together as leaders of such policy-planning groups as the Council of Foreign Relations and Committee for Economic Development. Although well-connected in both parties, we can see a power elite preference for the Republican Party, at least since 1968.[7]

What kind of politicians emerge from this individualistically-oriented electoral politics that has to curry favor with large contributors? The answer is available from several studies. Politicians are first of all people from the higher levels of the social ladder: "The wealthiest one-fifth of the American families contribute about nine of every ten of the elite of political economy."[8] They are secondly, at least among those who wish to go beyond local and state politics, quite ambitious men who are constantly striving for bigger and better things. They are thirdly people who are by and large without strong ideological inclinations; the exceptions to this statement are well known precisely because they are so unusual. Finally, with the exception of the local level, where businessmen are most likely to sit on city councils, they are in good part lawyers, an occupational grouping that by training and career needs produces ideal go-betweens and compromisers. The result of the candidate selection process, in short, is (1) men who know how to go along to get along, and (2) men who have few strong policy positions of their own, and are thus open to the suggestions put forth to them by the fat cats and experts who have been legitimated as serious leaders within the framework of the policy-planning network.

When we consider the interaction between the policy process and the political process, it is not surprising that there is a considerable continuity of policy between Republican and Democratic administrations. As columnist Joseph Kraft wrote about the Council on Foreign Relations, "the Council plays a special part in helping to bridge the gap between the two parties, affording unofficially a measure of continuity when the guard changes in Washington."[9]

I conclude that the notion of public policy being influenced to any great extent by the will of the people due to the competition between the two political parties is misguided. "Politics" is for selecting ambitious, relatively issue-

---

[7] G. William Domhoff, *Fat Cats and Democrats*, (Prentice-Hall, 1972), for the information in this paragraph.

[8] Kenneth Prewitt and Alan Stone, *The Ruling Elites* (Harper & Row, 1973), p. 137.

[9] Joseph Kraft, "School for Statesmen," *Harper's Magazine*, July 1958, p. 68.

THE POWER ELITE POLICY-MAKING PROCESS

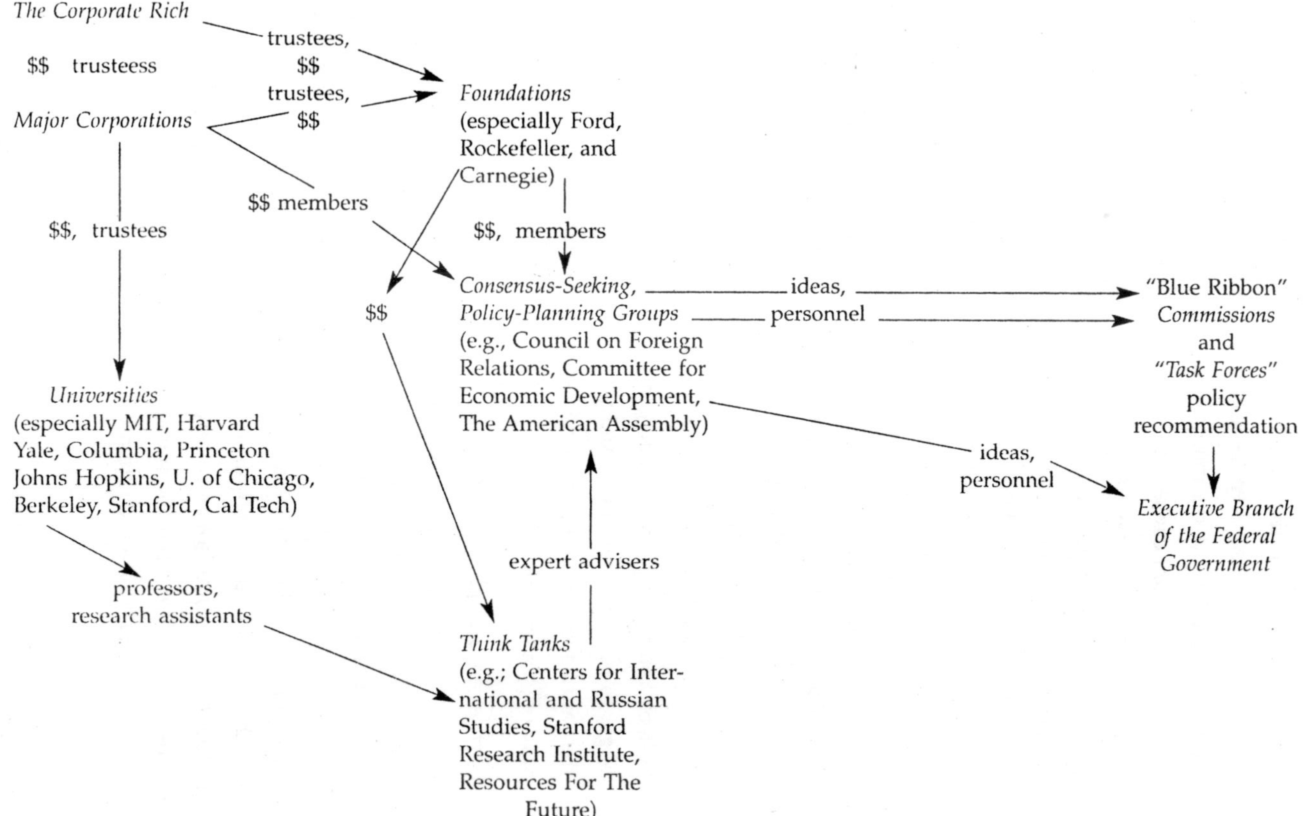

less middle- and upper-middle-class lawyers who know how to advance themselves by finding the rhetoric and the rationalizations to implement both the narrow and general policies of the bi-partisan power elite.

At this point I can hear the reader protesting that there is more to American politics than this. And so there is. I admit there are serious-minded liberals who fight the good fight on many issues, ecologically-oriented politicians who remain true to their cause, and honest people of every political stripe who are not beholden to any wealthy people. But there are not enough of them, for there is also a seniority system dominated by ruling class-oriented politicians who have a way of keeping the insurgents off the important committees and out of the centers of power. There is in addition a Southern Democratic delegation which retains its stranglehold on Congress despite all the claims of the mid-Sixties that its star was about to fade. Then there are the machine Democrats who aid the Southerners in crucial ways even while they maintain a liberal voting record. And finally, there are the myriad lobbyists and lawyers who are constantly pressuring those who would resist the blandishments of the power elite. As former Congressman Abner Mikva once said, the system has a way of grinding you down:

> The biggest single disappointment to a new man is the intransigence of the system. You talk to people and they say, 'You're absolutely right, something ought to be done about this.' And yet, somehow, we go right on ducking the hard issues. We slide off the necessary confrontations. This place has a way of grinding you down.[10]

In short, even though there is more to American politics than fat cats and their political friends, the "more" cannot win other than headlines, delays, and an occasional battle. The candidate-selection process produces too many politicians who are friendly to the wealthy few.

Contemplation of the ways in which the special-interest, policy-planning, and candidate-selection processes operate brings us to the $64 question: why do we, the general public, acquiesce in this state of affairs? Why is it, as Marx warned, the the ruling ideas of any age are the ideas of ruling class? Why does the ruling have what the Italian Marxist Antonio Gramsci called "ideological hegemony," by which he meant that "the system's real strength does

---

[10] Robert Sherill, "92nd Congress: Eulogy and Evasion," *The Nation*, February 15, 1971.

not lie in the violence of the ruling class or the coercive power of its state apparatus, but in the acceptance by the ruled of a "conception of the world" which belongs to the rulers?"[11] Unfortunately, no one has given an adequate answer to these interrelated questions. Such an answer would involve insights from a variety of disciplines including history, anthropology, and psychology as well as political science and sociology, and would quickly lead to age-old problems concerning the origins of the state and the general nature of the relationship between leaders and led.

However, at the sociological level which concerns me in this paper, we certainly can see that members of the ruling class work very hard at helping us to accept their view of the world. Indeed, we can be sure from past experience that they will stop at nothing – despite their protestations of "democracy" and "liberalism" – to get their views across.[12] Through the ideology process, they create, disseminate, and enforce a set of attitudes and "values" that tells us this is, for all its defects, the best of all possible worlds. At the fount of this process are the same foundations and policy-planning groups which operate in the policy process. For in addition to providing policy suggestions to government, these policy-planning organizations also provide the new rationales which make the policies acceptable to the general public. Thus, in the case of the ideology process we must link these organizations not to the government, as in the policy process, but to a dissemination network which includes middle-class discussion groups, public relations firms, corporate-financed advertising councils, special university and foundation programs, books, speeches, and various efforts through the mass media.

The dissemination apparatus is most readily apparent in the all-important area of foreign policy. Perhaps most critical here is the Foreign Policy Association and its affiliate, the World Affairs Council. Tightly interlocked with the Council on Foreign Relations, the Foreign Policy Association provides literature and discussion groups for the "attentive public" of upper-middle-class professionals, academics, and students. In addition to the Foreign Policy Association and the Committees on Foreign Relations, there are numerous

[11] Giuseppe Fiori, *Antonio Gramsci: Life of a Revolutionary* (NLB, London, 1970), p. 238.

[12] G. William Domhoff, "The Power Elite, the CIA, and the Struggle for Minds," *The Higher Circles* (Random House, 1970), for an account of how moderates and liberals within the power elite subverted various American institutions in their efforts to "save" an "open" society.

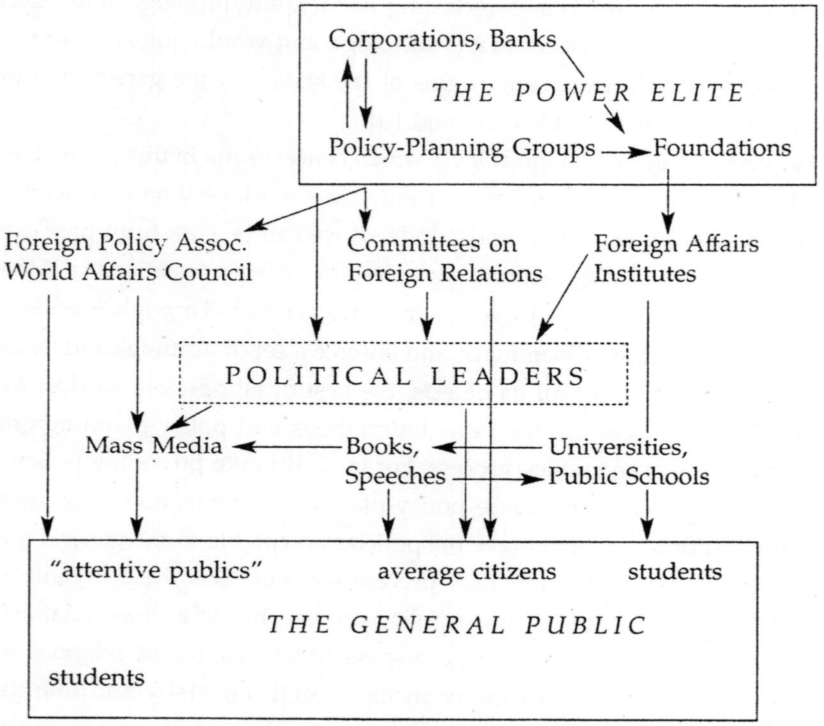


foreign affairs institutes at major universities which provide students and the general public with the perspectives of the power elite on foreign policy. Then too, political leaders often play an intermediary role in carrying foreign policy positions to the general public.

The enforcement of the ideological consensus is carried out in a multitude of ways that include pressure, intimidation and violence as well as the more gentle methods of persuasion and monetary inducement. Those who are outspoken in their challenge to one or another of the main tenets of the American ideology may be passed over for promotions, left out of junkets, or fired from their jobs. They may be excluded from groups or criticized in the mass media. If they get too far outside the consensus, they are enmeshed in the governmental law enforcement apparatus which is shaped in the policy-formation process with a special assist from the ruling-class dominated American Bar Association and its affiliated institutes and committees.[13] But I do not think we need spend much time considering the bitter details of ideology enforcement, for they are all too fresh in our minds after years of struggle over civil liberties and the war in Southeast Asia.

---

[13] The bottom level of the enforcement apparatus, the police, didn't do their job quite right in the late Sixties. While injecting the required amount of fear into many citizens, they also created many new dissenters among students, Blacks, and Chicanos by their heavy-handed tactics. So the Ford Foundation spun off a $30 million Police Foundation to fund the university programs, special institutes, consultants, and books which are being used to teach the police to be more sophisticated in their containment of dissent in the future.

Harvey Molotch

# Spilling Out (Again)

I had to satisfy the demand of a prominent leftist sociologist that I come up with a fitting presentation for a panel on the radical idea of "radical sociology" to be held at the 1969 meetings of the American Sociological Association. Marlene Dixon, who I considered a force to be reckoned with, warned me she did not want still another call for a radical sociology. She wanted a display of radical sociology itself. The great blowout in January fell into my hands.

I was already of the leftist persuasion, but other influences were just then seeping into my brain through UCSB colleagues of the time, especially Aaron Cicourel. I was already immersed in "conflict theory," but the move from Chicago to California increased my awareness and appreciation of interactionism of various sorts. Numbers of us were seeking a synthesis..The emerging result was a multi-perspectival view of the world – you make one truth if you are at the top and another if you are at the bottom – superordinate vs. subaltern in updated terminology. The world not only looks different depending on social position, but the tools to make reality for others are also differentially distributed.

In practical terms most relevant to my oil spill work, this means most "information" is systematically biased toward the interests of the privileged. This is not just a matter of individual perceptions but, in the terms used by Schattschneider, the way institutions external to individual perception "mobilize bias." Knowledge and power intertwine and their mutual production constitutes society, as Foucault, unknown to me at the time, so pervasively declared.

Beyond theorizing hegemony or more simply complaining about "bias," what can the sociologist do? Indicated in this article and in several successive pieces written in collaboration with Marilyn Lester, accidents and scandals have a special utility (Molotch and Lester 1974; Molotch and Lester 1975). First, they happen. Given institutional complexities and fickleness of the fates, no power base can control the future. Things "going wrong" introduce topics and reveal information otherwise out of view. Investigations of the related goings on can yield rich veins of information to inform ethnographic and historical cases. Our oil spill work aimed to demonstrate the usefulness of such an approach. Especially if repeated across researchers and their projects, we would gain systematic contrast between the reporting machinery ordinarily in place and what arises when things happen that are less predictable. The difference in accounting practices and information outcomes is a map for understanding hegemonic process.

The multi-perspectival viewpoint caught on in a big way, of course, thanks to an army of analysts coming from both sides of the Atlantic and from many disciplines, including literary theory. For me, Garfinkel's version was the most profound and intellectually disciplined. But whereas Garfinkel was, on principal, indifferent to politics, we were not. Marilyn Lester and I tried to show that Garfinkel's "bracketing" the mundane world could be a useful tool for applied work, a route to politically and morally relevant insights. For us, ethnomethodology – in addition to its profound insights of folk epistemology (Garfinkel's program) – worked as something like a good drug trip (not Garfinkel's program). Insights gained under its spell could be "brought back" into the world of politics, morals, and the ordinary stuff of daily life. The counter-culture celebrant, Theodore Roszak, thought this about drug trips of the psychopharmological type. He was distressed that users, partially in response to his own writings, tuned in and then dropped out (Roszak 1995). He considered drugs part of the process of gaining a heightened sense of possibility, worthwhile only when followed up with a return to the real world. Drugs (and the counter-culture in other of its aspects) had the potential to make people more, rather than less, practically effective.

In the intellectual arena, there are two ways that tripping out can do harm. First is solipsism. Scholars may actually believe (or write like they believe) there is "no real world" and advocate walking through walls – physical or social. Many have commented on the flows of nonsense to which this has led under the cover of post-modernism. The second danger has been partial solipsism. Morally conscious scholars come to see that the oppressors see and make worlds by virtue of their own position – versions of reality that then dominate everyone else. The antidote, so the reasoning goes, is to expose these linkages and in the process de-naturalize the received truths. The voice of those previously kept silent comes to stand-in for authentic knowledge. In extreme but quite frequent versions, the template for truth becomes the identity of the speaker rather than empirical evidence, logic, or what used to be thought of as *common* sense.

However much a research time-saver, this truth test is not good methodology, insurgent or otherwise. The "good people" may not see correctly and the "bad people" may know plenty. Blindness to this state of affairs affects research findings and political practice in a lousy way. We miss seeing strategically import divisions among elite groups, which makes it harder to understand the history of actual coalitions as well as the potential for future ones. Response to the Santa Barbara oil spill shows how odd bedfellows can indeed take form. Too monolithic a view also risks missing out on good insider informants. Ignoring divisions among the subaltern at the other end of the power spectrum leads to unnecessary surprise when they divide among themselves. False consciousness will simply not do to explain the Balkans, say, or American street crime. Ordinary people can construct troubled and troubling worlds pretty much on their own – or at least that is a possibility worth having on the agenda.

My point is that we need methods that go beyond looking at reality as socially constructed, indexical, or hegemonically managed. We need tools that can indicate the different ways that social construction occurs and also sustain our ability to hold on to a sense that reality does matter. Treating accidents and scandals as having different types of construction mechanisms "upstream" and consequences "downstream" can be a concrete way of investigating the power-knowledge process. Journalists use accidents and scandals as part of their craft, although they so often waste their energies on largely irrelevant disturbances, like the Lewinsky scandal and Princess Diana accident. Sociologists avoid the trivial but miss out on the methodological opportunity. When they combine the investigatory tool with substantive topic, we learn how the etiology of media coverage feeds into societal substance (Beamish 2002; Klinenberg 2003).

However much researchers have followed the trail proposed in the oil work (not so many, I don't think), scholars of various stripes certainly have engaged the topic of the environment. Thirty years ago, the natural world did not exist for sociologists, not because they were radical idealists but because they had just never thought about it much. Indeed, it was common for leftist intellectuals to refer to the whole issue as a diversionary "middle-class shuck," distracting attention from the important matters of race, class, and imperialism. But nature spoke for itself. If post-modernism means anything it is the realization that nature has its own agency, quite apart from modernist schemes of manipulating it or leftist disregard of its relative autonomy. Environmentalism is the result and is probably the sturdiest source of political activism in the U.S. and many other countries.

Environmental sociology still does not receive the attention it deserves. Increasingly, the public as well as insightful natural scientists understand that social organization is the key to sustainability. Sociology should be the lead discipline in understanding how people use the earth and what it might take to save it. Studies of the lesser accidents can point the way before the Big One, either in the form of a single blowout or a cumulating but irreversible disaster like global warming, makes it all moot.

Harvey Molotch and Marilyn Lester

# Accidents, Scandals, and Routines: Resources for Insurgent Methodology*

News is the information which people receive secondhand about worlds which are not available to their own experience. Out of a vast "glut of occurrences," a relatively few happenings are translated by mass media into things "fit to print," i.e., *the* important things worthy of constituting our conceptions of the community, state, nation, and world in which we live. News, and the process through which it is produced, determines the experience of publics; it is an important source of whatever ideological hegemony exists in a given society; those who make the news are crucial actors in making publics what they are.

The power of the media to create experience rests on what we'll term the "objectivity assumption," to which almost everyone pledges allegiance. This assumption has it that there is indeed a world "out there" and that an account of a given event reflects that world, or a piece of it, with some degree of accuracy. The "objectivity assumption" states not that the media are objective, but that there is a world out there to be objective about. Operating on the "objectivity assumption," lay people read a newspaper or listen to a news broadcast with the aim in mind of finding out about the world which is described in the produced account. People, in other words, read

* Article originally appeared in *The Insurgent Sociologist*, 3:4 (Summer, 1973), pp. 1–11.

newspapers to find out about an assumed objective state of the world. Sociologists in their work on power, on the media, and in their methods of content analysis, usually do much the same thing.

It's all very reasonable, to be sure, but there is an alternative possibility. Newspapers, instead of reflecting a world out there, might reflect the practices of those who have the power to determine the experience of others. Harold Garfinkel[1] has made a similar point about clinical records which he investigated. Rather than viewing an institution's records as standing for something which happened, as sociologists typically do, Garfinkle saw in those records the practices of people who make records: the hedges they play, the short-cuts they take, the theories in their heads, the purposes-at-hand with which they must deal. In other words, there are "good organizational reasons for bad clinical records." And those "good reasons" spell out the social organization of the clinic.

We think that mass media should similarly be viewed as one big, bad clinical record. Our present interest, however, does not lay in an opportunity for name-calling criticism, but rather in a possibility for understanding how the product comes to look as it does. We want to study media in order to see in them the methods through which the powerful come to determine the experience of publics. We look for the methods which accomplish ideological hegemony by examining the records which are produced.

We conceive of people doing news as people who are guided by a purpose at hand. In trying to explain what news is, we must meet the challenge of explaining how it is that certain phenomena are included as news while an infinite array of other phenomena are ignored. The traditional view, held by those who rely on the "objectivity assumption," inevitably falls back on the notion that some things are just more *important* than others. This, of course, begs the question: what determines what is or is not important? For our own answer, we begin by invoking the concept of selective perception from psychology. Selective perception teaches that individuals, when faced with a glut of stimuli in perceptable space, confront an analogous challenge in terms of discriminating the important from the trivial. The creation of a meaningful field of perception requires that this selection be accomplished. That accomplishment is carried out through *purposiveness*. We discriminate chairs from

[1] Harold Garfinkel, "Good Organizational Reasons for Bad Clinic Records," Chapter 6 in *Studies in Ethnomethodology*, Englewood Cliffs: Prentice-Hall.

other surrounding matter because of the recurrent need to sit. Carpenters discriminate among woods and eskimoes among snows. In all instances, the motive for discrimination and for meaning creation is present need. And since needs and purposes are not the same from one individual or culture to another, so it is that the meaningful worlds of individuals and cultures differ.

A sense of history, of community, of nation is created in the same way: purposes at hand carve up the *temporal dimension* of the perceptable field in order to make certain occurrences more important than others. When something happens which a given observer thinks is so important that *others* should hear it, he spreads the word – and that means there is *news*. We thus make news because *we* think something is important.

The summary of all this is that what is or is not news depends upon what we want others to think; and what we want others to think is guided by what we anticipate the consequences will be to our purposes. Thus, the newspaper and TV newscast are the results of purposive activities of certain actors who are trying to determine the experience of others. This purposiveness may be crude and transparently "selfish," or it may be absolutely unconsciously purposive and be viewed as "objective," without bias, and so forth. But all such newsmaking must emerge in some way from certain practical goals, simply because there is no other viable explanatory mechanism for the production of creative meanings.

We have inventoried three separate kinds of news events: Routine Events, Accidents, and Scandals. These differ in the ways in which the purposes of some people function to get them across on the printed page and in the newsbroadcast. We want to describe them here in order to help provide some alternative imageries which insurgent scholars and citizens can use to see the social system in the news. We will take up each in turn.

## Routine Events[2]

Definition: Routine Events are deliberately promoted occurrences which were originally deliberately accomplished by the promoter.

---

[2] Following Molotch (1970), Manela (1971) has developed a typology of events using similar terminology. Manela treats events as objective phenomena which are typed according to how well they fit or fail to fit established routines of formal organizations. Our treatment and purposes are distinct from Manela's, although certain intriguing parallels exist.

During the Santa Barbara oil spill in late January, 1969, President Nixon made an inspection tour of certain beaches and subsequently announced to the nation that the damage caused by the blow-out had been repaired. He did not announce that the stretch of beach he inspected had been especially cleaned for his arrival, while miles north and south of him remained hopelessly blackened. Let's take another example, drawn from the other side of the world: The supposed Gulf of Tonkin attack of 1964 by the North Vietnamese was promoted as a public event through news releases, press conferences, briefings, and speeches; it served to legitimize the escalation of American involvement in the Vietnam War.

These are examples of *routine events,* which partake of the most managed features of news-making. An individual or group promotes one or more of its activities as newsworthy because it is useful for them to do so. If that news is subsequently adopted by the media, we must assume then that they, also, have a use for publishing it. We learn from these events what others intend for us to learn: nothing hostile to the purposes of the event-makers, nothing useful to groups with conflicting purposes and interests. Public politics, public events, and what we read in the newspaper is in large part dominated by this type of event. Murray Edelman (1964) describes the dominance of routine events as the "symbolic use of politics":

> Basic to the recognition of symbolic forms in the political process is a distinction between politics as a spectator sport and political activity as utilized by organized groups to get quite specific tangible benefits for themselves. For most men most of the time politics is a series of pictures in the mind placed there by television news, newspapers, magazines, and discussions. The pictures create a moving panorama taking place in a world the mass public never quite touches, yet one its members come to fear or cheer. They are told of legislatures passing laws, foreign political figures threatening or offering trade agreements, wars starting and ending, candidates for public office losing or winning, decisions made to spend unimaginable sums of money to go to the moon. . . . Politics is for most of us a passing parade of abstract symbols. (p. 5)

Not only is routine event-making the standard fare of the mass media; it also provides the "data" for sociologists investigating the social structure. Edward Banfield, for example, in his classic study of community power, employs a decisional case study method in endeavoring to discover who influenced the outcomes of six "key" issues in Chicago (Banfield, 1962). He selects the issues which received the widest coverage in the media and assumes these to be synonymous with "key" political issues, uncritically letting the organized ways in which events get done determine his subjects of study. Consequently, the very "issues" Banfield studies are issues simply because his respondents made them such by promoting them as routine events, as material to fill the media's "news hole" and the public's mind. No contrast is made between routine events in the news and those events which Edelman considers to constitute the nonsymbolic political sector where tangible resources are actually distributed by and among members of the elites. No suggestion is made that what is published is done so for purposes that might have nothing to do with any "objective" importance or newsworthiness, if seen from other possible standpoints. Lost in this type of research are the ways in which powerful event makers are able to have their public agendas adopted by the media through their organized promotional activities (cf. Boorstin, 1961). Lost also is what Bachrach and Baratz (1962) term the "second face of power," the ability to create an event or public issue and the ability to prevent other options, activities, decisions, etc. from being publicly debated.

It is certainly not by chance that the kinds of issues to which we typically have access are of the sort which Banfield studies; e.g., where to locate the next branch of the University of Illinois or the next convention center. These are the kinds of issues which are deemed safe for public consumption, the kinds which will not significantly upset, challenge, or change the larger contextual basis of political life in America. They constitute, for the most part, all the news that's fit to print.

A routine public issue might best be described as *an event about which the elites divide*, where there is an agreement to disagree, because the stakes – although possibly important to some people – do not involve any critical restructuring of the social system and thus represent no threat to existing orders of power and privilege. When there exist competing definitions of events among powerful parties, or when an event can serve competing purposes, there is an *issue*. Since members of the elite disproportionately have the power to make all events, they also have disproportionate access to creating issues. He surfacing of public issues, especially through routine events, should thus be seen by critical content analyst or newspaper reader as inherently trivial, useful only as an index of splits among the routinely powerful.

Less powerful groups can have radically different uses for events; and they too try to cause issues to surface on the basis of positions, which if taken seriously, question basic socio-political structures. But by virtue of their lack of power, they must typically assemble themselves in an inappropriate place at an inappropriate time in order to be deemed "newsworthy." The fact that they are forced to resort to spectacular displays, e.g., sitins, allows those with easy access to the media to respond to the "inappropriate" display rather than to the questions which underlie it.

Thus, routine events are planned as events by those who have both a use for them and the ability to promote them as public. To select the media's "key events" for study is to employ a consensus methodology (cf. Young and Lehman, 1972); the researcher uncritically adopts a sample of events which fits the publicity needs of some small groups of people as his study topic.

## Accidents

> Definition: Accidents are unplanned occurrences which are promoted by a party other than the agent who inadvertently caused the underlying occurrence.

Accidents – occasions in which miscalculation or mistake leads to a breakdown in our conception of order – are specifically antithetical to the interests which produce routine event-making practices. Accidents are embarrassing; an accident occurs when those who were parties to an occurrence never intended to have that occurrence become a public event. Oil companies never intended, in drilling for oil, to cause a huge blow-out at Santa Barbara; those who designed our emergency alert system never intended for that system's total incompetence to be demonstrated through a false alert; those who built and deployed hydrogen bombs never intended for several to be "lost" in the Spanish countryside. At least in their early stages, accidents transcend and render inoperative the managed and contrived nature of routines. Nobody who ordinarily makes news is ready; the stories aren't straight; powerful people screw up. The accident's inherent features many problems for those who ordinarily make public events; their capacity to define the public agenda to serve their own interests and purposes is inhibited.

Moreover, the very appearance of accidents and the fact that large numbers of people often witness their direct consequences (oil on beaches, dead sheep strewn across two Utah valleys) demand that the media provide some minimal event-coverage. If they did not, censorship would be blatantly obvious. This would be inimical to the media's aura of objectivity which it needs to maintain and to its role definition as a mere reporter of what's "really happening," rather than as an active participant in the generation of news. Thus, in the case of accidents, the media become an ally, though often a reluctant one, and a resource for groups with competing uses for events (including sociologists seeking a radical perspective on the structure of American society).

The accident, quite unlike the routine event, provides access to normally obfuscated political structures – to decision-makers, to decision-making processes, and often to the private domains of individuals (e.g., Ted Kennedy at Chappaquidick Island) which in everyday life are kept far removed from the public events sector. The accident can serve as a high-powered microscope, a resource for generating information typically prevented from public consideration. If Banfield had selected his "key issues" on the basis of news surfacing as accidents, he (or some more reputable scholar) might have come away with other conclusions about power in American society.

Thus, as Molotch (1970) has described in a previous paper, we gain from the Santa Barbara oil spill a rare view of the oil companies' marriage to the federal government and the effects of that marriage upon local communities. We see how the latter come to be dominated by private decision-making in corporation board rooms and in the office of the Department of the Interior. As upper middle and upper class Santa Barbarans struggle to be heard, to gain access to key decision makers, they gained even more direct information about power in America and about the inefficacy of local protest. The discrepancy between pronouncement and practice on the part of corporate and federal officials was poignantly illustrated. Though the goal of getting oil out of Santa Barbara was thwarted, the President of the United States, heads of government departments, and corporations magnates stood naked before both investigators and citizens, and to a much lesser extent, before the country as a whole.

Similarly, we have been assured for years about the effectiveness of our early warning defense system. And yet, at the North American Air Defense Command located in Colorado Springs, Colorado, on February 21, 1971, an accident occurred which exposed the irrelevance of public assurances. Two IBM tapes hang on the wall there, one tape containing the code word for a real alert, the other a test tape. Twice each week the test tape is put on the teletype which automatically assumes control of the AP and UPI wire services. At 6:30 a.m. on that day, the operator mistakenly grabbed the tape for a real emergency alert. Since no procedure had ever been established to handle a false alert, a full forty minutes passed between the beginning and the end of the alert, a full forty minutes passed between the beginning and the end of the alert. The error was compounded at the local level: for example, in one place, paper was jammed in the teletype ticker, so the message was never received; in another, the broadcaster said he "just couldn't summon the courage to tell everybody there was a national emergency" and the message was not broadcast; in another, where the ticker is located in the basement, no one checked the wires until five hours after the alert had passed.

Were that to have been a real alert, it would have failed. Without the accident, no one would have realized how "unsafe" we all are, despite the rhetoric of public officials. The accident provided a view that contrasted sharply with previous speeches, press releases, and pronouncements.

A final example of the accident may be instructive. Dugway Proving Ground, located near Denver and Salt Lake City, spans one million acres. It is one of six military chemical and biological warfare installations where several different kinds of chemical and biological warfare weapons are tested, ranging from nerve gas and defoliants to synthetic versions of rattlesnake venom and Bubonic plague.

On March 13, 1968, a test involving the spraying of nerve gas "VX" from a jet airplane at a height of 150 feet was done. The objective was to determine "how the gas distributes itself in down winds between 5 and 25 miles per hour" (Hirsch, 1969; 13). As one of the planes zoomed up after a trial run, a valve on the two high explosive dispensers failed to snap firmly shut. The gas poured out, was picked up by winds, and was carried as far as 45 miles from the target area.

Within the next week 6400 sheep were dead. Two veterinarians called to the scene to assist ranchers suffered temporary illness. Although there were no other known effects on humans (the falling night snow of March 13 brought the gas to the earth and the combination of the hour and inclement weather kept exposed populations indoors), dead carcasses were clearly visible to citizens, reporters, Army personnel, and investigators; and the pictures which appeared in the press could not be obliterated with a slogan eliciting symbolic support against the "Reds." It was clear to all that chemical and biological warfare weapons could accidentally affect U.S. citizens as well as purposely destroy Communists.

These examples point out that, for social scientists, accidents provide a convenient resource for gaining entrance into unstudied and often hidden features of politics in America. Especially in the earliest stages of an accident, we have found few prohibiting factors to research save the ability to get a scene when an accident abruptly occurs. By virtue of the accident's internal characteristics, we can employ a case study technique which here becomes an insurgent methodology. That is, we now have access to an array of events and issues which defy the programmed character of routine events.

The situation changes, however, after the initial event, as those in power – e.g., the oil companies in the case of the oil spill, the defense department in the case of the false alert – seek to regain control of the event-making process.

One of the most important routinizing tactics is the deliberate complication of the issue so that final responsibility for the cause of the event is ambiguous. This was the strategy in the nerve gas case. For several months after the sheep carcasses were found, the Department of Defense, the U.S. Public Health Service, Utah State Departments of Health and Agriculture, as well as local scientists, conducted tests to discern the cause of death. The local scientists were positive that nerve gas "VX," sprayed accidentally from the plane, was responsible. But the other agencies first suggested that there was only an accidental correlation between the gas tests and sheep deaths; they searched for other causes – in poisonous plants, pesticides, and diseases, to name a few. When these tests proved negative, the Army advanced a multi-cause theory. They said that a variety of reasons were probably responsible, of which the nerve gas may have been one.

In routine events it is at best difficult, at worst highly arbitrary, to try to separate key background decision making from the cloaking activities of the elite; that whole scene has been neatly packaged for public consumption. With accidents, on the other hand, because the perpetrators are caught off guard, routinizing can occur only after the event and must be superimposed upon the consequences which have already been felt. Thus, we can directly observe endeavors to normalize the accident and to recapture hegemony on the part of the powerful. We can isolate, study, and publicize them for what they are: attempts to cover over the possible long-range ramifications of the accidents' relevations.

We can also use this understanding to study the way in which information is controlled in the first place. The tactics which actors use to normalize troublesome events are just more transparent examples of the everyday procedures of creating routine news.

In the accidents we have studied so far, one of the more exciting findings is that citizens are able to make connections between interest and power, between big business and governmental regulators. From these connections they can critically understand the discrepancy between public and private politics, an understanding heretofore restricted to the "insider." What citizens seem to lack, however, is the ability to move from what they learn from a specific accident to a more general conceptualization about how the entire society works. That linking activity is the work of the sociologist. Thus, the accident is a potential mobilizing force for publics which, after more work on the sociologist's part, might develop into a blueprint for change. As one Santa Barbara resident remarked:

> We, the people can protest and protest and it means nothing because the industrial and military junta are the country. They tell us, the people, what is good for the oil companies is good for the people. To that I say 'like hell'. . . .

Contrary to popular belief everyday people who have access to the necessary information are all too willing and able to draw the logical connections and to act on the basis of that knowledge. It is not that the issues are too complex for "mundane minds"; rather, the issues themselves are strategically complicated, and the thesis of the "dumb citizen" is itself an ideology for keeping publics at a distance.

Of course, accidents do not always mobilize vast groups of people for mass action. But they do provide some insight into the conditions under which a population can be roused. The fact that people do not overtly confront the perpetrators of an accident is an event in itself and should be contrasted with its opposite – where groups seize upon the accident's mobilizing potential. Such a contrast can pinpoint some of the obstacles which must be faced in trying to summon a mass movement for social change in the society.

For example, unlike Santa Barbarans, Utah citizens did not undertake an overt struggle against the Defense Department. While local elites in Santa Barbara were deeply involved in promoting the spill as a national public event and issue, local Utah elites were at best ambivalent in their response. The difference in attitude is to be found in the economic circumstances of the respective areas: Santa Barbara reaps few benefits from oil drilling in the channel; but the Utah economy is dependent on the Department of Defense and its hundreds of millions of dollars. Utah local elites could not afford to promote the occurrence as a public event; the local citizens had no difficulty in comprehending the predicament – that their lives are daily endangered by the hand which feeds them.

## Scandals

Definition: A scandal involves a deliberately planned occurrence which is promoted by a party different from the occurrence's agent.

The third type of event, the scandal is a kind of mixed case in our typology. Here are a few examples:

On May 1, 1971, an announcer at a local California radio station reported that Governor Ronald Reagan paid no state income taxes the previous year. The information was revealed through a "leak" in the confidential files of the Franchise Tax Board. For the next several days, this story was widely discussed, by newspapers and other media, by political opponents of Reagan, and by those on the left. It was a paradoxical revelation since the Governor was constantly on the warpath against cheats, rip-offs, hippie students, welfare recipients, and since he had opposed income tax withholding because, he said, "Taxes should hurt."

On the national level a similar type of event occurred on June 15, 1971, when *The New York Times* published an excerpt from the 47 volume secret study of the origins of the Vietnam war. In the next three weeks eight more excerpts were printed. Shortly after the publications began, however, the stories on the Pentagon Papers were in part overshadowed by the complex court battles which were taking place over the fact that a leak had occurred, over the right of the newspaper to print such government documents, and over the possible danger to national security posed by the publications. As typically occurs with accidents, the powerful were attempting to routinize the event by transforming the issue into one more compatible with their own purposes and fitting their own perspective on what is newsworthy, interesting, important, i.e., on what is "news."

Like the routine event, but unlike the accident, a scandal is planned, not by the central party involved, however, but by an informer – usually some sort of insider. Like the consequences of accidents, scandals can also be embarrassing: they provide insight into normally protected structures and activities. Reagan lost, at least temporarily, some of his support as a result of the publication of his tax status; and from the publication of the Pentagon Papers,

U.S. involvement in Vietnam became suspect. The scandal also allowed for issues to be raised concerning classification of government documents, freedom of the press, and private decision making in the execution of national policy.

What makes the scandal a type of event in its own right is the way in which it becomes a public event. Scandals involve persons who have at least some access to private sectors and who, for one reason or another, provide out-groups with information about that private sector. Scandals require "leakers" or "informant"; thus, they are contingent upon some dispute or disagreement among persons who are supposed to operate in substantial harmony. The scandal can only emerge when some insider is pissed-off or when some insurgent manages to be placed inside; and it can occur only if the media is willing to be a party to the exposure. The amazing thing about the Pentagon Papers, then, is not that Presidents tell lies, but that *The New York Times* was willing to expose that fact.

Nevertheless, scandals provide many of the same resources and research advantages as do accidents. We suggest a similar program of study: use scandals to accumulate otherwise obfuscated data about individuals, groups, and decision-making activities; attempt to pull together information gained from many scandals; try to draw profiles about the typical scandal, where it occurs, how it runs its course; make the resultant material and analysis available to groups who typically are unable to gain a foothold into the private political arena and who are working to contrast routine events with alternate conceptions.[3]

## Discussion

We can summarize: News is a constructed reality; newsmaking is political work. There does not exist "out there" a set of objectively important events waiting to be picked up by the mass media. Rather, newsmaking is a process

[3] There is a fourth type of event which logically flows from our schema: the serendipity event which takes place when a non-deliberate occurrence is deliberately promoted by the occurrence's agent. Put in informal language, a serenditipity event involves making hay out of what was accomplished accidentally, but without admission that there ever was an accident. Unfortunately, because of the very fact that a serendipity event is deliberately promoted in ways identical to the routine event, it is usually impossible to know in a given case whether or not the precipitating occurrence was accomplished purposively. It is for the reason of its invisibility that we treat serendipity events as a residual category, largely unretrievable to investigation.

whereby certain actors are able to create and thus to manage the news – "manage" in the largest sense. That is, individuals and groups do many things; those in powerful positions make many decisions. Only a small part of those are done with the intention of making news. Typically, activities are promoted as public events because they serve the actors' purposes or goals, while simultaneously these actors prevent any activity which would be inimical to their purposes from becoming a public event.

"Important" events are totally contingent on the makers' purposes at the time. Activities which are not promoted as events are *important* for keeping private although other groups may, of course, have use for those activities as events. Importance or "fitness," then, is conditioned and constituted by the relative positions of the actors; there are as many versions of "important" as there are variations in actors and actors' situations. When there are inconsistent versions among those with sufficient power to have media access, there is a public issue.

Similarly, the media is not an objective reporter of events but an active player in the constitution of events. Through their selection, they help to create public events. Their goals – profit, image, power – lead them to constitute events for news coverage. If they habitually cover the same kinds of events, made by the same small groups of actors, it is not because the latter are intrinsically more newsworthy. Rather, coverage is given to those actors whose goals and purposes correspond with those of the media. For newsmen, objectivity is, as Tuchman (1972) notes, "strategic ritual."

This work of selection and transformation by the actors and media, respectively, should be viewed as two levels of creative filtering which determines what becomes news and thus what we, as readers and researchers, have access to. Events and information hostile to the status quo are structurally blocked. To read the newspaper as a catalogue of the important happenings of the day, or to use the newspaper for selecting subjects of study, is to be duped into accepting as reality the political work by which events are constituted. Only by the accident and the scandal is that political work transcended, allowing access to "other" information and thus to a basis for practical action which is directly hostile to those groups who typically manage the public political stage.

A corresponding research activity involves investigations of how we as insurgent sociologists and as people seeking a radical transformation in society can best use accidents, scandals, and routines for our purposes. At least we have a new way to read papers and hear news broadcasts, as well as a new way to select research topics and do content analyses. More ambitiously, following T.R. Young (1972) and activists like Jerry Rubin, we suggest the possibility of the sociologist as methodological promoter of accidents and scandals – someone who does what can be done to upset routine news-making, simultaneously contributing to social reconstruction and gathering data on the impediments to such reconstruction.

# III. Class and Inequality

Samuel Bowles and Herbert Gintis

# Comments on "The Long Shadow of Work"

"The Long Shadow of Work" was part of a project that eventually resulted in the publication of *Schooling in Capitalist America* (Basic Books, 1976). This work began in 1968, stimulated by the then raging academic debates and social conflicts about the structure and purposes of education. Like many others we were then, and remain, hopeful that education can contribute not only to a more productive economy but to a flourishing life for all people and to the more equal sharing of its benefits. Our distress at how woefully the U.S. educational system was then failing these enlightened objectives sparked our initial collaboration. Its continuing failure has prompted our recent return to the subject.

The three basic propositions of our project concerned human development, inequality, and the process of social change.

Concerning human development we showed that while cognitive skills are important in the economy, the contribution of schooling to individual economic success lay elsewhere. We advanced the position that schools prepare people for adult work roles, by socializing people to function well (and without complaint) in the hierarchical structure of the modern corporation. Schools accomplish this by what we called the correspondence principle, namely by structuring social interactions and individual rewards to replicate the environment of the workplace. We thus focused attention not on the explicit curriculum but on the socialization implied by the structure of schooling. Our econometric investigations demonstrated that the contribution of schooling to later economic success is not explained by the cognitive skills learned in school.

Second, we showed that parental class and other aspects of economic status are passed on to children in part by means of unequal educational opportunity, but that the economic advantages of the children of the well-to-do go considerably beyond the superior education they receive. We used the then available statistical data to demonstrate that the U.S. fell far short of the goal of equal economic opportunity and that genetic inheritance of cognitive skill, as measured on standard tests, explains at most a small part of the high degree of intergenerational persistence of affluence and poverty within families.

Finally, our historical studies of the origins of primary schooling and the development of the high school suggested that the evolution of the modern school system is accounted for not by the gradual perfection of a democratic or pedagogical ideals but by a series of class and other conflicts arising through the transformation of the social organization of work and its rewards. In this process the interests of the owners of the leading businesses tended to predominate but were rarely uncontested. Later, in *Democracy and Capitalism* (Basic Books, 1986) we developed the idea that schools and the public sector generally are loci of conflicts stemming from the contradictory rules of the marketplace and the democratic polity.

How do we now view this work? For most of the intervening quarter of a century we have researched and taught subjects quite removed from the questions we addressed in *Schooling*. In recent years, however we have returned to writing about school reform, how economic institutions shape the process of human development, and the importance of schooling, cognitive skill, and personality as determinants of economic success and their role in the intergenerational perpetuation of inequality.

In light of the outpouring of quantitative research on schooling and inequality in the intervening years, the statistical claims of our project have held up remarkably well. In particular, recent research by us and others, using far better data than was available at the time "The Long Shadow of Work" was written, has entirely vindicated our estimates of high levels of intergenerational persistence of economic status, the unimportance of the heritability of IQ in this process, and the fact that the contribution of schooling to cognitive development plays little part in explaining why those with more schooling have higher earnings. Some additional research has supported our hypotheses concerning the role of personality traits (rather than skills per se) as determinants of labor market success. However progress has been halting in this area. We survey some of this recent research in "Intergenerational Inequality," *Journal of Economic Perspectives* 16:3 (Summer, 2002) and (with Melissa Osbourne) "The Determinants of Earnings: Skills, Preferences, and Schooling," *Journal of Economic Literature* (2002).

In "The Long Shadow of Work" and in *Schooling in Capitalist America* we illustrated the correspondence principle by the contrasting structures on elite private universities and public community colleges; but in *Schooling* (Chapters 8 and 9) we noted that during the 1960s, higher education had produced more rebels and flower children than middle-level managers and CEOs. We attributed this to the fact that colleges and universities had been created to serve social elites for whom learning to think critically and taking responsibility for controlling one's life was a preparation for one's economic future. However, in the 1950s and 1960s, higher education had become the training ground for middle class students who were destined to spend their work lives at middle levels in corporate bureaucracies. We suggested that the radical student movement, with its commitment to ending the Vietnam War, to civil rights for Black Americans, and to gender equality, was a response to this contradiction between education and work. In effect, the spirit of free inquiry, critical thought, and freedom of action fostered in the system of higher education fueled a student movement that contested various forms of unaccountable authority and illegitimate inequality. By 1980 we had expanded this insight beyond education, arguing that each of the major sites in society – family, state, educational system, economy – has its unique internal forms of social organization. These various social spheres do not fit together harmoniously, but rather represent different sets of values and foster diverse forms of behavior. Movements to combat the inegalitarian and autocratic nature of capitalism, we argued, took the form of "transporting" practices indigenous to one site – e.g., rights vested in persons and due process from the democratic state – to others – e.g., the capitalist economy and the patriarchal family – where they served as forces for liberation and equality. Our work in this area culminated in the book *Democracy and Capitalism*.

A major thrust in "The Long Shadow of Work," and in our writings of that period, was that individual preferences are not imposed on people by such cultural authorities as family, church, the state and the media or even by the explicit curriculum of the school. Culture, we argued, was a set of discourses used by people to achieve their individual and collective goals, rather than being simply a reflection of their material positions or an instrument of their subjugation. Thus, as in Marx's theory of alienation, preferences and values were developed through, and validated or contradicted by, the everyday life experiences of people. The correspondence principle in schooling, for example, works primarily by inducing students to engage in tasks the performance of which affected their values and personality.

Our subsequent research has considerably expanded the ways we think schools and economic institutions shape human development. In particular, we have applied the principles of Darwinian evolution to cultural practices, arguing that people's preferences and behaviors evolve through a process of differential replication of behaviors, beliefs and norms. Especially noteworthy here are Samuel Bowles and Herbert Gintis, "The Moral Economy of Community: Structured Populations and the Evolution of Prosocial Norms," *Evolution & Human Behavior* 19,1 (January 1998), Samuel Bowles, "Endogenous Preferences: The Cultural Consequences of Markets and Other Economic Institutions," *Journal of Economics Literature* 36 (March 1998), and Herbert Gintis, *Game Theory Evolving* (Princeton: Princeton University Press, 2000), "The Origins of Human Cooperation," in P. Hammersetin, ed. *Genetic and Cultural Origins of Cooperation* (Cambridge: MIT Press, 2003) and Samuel Bowles, *Microeconomics: Behavior, Institutions, and Evolution* (Princeton: Princeton University Press, 2004).

One aspect of this process of cultural evolution, we argue, tends to promote conformity to prevalent practices. But another aspect of the same process, however, promotes practices and values that appear to confer success on others, and hence are adopted by people even when flatly contrary to dominant cultural norms and the values professed by the dominant groups in society.

The erosion of traditional cultures under the influence of market institutions is an example. Economic institutions shape this evolutionary process by influencing the cultural models individuals meet, which behavioral traits confer success, and for other reasons.

On current reflection, the main shortcomings of our intellectual project of the early 1970s reflect the times in which we wrote. The long 1960s economic boom and the anti-materialist counter-cultural currents that it fostered perhaps led us to understate the value of schooling in contributing to productive employment. The more important shortcoming, we think, is programmatic.

We avoided for the most part the question of what schools should be, focusing instead on what schools actually are and do. Nor did we devote much attention to how economic systems other than capitalism might better facilitate achieving the enlightened objectives of schooling. We took it as obvious that a system of democratically-run and employee-owned enterprises coordinated by both markets and governmental policies was both politically and economically viable as an alternative to capitalism. We remain convinced of the attractiveness of such a system, but are less sanguine about its feasibility, and more convinced that reforms of capitalism may be the most likely way to pursue the objectives which we embraced at the outset. While the book endorses the idea that radicals (even revolutionaries) must also be reformers, we provided little guidance to either policy makers, teachers, or students seeking practical positive steps to bring about long term improvements in educational structure and practice.

Partly because we are now reasonably certain that we had the facts right, we remain committed to our overall approach to schooling – embedding the analysis of education in the evolving structure of the economy and the polity, and giving attention to the non-cognitive as well as conventional effects of education. Today, no less than during the stormy days when *Schooling* was written, schools express the conflicts and limitations as well as the hopes of a divided and unequal society. They continue to be both testing grounds and battlegrounds for building a more just and freer society.

Samuel Bowles, Herbert Gintis and Peter Meyer

# The Long Shadow of Work: Education, the Family, and the Reproduction of the Social Division of Labor

> Every child born into the world should be looked upon by society as so much raw material to be manufactured. Its quality is to be tested. It is the business of society, as an intelligent economist, to make the best of it.*
>
> Lester Frank Ward, "Education," 1872

## Introduction

A central tenet of Marxist social theory is that consciousness develops through the social relations into which people enter in their daily lives. Among the manifold relations formative of consciousness, those involving the production of material life hold a preeminent position. Thus in the *Manuscripts*, Marx says:

> [Labor is] a process going on between man and nature, in which man, through his own activity initiates, regulates and controls the material reactions between himself and nature. He confronts nature as one of her own forces. . . . By thus acting on the external world and changing it, he at the same time changes his own nature.[1]

---

* The original version of this article appeared in *The Insurgent Sociologist* 5:4 (Summer, 1975), pp. 3–22.

[1] Marx (1963).

The vision of a perfect dialectic between individuals and nature, in which each acquires its character from its interaction with its antagonist, Marx notes in his later writings, is broken in class societies. The existence of dominant and subordinate classes produces on the one hand history as class struggle rather than the embodiment of communal wills; and on the other hand, consciousness as class-specific, class-differentiated, and alienated according to the way people enter into the social division of labor.

This paper treats an area in the reproduction of consciousness relatively unexplored in the Marxist literature: the role of such institutions of reproduction as the educational system and the family. We shall argue that consciousness is reproduced not only directly through the individual's contact with work and membership in a particular class, but also through these institutions of reproduction. Thus both inequality and repressiveness in the educational sphere, to take a case in point, are best understood as reflections of the social relations of hierarchy and subordination in the capitalist economy.

We shall here suggest that the key which unlocks the secret of the social relations of U.S. education lies in the capitalist economy itself.

The most fruitful way to understand the relationship between schooling and economic life in the U.S. is to grasp the essential structural similarity between their respective social relations. The *correspondence*, between these social relations is pervasive, and accounts for the ability of the educational system to *reproduce* the social relations of production by reproducing an amenable labor force. The *experience* of schooling, and not merely the *content* of formal learning is central to this process, and the process is efficacious because the structures of the schooling and work experiences are conformable.

In our view, it is fruitless to ask if the net effect of U.S. education is toward equality or inequality, repression or liberation. These issues pale into insignificance before the major fact: the educational system is an integral element in the reproduction of the class structure. The liberal educational creed is mistaken because the stance of schooling vis-à-vis equality and liberation are molded by its role in the reproduction of the social relations of production. The experience of work and the articulation of the class structure are the fixed points around which educational values are formed, social justice assessed, the realm of possible delineated in people's consciousness, and the social relations of the educational encounter historically transformed. Educational and economic transformation go hand in hand.

The theme of this paper is the unity of lived experience through the structural similarities of its diverse spheres. Structural correspondence lies at the heart of the reproduction of social life. Yet at the base of reproduction lies contradiction, and the correspondences we shall describe have arisen through struggle. Both the evolution of the educational system and the prospects for a liberated future must be analyzed in terms of both reproduction and contradiction. But here we shall stress the former.

In the next section we argue that the economic system must be understood in light of the need to reproduce consciousness and modes of personal interaction through the lived experiences of daily activity. In the section following we suggest that the stability of the economic system in this reproduction process is facilitated by the prior experiences which individuals undergo in the educational system. Thus, that section presents the basic descriptive, analytical, and statistical support for our principle of the correspondence between the social relations of schooling and work. We then turn to the role of the family in the reproduction of the class structure. In the third section we shall argue that the social relations of the educational encounter are predicated on prior experiences in family life. In the contemporary U.S., education works because, and insofar as, the family works. Finally, we shall argue that there is also a tendency for the social relations of family life to correspond to the social relations of production, in the sense that the positions individuals hold in the hierarchy of production influence the structure of family life and the mode of raising children. In light of this, the role of family life in reproducing the class structure and affecting the transmission of economic status from one generation to the next can be understood, as well as the interaction of social background and education in the individual's maturation process.

## On Reproducing Consciousness

Economic life exhibits a complex and relatively stable pattern of interactions and power relations among individuals and groups. The stability of social intercourse is by no means automatic. As with a living organism, it is the result of explicit mechanisms constituted to maintain and rejuvenate these systemic relationships. We call these *mechanisms of reproduction.*

Amidst the various types of social relations experienced in daily life, a few stand out as central to our analysis of education. These are (a) inter-class relations: the social relations obtaining among classes defined by the capitalist mode of production; (b) intra-class relations: the social relations obtaining among members of the same class, and in particular the degree of solidarity, mutuality, and social distance they normally exhibit; (c) production relations:

the social relations of cooperation, competition, dominance, and subordination obtaining in the production process itself.

Under normal circumstances, the efficacy of coercive power is based at least on the inability or unwillingness of those so subjected to join together in its opposition. More auspiciously, the economic system enjoins their positive acceptance and approbation. Laws generally considered illegitimate lose their coercive power, and force too frequently applied tends to contradict its intended effect. The consolidation and extension of the capitalist relations of production have engendered struggles of furious intensity no less today than in past times. Yet instances of force deployed against a united and active opposition are sporadic. They have usually given way to detente through the annihilation of opposing forces, through structural change, and through ideological accommodation. Thus it is clear that the consciousness of workers – beliefs, values, self-concepts, types of solidarity and fragmentation, as well as modes of personal behavior and development – is integral to the perpetuation, validation and smooth operation of economic institutions. The reproduction of the social relations of production depends on the reproduction of consciousness.

Under what conditions will individuals accept the pattern of social relations that frame their lives? Believing that the long-run development of the existing system holds the prospect of fulfilling their needs, they might actively embrace these social relations. Failing this, and having no vision of a fundamental transformation of economic life that might significantly improve their situation, individuals might merely *accept* their condition with some resignation. Even with such a vision, vaguely adumbrated or fully articulated, they might passively *submit* to the framework of economic life and seek individual solutions to social problems, believing that the possibilities for forging a powerful movement for change are remote. The issue of the reproduction of consciousness enters each of these three assessments.

First, the economic system will be embraced when the *perceived* needs of individuals are congruent with the types of satisfaction the economic system can objectively provide. While perceived needs may be in part biologically determined (e.g., minimal physical and psychological requisites), in larger part needs arise through the aggregate experiences of individuals in society itself. That is, the social relations of production are reproduced in part through a harmony between the perceived needs which the social system generates, and the means at its disposal for satisfying these needs.

Second, the assessment of fundamental social transformation as infeasible, unoperational, and utopian is normally supported by a complex web of ideological perspectives deeply embedded in the cultural and scientific life of the community, and reflected in the structure of consciousness of its members. But fostering the "consciousness of inevitability" is not the office of the cultural system alone. In addition, mechanisms systematically thwarting the spontaneous development of social experiences of contradicting these beliefs must exist. Such mechanisms include direct suppression of counter-institutions (e.g., workers' or consumers' co-ops and communes) by dominant classes, as well as channelling their development in directions compatible with the prevailing constellation of power prerogatives and consciousness.

Third, the belief in the futility of organizing for fundamental social change is facilitated by social distinctions which fragment the conditions of life and consciousness of subordinate classes. Thus the strategy of "divide and conquer" has been basic to the maintenance of power of dominant classes since the dawn of civilization. Once again the splintered consciousness of a subordinate class is not the product of cultural phenomena alone. Rather, the fragmentation of subordinate groups, with its consequent chaotic pattern of divergent interests, must be reproduced through the social relations of daily life.

The reproduction of consciousness develops in part through the individual's direct perception of and participation in social life.[2] For instance, when the social division of labor stratifies the working class, individual needs and self-concepts develop in an accordingly fragmented manner. Youth of different racial, sexual, ethnic or economic backgrounds directly perceive the economic positions and prerogatives of "their kind of people," and by appropriately adjusting their aspirations, not only reproduce stratification on the level of personal consciousness, but bring the development of their needs into (at least partial) harmony with the objective conditions of economic life. Similarly, individuals tend to gear the development of their personal capacities – cognitive, emotional, physical, aesthetic, and spiritual – in directions where options for their exercise are available. For instance, the alienated character of work leads people to guide their creative and human potentials to areas outside economic activity: consumption, travel, sexuality, and family life. Thus needs and need-satisfaction again tend to fall into congruence. Alienated labor is reproduced on the level of personal consciousness.[3]

---

[2] Gintis (1974); Berger and Luckmann (1966); Schutz (1973).
[3] For an extended treatment of these issues, see Gintis (1972).

But this congruence is continually disrupted; the satisfaction of needs give rise to new needs – which derive from the logic of personal development and in turn undercut the social integration of consciousness. Thus the reproduction of consciousness cannot be the unintended by-product of social experience. On a deeper level, social relations are often organized to *facilitate* the reproduction of consciousness through the day-to-day activities of the individual. For instance, power configurations, job contents, inter-personal relations and hiring criteria in the enterprise are organized to *reproduce* the workers' self-concepts, the legitimacy of their assignments within the hierarchy, the technological inevitability of the hierarchical division of labor itself, and their social distance from other workers in the organization. Indeed, workers' participation in decision-making becomes a threat to profits because it tends *not* to reproduce patterns of consciousness compatible with capitalist control. By generating new needs and possibilities, by demonstrating the feasibility of more thoroughgoing economic democracy, by increasing worker solidarity to a potentially threatening degree, worker involvement in decision-making may undermine the power structure of the enterprise.

But the reproduction of consciousness cannot be insured through the direct mechanisms alone. In addition, the initiation of youth into the economic system is facilitated by a series of institutions more immediately related to the formation of personality and consciousness. Among these institutions are the family and the educational system.

How does the educational system reproduce consciousness? In a very general way, schooling fosters and rewards the development of certain capacities and the expression of certain needs, while thwarting and penalizing others, and by tailoring the self-concepts, aspirations, and social class identifications of individuals to the requirements of the capitalist division of labor. The educational system accomplishes this through the institutional relations to which students are subjected.

More concretely, we may isolate four main functions of the educational system. First, schooling produces many of the technical and cognitive skills required for adequate job performance. This process is well understood and, as we have suggested elsewhere, cannot account for either the association between schooling and economic success or the repressive nature of U.S. education.[4] We shall not pursue it further. Second, the educational system helps legitimate economic inequality.

---

[4] Bowles and Gintis (1975).

The objective and meritocratic orientation of U.S. education, the cumulative process of reconciling the aspirations of individuals with their future positions, reduces discontent over both the hierarchical division of labor and the process through which individuals attain position in it. Once again, the generation of needs is rendered compatible with the means of satisfying them – in this case the personal need for the attainment of valued social positions. Third, the school generates rewards, and selects personal characteristics relevant to the staffing of positions in the hierarchical division of labor. Fourth, the educational system, through the pattern of status distinctions it fosters, reinforces the stratified consciousness on which the fragmentation of subordinate economic classes is based.

What aspects of the educational system allow it to serve these various functions? We shall suggest that the educational system's ability to reproduce the consciousness of workers lies in a straightforward *correspondence principle*: for the past century at least, schooling has contributed to the reproduction of the social relations of production largely through the correspondence between school structure and class structure.

## Education and Consciousness: the Correspondence Principle

The oft discussed tension between "business" and "academic" values obscures an underlying communality: the structure of social relations in education – including sources of motivation, authority, and control, and types of sanctioned interpersonal relations – not only inure the student to the discipline of the work-place, but develop the types of personal demeanor, modes of self-presentation, self-images, and social class identifications which are the crucial ingredients of job adequacy.

Specifically, the social relations of education – the relations between administration and teachers, teachers and students, students and students, and students and their work – replicate the hierarchical division of labor. Hierarchical relations are reflected in the vertical authority lines from administrators to teachers to students. Alienated labor is reflected in the student's lack of control over his or her education, the alienation of the student from curriculum content, and the motivation of school work through a system of grades and other external rewards rather than the student's integration with either the process (learning) or the outcome (knowledge) of the educational "production process." Stratification and fragmentation in work is reflected in the institutionalized and rarely constructive competition among students, continual and ostensibly meritocratic ranking and evaluation of students. By attuning young people to a set of social relations similar to those of the workplace, schooling gears the development of personal needs to its requirements.

The correspondence of schooling with the social relations of production goes beyond this aggregate level, however. First, different levels of education feed workers into different levels within the structure of production and correspondingly tend towards an internal organization comparable to levels in the hierarchical division of labor. The lowest levels in the hierarchy of the enterprise emphasize rule-following, middle levels dependability and capacity to operate without direct and continuous supervision, and the higher levels internalization of norms of the enterprise and sensitivity to interpersonal relations without the organization.[5] Similarly, lower levels of education (junior and senior high school) tend to severely limit and channel the activities of students; junior colleges, teacher colleges, and community colleges allow more breadth for independent activity and less overall supervision, with the four-year colleges tending toward social relations conformable with the higher levels in the production hierarchy. Thus schools continually maintain their hold on students. As they "master" one type of behavioral regulation, they are either allowed to progress to the next, or tend to be channeled into the corresponding level in the hierarchy of production.

Second, even within a single school, the social relations of different tracks tend to conform to different behavioral norms. Thus high school vocational and general tracks emphasize rule-following and close supervision, while the college track tends toward a more open atmosphere emphasizing the internalization of norms.

These differences in the social relations among and within schools, in part reflect both the social backgrounds of the student body and their future economic positions as well. Thus blacks and other minorities tend to concentrate in schools with the most repressive, arbitrary, and coercive authority structures, and which offer the most minimal possibilities for advancement – in all respects mirroring the characteristics of secondary job structures. Similarly, predominantly working class schools tend to emphasize behavioral control and rule-following, while schools in well-to-do suburbs utilize relatively open systems involving greater student participation, less direct supervision, more student electives, and in general a value system stressing internalized standards of control.

[5] Edwards (1975); Bowles and Gintis (1975).

The differential socialization patterns of schools attended by students of different social classes, and even within the same school, do not arise by accident. Rather, they stem from the fact that the educational objectives and expectations of administrators, teachers and parents, and the responsiveness of students to various patterns of teaching and control, differ for students of different social classes.

At crucial turning points in the history of U.S. education, changes in the social relations of schooling have been structured in the interests of a more harmonious reproduction of the labor force, and usually through the direct intervention of elites most highly, benefited by these changes. But in the day-to-day operation of the schools, the consciousness of social classes, derived from their cultural milieu and work experience, is crucial to the maintenance of the correspondences we have described. That working class parents seem to favor stricter educational methods is a reflection of their own work experiences, which have demonstrated that submission to authority is an essential ingredient in one's ability to get and hold a steady, well-paying job. That middle class parents prefer a more open atmosphere and a greater emphasis on motivational control is likewise a reflection of their positions in the social division of labor. Thus Burton Rosenthal has shown that when given the opportunity, higher status parents are far more likely than their lower status neighbors to choose "open classrooms" for their children.[6]

Further, differences in the social relations of schooling are reinforced by inequalities in financial resources. The paucity of financial support for the education of children from minority groups and working class families leaves more resources to be devoted to the children of those with commanding roles in the economy; it also forces upon the teachers and school administrators in the working class schools a type of social relations that fairly closely mirrors that of the factory. Thus financial considerations in poorly supported working-class schools militate against small intimate classes, against a multiplicity of elective courses and specialized teachers (except disciplinary personnel), and preclude the amounts of free time for the teachers and free space required for a more open, flexible educational environment. The lack of financial support all but requires that students be treated as raw materials on a production line; it places a high premium on obedience and punctuality; there are few opportunities for independent, creative work or individualized attention

[6] Rosenthal (1972).

by teachers. The well-financed schools attended by the children of the rich can offer much greater opportunities for the development of the capacity for sustained independent work and the other characteristics required for adequate job performance in the upper levels of the occupational hierarchy.

Our correspondence principle should help us explain the observed association between educational attainment (years of schooling) and economic success (income and occupational status). This association *cannot* be accounted for in terms of the acquisition of cognitive skills alone.[7] We shall now show that much empirical evidence points to the importance of work-related personality traits in accounting for this association.

We have referred to the research of our colleague Richard Edwards, who found that job performance could be quite well predicted by three personality factors – rule-following, dependability, and internalization of norms – with the first relatively more important at the lowest levels of the hierarchy of production, internalization of norms predominant at the highest, and with dependability salient at intermediate levels. Are these traits in fact rewarded in schools? Our discussion certainly suggests that they are. In addition, we have surveyed the literature on the personality correlates of school success and have found that the best predictors consistently fall into four categories quite similar to Edwards' factors: Subordinacy, Discipline, Emotionally Neutral Orientation to Interpersonal Relations, and Motivation by External Reward.[8]

A more direct confirmation of the proposition that the personality traits rewards in schools (through grading) are similar to those conducive of performance in the hierarchical division of labor can be obtained by using these same personality measures employed in Edwards' study on a group of school students, thus obtaining direct comparable evidence.[9]

We began with the personality measures used by Edwards. Gene Smith, the originator of these types of personality measures, had previously shown them to be excellent predictors of educational success (grade point average) in a series of well-executed studies.[10] Noting that personality inventories suffer from low validities due to their abstraction from real-life environments, and low reliabilities due to the use of a single evaluative instrument, Smith turned to student peer-ratings of 42 common personality traits, based on each

[7] Gintis (1971); Bowles and Gintis (1975).
[8] Gintis (1971).
[9] Meyer (1972).
[10] Smith (1967a, 1967b, 1970).

student's observation of the actual classroom behavior of his or her classmates. Factor analysis allowed the extraction of five general traits, stable across different samples. These five traits may be labeled Agreeableness, Extroversion, Work-orientation, Emotionality and Helpfulness. Of these only the Work-orientation factor, which Smith calls "Strength of Character" – including such traits as "not a quitter, conscientious, responsible, insistently orderly, not prone to daydream, determined-persevering" – was related to school success. Smith then showed that in several samples Work-orientation exhibited three times the power to predict post-high school academic performance than any combination of thirteen cognitive variables, including SAT-verbal, SAT-mathematical, and high school class rank. Edwards' success with this test in predicting supervisor ratings of workers convinced us that applying the same forms to high school students would provide a fairly direct link between personality development in school and the requisites of job performance.

We chose for our sample the 237 members of the senior class of a single New York state high school, of whom most participated in the study.[11] Analysis of this data provides striking confirmation of the correspondence principle. Following Edwards (1972), we created sixteen pairs of personality traits,[12] and obtained individual grade-point averages, IQ scores, and College Entrance examination SAT-verbal and SAT-mathematical scores from the official school records.[13]

As was expected, the cognitive scores provided the best single predictor of grade point average – indeed, that grading is based significantly on cognitive performance is perhaps the single valid element in the "meritocratic ideology." Yet the sixteen personality measures possessed nearly comparable predictive value, having a multiple correlation of .63 as compared to .77 for the cognitive variables.[14] More important than the overall predictive value

---

[11] Personality data was collected for 97% of the sample, grade-point average and test-scored data was available for 80% of the sample, and family background data was available for 67%. Inability to collect data was due usually to students' absences from school during test sessions.

[12] These are described fully in Bowles and Gintis (1975), Appendix B.

[13] The school chosen was predominantly higher income, so that most members had taken college entrance examinations.

[14] The multiple correlation of IQ, SAT-verbal, and SAT-mathematical with grade-point average (GPA) was r = .769, while their correlation with the personality variables was r = .25, which is quite low.

Table 1. The Importance of Personality Traits in Predicting Grades.

| Rewarded Traits | | Penalized Traits | | Neutral Traits | |
|---|---|---|---|---|---|
| Perseverant | .42* | Creative | –.33* | Frank | .11** |
| Dependable | .40* | Aggressive | –.27* | Loner | –.07** |
| Consistent | .39* | Independent | –.23* | Temperamental | –.02** |
| Identifies with School | .38* | | | | |
| Empathizes Orders | .37* | | | | |
| Punctual | .35* | | | | |
| Defers Gratification | .31* | | | | |
| Externally Motivated | .29* | | | | |
| Predictable | .25* | | | | |
| Tactful | .17* | | | | |

*p < .01 **p > .05
*Note*: These are partial correlations controlling for IQ, SAT-Verbal and SAT-Math.
*Source*: Meyer (1972); Bowles and Gintis (1975).

of the personality traits, however, is their pattern on contribution to grades. To reveal this pattern, we first eliminated the effect of differences in cognitive performance in individual grades, and then calculated the correlation between grades and the personality measures.[15] The results are presented in Table 1.

The pattern of resulting associations clearly supports our model. First, the only significantly penalized traits are precisely those which are incompatible with conformity to the hierarchical division of labor – Creativity, Independence, and Aggressivity. Similarly, all the personality traits we would expect to be rewarded are, and highly significantly so while those which are more or less neutral from the social relations of production framework are insignificant (lines 13 through 16).

As a second stage in our analysis of this data, we used the technique of "factor analysis" to consolidate the sixteen personality measures into three "personality factors." Factor analysis allows us to group together those measured traits which are normally associated with one another across all individuals in the sample The first, which we call Submission to Authority, includes Consistent, Identifies with School, Punctual, Dependable, Externally Motivated, and Persistent. In addition, it includes Independent and Creative weighted *negatively*. The second, which we call Temperament, includes Not Aggressive, Not Temperamental, Not Frank, Predictable, Tactful, and Not Creative. The

[15] That is, we created partial correlation coefficients between GPA and each personality measure, controlling for IQ, SAT-V and SAT-M.

Table 2. Factor Analysis of High School Personality Traits.

| Submission to Authority | | Temperament | | Internalization of Norms | |
|---|---|---|---|---|---|
| Consistent | .83[a] | Aggressive | –.80[a] | Empathizes Orders | .74[a] |
| Identifies with School | .81 | Temperamental | –.78 | Defers Gratification | .71 |
| Punctual | .80 | Frank | –.74 | | |
| Dependable | .78 | Predictable | .58 | | |
| Externally Motivated | .77 | Tactful | .54 | | |
| Perserverant | .73 | Creative | –.51 | | |
| Independent | –.69 | | | | |
| Creative | –.52 | | | | |

*Note*: [a] Numbers are factor loadings. The factor analysis was by principal components and quartimax rotation. The first factor accounts for 43.7% of the variance, the second for 15.9% of the variance, and the third for 11.8% of the variance.

third, which we call Internalization of Norms, includes Empathizes Orders and Defers Gratification. Factor Loadings are presented in Table 2.[16]

These three factors are not perfectly comparable to Edward's three factors. Rather, our Submission to Authority seems to combine Edwards' Rules and Dependability factors, while our Internalization is comparable to Edwards' Internalization factor. In the case of the latter factor, both Edwards' and Meyer's data depict an individual who sensitively interprets the desires of his or her superior, and who operates adequately without direct supervision over considerable periods of time.

Our theory would predict that on the high school level Submission to Authority would be most predictive of grades, while Internalization, which becomes important on the post-high school level, would be less important. The Temperament factor is essentially irrelevant to our theory, and might be expected to be unimportant. In Table 4, this prediction is confirmed. This Table exhibits the independent contributions of both cognitive measures and personality factors to the prediction of grades. We see that SAT-math is the most important, with Submission to Authority and SAT-verbal being equally important, and Internalized Control significantly less so. The Temperament and IQ variables have no independent contribution.

Thus the personality traits rewarded in schools, at least for this sample, seem to be quite closely related to those indicative of good job performance in the capitalist economy. Since both Edwards and ourselves used essentially the same measures of personality traits, this assertion can be tested directly.

[16] This is taken from Meyer (1972) and Bowles and Gintis (1975), Appendix B.

We may take the three general traits extracted by Edwards in his study of workers – Rules-Orientation, Dependability, and Internalization of Norms – and find the relation between grades and those traits in our school study. This is exhibited in Table 4, which shows a remarkable congruence.[17]

Hence the correspondence principle stands up well in the light of grading practices. We must stress, however, that the empirical data on grading must not be conceived as revealing the "inner workings" of the educational system's reproduction of the social division of labor. First of all, it is the overall *structure* of social relations of the educational encounter which reproduces consciousness, and not merely grading practices. Second, personality traits are not the only relevant personal attributes – others being modes of self-presentation, self-image, aspirations, and class identifications – which are not captured in this data. Third, the measuring of personality traits is tricky and difficult, and the studies mentioned probably only capture a small part of the relevant dimensions. Fourth, both traits rewarded in schools and relevant to job performance differ by educational level, class composition of schools, and the student's particular educational track. These subtleties are not reflected in the data.

For these reasons we would not expect student grades to be a good predictor of economic success. In addition, grades are clearly dominated by the cognitive performance of students, which we have seen is not highly relevant to economic attainment. Yet we might expect that in an adequately controlled study in which work performances of individuals on the job and with comparable educational experience are compared, grades would be good predictors. We have managed to find only one study meeting these requirements – a study which clearly supports our position, and is sufficiently interesting to present in some detail. Marshall S. Brenner studied 100 employees who had joined the Lockheed-California Company after obtaining a high school diploma in the Los Angeles City School Districts. From the employees' high school transcripts, he obtained their grade-point averages, school absence rates, a teachers' "work habits" evaluation and a teacher' "cooperation" evaluation. In addition to this data, he gathered three evaluations of job performance by employees' supervisors; a supervisors' "ability rating," a supervisors' "conduct rating" and "productivity rating." Brenner found a significant correlation between grades and all measures of supervisor evaluation. We have

[17] This is taken from Edwards (1975), Table 2.

reanalyzed Brenner's data to uncover the source of this correlation. One possibility is that grades measure cognitive performance and cognitive performance determines job performance. How-ever, when the high school teachers' "work habits" and "cooperation" evaluations as well as "school absences" are controlled for by linear regression, grades have no additional predictive value. Hence, we may draw two conclusions: first, grades predict job adequacy only through their non-cognitive component; and second, the teachers' evaluations as to behavior in the classroom is strikingly similar to the supervisor's ratings as to behavior on the job. The cognitive component of grades predicts only the supervisors' "ability rating" – not surprising in view of the probability that both are related to employee IQ.[18]

In closing, we wish to emphasize that the correspondence principle has been introduced not only as the structural relationship between the economy and the educational system, but as the framework for understanding why individuals with greater educational attainment achieve higher levels of economic success. The question arises because the most obvious candidate for an answer – the difference in cognitive skills attained – actually accounts for only a small portion of this association.

Why then the association? Elsewhere we surveyed the reasoning and evidence indicating the importance of four sets of non-cognitive worker traits – work-related personality characteristics, modes of self-presentation, ascriptive characteristics and credentials.[19]

We believe all are involved in the association between educational level and economic success. We have emphasized that personality traits opposite to performance on different hierarchical levels are fostered and rewarded by the school system. A similar, but simpler argument can be made with respect to modes of self-presentation. Individuals who have attained a certain educational level tend to identify with one another socially and differentiate themselves from their "inferiors." They tend to adjust their aspirations and self-concepts accordingly, while acquiring manners of speech and demeanor more or less socially acceptable and appropriate to their level.[20] As such, they

[18] Brenner (1968).

[19] Bowles and Gintis (1975).

[20] See Offe (1970). Offe quotes Bensen and Rosenberg from *The Meaning of Work in Bureaucratic Society* (in M. Stein et al. [eds.], *Identity and Anxiety*, New York: Free Press, 1960), pp. 183–184: "Old habits are discarded and new habits are nurtured. The would-be success learns when to simulate enthusiasm, compassion, interest, concern, modesty, confidence, and mastery; when to smile, and with whom to laugh and how

Table 3. Contribution of Personality Factors to the Prediction of Grades.

| | |
|---|---|
| SAT-Math | .43* |
| Submission to Authority | .29* |
| SAT-Verbal | .31* |
| Internationalization of Norms | .16* |
| Temperament | .08* |
| IQ | .01** |

*p < .01 **p > .05
*Note*: The numbers represent normalized regression coefficients when all variables are entered into a single regression.

Table 4. Predicting Job Performance and Grades from the Same Personality Factors.

| | Rules-Orientation | Dependable | Internalizes Norms |
|---|---|---|---|
| Supervisor Rating | .28 (6.96) | .28 (7.19) | .29 (7.07) |
| GPA | .22 (3.25) | .25 (3.87) | .17 (2.65) |

*Note*: The Multiple R in the first equation is R = .613, and in the second equation, R = .523. The figures in parenthesis are beta coefficients.
*Source*: Edwards (1975); Bowles and Gintis (1975).

are correspondingly valuable to employers interested in preserving and reproducing the status differences on which the legitimacy of the hierarchical division of labor is based. In addition, insofar as educational credentials are an independant determinant of hiring and promotion,[21] they will directly account for a portion of this association.

Finally, family background effects also account for a significant portion of the association between educational and economic attainment. For white males about 33% of the correlation between education and income is due to their common association with socio-economic background, even holding constant childhood IQ. That is, children whose parents have higher status economic positions tend to achieve more income themselves independent of their education, but they also tend to get more education. Hence the observed association is reinforced.

---

intimate and friendly he can be with other people. He selects his home and his residential area with care; he buys his clothes and chooses styles with an eye to their probably reception in his office. He reads or pretends to have read the right books, the tight magazines, and the right newspapers. All this will be reflected in the 'right line of conversation' which he adapts as his own. . . . He joins the right party and espouses the political ideology of his fellows."

[21] See Berg (1971), and Taubman and Wales (1972) for some evidence on this point.

Indeed, there is a strong independent association between family background and economic success. What is the origin of this effect? We shall argue in the following section that the experiences of parents on the job tend to be reflected in the social relations of family life. Thus, through family relations children tend to acquire orientations toward work, aspirations, and self-concepts preparing them for similar economic positions themselves.

## Family Structure and Job Structure

Family experience has a significant impact on the welfare, behavior and personal consciousness of individuals, both in their period of maturation and their daily adult lives. The social relations of family life – relations between husband and wife as well as between parents and children and among children – have undergone important changes in the course of U.S. economic development. The prospect for future changes is of crucial importance in the process of social transformation.[22]

The analysis of family life is not only of basic importance, but is of subtle and dynamic complexity. Compared to the social relations of family life, the economic and educational phenomenon we have been discussing appear as straightforward and rather mechanical. Hence rather than entertaining a broad analysis of family life we shall limit our discussion to a few issues directly linked to our central concern: the reproduction of the social relations of production. Like the educational system, the family plays a major role in the preparation of the young for economic and social roles. In particular, the family's impact on the reproduction of the sexual division of labor is distinctly greater than that of the educational system.

We maintain that the reproduction of consciousness is facilitated by a rough correspondence between the social relations of production and the social relations of family life. This correspondence is affected by the experiences parents encounter through their participation in the social division of labor. Thus there is a tendency for families to reproduce in their offspring not only a consciousness tailored to the objective nature of the work world, but to prepare them for economic positions roughly comparable to their own. These tendencies can be countered by other social forces (schooling, media, shifts in

---

[22] See Benston (1969), Goldberg (1971), Gordon (1971), Mitchell (1972), and Zaretsky (1973).

aggregate occupational structure), but they remain sufficiently strong to account for a significant part of the observed intergenerational status transmission processes.

The case of the sexual division of labor is particularly straightforward. The capitalist division of labor promotes the separation between wage labor and household labor, the latter being unpaid and reserved almost exclusively for women. This separation is reflected within the family as a nearly complete division of labor between husband and wife. The occupational emphasis on full-time work, the dependance of promotion upon seniority, the career-oriented commitment of the worker, and the active discrimination against working women, conspire to shackle the woman to the home while minimizing the possibility of sharing of domestic duties between husband and wife.

But how does the family help *reproduce* the sexual division of labor? First, wives and mothers themselves normally embrace their self-concepts as household workers. They then pass these onto their children through the differential sex role typing of boys and girls within the family. Second, and perhaps more important, children tend to develop self-concepts based on the sexual divisions which they observe around them. Even families which treat boys and girls equally in important respects cannot avoid sex role typing when the male parent is tangentially involved in household labor and child-rearing. In short, the family as a reproduction unit cannot but reflect its division of labor as a production unit – as the locus of household production and the sexual division of labor. This sex typing, unless countered by other social forces, then facilitates the submission of the next generation of women to their inferior status in the wage labor system and lends its alternative – child-rearing and domesticity – an aura of inevitability, if not desirability. Yet in essential respects, the family exhibits social patterns quite a typical of the social relations of production. The close personal and emotional relations of family life are a far cry from the impersonal bureaucracy and autocracy of the wage labor system. Indeed, the family is often esteemed as a refuge from the alienation and psychic poverty of work life. The fact that family structure and the capitalist relations of production differ in essential respects lies at the heart of our explanation of the necessary role of schooling in the integration of young people into the wage labor system.[23]

[23] Bowles and Gintis (1975), Chs. 6–9.

Despite the tremendous structural disparity between family and economy, we shall argue there is a significant correspondence between the authority relations of production and child-rearing. This flows in part from the overall tenor of family life common to all social levels. The work-dominated family with its characteristically age-graded patterns of power and privilege replicates many of the aspects of the hierarchy of production in the firm. Yet we shall be more concerned with the difference among families whose income earners hold distinct positions in this hierarchy.

Successful job performance at low hierarchical levels requires the worker's orientation toward rule-following, or conformity to external authority, while successful performance at higher levels requires behavior according to internalized norms.

These traits are not confined to work alone, but affect the individual's fundamental social values and orientations generally. It would be surprising indeed if these general orientations did not manifest themselves in parental priorities for the rearing of their children.

## Conclusion

The economic system is stable only if the consciousness of the strata and classes it engenders remain compatible with the social relations which characterize it as a mode of production. Hence, the social division of labor must be *reproduced* in the consciousness of its participants. The educational system is one of the several reproduction mechanisms. By providing skills, legitimating inequalities in economic positions, and facilitating certain types of social intercourse among individuals, U.S. education patterns personal development around the requirements of alienated work. The educational system reproduces the capitalist social division of labor in part through a *correspondence* between its own internal social relations and those of the workplace.

We believe that the tendency of the social relations of economic life to be reproduced in the educational system and in family life lies at the heart of the failure of the liberal educational creed, and must form the basis of a viable program for social change. Patterns of inequality, repression, and forms of class domination cannot be restricted to single spheres of life, but reappear in substantially altered yet structurally comparable form in all spheres. Power and privilege in economic life surface not only in the core social institutions which pattern the formation of consciousness (family and school), but even in face-to-face personal encounters, leisure activities, and philosophies of the world. In particular, the liberal goal of employing the educational system as a corrective device, overcoming the "inadequacies" of the economic system is vain indeed. Transformation of the educational system and the pattern of class relations, power, and privilege in the economic sphere must go hand in hand as part of an integrated program of action.

To speak of social change is to speak of making history. Thus, we are motivated to look into the historical roots of the present educational system, to better understand the framework within which social change takes place and has taken place in the past. Our major question will be: what were the historical forces giving rise to the present correspondence between education and economic life, and how have these been affected by changes in the class structure and concrete peoples' struggles?

We believe that the historical development of the educational system reflects a counterpoint of reproduction and contradiction, as capitalist economic development leads to continual shifts in the social relations of production and the attendant class structure. These social relations have involved class conflicts which throughout U.S. history have periodically changed in both form and content. A major role of the educational system has been to defuse and attenuate these conflicts. Thus the changing character of social conflict, rooted in shifts in the class structure, has demanded periodic reorganizations of the network of educational institutions. We perceive the recurrent phenomenon of an educational system whose social relations are geared to a disappearing pattern of economic relations thrown into contradiction with the reproduction needs of the ascendent economic structure. Out of this recurrent contradiction have come structural transformations characterizing the "crucial turning-points" in U.S. educational history.

Val Burris

# The Future of Class Analysis: Reflections on "Class Structure and Political Ideology"

The concept of "class" is, at once, one of the most central and one of the most contested concepts in sociological theory and research. Despite its Marxist heritage and association with the theoretical and political aspirations of Marx's critique of capitalism, the concept of class has survived all efforts to expunge it from the lexicon of sociology – including mainstream, non-Marxist sociology. Proclamations of the death or irrelevance of class analysis are a recurrent theme within the sociological literature (Nisbet 1959; Gorz 1982; Laclau and Mouffe 1985; Clark and Lipset 1991; Kingston 1994; Paluski and Waters 1996). In an earlier day such obituaries were issued mainly by representatives of the avowedly anti-Marxist mainstream, whereas today they are as likely to emanate from the ranks of the self-styled "post-Marxist" left. Nevertheless, the concept of class refuses to give up the ghost, but, like the specter hailed by Marx and Engels in the opening lines of the *Communist Manifesto*, continues to haunt the discipline of sociology.

The resiliency of the concept of class and the attraction that it holds over Marxist and non-Marxist sociologists alike can be attributed to its ability – or, more realistically, its plausible promise – to reconcile many of the theoretical antinomies that animate the discipline: self and society, structure and agency, being and consciousness, social reproduction and social change. The discipline of sociology and the concept of class are both offspring of the rise of industrial capitalism and, as such, share a common historical legacy. C. Wright Mills' (1959), who so elegantly defined the task and the promise of sociology in terms of enabling people to see the connection between their personal troubles and the larger socio-historical context, considered class to be among the most powerful concepts in the sociological toolkit. Arthur Stinchcombe, using the less elegant language of causal modeling, has said that "sociology has only one independent variable, class" (quoted in Wright 1979). While this may be something of an exaggeration, it does capture the fact that deeply structured inequality is one of the defining concerns of sociology and that class is arguably among the most refined and fully developed concepts for exploring this issue.

Within the Marxist tradition the concept of class is not only an explanatory concept but also a normative one that is linked to the critique of capitalism as an inherently exploitative system and with political movements seeking a more democratic and egalitarian (classless) society. There have been periods during which – owing to the association between class analysis and political radicalism – theoretical and empirical work on class has been pushed to the margins of the discipline, where it has been sustained mainly by critical or alternative journals like *The Insurgent Sociologist*. Such was the case in the U.S. from roughly the late 1950s through the late 1970s. By contrast, in Europe, and especially England, where class divisions were more readily acknowledged within the popular consciousness, where Marxism was more academically respectable, and where there existed a Fabian tradition of class analysis that avoided incendiary talk of proletarian revolution, mainstream sociology remained receptive to research on social class throughout these years (Lockwood 1958, Goldthorpe et al. 1969, Giddens 1973).

The essay on "Class Structure and Political Ideology," which is based on work done in the early and mid-1980s, bears the mark of this marginalization of class analysis in U.S. sociology during the immediately preceding period. Most of the references in this article are to research published in alternative journals like *The Insurgent Sociologist*, *Politics and Society*, *New Left Review*, *Radical America*, *Capital and Class*, and the *Review of Radical Political Economics*. By the time the essay was published, however, the situation had begun to change and mainstream sociology journals were becoming more open to research on social class, including research from an explicitly Marxist perspective. Since the early 1980s class analysis has continued to be contested within the discipline of sociology, but it has not been relegated back to the margins.

Much of this greater openness among sociologists to research on class and class structure can be attributed to the wave of New Left activists who entered the discipline in large numbers starting in the mid-1970s. But part of the credit must also be given to the dogged efforts of individual scholars who have devoted their careers to demonstrating the theoretical rigor and explanatory power of class analysis. Here I have in mind especially the work of Erik Wright (1979, 1985, 1997) within the Marxist tradition and John Goldthorpe (1982, 1987, 1996; Goldthorpe and Marshall 1992; Erikson and Goldthorpe 1992) among the not-so-Marxist (quasi-Weberian) proponents of class analysis.

Since the early 20th century, a central preoccupation of class analysis has been the class position, social consciousness, and political behavior of salaried white-collar workers – variously referred to as the "new middle class," "new working class," "new petty bourgeoisie," "professional-managerial class," or "service class" (see Burris [1986] for an overview). The reasons for this preoccupation are not hard to identify. As salaried professionals, most social theorists would themselves qualify as members of a new middle class. Their concern with this group is thus motivated by an interest in self-understanding, if not by an inflated sense of their own importance. In addition, the growing proportion of salaried white-collar workers in advanced capitalism naturally lends itself to speculation about the future trajectory of class society. Beyond these factors is the genuine challenge that salaried white-collar workers pose to class analysis, given the complex and heterogeneous roles that they occupy within the social relations of modern capitalism. Efforts to clarify the class location of salaried white-collar workers inevitably bring into play many of the broader theoretical issues that lie at the root of competing paradigms of class analysis – e.g., the relative importance to be given to mental labor versus manual labor, production relations versus market relations, authority versus property ownership, and objective class positions versus subjective class identities.

"Class Structure and Political Ideology" presents a critical overview of some of the more influential Marxist and neo-Marxist theories of the time, including those advanced by Nicos Poulantzas, Erik Wright, Guglielmo Carchedi, and John and Barbara Ehrenreich, with a focus on how these different theories conceptualize the distinction between the working class and salaried intermediate classes. The original version of the article also included an empirical section (omitted here for reasons of space) that used national survey data to assess the degree to which different theories of class structure corresponded (or failed to correspond) to actual cleavages in patterns of subjective class identity and political ideology. Both the theoretical and empirical discussions converged on the conclusion that the most salient class cleavage among wage and salary workers is one that classifies the majority of manual and routine nonmanual wage-earners as working class and some combination of managers, professionals, and technical employees as middle class. Descriptively, this model of class structure has arguably become the dominant view today among Marxist and non-Marxist theorists alike, although there are important differences in the underlying theories of class associated with this general map of class divisions.

Many of the foundational questions of class analysis that were once discussed primarily in the pages of alternative journals like *The Insurgent Sociologist* have lately become the focus of debate within the sociological mainstream. Here I would point specifically to the debates initiated by Aage Sørensen's proposal to reconceptualize class relations in terms of the distribution of rent-producing assets (A. Sørensen 2000; Wright 2000; Goldthorpe 2000; Rueschemeyer and Mahoney 2000) and by David Grusky and his co-authors' argument in favor of a disaggregated approach to class analysis based on detailed occupational categories (Grusky and J. Sørensen 1998; Grusky and Weeden 2001; Goldthorpe 2002; Birkelund 2002; Therborn 2002). Although I am inclined to agree more with the critics than with the advocates of either of these reformulations of class analysis, it must be said that the theoretical acuity shown by these proponents of new ways of conceptualizing class is impressive, and the debates they have spawned have done much to sharpen the focus of contemporary class analysis. Unlike many earlier treatments of Marxist class analysis within mainstream sociology, these recent interventions have generally shown an appreciation of the logic and explanatory power of the Marxist perspective, even when they have challenged aspects of that perspective.

Corresponding to the greater openness of mainstream sociology to class analysis there has also developed a more fruitful dialog between the proponents of broadly Marxist and broadly Weberian perspectives on class (Burris 1987). At the time that "Class Structure and Political Ideology" was written these theoretical camps remained much more polarized – sometimes artificially so – with Marxists arguing for the wholesale rejection of Weberian ideas about bureaucratic authority, market-based inequality, social closure, and status cultures, and Weberians likewise polemicizing against an overly simplistic, if not entirely fictional, caricature of Marxist class theory. Today, as a reading of the contributions to the above mentioned debates will reveal, there is much more cross-fertilization between these two theoretical traditions and a more honest appreciation of the relative strengths and weaknesses of each.

Another positive development in the treatment of class in contemporary sociology is the level of methodological sophistication that has been achieved in empirical research on class and its consequences. I have already mentioned the important role that Erik Wright and John Goldthorpe have played in this regard, but the list of contributors to this collective endeavor is now quite extensive. Despite the sometimes divergent theoretical viewpoints that are represented in this literature, the cumulative impact of a growing body of empirical research demonstrating the significance of class for a variety of social outcomes and behaviors makes it increasingly difficult to ignore or marginalize class analysis as a framework for sociological explanation.

There is a certain irony that, as class analysis has made increasing inroads into the sociological mainstream, it has declined in favor among many of those who have sought to position themselves to the left of the mainstream. The hegemony that concepts of race and gender enjoy within mainstream sociological theory and research on social inequality is, if anything, amplified among those committed to a critical or radical sociology. This reflects, among other things, the declining credibility of socialism conceived as a class-based historical project, the fragmentation of the left into single-issue movements, the sway that identity politics hold over the political imagination, and the postmodern turn toward subjectivist and relativist epistemologies. At the same time, one can point to ongoing trends – most notably the impact of globalization, economic polarization, and the increasingly naked exercise of corporate power – that make it impossible for left or critical sociology to ignore questions of control over the means and processes of social production and, hence, of the nature and consequences of class inequality.

The future of class analysis as an area of sociological theory and research is thus filled with both opportunity and challenge. Although we can be assured of continuing prophesies of the death of class, the fact is that the discipline of sociology is much more open to class analysis, including critical or Marxist approaches to class analysis, than it was only a few decades ago. The conceptual tools of class analysis have been refined both through theoretical debate and empirical investigation. At the same time, it would be folly to pretend that the conceptual and epistemological issues that lie at root of the debate over class have been resolved once and for all time. The contested nature of class analysis provides, in microcosm, a reflection of the contested nature of the sociological enterprise. And for those who share C. Wright Mills' vision of the task and the promise of sociology, the challenge of bridging the gap between the sometimes abstract and highly technical discussions of class within the sociological literature and the personal experience of class inequality within the larger society has never been greater.

Val Burris

# Class Structure and Political Ideology*

Marxist theorists have devoted much effort recently to the clarification of the concept of class and the elaboration of alternative models of class structure. The main focus of this theorizing has been the class position of salaried intermediaries and their role in the class struggle. With a few exceptions, most Marxists today recognize the existence in advanced capitalist society of a significant group of people who cannot be included in the working class, even though they work for a salary or wage. Various names have been applied, to this group – "new middle class," "new petty bourgeoisie," or "professional-managerial class" – and competing theories have been advanced to explain the nature and significance of these positions within the class structure. Disagreements over how to conceptualize intermediate class positions have prompted extensive debates over the basic principles of Marxist class analysis and the application of those principles to modern capitalist society.

Three issues have been central to this debate. First is the definitional question of specifying the boundaries of classes – especially the boundary which separates intermediate class positions from the working class. Second is the conceptual issue of clarifying the nature and identity of these intermediate class positions. Do they qualify as a "class" in the full sense of

* The original version of this article appeared in *The Insurgent Sociologist*, 14:2 (Summer, 1987), pp. 5–46.

the term? If so, do they constitute a new class within advanced capitalism or the evolution of some earlier intermediate class? Third is the political question of predicting the alignment of this group in the struggle between capital and labor. Will it side with the proletariat or the bourgeoisie, establish an independent third course, or fragment under the strain of competing pressures?

On the question of class boundaries, at least four different lines of demarcation have been proposed to distinguish intermediate from proletarian class positions. The first and most restrictive definition of the proletariat assigns a nonproletarian status to all salaried employees except manual workers in industry. The second identifies the boundary between proletarian and nonproletarian positions as a division between manual and nonmanual workers. The third excludes only professionals and managers from the proletariat. The fourth excludes only managers who directly supervise other workers.

On the question of the identity of these intermediate positions, three alternative theories can be distinguished. The first interprets these positions as a heterogeneous intermediate stratum which lacks the coherence or unity of a true class. The second and third perspectives attribute a common class identity to these positions – one viewing them as a new middle class and the other seeing them as an extension of an older intermediate class, the petty bourgeoisie.

Distinctive conceptions of political strategy are associated with different models of class structure. Theorists who classify the vast majority of wage workers as members of the proletariat tend to favor an parliamentary strategy of socialist transition based on the preponderant numerical strength of the working class. Those who adopt a narrower definition of the working class are more likely to affirm the necessity of an extraparliamentary strategy and/or to identify the prospects for socialism with the possibility of alliances between the proletariat and other classes. Different conceptions of the identity of intermediate classes yield different conclusions regarding the possibility of such alliances. Theorists who interpret these intermediate positions as part of a heterogeneous stratum usually characterize this group as incapable of independent political organization and therefore open to the competing political appeals if the proletariat and the bourgeoisie. Because they view this group as having no unifying class interests antagonistic to those of the proletariat, they perceive few barriers to the incorporation of large segments of this stratum into a popular alliance with the working class. Theorists who view these intermediate positions as belonging to a separate class are usually more skeptical about the possibility of class alliances. This is particularly true of those who identify these intermediate positions as a fraction of the traditional petty bourgeoisie – a class which is associated historically with fascism and other reactionary right-wing movements. Such theorists typically place a greater emphasis on the working class as the leading force in the transition to socialism, regarding all other classes as, at best, temporary or unstable allies in this struggle. The question of how to conceptualize intermediate class positions is therefore of more than theoretical interest; it poses issues which go to the very heart of socialist political strategy.

In this paper I examine the question of intermediate class positions from both a theoretical and an empirical direction. The first part of the paper presents a critical overview of alternative Marxist theories of class structure. Five specific theories are examined: Nicos Poulantzas' theory of the new petty bourgeoisie, Erik Olin Wright's theory of contradictory class locations, Wright's more recent theory of class structure and exploitation, Guglielmo Carchedi's theory of the new middle class, and Barbara and John Ehrenreich's theory of the professional-managerial class. In the conclusion of the paper I outline the model of class structure which, for both theoretical and empirical reasons, I believe best captures the existing pattern of class relations in American society.

## Poulantzas: The New Petty Bourgeoisie

Few theorists have exercised greater influence over the development of Marxist class analysis than Nicos Poulantzas. Indeed, much of the recent Marxist debate over the class location of salaried intermediaries has been directly inspired by Poulantzas' theory of the "new petty bourgeoisie" and the broader principles of class analysis upon which that theory is based.

Poulantzas' analysis of class rests on several basic premises. First, Poulantzas argues that *classes cannot be defined apart from class struggle.* By this Poulantzas emphasizes the relational nature of classes: classes refer neither to positions within a static classificatory scheme nor to groups of similar individuals composed through simple addition, but to the system of antagonistic relations which comprise the social division of labor. Second, *classes are structurally determined*; they exist objectively, independent of the will or consciousness of individuals. Class analysis is therefore concerned with the structure of "empty places" within the social division of labor, and only secondarily with the identity of the social agents who occupy such places. Third, in the determination of classes, *the principal role is played by the social relations of production.* By this, Poulantzas distinguishes the Marxist theory of class from those who define classes in terms of the social relations of distribution (income categories) or who derive classes from the technical organization of production (occupational categories). Finally, while the economic place of social agents has the principal role in defining classes, Poulantzas maintains that *political and ideological relations are also part of the structural determination of class.* In Poulantzas' model of class structure there are thus three criteria – economic, political and ideological – which define the boundary between proletarian and nonproletarian class positions.

In analyzing the economic determinants of class, Poulantzas rejects the criterion of wage-labor (nonownership of the means of production) as a sufficient condition of proletarian class position. The wage relation, Poulantzas argues, is a form of distribution of the social product rather than a social relation of production. Ownership or nonownership of the means of production acquire significance only insofar as they correspond to determinate relations of exploitation. In place of wage-labor, Poulantzas substitutes the criterion of productive labor (labor which produces surplus value) as the distinctive economic characteristic of the working class. Productive labor is defined narrowly by Poulantzas to include only that labor which directly produces surplus value through the production of *material* commodities, thereby excluding service workers as well as state and commercial workers from the working class. Wage-earners in these sectors are considered to be outside of the dominant capitalist relation of exploitation and are therefore classified as part of a separate class, the "new petty bourgeoisie."

The political and ideological determinants of class serve to exclude further positions from the proletariat. By political and ideological relations, Poulantzas refers to those social relations which secure the reproduction of the dominant mode of exploitation. At the political level this is accomplished through the relations of supervision and authority within the capitalist enterprise. According to Poulantzas, the work of management and supervision under capitalism entails not only the technical coordination of the labor process, but also the enforcement of capitalist domination over the working class. This 'places salaried managers and supervisors in an antagonistic relation to the working class, even when they are engaged in productive labor. At the ideological level Poulantzas identifies the basic class relation as the division between mental and manual labor. Poulantzas argues that this division also reproduces the subordination of the working class by excluding them from the "secret knowledge" of the production process and thereby reinforcing their dependence upon capital. Professionals, technicians and other mental workers are the bearers of this relation of ideological domination and are therefore classified as part of the new petty bourgeoisie along with managers and supervisors.

The new petty bourgeoisie is thus defined by Poulantzas as those salaried workers who are not exploited in the form of the dominant capitalist economic relation (unproductive workers) or who participate in the domination of the working class either politically (managers, supervisors) or ideologically (mental workers). Comparing these intermediate positions to those of the traditional petty bourgeoisie (small shopkeepers, artisans), Poulantzas concludes that the two groups are both part of a single heterogeneous class, the petty bourgeoisie. Even though they occupy different structural positions, the traditional and the new petty bourgeoisie are similarly located in relation to the dominant class antagonism between the proletariat and the bourgeoisie. This common situation within the class struggle results in a rough ideological unity, characterized by competitive individualism, reformism, and a belief in the neutrality of the state as an arbiter of competing class interests. Poulantzas maintains that this ideological affinity is sufficiently strong to justify placing both the traditional and the new petty bourgeoisie in the same class.

Numerous criticisms have been raised against Poulantzas' model of class structure (Wright, 1976; 1980; Hunt, 1977; Skotnes, 1979). Probably the most controversial aspect of Poulantzas' theory is his use of productive labor as a criterion of proletarian membership. Apart from the arbitrariness of Poulantzas' restriction of productive labor to those who produce surplus value in *material* goods production only, the productive/unproductive distinction is problematic as a boundary between classes since, by any definition, most concrete positions within the social division of labor combine a mix of productive and unproductive activities. More important, it is not clear why the distinction between productive and unproductive labor should correspond to any fundamental differences in worker interests or experience. It is true that *some* unproductive workers are exempt from exploitation. But *most* unproductive workers are exploited no less than productive workers; only the mechanism of their exploitation differs. The labor of productive workers is expropriated in the form of surplus value; that of unproductive workers is expropriated in the form of unpaid labor time which reduces the cost to the capitalist of appropriating part of the surplus value produced elsewhere (Marx, 1967: 300). For most routine commercial and clerical workers the concrete experience of exploitation is essentially identical to that of productive workers. In both cases workers are engaged in an antagonistic relation with capitalists over the rate of exploitation and control of the labor process. If, as Poulantzas argues, classes are defined by their position in the class struggle, it is difficult to see why unproductive labor should be a sufficient condition for exclusion from the proletariat.

Further objections can be raised against Poulantzas' interpretation of the political and ideological determinants of class position. While it makes sense to view the monopolization of productive knowledge as a form of class domination, thereby placing those who monopolize such knowledge in an antagonistic relation to the working class, it does not follow that *all* mental workers, including routine clerical and commercial employees, should be placed in this category. As Braverman (1974: 293–376) has documented, the labor processes in many offices and commercial enterprises are just as rationalized, as despotically controlled, and as mechanized as those of industry. The fact that routine mental workers participate in certain "rituals" and "cultural practices" which symbolize their ideological distance from manual workers does not demonstrate their domination over those workers, particularly when they themselves are no less separated from the knowledge necessary for the direction of the production process.

Finally, the fact that political and ideological criteria override the importance of economic criteria in Poulantzas' model draws into question his assertion of the primacy of economic relations over political and ideological relations. Salaried managers and technicians who share with workers the common economic practice of productive labor are excluded from the working class solely on the basis of political and ideological criteria. Conversely, the traditional and the new petty bourgeoisie, which occupy different economic positions, are classified as part of a single class on the basis of "common ideological effects." The unity which Poulantzas attributes to the traditional and the new petty bourgeoisie is especially problematic, since the economic positions occupied by these classes are not only divergent but objectively *antagonistic*. The concentration and centralization of capitalist enterprise, upon which the growth of the new petty bourgeoisie is based, poses a vital threat to the petty commodity forms of production from which the traditional petty bourgeoisie derives its livelihood. Given the opposed economic interests of these two groups, their fusion into a single class on the grounds of common ideological tendencies contradicts the fundamental Marxist premise of the primacy of economic relations in the determination of classes.

## Wright: Contradictory Class Locations

One of the most rigorously developed alternatives to Poulantzas' theory of the class structure is Erik Olin Wright's theory of contradictory class locations. Like Poulantzas, Wright (1980: 325) begins by setting out the basic theoretical premises of the Marxist conception of class. First, classes are defined in *relational* rather than *gradational* terms. Second, classes are determined by the *social* organization of economic relations rather than the *technical* organization of economic relations. Third, within the social organization of economic relations, classes are defined by the social relations of *production* rather than the social relations of *exchange*. In contrast to Poulantzas, Wright excludes political and ideological relations from the structural determination of class position, although he views these as important factors in determining the concrete alignment of class positions within the class struggle.

In Wright's model, class positions are defined by three economic criteria: control over investments and resource allocation, control over the physical means of production, and control over labor. The first of these designates the relations of "real economic ownership" (as opposed to mere legal ownership); the second and third comprise what Wright calls the economic relations of "possession." In terms of this model, the fundamental class division between capital and labor is viewed as a polarized, antagonistic relation in which the capitalist class occupies a dominant position (full control) and the working class a subordinate position (no control) on all three of these dimensions. These constitute the two basic classes of the capitalist mode of production. In addition, Wright recognizes a third class – the traditional petty bourgeoisie – which is distinguished by its location in a different mode of production: the petty commodity mode of production. Petty bourgeois positions involve both real economic ownership and control over the physical means of production, but not control over the labor of other workers, since none are employed. All remaining positions for which the three dimensions of class relations do not coincide perfectly are classified by Wright as "contradictory class locations," i.e., as social positions that are not firmly rooted in any single class, but occupy objectively contradictory locations "between" classes.

Wright identifies three groups of contradictory locations. *Managers and supervisors* occupy a contradictory location between the working class and the capitalist class. Like workers they are excluded from control over investments and resource allocation, but like capitalists they exercise a degree of control over the physical means of production and over the labor of others. *Semi-autonomous employees* occupy a contradictory location between the working class and the petty bourgeoisie. Like the working class they are excluded from both the control over investment capital and over the labor of others, but like the petty bourgeoisie they retain a degree of control over their immediate physical means of production within the labor process. *Small employers* occupy a contradictory location between the petty bourgeoisie and the capitalist class since they employ and control a minimal amount of labor power, but not sufficient to accumulate large masses of capital. Each of these groups combines characteristics of two classes and is therefore viewed as being objectively torn between two opposing class locations.

As a general strategy for conceptualizing the class position of salaried intermediaries, Wright's notion of "contradictory class locations" is appealing. It captures the ambiguity of these class locations as well as the complexity of their relationship to other classes. The particular criteria by which Wright defines these contradictory locations, however, are open to criticism. Although presented in Marxist terms, Wright's model, draws upon a Weberian conception of occupational stratification as much as a Marxist conception of class relations. This can be seen by comparing Wright's model with his own statement of the basic premises of Marxist class analysis. Wright maintains that classes must be analyzed in terms of the *social* relations of production rather than the *technical* organization of production; however, his own criteria of class position are specified essentially in terms of the technical characteristics of occupational positions: which activities and decisions they participate in, how much autonomy they exercise, etc. Wright also maintains that, in order to grasp the class contradictions which motivate social change, classes must be defined in *relational* rather than *gradational* terms; yet, he immediately proceeds to define classes in terms of forms of control that are inherently gradational. Control over investments, control over the physical means of production and control over the labor process are inherently matters of degree, as Wright (1980: 332) himself recognizes by specifying four general levels of control for each of these dimensions: "full control," "partial control," "minimal control," and "no control." The result is that, logically, Wright's criteria imply an indeterminate number of contradictory class locations, stratified along three separate dimensions, with no meaningful line of demarcation between them and the "noncontradictory" positions of the basic classes. In his pursuit of a rigorous system of classification, Wright defines classes virtually out of existence, since, by his own estimates, as much as 56 per cent of the U.S. labor force does not belong to any particular class, but is located somewhere outside of or between the three basic classes (Wright, 1976: 37).

These problems are most pronounced in Wright's treatment of salaried intermediate positions – especially the contradictory class location which he refers to as "semi-autonomous employees." First, there is the question of why these positions should be located between the proletariat and the petty bourgeoisie while managers and supervisors are located between the proletariat and the capitalist class. In terms of his three criteria of class position, semi-autonomous employees could just as well be viewed as combining characteristics of the proletariat and the bourgeoisie. Wright suggests that semi-autonomous employees represent an historical residuum of formerly petty-bourgeois positions which, although they now work for a salary, have not yet been fully proletarianized under capitalist relations of production. Yet, this is hardly an accurate description of the majority of salaried professional and technical positions which only came into existence with the growth of capitalism, and is probably more true of many salaried managers (e.g., managers in retail trade, farm managers, etc.) which Wright locates between the proletariat and the bourgeoisie even though they did indeed originate out of the expansion of capitalism into previously petty-bourgeois domains.

Second, since Wright defines autonomy as a technical relationship between workers and their physical means of production, his model fails to specify any social relationship between those who possess a certain level of autonomy and those who do not. The boundary between the working class and semi-autonomous employees is therefore merely a point on a scale, not a division between two groups of class positions which are defined by their antagonistic relation to one another. In this regard, Poulantzas' concept of the monopolization of strategic knowledge would seem to provide a sounder basis for identifying the class interests of nonsupervisory mental workers, even if Poulantzas himself applies this concept much too widely.

Finally, of Wright's three dimensions of control, the criterion of autonomy is most obviously a gradational characteristic. Virtually all workers retain at least some control over their immediate instruments of production. At what point does their level of control become sufficient to exclude them from the working class? Certainly the industrial workers of Marx's day exercised, by contemporary standards, a considerable degree of control over the labor process. Does this mean that they were not proletarians? The problem here is not just one of a degree of indeterminacy in the application of the autonomy criterion, since any definition of class boundaries will confront ambiguous or borderline cases, but the fact that the criterion in question implies *no* logical basis for drawing the boundary at one point rather than another. To operationalize the autonomy criterion, Wright (1978: 82) proposes that sufficient autonomy exists to warrant exclusion from the working class whenever an employee exercises some control over *what* is produced, and not merely over *how* it is produced, but this dividing line is never defended theoretically, nor is there any explanation offered as to why distinctive class interests should be associated with the first form of autonomy and not the latter.

## Wright: Class Structure and Exploitation

In his more recent writings, Wright (1985) himself has raised a number of objections to his original theory of contradictory class locations and suggested an alternative approach to the analysis of salaried intermediate classes. The basic problems with his earlier theory, Wright now argues, derive from its misguided attempt to incorporate relations of domination and subordination into the Marxist definition of class – an error which it shares with other contemporary Marxist theories of class structure. From a Marxist standpoint, Wright argues, the introduction of class criteria like the exercise of supervisory authority or autonomy from such authority creates two kinds of problems. First, such relations do not, in and of themselves, imply any necessary asymmetry of class interests. This is a problem I have already noted in my critique of Wright's criterion of autonomy. In Wright's view, however, it is a deficiency common to all criteria of class position which are framed in terms of relations of domination and subordination. Second, Wright argues that incorporating relations of domination and subordination into the definition of class obscures the distinctiveness of class oppression by placing it on the same plane as numerous other forms of domination – sexual, racial, national, etc. This renders problematic the basic Marxist claim of the explanatory primacy of class relations in social and historical analysis.

In order to overcome these problems, Wright now argues that class must be conceptualized exclusively as a relationship of *exploitation*, rather than a complex unity of exploitation and domination relations. Building upon the work of John Roemer (1982), Wright maintains that exploitation (the transfer of labor from one class or individual to another) is essentially a product of the unequal distribution of property rights in the means of production. Relations of domination and subordination at the point of production may enhance or reinforce such exploitation, but they are basically incidental to its operation. In any society it is possible to distinguish multiple forms of exploitation. The dominant form of exploitation in capitalist society is that based on the private ownership of the material means of production, but there are also subsidiary forms of exploitation which derive from the unequal distribution of other productive assets. One such asset is skills – especially those whose supply is artificially restricted through credentials. A second is what Wright calls "organization assets," by which he means control over the conditions for the coordination of labor. Within this framework, salaried intermediaries are distinguished from the working class by their ownership of one or the other (or both) of these subsidiary assets. Such differentials in skill and organization assets, Wright argues, enable them to exploit the labor of other workers, even as they themselves are exploited by capitalists.

This new theory of class structure has important continuities with Wright's earlier theory of contradictory class locations. The class location of salaried intermediaries can still be viewed as "contradictory" in the sense that they occupy both dominant and subordinate positions on different dimensions of class structure. What is new is Wright's claim that these dimensions should be conceptualized as relations of exploitation based on differential *ownership* of productive assets, rather than as differential *control* over various elements of the production process. Descriptively the new theory also yields roughly equivalent class groupings. On the boundaries of the working class stand two kinds of contradictory class locations. The first are salaried managers, which Wright now distinguishes by their ownership of organization assets rather than by their control over the physical means of production and the labor of others. Second are various nonsupervisory intermediaries (mainly salaried professionals and technicians), which Wright once distinguished by their autonomy, but now argues are distinguished by their ownership of skill assets.

Wright argues that this new formulation has advantages over his earlier theory of contradictory class locations. First, it dispenses with the problematic notion of autonomy as a criterion of class position. Second, Wright argues, by reconceptualizing the different dimensions of class structure as relations of exploitation, the new model enables him to specify the class interests of intermediate classes more clearly. Their interests both within capitalism and with respect to various noncapitalist alternatives can now be analyzed in terms of "their material optimizing strategies given the specific kinds of assets they own/control" (Wright, 1985: 91). The prospects for class alliances between salaried intermediaries and either capitalists or workers can thus be derived in a more straightforward fashion from the nature of their class location. Finally, Wright argues that the new theory has a stronger historical thrust in that, by recombining the component dimensions of exploitation in different ways, it is possible to conceptualize a variety alternative class structures which may be viewed as potential successors to capitalism. "Bureaucratic statism," for example, is understood by Wright as a class society in which the ownership of organization assets becomes the dominant form of exploitation, while "socialism" is understood as a society in which both private property and organization assets have been democratized and skill differentials remain the only basis of exploitation.

These are certainly worthwhile aims of any Marxist theory of class structure. Wright is also correct, I believe, that the incorporation of relations of domination and subordination into the Marxist definition of class tends to undermine the distinctiveness of the concept. In the abstract, the development of a more elaborate model of exploitation relations would seem to be a promising strategy for clarifying the class position of salaried intermediaries. I would question, however, whether the particular model proposed by Wright is indeed an advance over his earlier theory. On the contrary, I would argue that Wrights attempt to reassert the primacy of exploitation relations is accomplished mainly by definitional fiat and by the incorporation of concepts that are themselves at variance both with Marxism and with what we know empirically about the functioning of the class system.

Consider Wright's concept of "organization assets" as a basis of exploitation. Wright argues that the coordination of the technical division of labor is itself a source of productivity. This is plausible. He further argues that "organization" can therefore be viewed as a productive asset which is controlled by managers and bureaucrats and which enables them to exploit the labor of those who are without such assets. This claim is much more dubious. In what sense can organization be treated as an "asset" akin to property or skills?

Wright admits that the asset of organization cannot be owned in the same way as property or skills; it has no existence apart from the positions within which it is exercised and cannot be transferred by its owner from one use to another. The "ownership" of organization assets is therefore indistinguishable from the exercise of hierarchical authority. Operationally, the two concepts identify identical class groupings. What then is gained by redefining the exercise of hierarchical authority as the ownership or control of organization assets?

The crucial difference, it seems to me, is that the first view treats managerial authority as a power relation which is ultimately *subordinate* to capitalist property relations, while the latter defines it as a *separate* kind of property relation. From the standpoint of class interests, the first view interprets the privileges of managers as a dividend which they reap because of their strategic importance to the process of capitalist exploitation, while the latter treats them as the fruits of a different form of exploitation which is independent of (and potentially *antagonistic* to) capitalist exploitation. The latter perspective, in my opinion, is problematic for at least two reasons. First, it posits a degree of conflict between capitalists and managers that is nowhere evident. Second, it assumes that the economic returns to managerial status exist only because of the contribution of managers to productivity – an assumption which becomes more tenuous the higher one goes in the managerial hierarchy and the farther one gets from direct involvement in the production process.

Wright's concept of "skill-based exploitation" poses similar problems. As with exploitation based on organization assets, Wright assumes that the rewards accruing to credentialed employees reflect the greater contribution of more skilled employees to the total social product. This is similar to the argument of human capital theory, and there is undoubtedly a partial truth to this proposition. But Wright's wholesale acceptance of such a viewpoint ignores a wealth of empirical evidence demonstrating the tenuousness of the relationship between credentials and productivity or between productivity and market rewards (Bowles and Gintis, 1976; Collins, 1979).

Apart from this problem, even if one assumes that credentials by and large serve as a means of restricting and certifying truly productive skills, the concept of skill differentials is still a questionable criterion by which to define classes. Like the notion of autonomy which it replaces in Wrights conceptual scheme, skill differentials are inherently gradational and, in and of themselves, imply no necessary boundaries between classes. If a salaried professional occupies a different class position than a craft worker for reasons of skill, then shouldn't a craft worker occupy a different class position than a factory operative? Here once again Wright's model begins to look more like a theory of occupational stratification than a Marxist theory of class relations.

Finally, Wright's claim that credential exploitation is *independent* of capitalist exploitation is open to question. Credentials (or the lack thereof) are certainly important as a mechanism mediating between class positions as "empty places" within the social division of labor and social classes as concrete collectivities with a degree of intergenerational continuity. By restricting labor market competition they may also limit the exploitation of certain occupations. But credentials are basically valueless unless they provide entry into occupational positions that entail strategic responsibilities, are not easily rationalized, and therefore command special compensation. The structure of such positions may be influenced by the distribution of skills within the labor market, but it is also and more fundamentally conditioned by the powers and interests invested in the private ownership of the means of production. The dependent status of skill-based privilege is demonstrated nowhere more clearly than when the interests of capital dictate the deskilling of once privileged occupations as a means of increasing the rate of exploitation. Like supervisory authority, credentials are better understood from the standpoint of their articulation with capitalist relations of production, than as an independent basis of privilege.

## Carchedi: The New Middle Class

A simplified conception of the theory of contradictory class locations that avoids some of the difficulties of Wright's analysis is presented by Guglielmo Carchedi. Carchedi (1977) defines class positions in terms of three types of dichotomous social relations. (1) *Ownership relations* distinguish those who own the means of production from nonowners. Like Wright, Carchedi refers here to real economic ownership, which he defines as "the power to dispose of the means of production," rather than strictly legal ownership. (2) *Expropriation relations* distinguish those who expropriate surplus labor from those who are expropriated of surplus labor. Contrary to Poulantzas, Carchedi does not differentiate between labor which is expropriated in the form of surplus value (productive labor) and labor which is expropriated directly as unpaid labor time (unproductive labor); for the purpose of defining classes the two are treated as equivalent forms of exploitation. (3) *Functional relations* distinguish those who perform the "global function of capital" from those who perform the "function of the collective worker." Carchedi defines the function of the collective worker as the production of use-values (either material or nonmaterial) within a complex and differentiated labor process. The global function of capital is defined as "the control and surveillance of the labor process" – a function which is essential to the expropriation of surplus labor and which he distinguishes from the technically necessary work of coordination and unity of the production process (which is part of the function of the collective worker).

Carchedi views these three aspects as bound together in a relation in which the ownership element is dominant over the expropriation and functional elements. In the pure case, there is a correspondence between ownership, expropriation and functional relations. This correspondence determines the two basic classes of the capitalist mode of production: the bourgeoisie, which owns the means of production, expropriates surplus labor and performs the global function of capital; and the proletariat, which does not own the means of production, is expropriated of surplus labor and performs the function of the collective worker. The correspondence between these three aspects is not perfect, however. There are historical reasons, in particular, why a degree of noncorrespondence has developed between the ownership and functional elements. In the course of the capitalist development the function of the individual capitalist (control and surveillance of the labor process) has been taken over by a differentiated managerial apparatus (the "global capitalist"), while the function of the individual worker (the production of use-values) has been broken down and reorganized into a complex division of labor (the "collective worker"). This creates the possibility of a noncorrespondence between ownership and functional relations in the form of agents who, while not owning the means of production, nevertheless perform the global function of capital, or who perform in a varying balance both the global function of capital and the function of the collective worker. These contradictory positions – essentially salaried managers and supervisors – are classified by Carchedi as belonging to the "new middle class."

Carchedi's conception of contradictory class locations has certain advantages over Wright's initial model. First, his criteria of class position are more explicitly relational. For example, whereas Wright conceptualizes the supervisory hierarchy as a continuum of degrees of control over the means of production,

Carchedi emphasizes the antagonistic *relation* between those whose function is to ensure the appropriation of surplus labor and those whose labor is appropriated. Second, the fact that Carchedi defines contradictory class locations exclusively in terms of a noncorrespondence between ownership of capital and surveillance of labor (and not between ownership of capital and control of the physical means of production) means that he avoids the problems associated with Wright's conception of autonomy. Compared with Wright's revised theory of class structure, Carchedi avoids the dubious separation between capitalist exploitation and managerial (organization asset) exploitation by treating the latter as a function subsumed under the dominance of the former. Similarly, the exercise of skill is treated by Carchedi as a function of the (internally differentiated) collective worker, rather than as an independent asset which confers a nonproletarian status on those who exercise it, thereby avoiding the problems I have noted with Wright's concept of skill exploitation.

Carchedi is able to avoid the conceptual difficulties of Wright's model, however, only at the cost of considerable oversimplication. The main problem with Carchedi's model is that his notion of the global function of capital is too narrow. Noticeably absent from Carchedi's conception of class relations are any forms of capitalist domination that go beyond the direct control and surveillance of the labor process. Certainly there are other forms of domination (e.g., those described by Poulantzas as the monopolization of strategic knowledge of the production process) that are also integral to the expropriation of surplus labor and should therefore be included in the global function of capital. Restricting his attention to the labor process and to those who perform the delegated capitalist function of control over the expropriation of surplus labor, Carchedi also ignores those who perform delegated capitalist functions of control over the accounting and realization of surplus value (corporate lawyers, accountants, market analysts, etc.). As Wright (1980: 363) has noted, this narrow definition of the global function of capital produces some curious results. According to Carchedi's criteria, for example, foremen and other low-level supervisors would be placed within the new middle class, while many top corporate professionals, planners and technocrats would be classified as proletarians since they do not directly supervise the labor of others. The class position of nonsupervisory professional and technical workers is therefore something of an anomaly in Carchedi's conception of class structure.

## Ehrenreichs: The Professional-Managerial Class

The final conception of class structure to be considered is Barbara and John Ehrenreichs' theory of the professional-managerial class. For the Ehrenreichs (1977: 12), classes are defined by two general characteristics: (1) by a "common relation of the economic foundations of society – the means of production and the socially organized patterns of distribution and consumption;" and (2) by a "coherent social and cultural existence," including such things as a shared life-style, educational background, kinship networks, consumption patterns, work habits and ideology. The Ehrenreichs argue that in the course of capitalist development a distinctive new class has emerged, which they call the "professional-managerial class" (PMC for short). The PMC is defined as "consisting of salaried mental workers who do not own the means of production and whose major function in the social division of labor may be described broadly as the reproduction of capitalist culture and class relations" (Ehrenreichs, 1977: 13). This includes both those who carry out this reproduction function in their roles as agents of social control or as producers and propagators of ideology (teachers, social workers, psychologists, entertainers, advertising copy writers, etc.) and those who do so through their performance of administrative and technical roles which perpetuate capitalist relations of production (managers, engineers, college-trained technicians, etc.). Despite the wide range of occupations included within this category and the somewhat fuzzy boundaries separating it from the ruling class above and the working class below, the Ehrenreichs maintain that the PMC nevertheless constitutes a single, coherent class. Its members share not only a common economic function, but also a common cultural existence, characterized by distinctive patterns of family life (emphasizing individual achievement), their own forms of self-organization (professional associations), their own specific ideology (technocratic liberalism), and their own institutions of class reproduction and socialization (colleges and universities).

Historically, the Ehrenreichs argue, the PMC emerged with the rise of monopoly capitalism as part of a broader transformation of capitalist class relations. The formation of the PMC depended upon the coexistence of two conditions which were only met during the early part of the twentieth century: (1) the expansion of the social surplus to a point sufficient to sustain a new unproductive class; and (2) the development of the class struggle to the point that a class specializing in the reproduction of capitalist class relations became a necessity to the bourgeoisie. The expansion of professional and managerial positions satisfied this need by extending capitalist control over the actual production process, creating mass institutions of social control, and reorganizing working-class life within a framework of mass consumer culture. Forged out of the heat of class struggle between the proletariat and the bourgeoisie, the PMC is enmeshed in a complex web of partly complementary, partly antagonistic class relations. As an agent of bourgeois cultural and technological hegemony, the PMC exists "only by virtue of the expropriation of skills and culture once indigenous to the working class" (Ehrenreichs, 1977: 17). It is therefore in an objectively antagonistic relation to the working class. However, as salaried employees, members of the PMC share with other workers a common antagonism to the bourgeoisie, which they confront as a limit to their professional autonomy and an obstacle to their vision of a technocratic society. The PMC is therefore also a reservoir of anti-capitalist sentiment, albeit of an elitist and reformist variety.

What is most attractive about the Ehrenreich's analysis is their attempt to weave together threads of historical, economic, and cultural analysis in a coherent account of the contradictions of middle class life and politics. Their concept of the PMC is historically grounded in the process of class struggle. Although based on relations of production, it is not limited to a description of occupational roles but extends to broader aspects of class experience. This multidimensional aspect of their analysis is its greatest strength, but it is also the source of several problems. These derive, most basically, from the eclecticism of their model of class structure and the theoretical limitations of their concept of "reproduction."

Like Mills before them, the Ehrenreichs draw freely upon both Marxist and Weberian traditions in their analysis of the salaried middle class. From Marx they take the notion of the PMC as an economic class, defined by a "common relation to the economic foundations of society." From Weber they take the notion of the PMC as a social class or status group, defined by a "coherent social and cultural existence." Their initial definition of class assumes a correspondence between these two dimensions of class structure, yet this point is never adequately demonstrated in their analysis of the PMC.

The Ehrenreichs are most persuasive in arguing that there exists a coherent *social* class, as measured by common educational background, lifestyle, consumption patterns, mobility closure, and intermarriage, that is roughly coterminous with professional and managerial occupations. They are much less persuasive in arguing that the members of this occupational group can also be viewed as an *economic* class in the Marxist sense or that they share a common class interest based on their relation to the means of production. The criterion given by the Ehrenreichs for assigning managers and professionals to a common economic class is that such positions are all implicated in the "reproduction of capitalist culture and class relations." This functional definition has serious shortcomings. As other critics have pointed out, there is no strict correspondence between the function of reproduction and positions within the social division of labor (Noble, 1979; Wright, 1980). The function of reproduction is not a separate task restricted to specific social positions; it is an *effect* of the production process in general. As Marx demonstrates in *Capital*, workers themselves function to reproduce capitalist class relations simply by their participation in the capitalist production process.

A further problem with the concept of reproduction is that it lends itself to a functionalist conception of social order and a teleological view of social change. Separating reproduction from production and treating it as a specialized function of a specific social agency exaggerates the self-perpetuating capacity of the system. By positing a functional effect, reproduction, as the cause of PMC expansion, the Ehrenreichs present an overly rational, almost conspiratorial, interpretation of the rise of the PMC.

This is not to say that functional criteria have no place in class analysis. Carchedi's "global function of capital," defined as the control and surveillance of the labor process, is sufficiently specific and sufficiently identified with particular locations to be a meaningful criterion of class position. The Ehrenreich's function of "reproduction," however, is too vague to serve as anything more than a terminological gloss for intuitively assigning the "PMC" label to whatever groups appear to have some modest privilege or stake in the established order.

Particularly questionable is the equation the Ehrenreichs make between the function of managers and that of nonsupervisory professional and service workers. Whatever their cultural similarities, these two groups have very different relations to both the capitalist and the working classes. The first is directly hired by capitalists, granted delegated authority over the labor process, and rewarded for their role in the appropriation of surplus. The second is frequently employed outside of capitalist organizations, derives what authority it exercises from the state or its claim to professional expertise, and has a much more indirect relationship to the appropriation of surplus. Wright attempts to grasp this distinction in terms of his dual criteria of supervision and autonomy (and later in terms of organization assets and skill assets), while Carchedi argues that only the first of these groups qualifies as middle class, while the latter belongs to the more skilled sector of the working class. The Ehrenreichs themselves acknowledge the importance of this distinction when they note that, historically, the deepest rift within the PMC has been "between the managers, administrators and engineers on the one hand, and those in the liberal arts and service professions on the other" (Ehrenreichs, 1977: 27). It is doubtful, however, whether the significance of this rift can be clarified without going beyond the Ehrenreich's simple functional definition of intermediate class positions.

## Conclusion

I would like to summarize by presenting some tentative conclusions about the class structure of American society. This will be done by addressing, in turn, each of the basic divisions which has been proposed as a boundary between the proletariat and intermediate class positions.

First, I would argue that there is no justification, empirical or theoretical, for viewing the distinction between productive and unproductive labor as a criterion of class position. It is true that *most* salaried intermediate positions are *largely* unproductive. The expansion of unproductive labor is therefore an important factor in explaining the historical growth of intermediate class positions (Nicolaus, 1970; Przeworski, 1977; Burris, 1980). The majority of unproductive workers, however, occupy class positions that are identical to those of productive workers in the sense that they neither exercise domination over other workers nor avoid the expropriation of their surplus labor.

For similar reasons, I would reject the distinction between manual and nonmanual labor as a boundary between proletarian and nonproletarian class positions. There may have been a time, early in the twentieth century, when the manual/nonmanual division did approximate a boundary between classes. The expansion and rationalization of clerical and sales occupations, however, has long since altered the class position of routine white-collar employees. At the present time, the manual/nonmanual division is better understood as an fractional division within the working class than as a boundary between classes.

The division between supervisory and nonsupervisory positions is more appropriate as a criterion of class position. All four of the theorists surveyed agree that salaried managers and supervisors should be excluded from the working class. The clearest justification for this exclusion is provided by Carchedi who conceptualizes management as a delegated capitalist function of enforcing the expropriation of surplus labor through the control and surveillance of the labor process. Roughly similar criteria are given by Poulantzas and Wright in his original theory of contradictory class locations. Except at certain subordinate levels where supervision entails no more than technical coordination and/or the routine transmission of higher directives, managers and supervisors occupy positions which are objectively antagonistic to those of the working class, even while they themselves are subordinate to capital. Empirically, this class antagonism is confirmed by the consistency with which managers and supervisors occupy opposing positions to other salaried employees on a wide range of political issues.

Whether *nonsupervisory* professional and technical positions should also be excluded from the working class is a more difficult question. The various theorists surveyed propose a number of criteria by which such positions might be differentiated from the working class. Poulantzas argues that they reinforce the subordination of other workers through their monopoly of strategic knowledge. Wright argues that are autonomous from direct capitalist domination and/or exploit other workers through their disproportionate ownership of skill assets. The Ehrenreichs argue that they reproduce the subordination of workers in their roles as agents of social control and purveyors of bourgeois ideology. Each of these criteria has been criticized as inadequate to define the boundary between proletarian and nonproletarian class positions. Nevertheless, I believe that each of them captures a partial truth about the nature of intermediate class locations. Hence, it may be possible to incorporate the insights of several of these theories within a revised model of the class structure.

In analyzing the class position of salaried professional and technical workers, the crucial question we must ask is: what is the place of these positions within capitalist relations of exploitation. On this point, I believe that Wright (1985: 36–37) is correct when he argues that exploitation is fundamental to the Marxist concept of class and that domination *alone* does not define distinctive class positions. Contrary to Wright, however, and more in line with the arguments of Poulantzas, Carchedi, and the Ehrenreichs, I believe that exploitation cannot be specified independently of the relations of domination through which it is maintained and reproduced. Relations of domination that are integral to the process of exploitation must therefore be included in the definition of classes. Rather than exclude relations of domination from the definition of class, we must give closer attention to the functional relation between specific forms of domination and the process of exploitation.

Most disagreements over the class position of salaried professionals and technicians boil down to a debate over whether and how such positions are integral to the process of capitalist exploitation. To sort out the issues in this debate, I would propose that we distinguish two different ways in which salaried positions might be differentiated from the working class: (1) because they are exempt from exploitation by capitalists, and (2) because they participate in and share the fruits of capitalist exploitation of workers. Although he does not express it in quite this fashion, I believe that this is the rational kernel to Wright's notion that (salaried) contradictory class locations can be grouped into two relatively distinct clusters: one which is *tangential* to the capitalist-worker relation and one which is *intermediate* between these two classes. This distinction also provides a framework for theorizing the rift which the Ehrenreichs acknowledge, but fail to explain, between "managers, administrators and engineers on the one hand, and those in the liberal arts and service professions on the other" (Ehrenreichs, 1977: 27).

Managers and supervisors are typically differentiated from the working class in the latter, more antagonistic, sense. Managers exercise delegated functions of capitalist authority over the means of production and the labor process. Because of their strategic importance to the process of exploitation, and because their functions are not easily monitored in a direct and detailed fashion, managers can demand and typically receive a share of the fruits of exploitation to ensure their loyalty to the interests of capital. This pattern is confirmed by the strong association between the managerial/nonmanagerial dichotomy and the pattern of income differences among wage and salary workers. The domination managers exercise over workers is thus tied to the process of exploitation in two ways: it is delegated for the purpose of enforcing the extraction of surplus and it is typically compensated with a share of that surplus.

Poulantzas and the Ehrenreichs try to apply the same kind of argument to nonsupervisory professional and technical workers, but their concepts of the "monopolization of strategic knowledge" and the "reproduction of capitalist class relations" are stretched far beyond the range of occupations that can reasonably be viewed as integral to capitalist exploitation. Without question, *some* categories of nonsupervisory professionals occupy strategic roles with respect to the accumulation of capital (corporate lawyers, financial managers, some types of engineers). These positions ought to be viewed as functionally analogous to managers and supervisors. More commonly, however, nonsupervisory professional and technical employees are differentiated from the working class (if at all) only in the weaker sense of being relatively exempt from exploitation by capital.

This exemption is typically due to a combination of factors. Generally speaking, capitalist relations of exploitation, while rooted in the capitalist's ownership of the means of production, depend in their operation on a combination of market and domination relations. Workers must be subjected to competition from a reserve army of labor in order to drive down the value of their labor power, and jobs must be rationalized and/or subjected to surveillance in order to ensure that the labor expended exceeds the value of the wage. Salaried professionals and technicians are typically insulated from one or both of these aspects of proletarianization, thereby limiting their exploitation by capital. As Wright points out, such positions are typically characterized by the exercise of skill and/or autonomy; however, it is not skill or autonomy *per se* that distinguishes them from the working class – only those forms of skill and autonomy which function as a barrier to exploitation.

Of course, this distinction between salaried intermediaries who are integral to capitalist exploitation and those who are merely exempt from capitalist exploitation does not yield a sharp boundary between two mutually exclusive groups. As with any criterion of class position, there will be ambiguous and borderline cases. But this in itself does not invalidate the logic of the distinction. The greater problem lies in the fact that intermediate positions that are distinct from the standpoint of their place within capitalist relations of exploitation tend to be much more integrated at the level of social and market relations. From the perspective of the individual social agent, the main avenue of entry into to either type of intermediate class position is the possession of educational credentials. Differential access to educational credentials limits competition for privileged occupations, secures the intergenerational reproduction of nonproletarian status, and contributes to the internalization of a common culture. Herein lies the rational kernel to the Ehrenreich's notion that nonsupervisory professionals and technicians should be classified *together* with managers as members of a single social class. As we have seen, this model corresponds most closely to the commonsense understanding of "middle class" in our society as measured by subjective class identification. Other research has shown that, in terms of intergenerational mobility, friendship networks, and residential patterns, the most significant class cleavage among salaried employees is also one which places managers and professionals together on one side and all other categories of wage and salary workers on the other (Vanneman, 1977).

Nonsupervisory professional and technical positions can thus be viewed as the most contradictory of "contradictory class locations." In terms of ownership relations they resemble the working class. Nevertheless, they typically retain a degree of control over their own labor and their immediate conditions of production. This fact, together with their relative insulation from labor market competition, serves as a barrier to their exploitation by capital. From the standpoint of social and market relations, they share much in common with salaried managers. From the standpoint of their function within the social division of labor, however, nonsupervisory professionals and technicians differ from managers in that they are generally less implicated in the exploitation of workers by capital. At this level their class positions are less sharply differentiated from other wage and salary workers and their class interests are more tangential than antagonistic to those of the working class.

Viewed in this light, the shifting political alignments of nonsupervisory professional and technical employees are less confusing than they might appear. Given their dependence on credentials and other individualistic forms of market closure, salaried professionals are understandably unsympathetic toward competing (collective) closure strategies like unionization. Their social and educational background leads them to view themselves subjectively as "middle class." But, compared with managers and supervisors, their alignment on most political and economic issues is much less opposed to that of the working class. On such questions as political party preference, confidence in corporations, support for income redistribution, and support for state welfare spending, they tend to be aligned more closely to rank-and-file workers than they are to managers and supervisors.

The model of class structure advanced in this paper can thus be summarized as follows. Most wage and salary earners belong to the working class. This includes manual workers (both productive and unproductive) and routine nonmanual workers. Salaried managers and most nonsupervisory professionals, however, should be excluded from the working class. At a minimum, such positions are relatively exempt from exploitation by capital. In some cases (most clearly in the case of managers) they participate in and share the fruits of capitalist exploitation of workers. Whether these nonproletarian positions should be classified as a discrete intermediate class, or a more heterogeneous intermediate stratum, depends on which aspect of class relations one chooses to emphasize. From the standpoint of social characteristics and market relations, such positions are sufficiently similar to warrant their treatment as a single *social* class. But, from the standpoint of their location within capitalist relations of exploitation – the standpoint emphasized in Marxist theory – such positions vary considerably in the manner and extent to which they are implicated in the process of exploitation. As a consequence, the cohesion and political alignment of these intermediate class locations tends to vary according to the issue in question.

For those who desire an unambiguous model of class structure, with neatly defined categories and clear implications for political strategy, these conclusions will come as a disappointment. Although the basic outlines of the class structure are conceptually clear, we are left with somewhat imprecise boundaries between proletarian and nonproletarian class positions and between different types of nonproletarian positions. Capitalist relations of exploitation provide the ultimate litmus test for assigning class position; however, the recognition that exploitation is articulated with diverse relations of domination (both within the market and at the point of production) makes the unraveling of exploitation relations an extremely complex task. Any attempt to reduce this complex structure to a small number of readily operationalizable criteria of class position will always be open to criticism. Further theoretical work on this topic may help to resolve some of these issues. Judging from the inconclusiveness of recent debates, however, I suspect that the ambiguity of intermediate class locations is but a reflection of the real complexity of the contemporary class structure and that further advance in this area will depend as much on careful empirical study as on pathbreaking new theorizations.

Martha E. Gimenez

# Reflections on "The Feminization of Poverty: Myth or Reality?"

The concept, feminization of poverty, not only indicates that the greater proportion of the poverty population is female but also connotes the idea of continuous growth and novelty as if the feminization of poverty were an unprecedented process bound to intensify in the future. This concept also implies that in an unspecified earlier time, the gender composition of the poverty population had been different, with an equal or greater proportion of men. The feminization of poverty, then, is a concept that purports to identify a new trend of a greater proportion of the poverty population being women.

The data, on the other hand, indicate that the sex composition of the poverty population has not changed a great deal since the earliest available data was gathered by the U. S. Bureau of the Census. The female proportion of all ages of the population below the poverty level has remained relatively constant since 1966, when it was 57.1 percent, fluctuating between 57 and 58 percent in the 1970s and early 1980s, but remaining mainly a little over 57 percent since 1982. In 1987, the year this article was first published, it had declined to 56.1 percent. Its highest peak (59.1 percent) was reached in 1978; 20 years later it was 57.3 (U.S. Bureau of the Census, Historical Poverty Tables – Table 7, www.census.gov/hhes/poverty/histpov7.html). It was 56.5 percent in 2001 (http://ferret.bls.census.gov/macro/032002/pov/new01_001.htm) and there is no reason to believe that more recent data will show a drastic change.

Given this relative stability in the female proportion of the poverty population, why was it possible to speak of the feminization of poverty as a novel and intensifying process? Why is this concept uncritically accepted and still used today? The perception of increasing female poverty was the product of several factors.

Ideologically, the aftermath of the women's movement sensitized researchers to the economic inequality between men and women. Women's earnings relative to men's, women's place in the occupational structure, women's educational and occupational opportunities, the economic effects of divorce, and women's poverty became and continue to be important areas of research and policy concerns. Research demonstrating that a large proportion of women experienced downward social mobility and even poverty after divorce led to the observation that even "middle-class" women were "a man away from poverty." But there were also important economic factors shaping the perception that women were becoming poorer. Changes in the economy, including de-industrialization, altered the opportunity structures for male and female workers so that poverty and near poverty increased for male and female adult workers (aged 18–44), while it decreased for older workers (aged 45–64) and those 65 and older. In addition, coupled with the better economic opportunities enjoyed by older Americans after WWII, the Social Security tie to the consumer price index helped to lower the proportion of the poor aged 65 and over. This change in the age structure of the poverty population made more visible the poverty of single adult women, with and without children. This increased visibility combined with the widespread dissemination of research documenting the relationship between divorce and women's economic well being to strengthen the perception that women were becoming increasingly poorer and that poverty was being feminized. A recent study (NcLanahan and Kelly, http://www.olin.wustl.edu/,acarthur/working%20 papers/wp-Mclanahan3.htm) examining trends in men's and women's absolute and relative poverty between 1950 and 1996 concludes that even as the poverty rate declined, the gap between men's and women's poverty varied among age groups. The feminization of poverty reflected declines in marriage, increases in divorce and out of wedlock births, government policies and economic changes which in the last two decades affected wages and employment in ways first detrimental but later favorable to women. The decline in the poverty of adult women in recent years is due, in part, more to declining male wages and economic opportunities than to increases in women's earnings. Examining the poverty of women in three Western European countries, they conclude that the feminization of poverty is avoidable through state policies (Sweden and the Netherlands) and high marriage rates (Italy).

Given that near 60 percent of the poverty population is female in the U.S., and that the pervasiveness of gender inequality everywhere suggests that this proportion is likely to characterize the situation of women in the rest of the world, it would seem that the concept, feminization of poverty, captures the empirical reality of women's lives while illustrating the theoretical importance of gender to explain women's plight.

While it is undoubtedly true that there are more poor females than males, I have presented in my paper an argument against the theoretical adequacy of the concept, feminization of poverty, that continues to be relevant today. I argued that it is misleading to characterize this phenomenon as the "feminization of poverty" because gender is a relevant correlate of poverty only among women located in the working class, in the classical marxist sense; i.e., women who, regardless of skills or credentials, depend on the sale of their labor power – whether for wages or salaries makes no difference – for economic survival. Expanding this analysis to include women in Latin America, Asia and Africa, it entails the inclusion of working women who make a living producing food for the market and their households' consumption, or selling products or services in the market. While gender, in light of this argument, is an important individual characteristic of people as well as a key axis of social inequality, in capitalist societies it is not the major determinant of everyone's economic fate; gender affects economic survival and well being among those whose social class location compels them to work to make a living. Women who do not depend on marriage or a job for economic survival – women who are economically independent – are unlikely to fall into poverty if they become single mothers or divorce, unless changes in the economy devalue their assets. Most propertyless women, on the other hand, if they do not hold tenured, well paid jobs, are at the risk of becoming poor, especially if they are born in poor families.

A focus on women's poverty turns poverty into a gender effect and overlooks that gender is only one of the important social relations that shape people's fate. People, as Marx once wrote, are "ensembles of social relations," and their social conditions cannot be understood in isolation from the social relations within which they live their lives. Among those relations, class relations are fundamental and this is why it is inappropriate to make generalizations about the correlation between poverty and gender that overlook the qualitative differences between capitalist women, economically independent women, and the vast majority of women whose economic survival depends on marriage, employment, or a combination of the two.

As economic conditions change, men's opportunities also change. At the time the feminization of poverty was becoming a popularized way to understand poverty, the number of poor men almost doubled between 1978 and 1983. There are, furthermore, important links between the poverty of men and the poverty of women that must be taken into account. The declining employment opportunities and earnings of men affect the economic basis for marriage and family formation and, therefore, the economic status and opportunities of women. Married women can become the main breadwinners, a role reversal which may be a source of marital stress and even separation or divorce. Single women might remain single and become single mothers by necessity, not by choice, unable to find men able to earn enough to support a family.

Gender, race, and age, are undoubtedly important social relations that shape individuals' economic fate. But, as I argued in 1987 and continue to argue today, to focus on the poverty of the disproportionately poor (e.g., the poverty of women, children, the elderly, or adult younger workers, etc.) as the media, policy makers and social scientists tend to do, overlooks the class location of the poor and, consequently, the main causes of their poverty. Structurally, poverty is a class issue and to overlook this fact results in the conceptualization of poverty as an identity issue to be ameliorated through policies targeted to the needs of specific sectors of the poverty population – sectors defined on the basis of identities, rather than class location – thus detracting from the examination of the complex ways in which changes in the mode of production affect family formation and basic survival among the most vulnerable sectors of the working class. It is not my intention to deny that women are disproportionately poor, nor to fall into "class reductionism" by denying the effects of gender. My argument is that gender, as an objective structure of inequality and as an individual characteristic and identity, matters to understand the poverty and the downward mobility of propertyless or working class women, so that the appropriate way to refer to the phenomenon in question might be the feminization of working class poverty, thus avoiding the overgeneralization that most women, unlike men, are at a greater risk of becoming poor.

The dominant thinking about poverty separates it from its class determinants, so that we think of the poor as having no social class at all, or as the marginal sectors of the population or "underclass." We need to think of the poor as the most vulnerable, the most oppressed layers of the working class (understood as the vast majority of the population that is compelled to work for a living, whether its members are able to find work or not) and then examine the ways other oppressions and exclusions based on age, gender, race, ethnicity, citizenship status and other social divisions, cause disproportionate poverty. This is why I ended my article suggesting that the feminization of poverty is a concept that partially captures and obscures the effects of the increasing and deepening poverty of the lower layers of the working class.

At the time this article was originally published, the world was still divided between the capitalist West and the socialist East; two years later the Berlin Wall came tumbling down and in 1991 the Soviet Union ceased to exist. The world entered the era of "globalization," a euphemism for the spread of capitalism in Eastern Europe and the adoption, by most nation states, of neo-liberal economic policies which entailed the implementation of export development strategies and the collapse of economic sovereignty under the demands of the I.M.F., the World Bank, and the iron laws of the world market. Globalization became the lens through which everything has to be examined, the deus ex machina for everything that goes wrong in the world. It is not surprising, then, that the effects of globalization on the feminization of poverty or on women have become the topic of an ever increasing professional literature. Globalization, it is argued, increases the feminization of poverty at a global level, and the feminization of the proletariat as well. This means that the same critical questions asked when the feminization of poverty emerged as a new way to talk about women's poverty have to be asked today; if poverty and the proletariat are being feminized, what is happening to men? Are they all becoming better off than women? Both at the national and global levels of analysis, the discourse is formally the same: it is about the poverty of women, about the feminization of the proletariat, as if gender were the main reason for women's economic status. In this area of research and social policy, radical sociology has not had a noticeable effect except, perhaps, in the emergence of a social science perspective, the Race, Gender & Class perspective, that attempts to be all inclusive but which ends relegating class to one among other equally important sources of oppression. While it is important to examine all the sources of inequality, if the purpose of social science research is to provide solid foundations for policy making, a focus on women or on gender inequality narrows possible policies to those likely to enhance the opportunities of women as if all women were equally vulnerable to the risk of poverty and as if the economic status of women were analytically and empirically independent from the economic status and opportunities of men. By acknowledging that it is working women, women who need to work for a living, who are at risk of poverty and that their risk varies not so much because of the actions or intentions of men in general or of patriarchal structures, but because of the effects of macro level economic changes on the opportunities of male and female workers, more effective social policies could theoretically be devised to mitigate, at least, the effects of ongoing macro level changes in the world capitalist economy. The circulation of capital, for example, has its counterpart in the circulation of labor power; male migrant workers searching for jobs in the wealthier regions of their countries or in other countries leave behind women and children, who then become poorer than they would have been otherwise. As the search for economic survival separates husbands from wives, parents from their children, leaving behind the elderly and the very young, the poverty of working women increases and becomes visible in a way that hides the connections between their fate and the economic fate of working men. Politically, the effect of the feminization of poverty or feminization of the proletariat discourse has the effect of dividing the working population while making it difficult for workers to conceptualize economic and social goals that would benefit them regardless of their gender.

While the study of the effects of globalization on the feminization of poverty or the feminization of the proletariat calls attention to an important phenomenon, radical sociology, in the tradition started with the *The Insurgent Sociologist*, calls for the theorization of the effects of globalization on the material conditions necessary for the generational and daily reproduction, physical and social, of the working classes both within nation states, in regions and in the world as a socio-economic totality. Asking questions from the standpoint of the reproduction of labor power and the working class shifts the analysis from the poverty of women or from the proletarianization of women, to the analysis of the different effects of economic and political processes on male and female workers. For example, it is likely that the counterpart of the feminization of the proletariat in Mexico, might be the "masculinization" of the agricultural proletariat in the U.S.

From the standpoint of radical sociology, then, the "feminization of poverty" remains only a first approximation to the study of the differential effects of capitalist macro level processes upon the economic opportunities of female and male workers which may "feminize" the working class in one place while "masculinizing" it in another as technological changes inexorably increase the size of the reserve armies of labor and, consequently, the poverty and near poverty of the world's working classes.

Martha E. Gimenez

# The Feminization of Poverty: Myth or Reality?

The 'feminization of poverty' is a phenomenon of great concern to the government, social scientists, politicians, and feminists of all political persuasions. This phrase attempts to capture the essence of the following facts: in the United States, the fastest growing type of family structure is that of female-headed households and, because of the high rate of poverty among these households, their increase is mirrored in the growing numbers of women and children who are poor; almost half of all the poor in the U.S. today live in families headed by women. In 1984, 16 percent of all white families, 25 percent of all families of Spanish origin, and 53 percent of all black families were headed by women (Rodgers, 1986: 5). In the same year, the poverty rate for white, Spanish-origin and black female-beaded households was 27.1 percent, 53.4 percent, and 51.7 percent respectively (Rodgers, 1986: 12). Poverty affects not only young and adult women with children but also older women; in 1984, the median income of women 65 years and over was $6,020 (while it was $10,450 for men in the same age category) and 15.0 percent of all women age 65 and over had incomes below the poverty line (Sidel, 1986: 158). The poverty of women is reflected in the poverty of children. There are almost 13 million poor children in the U.S.; 52 percent

---

The original version of this article appeared in *The Insurgent Sociologist*, 14:3 (Fall, 1987), pp. 5–30.

of them live in families headed by women and the poverty rate for white, black, and Spanish-origin children living in female-headed households is 46 percent, 66 percent, and 71 percent respectively (Rodgers, 186: 32–33).

The facts and figures documenting the increased immiseration of women and children can be found in many recent publications (e.g., Stallard et al., 1983; Sidel, 1986; and Rodgers, 1986), together with analyses that put forth the notion that it is women, *as women*, who are peculiarly vulnerable to poverty. Poverty is being 'feminized' and this idea is nowhere expressed more clearly than in an often quoted statement from the President's National Advisory Council on Economic Opportunity (1981):

> All other things being equal, if the proportion of the poor in female-householder families were to continue to increase at the same rate as it did from 1976 to 1978, the poverty population would be composed solely of women and their children before the year 2000 (Rodgers Jr., 1986: 7).

Critics have rightly pointed out that this statement suggests that "by the year 2000 all of those men who are presently poor will be either rich or dead" (AAWO, 1983: 6). While those who quote it acknowledge that society does not keep still, that poverty affects men also and falls more heavily among nonwhites, nevertheless the main thrust of the analysis of present trends continues to interpret them as 'feminization of poverty.'

Is this a theoretically adequate notion? What can we learn from it? What are its shortcomings? Does it adequately convey the nature of the processes it describes? Is the 'feminization of poverty' a real phenomenon or a mystification that obscures the unfolding of other processes? These are some of the questions I will seek to answer in this essay. I will examine, from the standpoint of Marxist-feminist theory, the strengths and shortcomings of current explanations to establish whether recent changes in the size and composition of the poor population, growth in female-headed families, and the increased vulnerability of women to poverty can be adequately understood as the 'feminization of poverty.'

## Factors Accounting for the Feminization of Poverty

The definition of a social phenomenon shapes the questions that can be asked about its possible determinants and, of course, the questions in turn shape the answers. In this case, it is unavoidable to center such questions around women: why are women more likely to be poor than men? Why are female-headed households and families more likely to be poor? Why is the number of those households and families increasing? This leads researchers to focus on factors which are specific to the situation of women in modern society and conclude that women, as a group and regardless of class, are more vulnerable to poverty than men and that, consequently, women's poverty has different causes than the poverty of men.

The conceptualization of women *as a group* characterizes most discussions of the feminization of poverty. This tendency is encouraged by the manner in which poverty statistics are compiled. Census data do not differentiate between social classes; researchers have information about income, sex, racial and ethnic categories of analysis and this reinforces and tendency to frame the discussion in terms of statistical rather than theoretically significant categories of analysis. The determinants of women's poverty, it is therefore implied in the analysis, are factors that affect *all* women and place *all* women at risk.

What are these factors? Changes in mortality and marriage rates, divorce and separations, and out of wedlock births contribute to the increase in female-headed households (Rodgers, 1986: 38–42). Women's higher life expectancy contributes to the increasing number of women over 65 years of age living alone and a substantial proportion of these women are poor. Younger women become heads of households through out-of-wedlock childbearing, separation, divorce, or the decision to live alone while they work and postpone marriage until they consider it appropriate.

Male unemployment, lay-offs, and decline in wages are also crucial correlates of women's poverty. Such factors correlate with marital stress and violence, separation or divorce, and can make family formation impossible. Poor men who are chronically unemployed or underemployed cannot form families or stay with their families, particularly in states where welfare policies deny eligibility to two-parent families. Because of the heritage of racial and economic discrimination, these factors are intensified in the black and Spanish origin populations which have a higher proportion of poor female-headed families than the white population.

In addition to these structural factors and the lack of adequate welfare policies, Ruth Sidel argues that women's poverty is also the result of ideological and structural constraints peculiar to women. Women socialized to put family obligations first, to see themselves primarily as wives and mothers and seek in marriage and the family their fulfillment as adult members of the society, are likely to neglect or overlook the need to develop occupational and educational skills that will help them support themselves if they remain single or their marriage breaks up. Women's domestic activities, in spite of their social, economic, and psychological significance, are devalued and time consuming, and interfere with their full participation in the labor force. The domestic division of labor thus interacts with the sex-segregated nature of occupations to restrict the economic and educational opportunities of women. The negative effects of this situation become more salient once women become single heads of families (Sidel, 1986: 25–35).

As the preceding discussion indicates, the feminization of poverty is associated with many interrelated structural and ideological variables. Stallard et al. (1983) sum up the determinants of the feminization of poverty as follows:

> [It] is a direct outgrowth of women's dual role as unpaid labor in the home and underpaid labor in the work force. The pace has been quickened by rising rates of divorce and single motherhood, but the course of women's poverty is determined by the sexism – and racism – ingrained in an unjust economy (Stallard et al., 1983: 51).

It would seem that recent literature has produced not only a detailed description but also some plausible and, some may even say, obvious explanations of the feminization of poverty. That this is really the case, in spite of the impressive documentation and well developed arguments, is not a self-evident as it may seem. The identification of the determinants of the feminization of poverty in sexism, racism, and the operation of the economy does not really tells us much beyond that which is empirically obvious and observable. What is questionable is the meaning given to the trends: are we witnessing the feminization and the minoritization of poverty or something else? I will introduce some additional facts and figures about poverty to highlight the complexity of these issues, and the problems inherent in the 'feminization of poverty' perspective.

## Who Are the Poor?

A recent analysis of poverty in the U.S. indicates that, while it is the case that women are more likely to be poor than men and that, in absolute numbers, there were more poor women in 1983 than men (20,084,000 vs. 15,182,000), *"the female share of the overall poverty population was the same in 1983 as it was in 1966 [the earliest available data] – 57 percent"* (O'Hare, 1985: 18, my emphasis).[1] Poverty trends since 1983 have modified this conclusion only slightly. Between 1983 and 1986, the female share of the poverty population increased slightly from 57.0 percent to 57.6 percent (Bureau of the Census, 1987: 30).

The female and male shares of the poverty population from 1966 to 1986 show remarkable stability: the female share increased gradually, rising to 59.1 percent in 1978, declining to 57.0 percent in 1983 and 1984, rising to 57.6 percent in 1986 (see Table 1). If only adults over 21 are considered, in 1983 – *as it was in 1966* – women comprised 62 percent of the poor (O'Hare, 1985: 18). This percentage increased to 62.1 in 1984, 62.7 in 1985, and 64.2 in 1986 (Bureau of the Census, 1986a: 28; 1986b: 27; 1987: 30).[2]

Mortality differentials increase the numbers of older women living alone, and 27.7 percent of the 6.7 million women age 65 and over who in 1983 lived as 'unrelated individuals' were below the poverty level. In 1984, the number of women in that category increased to 6.8 million, but the percent below the poverty level declined to 25.2 percent (Bureau of the Census, 1985: 41, 1986a: 29). By comparison, in 1984, 20.8 percent of 'unrelated males' age 65 and over fell below the poverty level. The differences between the poverty rate of younger 'unrelated' women reflects the sharp fluctuations associated with

---

[1] The lower proportion of poor men in the population below the poverty level might be partially correlated with sex differential mortality. This is a complex issue that cannot be fully examined here, but it is possible, nevertheless, to present some pertinent observations. Occupationally caused mortality and disability are disproportionately high among working class men and women (Berman, 1978; Chavkin, 1984). Death rates among working age males (15–64) are considerably higher than among females of the same age. Death rates from accidents and violence are also exceedingly high for younger males, particularly for blacks (Bureau of the Census, 1986: 72, 76). As mortality varies inversely with socioeconomic status, it is reasonable to suppose that death rates for occupational accidents, disease and violence are likely to be higher for working class men, than the reported rates which do not take class differences into account.

[2] Bureau of the Census, "Supplementary Report on the Low Income Population: 1966–1972," Current Population Reports Series P-60, No. 95, July 1974, Table 1; "Characteristics of the Low Income Population: 1973" Current Population Reports Series P-60, No. 98, January 1975, Table 6; "Characteristics of the Population Below the Poverty Level: 1974," Current Population Reports Series P-60, No. 102, January 1976, Table 6; Table 11 in "Characteristics of the Population Below the Poverty Level" for the years 1975 and 1976, 1977, 1978, 1980, 1981, 1982, 1983, Current Population Reports Series P-60, No. 106, June 1977; No. 115, July 1978; No. 119, March 1979; No. 124, July 1980; No. 130, December 1981; No. 133, July 1982; No. 138; No. 144, March 1984; No. 147, February 1985; No. 152, June 1986; Table 8; "Money Income and Poverty Status of Families and Persons in the United States: 1985," Current Population Reports Series P-60, No. 154, August 1986, Table 18; No. 157, July 1987; Table 11 and 18.

the 1981–82 recession. However, an examination of the average annual percentage changes in the number of men and women below the poverty level between 1975 and every year until 1985, for all ages, shows a greater increase in male poverty in every year from 1982 on. At ages 18–44, there is a higher rate of increase in male poverty for every year from 1979 on.[3] The lower proportion of men below the poverty level makes the percent changes in male poverty higher than what they would have been had sex ratios been closer to unity. On the other hand, the higher percent changes in male poverty cannot be dismissed lightly as statistical artifacts; and it must be remembered that male poverty is an important correlate of female poverty. The sharp increases in male poverty between 1978 and 1983 were real and seem to have lingered on after the "economic recovery" that followed the 1981–82 recession. They reflect the vulnerability of men to unemployment at times of rapid economic decline, whereas women tend to work in more "recession proof" sectors of the economy (Smith, 1986: 3; Sparr, 1987: 11).

As indicated earlier, the proportion of men and women in the 18–44 age group who become poor has been steadily increasing. While in 1983 the poverty rate for families with a householder aged 45–64 was 8.7 percent (up from 6.4 percent in 1978) and 14.2 percent (up from 10.2 percent in 1978) for families with a householder age 25–44, it was 29.5 percent (up from 18.5 percent in 1978) for families with a householder under 25 (O'Hare, 1985: 13). In 1984, the poverty rate for householders under 25 remained practically unchanged at 29.4 percent, while the rate for householders aged 25–44 declined slightly to 13.2 percent (Bureau of the Census, 1986a: 14).

The faster increase in the poverty rate of younger workers of both sexes indicates that the working class is experiencing substantial downward mobility (O'Hare, 1985: 13–14; Harrington, 1984: 46–48). The increase in the poverty of children, usually linked to the increase in the number of female-headed families, is actually the result of the increase in poverty among young adult workers. While in 1983, 49 percent of poor children lived in female-headed households, 81 percent of poor children lived in families where the house-

[3] The decline in the poverty rate after 1975 is reflected in the decline, for all ages and both sexes, in the numbers below the poverty level during the next four years. In 1978, the year chosen by O'Hare as the base year, the poverty rate was low (11.3 percent) and the number of poor men of all ages (10,017,000) was the lowest ever since 1966, while the number of poor women (14,381,000) was relatively low if compared to most of the preceding years, but certainly higher than the lowest number recorded since 1966: 13,316,000 in 1973.

holder was under 45. Between 1978 and 1983, 4 million children under 18 joined the poverty population and only 25 percent of them lived in female-headed households (O'Hare, 1985: 13–17).

Real average earnings of young male workers aged 20–24 have declined 30 percent since 1973. A comparison between the earnings of men who turned 30 in 1973, and in 1983, shows that the average real income of the older men kept pace with inflation while that of the younger men declined 35 percent (*Dollars & Sense*, 1987: 10). Income inequality among young men is related to education; those without a college degree are reduced to taking whatever the economy offers them, which, in these days, are jobs that pay relatively little. While college attendance by low income men is declining, the gap in earnings between college graduates and high school dropouts is growing: "in 1973, the average earnings of a 20 to 24-year-old male high school dropout were three-quarters of the earnings of a college graduate. By 1984, this fraction dropped to two-thirds" (*Dollars & Sense*, 1987: 11).

In light of this information, it must be acknowledged that the 'feminization of poverty' is only one dimension of a broader process that also affects men, children, and the elderly in different degrees and for reasons that are fundamentally interrelated. *Just as an exclusive focus on 'women' leads to a one-sided analysis that seems to give lesser importance to other dimensions of poverty, it would be equally misguided to focus on the poverty of 'men' or of 'young adult workers.'* These are simple descriptive categories that indicate the composition of the poor population, but cannot serve as the basis for developing a theoretical analysis of the meaning of present poverty trends. Poverty is, furthermore, only a descriptive concept that does not help us understand the nature of the phenomena captured by these and many other statistics.

An important statement critical of the 'feminization of poverty' perspective (AAWO, 1983) convincingly argues that it offers an inaccurate empirical and political analysis of the situation because it ignores, for all practical purposes, the class differences between women and the common basis for class, racial and ethnic solidarity between men and women. Because the focus of analysis is the poverty of women *as women*, their class and race are not considered as crucial in determining their poverty as the fact they are women. It is the case, however, that not all women are in danger of becoming poor; only those who are working class or members of racial and ethnic minorities are thus threatened. Many women are becoming richer and, of course, ruling class women have never been at risk if becoming poor (AAWO, 1983:

2). Poverty is not a phenomenon affecting primarily women; it is a structural component of the capitalist economy that affects people regardless of age and sex and falls disproportionally upon minorities. It is racism, more than sexism, that determines who works in the worse sectors of the economy. Racism excludes large numbers of minority men from employment and the possibility of forming families, this changing the conditions faced by working-class women of color in ways which the 'feminization of poverty' perspective cannot adequately account for as long as it views all women as an oppressed class (AAWO, 1983; Staples, 1985; Center for the Study of Social Policy, 1985; Sparr, 1987).

This critique of the 'feminization of poverty' interpretation of current trends identifies important issues for further theoretical and empirical investigation. These insights, as well as those presented previously, have to be connected to their underlying capitalist structural determinants in production and reproduction, to more clearly understand the significance of these empirically observable phenomena. This process entails the examination of the relationship between capitalist structures, processes, and contradiction, which are not readily observable, and empirically observable changes in the size and composition of the poverty population. *It is my contention that the feminization of poverty is an important dimension of a larger process: the immiseration of the working class brought about by the profound structural changes undergone by the U.S. economy during the 1980s.* It would be beyond the limits of an essay to do justice to the complexity of these issues. The remarks that follow ought to be taken as tentative statements that will provide guidelines for future theoretical and empirical investigation.

## Beyond Women as a Category of Analysis: Class Differences Among Women and their Impact on Poverty

The feminization of poverty perspective focuses mainly on the poverty of women *as women*. This starting point introduces problems in understanding why some women become poor, while others do not. In this section, I will argue that gender related factors are relevant correlates (not determinants) of poverty only among women whose class location already makes them vulnerable to poverty. If no class differences (in the Marxist sense) are taken into account in the analysis of the feminization of poverty, it does appear as if it were caused primarily by sexism. It is necessary, therefore, to examine the concept of social class and explore its implications for the life chances of women in different social classes.

From the standpoint of Marxist theory, class is a relation between people mediated by their relationship to the means of production. Ownership of means of production, even in a modest scale, gives political and economic control over others, and economic independence. Lack of means of production places workers – male and female – in a dependent situation, vulnerable to the decisions taken by those who, in controlling capital, control their access to the conditions indispensable for their physical and social daily and generational reproduction: employment. Changes in the occupational structure and quantitative and qualitative changes in the demand for labor divide the propertyless class in terms of occupation, income, and education, which are precisely the building blocks with which the average person and most social scientists construct socioeconomic status categories.[4] This is the material basis for the common sense division of people into a variety of 'classes,' in a ranking that ranges from 'the poor' and the 'lower class' at the bottom, to the 'upper class' at the top, with the 'working class,' 'middle' and 'upper-middle class' in between. This is an empiricist understanding of social class that mystifies the sources of women's poverty; it is a simple ordering or gradational concept of class, that focuses only on the different power and resources individuals bring to the sexual and economic markets (Ossowski, 1963: 41–57, Weber, 1982: 61–62). It is a central contention in my argument that, if the social class location of women (not their socioeconomic status) is taken into account, it becomes obvious that it is not sex but class that propels some women into poverty.

*Capitalist women and petty bourgeois women are not at risk of becoming poor*

Being a capitalist or a petty bourgeois women entails, theoretically, having capital of one's own and, therefore, a source of income *independent* from marriage or from paid employment. Women who own wealth are unlikely to

[4] I am aware of the complexity of the issue of class and class structure within Marxist and neo-Marxist theory. Nevertheless, for the purposes of developing my argument in this essay, I consider that it is enough to point out the crucial differences between classes defined at the level of production relations and classes defined at the level of market relations. If relationship to the means of production is overlooked, it is possible to argue that most women, regardless of social class, could become poor; if the impact of propertylessness is taken into account, it becomes obvious that is the working class women who are at the greatest risk of becoming poor.

become poor for gender related factors, though inheritance practices and family accumulation strategies might deny them full control of their property.

Of the top wealth-holder with gross assets of $300,000 or more in 1982, 39.3 percent (1.85 percent of the total female population) were women. Between 1985 and 1986, the proportion of women aged 21 and over in the poverty population rose 1.5 percentage points (from 62.7 percent to 64.2 percent); in the same period of time, the number of women workers (full- and part-time) earning more than $35,000 increased 32 percent; those earning between $50,000 and $75,000 increased 34.5 percent, while the number of full-time women workers earning more than $75,000 increased 55.4 percent. As some women fell into poverty, others certainly became more affluent, although only 3.2 percent of all women workers earn more than $35,000 a year and only 0.3 percent of full-time working women earn more than $75,000 (Bureau of the Census, 1987: 19; 1986c: 447). Women earning over $35,000 a year are certainly far less likely to fall into poverty if they become single mothers, divorce or separate. On the other hand, if they lose their jobs, *lack an independent source of income*, and are unable to find a job with similar pay, they will experience downward social mobility and might even become poor.

Patterns of income distribution and wealth ownership indicate the existence of extreme socioeconomic status differences (income based) and class differences (based on wealth ownership) among women, which constitute the underlying material basis for the notion that virtually all women are vulnerable to poverty: that is so because most women (and most men as well) are propertyless.

### *Propertyless women (and propertyless men) are always at the risk of becoming poor*

As economist Ferdinand Lundberg has trenchantly observed: "anyone who does not own a substantial amount of income-producing property, or does not receive an earned income sufficiently large to make substantial regular savings or does not hold a well-paid securely tenured job is poor. . . . By this standard at least 70 percent of Americans are poor, although not all of these are by any means destitute or poverty stricken" (Lundberg, 1969: 23).

Propertyless women may attain, at the level of market relations, through family-transmitted advantages (e.g., real estate property, higher education) and/or marriage, a socioeconomic status that appears to place them above the working class. When it is argued that the feminization of poverty places all or most women at risk, including 'middle,' and 'upper-middle class' women, a very important observation is made which does not apply to women across social classes. The often made statement, "most women are just a man or a divorce away from poverty," reflects the conditions of existence of most *propertyless* women whom the capitalist organization of production and reproduction makes dependent on marriage and/or employment for economic survival.

Working-class women with substantial 'human capital' of their own are still a tiny minority; they, and women with stable jobs face a lower probability of poverty than women with less skills or with precarious working conditions. Data on women's income and employment indicate that the vast majority of propertyless women are working class, not only in terms of their location in the relations of production (i.e., they are propertyless and depend on a wage or salary for the economic survival of themselves and their families) but also at the level of socioeconomic stratification (i.e., the vast majority of women work in low paid, low status, blue- or white-collar jobs). Of the 39,214,000 women who worked full-time in 1986, 72.3 percent earned less than $20,000; 32.3 percent earned less than $10,000 (Bureau of the Census, 1987: 19). On the other hand, there are more men than women in 'middle class' and 'upper-middle class' occupations and in the better paid skilled blue collar jobs. Consequently, most women experience some form of 'upward mobility' through marriage and, if they lack skills or resources of their own, are likely to return to their previous place in the socioeconomic structure in case of separation, divorce, or widowhood.

Most of the 'social mobility' propertyless men and women experience in their life time is not social class mobility in the Marxist sense (e.g., changing from being propertyless to becoming petty bourgeois, small or big capitalist, etc.) but occupational mobility. It is important to realize that men and women can experience mobility at the market level while remaining, at the same time and whatever their socioeconomic status may be, located in the working class or propertyless class. Intra-class differences (i.e., differences within the propertyless class) in the socio-economic status and individual resources that men and women bring to the market is at the core of women's greater vulnerability to poverty and the transformation of marriage into the major source of economic survival for vast numbers of women.[5]

[5] Intra-class differences in the market resources of propertyless men and women reflect, in turn, differential patterns in the intergenerational transmission of socio-

The feminization of poverty is a market level structural effect of intra-class differences in male and female socioeconomic status and mobility; it is fundamentally a class issue although it is experienced and analyzed as an effect of sex and race discrimination. Sexism and racism unquestionably intensify the effects of economic changes upon the more impoverished layers of the working class (AAWO, 1983; Sparr, 1987). Nevertheless, the ultimate determinant of individuals' relative vulnerability to poverty is their class location: "if sexism (and, I add, racism) were eliminated, there would still be poor women (and poor non-whites). The only difference is that women (and non-whites) would stand the same chance as men (and whites) of being poor" (Sparr, 1987: 11).

## Conclusion

The data discussed earlier in this essay show that the sex ratio of the poverty population has changed little since 1966; its age composition, however, did change. Today, the majority of the poor are children under 18 and adults under 44 (see Table 1). While, in absolute numbers, there are still more poor women than poor men, the dramatic increase in poverty between 1978 and 1983 was felt more heavily among men than among women. Since 1983, the modest decline in poverty has also been more rapid among men than among women.

Theoretically, these trends are empirical indicators of the immiseration of the working class. The essence of this argument is that people do not fall into poverty because of their age, sex, or racial/ethnic characteristics, but because of their social class. Age sex, and ethnic/racial groups are not socially homogeneous; they are divided in social classes which, in turn, are stratified on the basis of income, education and occupation. The fact that poverty falls disproportionately upon the young, women and minorities does not invalidate the analysis; those who become poor share a common relationship to the means of production that cuts across age, sex, and racial/ethnic differences.

Sexism and racism are important in determining who gets the worst jobs or is most likely to be affected by unemployment (AAWO, 1983). But sexism and racism are not unchanging entities standing on an independent mater-

economic status which, in turn, are determined by the articulation of production and reproduction within the propertyless class, a topic which cannot be examined within the limitations of this essay.

ial base; they are shifting structural effects of capitalist processes of labor allocation designed to increase profit margins and enhance economic and political control over the working class. The general determining dynamics of poverty are, from this standpoint, located in capitalist processes which racialize, ethnicize and sexualize the work force on national and world-system levels – processes whose ideological, political and legal effects, in turn, perpetuate them through time, endowing them with a deceptive universality and antiquity (Wallerstein, 1983; 1985). The specific determinants of recent poverty trends are to be found in the interplay between the historical effects of sexism and racism and recent political and economic changes which have drastically altered the U.S. economic structure. Some sectors of the capitalist class, to become competitive at the international level are lowering the average price of labor; cuts in wages, union busting, right to work laws, 'give backs,' cuts in social services, and recent changes in immigration laws that allow the legalization of undocumented workers under certain conditions are all efforts aimed at cheapening the overall costs of labor (Piven and Cloward, 1986; Harrington, 1985).

Lacking access to the material conditions for their physical and social reproduction on a daily and generational level, over 32 million members of the working class below the poverty level barely survive under the restrictive conditions imposed by the welfare state. Altogether, 43.4 million people live below 125 percent of the poverty level; this includes 9.4 million families (45.9 percent headed by women) and 15.5 million children under 18 (51.1 percent of which live in families headed by women) (Bureau of the Census, 1987: 28). Nutrition levels and health among the poor have deteriorated; between 1982–85, the food-stamp program was cut by $7 billion and child-nutrition programs by 5 billion. In spite of the large number of people below the poverty level, only 19 million today receive food stamps; 12 million children and 8 million adults suffer from hunger (Brown, 1987: 37–41).

Lack of access to the basic material conditions necessary for physical and social reproduction on a daily and generational basis threatens the intergenerational reproduction of the working class among all races, particularly among racial and ethnic minorities. The immiseration of the working class culminates in the breakdown of its inter-generational reproduction. Poor parents, particularly poor single mothers, are placed under conditions that deprive them of their ability to reproduce people with marketable skills. This situation may be 'functional' for the economy, in so far as the demand for skilled and educated workers is not likely to rise dramatically during the near future. From the standpoint of the working class and minorities, in particular, this is a very serious situation which civil rights, better educational opportunities, and measures designed to help women combine work and parenting, *in themselves*, can not possibly solve.

William Julius Wilson (1978) has written of the 'declining significance of race' and the need to recognize the primarily economic and class-based determinants of the poverty and deprivation of most black Americans. By the same token, *the recent increase in both male and female poverty should alert us to the declining significance of sex as a cause of women's poverty.* The feminization of poverty reflects the fact that women are more than half of the U.S. propertyless class and that the standard of living of this class is noticeably declined in the last ten years (for a thoughtful statement about the need to overcome the limits of an exclusive focus on sex, to the detriment of class and race, as sources of women's oppression, see Thornton Dill, 1987: 204–213).

The media, social scientists, politicians and activists give – depending on their specific concerns, political agendas and the theoretical commitments – greater importance to different sectors of the poor. The notoriety of the 'feminization of poverty,' the poverty of the minorities, the elderly, or children contrasts with the relative silence about the erosion in the standard of living and the growing poverty of the working class. While it is important to uncover the correlates of poverty pertinent to each of these sectors, to the extent the analysis stops there it can lead to the development of theoretically flawed explanations and policies that pit the interests of women against the interests of men, the young versus the old, whites versus nonwhites.

Stress upon the poverty of those who are disproportionately poor produces a misleading perception of poverty as something that affects mainly women, the elderly, ethnic/racial minorities, and welfare recipients and could, theoretically, be effectively dealt with by measures addressing the needs of women workers, civil rights enforcement, and the welfare reforms. In fact, most of the poor are white (69 percent in 1986), most of the poor between the ages of 22 and 64 are working or looking for work, and only 35 percent of the poor families receive welfare benefits (O'Hare, 1985: 4). Only 10.5 percent of the elderly aged 65 and over are poor and 55 percent of the poor who live in families do not live in families headed by women (Bureau of the Census, 1986b: 22–24). Furthermore, of the 2,453,000 families between the poverty level and 125 percent of the poverty level, only 30 percent are headed by women (Bureau of the Census, 1987: 28–29).

To speak of the immiseration of the working class does not entail the adoption of a mindless economic reductionism nor the callous denial of the plight of minorities, women, children, and the elderly. It simply entails the recognition of the fact that those sectors of the poor population, including men, do not live as isolated individuals but are linked to each other through common relations of production and reproduction. The fate of each sector is tied to the fate of the others because they are all part of the same social class, just as the fate of individuals is tied to the fate of those with whom they share a kinship or emotional and social bonds. People are "an ensemble of social relations" (Marx, 1969: 198) and cannot be meaningfully understood in isolation of those relationships that give them their historically specific place in the world they live.

It is not by reducing people to age, sex, racial or ethnic categories that poverty and its determinants can be best understood; people are poor or become poor because they are subject to common 'socioeconomic and political processes that deprive them of access to their material conditions of existence, tear families apart, or make family formation impossible for vast numbers of working-class men and women, particularly those who are also members of racial and ethnic minorities. Placed in its historical context, the feminization of poverty is a real, important, albeit partial dimension, of a vast process of social transformation resulting in a drastic decline in the overall level of wages and standard of living of the U.S. working class, a significant increase in the size of the reserve army of labor, the intensification of the proletarianization of women,[6] and the undermining of the material conditions necessary for the maintenance of 'middle class' illusions and for the intergenerational physical and social reproduction of the lower strata of the working class – particularly its racialized, ethnicized, and feminized sectors.

[6] This process in not equivalent to the 'feminization of the proletariat' (Ehrenreich, 1987: 12). Because of demographic reasons (high male mortality) women have always been more than half of the proletariat, whether they were aware of it or not. I refer here to the erosion of 'middle class' and 'upper-middle class' statuses among growing numbers of propertyless women. It in also true that working women are concentrated in the more poorly paid jobs and the demand for female (and male) cheap labor is increasing. These trends can be best understood not in demographic terms (giving emphasis to the sex or age composition of the proletariat), but as effects of current processes of wealth concentration and class proletarianization.

# IV. Race and Gender

Edna Bonacich

# Comments on "Class Approaches to Ethnicity and Race"

It is scary to read something you wrote over twenty years ago. My reactions to reading this paper again after all this time veer between embarrassment at the chutzpah it took to write about such a huge topic from a position of considerable ignorance, and pleasure at the fact that I was trying to grapple with some big issues, issues that are still my central concerns. I feel some continuity with this young author, as well as a bemused distance from her.

I can't hope to review all that has happened in the field of race and racism since 1980, so I will only make a few observations:

- The independence of race from class has been boldly asserted, starting with the influential book by Omi and Winant (1986). Race and racism, it is claimed, cannot be "explained away" by capitalism, and stands on its own as an equal and independent force.
- The idea that "race" is socially constructed, and not primordial in any sense, is widely accepted. Race is seen as politically contested. Despite the fact that it has no biological reality, its social importance is huge. Certainly U.S. society is structured around race down to every detail of life.
- Race has come to be seen by a number of authors as more important that class. People often have difficulty recognizing class forces, but they experience

race vividly on a daily basis. The fact that the white working class has so frequently engaged in racism has led to a questioning of the possibility of any overarching "working class" solidarity.

- The concept of class seems to have suffered a decline. In numerous books on race, class and gender, class is treated as an identity equivalent to race and gender. For example, an article will describe how hard it is for a student with a working class background to feel comfortable in the university. Class as a property relation seems too often to have disappeared.
- Some authors criticize these trends, claiming that people have stooped to a divisive "identity politics." Each particular ethnic, racial, gender, sexual, age and disability category is seen as forming its own organizations, proclaiming its special suffering, and demanding its own reparations.
- These developments are all consonant with the emergence of post-modernism, including a critique of Marxism as a "master narrative" by a dead white guy that imposes class categories on people. It is felt that this imposition is an infliction, somehow negating people's freedom to define themselves.

Maybe I'm stuck in the past, but I still find Marxism incredibly useful for understanding our world, as well as for trying to change it. I see "class" not solely as a subjective phenomenon (though, of course, it can be), but as an objective feature of society, of which people can become more or less aware. Whether people realize it or not, the overarching goal of our system is to accumulate capital, and this is achieved by the exploitation of labor. When this is revealed to people, they often experience a deep sense of understanding, and feel they now have a guide to the kinds of struggles that need to be waged. It is no surprise that many people don't see class operating in their lives since capitalists and their allies, especially in government, work hard to obscure this reality.

Now, having an analysis of how capitalism operates does not negate the importance of race in the world. It seems to me that capitalism and racism are deeply intertwined, as shown in the mutual relationship between capitalism and slavery in the Atlantic economy (Williams, 1944; Blackburn, 1997). There is no question that race has been a major division in the working class, with white workers tied to "free labor" and workers of color often denied full citizenship and working under various forms of coercion. Unity around "whiteness" has been a political expression of this division (Roediger, 1991; Saxton, 1990).

Put another way, in my way of thinking, race is not secondary to class in importance, nor can we expect an easy working class unity that transcends race. Racial division, competition and manipulation all require a frontal assault. Nor can all racial issues be assumed to be connected with labor exploitation – though I personally think it remains one of the key forces behind racism. I look at Southern California (where I live) today and see an almost total structuring of the labor force and the unemployed along racial lines. Low-wage jobs are almost entirely filled by immigrant Latinos, and to a lesser extent, Asians. The capitalist class is almost entirely white, with a few Asians, and these two groups are also highly over-represented among the professional-managerial strata that run the global economy. African Americans are disproportionately unemployed and criminalized. Asians are overrepresented among the smaller businesses that service and employ Blacks and Latinos. This ethnic/racial economic structuring breeds antagonisms not only between whites and people of color, but also between Blacks, Latinos and Asians. That capitalists pit these groups against each other, and benefit from their divisions, seems indisputable.

Looking back at my 1980 article, I see a few good ideas. I still think that Figure 3 is useful for laying out the basic class/race relations associated with imperialism, though it omits important class components, notably the various "middle" classes. Of course, it is very sketchy. But I am happy to be able to say that I don't feel the need to disown it.

Edna Bonacich

# Class Approaches to Ethnicity and Race

The field of ethnic and race relations has recently tended to be dominated by an assumption that race and ethnicity are "primordial" bases of affiliation, rooted in "human nature." This assumption is increasingly being challenged by authors who contend that, while race and ethnicity may appear to be primordial attachments, in fact they reflect a deeper reality, namely, class relations and dynamics. I believe that class approaches are the most fruitful way to study ethnicity and race. Not only are they more in accord with a "deeper" level of reality that enables us to understand phenomena at the surface of society, but they also provide us with the tools for changing that reality. The purpose of this paper is to briefly review and criticize primordial assumptions about ethnicity and race, to present several class approaches to the subject in an effort to demonstrate the richness of available ideas, and finally, to attempt a tentative synthesis of some of these ideas.

Before we start, let us define our terms. Ethnicity and race are "communalistic" forms of social affiliation, sharing an assumption of a special bond between people of like origins, and the obverse of a negative relation to, or rejection of, people of dissimilar origins. There are other bases of communalistic affiliation as well, notably, nationality and "tribe". For the

---

The original version of this article appeared in *The Insurgent Sociologist*, 10:2 (Fall, 1980) pp. 9–23.

Figure 1. Ethnicity* and Class in the Capitalist Mode of Production.

| | Ethnic Group 1 | Ethnic Group 2 |
|---|---|---|
| Class Division | Bourgeoisie | Bourgeoisie |
| | Proletariat | Proletariat |
| | Ethnic Division | |

* Nationality, race, or tribe could be substituted for ethnicity.

sake of this discussion, I would like to treat all of these as a single phenomenon. Thus, ethnocentrism, racism, nationalism, and tribalism are similar kinds of sentiments, dividing people along lines of shared ancestry rather than other possible lines of affiliation and conflict, such as common economic or political interest.

Obviously there are other important bases of affiliation besides communalism. One important alternative form of solidarity is along class lines. Figure 1 presents schematically these two forms of affiliation and their interaction for capitalist societies. Needless to say, it is a very simplified sketch and could be elaborated along both dimensions, as well as by the addition of other dimensions. Still, the point to be made is that ethnic (or communalistic, or "vertical") forms of solidarity cross-cut class (or "horizontal") bases of affiliation. They represent competing principles, each calling on people to join together along one or two axes.

## Primordialism

The sociology of race and ethnic relations grew in reaction to a tradition that underplayed the importance of communalistic affiliations.[1] As many authors have pointed out, the early "classic" writers in sociology paid little heed to ethnicity.[2] They assumed that it would disappear with modernization and industrialization. The exigencies of modern society would "liberate" people

[1] Perhaps this position was itself a reaction to the belief that race and ethnicity were "real" and marked off some nationalities from others as biologically superior or inferior.

[2] Cf. Banton, 1974; Glazer and Moynihan, 1975; Rex, 1970.

from these traditions.[3] It should be noted that this expectation was also held by early Marxists, who assumed that class solidarity would override national chauvinism (Nairn, 1975; Blauner, n.d.).

The obvious falseness of this premise, perhaps especially realized by American sociologists in the face of Nazi Germany, when one of the worlds's most "modern" societies proved capable of extreme racism, forced a reassessment. Similarly, the black uprising of the 1960s in the United States reawakened sociologists to the fact that the "race problem" was not simply disappearing. Clearly these "traditional" sources of solidarity were far more resistant to change than had been realized.

Several authors began to call for revisions in our thinking. Criticizing earlier writers, they demanded that race and ethnicity be given prominence as phenomena that could not be ignored.

The polemic against the obvious inadequacies of the belief that ethnicity would disappear has led to another extreme position: the view that it is such a "natural" bond between people as to be immutable or "primordial" (Geertz 1963: 109).

The primordial ethnic bond is assumed to have two faces. On the one hand, it leads to a special attachment to an "in-group" of similar people, on the other, to feelings of disdain or repulsion towards the "out-group" or people of dissimilar origins. "Ethnocentrism" is believed to be a "natural" human sentiment.

This idea derives from a biologically rooted conception of "human nature."[4]

Accepting the primordialness of ethnicity leads to a certain logic of inquiry. Since ethnic and racial affiliation requires no explanation in itself, one concentrates on its consequences.[5] These may be negative, in the form of prejudice and discrimination against "out-groups."[6] Or they may be positive, providing people with a meaningful and rich group life.[7] In the process of

---

[3] For a more complete exposition of this position, see Blumer, 1965; pp. 220–253. For a criticism of this position see Wolpe, 1970, pp. 151–179.

[4] For a similar position see Isaacs, 1975, pp. 29–52.

[5] Perhaps I am overstating this case. Even authors who concentrate on the consequences of ethnic affiliations give some attention to origins. But these tend to be seen as rooted in the distant past, and firmly embedded in long-established cultural traditions, rather than requiring explanation in the present. Class theorists, in contrast, believe that ethnic affiliation must be created or reproduced in the present for its persistence to be understood.

[6] See for example: Simpson and Yinger, 1972.

[7] See for example, Gordon, M., 1964. In addition, see authors interested in the rise of "white ethnicity," such as Greeley (1974); Novak (1971).

concentrating on intra-"group" solidarity and inter-"group" hostility, little attention is paid to intra-ethnic conflict let alone cross-ethnic alliances.

There are at least three reasons for questioning the primordial nature of communalistic ties. First, there are boundary problems in defining ethnic and racial groups (cf. Barth, ed., 1969; Patterson, 1977). Because of the pervasive tendency for human beings to interbreed, a population of mixed ancestry is continually being generated. To consign these people to an ethnic identity requires a descent rule. There are a variety of such rules, including: tracing descent matrilineally (as found among the Jews), or by the presence of one particular ancestry (as in U.S. blacks), or by treating mixed ancestry as a separate ethnicity (as in the case of South African Coloureds), and so on. The variability in descent rules suggests their social rather than primordial nature. They reflect social "decisions," not natural, kin-like feeling.[8]

Apart from mixed ancestry problems, ethnic groups can redefine their boundaries in terms of whom they incorporate. As many authors (e.g. Yancey et al., 1976) have pointed out, several of the European immigrant groups to the United States, such as Italians, had no sense of common nationality until they came here. And the construction of "whites" out of the enmity between old and "new" European immigrants took decades to achieve. Similarly today a new ethnic group, Asian-Americans, is being constructed out of previously quite distinctive, and often hostile, national elements. That such a creation is social and political, rather than primordial, seems clear.

A second reason for questioning the primordial nature of ethnicity is that shared ancestry has not prevented intra-ethnic conflict, including class conflict. If one considers the history of societies which were relatively homogeneous ethnically, such as France or England, one finds not only intense class conflict, but even class warfare. Even in ethnically diverse societies such as the United States, within ethnic groups, class conflict is not unknown. White workers have struck against white-owned plants and been shot down by co-ethnics without concern for "common blood." Chinese and Jewish businessmen have exploited their ethnic "brothers and sisters" in sweatshops and have bitterly resisted the efforts of their workers to gain independence. The prevalence of intra-ethnic conflict should lead us to question the idea that ethnicity necessarily provides a bond between people, let alone a primordial one.

---

[8] A good example of an effort to uncover the social or class meaning of descent rules is M. Harris, 1964, in which he contrasts the United States' and Latin American descent rules for determining who is black.

Third, conflicts based on ethnicity, race, and nationality, are quite variable. In some cases they are fierce; in others, despite the presence of groups with different ancestry, conflict is limited or non-existent. A full range of ethnic relations is found in the world, extending from complete assimilation of diverse ethnic elements (as in the case of various European nationalities which came to make up the "WASP" group in the United States), to the total extermination of one ethnic group by another (as in the genocide of the Tasmanians). This variability should, again, lead us to question the primordial nature of ethnicity for if ethnicity were a natural and inevitable bond between people it should always be a prominent force in human affairs.

Recently a new school of thought has emerged. While not moving back to the earlier errors of the "founding fathers" in ignoring the importance of ethnicity, racism, and nationalism it nevertheless holds that these phenomena cannot be taken for granted as natural; they need to be explained. Without ignoring communalistic affiliations we can ask: Under what conditions will ethnic or racial affiliation be invoked? Under what conditions will this lead to extreme conflict? And under what conditions will ethnicity or race subside as major axes of social organization and conflict? And under what conditions will ethnicity or race subside as major axes of social organization and conflict? Class theories constitute one broad category of attempted explanation of the ethnic phenomenon. They share in common the notion that ethnic movements are not only essentially political rather than primordial, but that they have *material* roots in the system and relations of production.

## Class Theories of Ethnicity

There is no single class approach to the question of ethnicity. Indeed, in recent years, considerable creative work has proceeded on several fronts not all of which are in communication with one another. Different disciplines and subdisciplines, such as economic anthropology, urban sociology, and immigrant history, are all developing class approaches to ethnicity. Scholars interested in different areas of the world tend to communicate poorly with one another. Thus there are class theories of ethnicity in African or Latin American studies, about South Africa, the U.S.-Mexican border, about guest workers in Europe, and so on. In addition, an abundance of theoretical models is available, some of which operate at different levels, but all of which address ethnicity to some extent. These include: theories of labor migration and immigration, dependency theory, dual labor markets, split labor markets, internal colonialism, theories of middleman minorities, labor aristocracy theories, world systems theory, and more. Bringing all these literatures together is a huge task, well beyond the scope of this paper. My goal here is to present a few of the available ideas.

Before examining particular theories, let us briefly return to Figure 1 to define what is being talked about. Positive (integrative) movements along the vertical axis may be termed "nationalist" movements. These are efforts to mobilize people of different classes within the same ethnic group to join together. Negative (conflictual) movements along the horizontal axis represent within-class inter-ethnic antagonisms. These two types of movements constitute the two faces of ethnicity: in-group solidarity and out-group rejection. In contrast, negative movements along the vertical axis represent intra-ethnic class struggle, while positive movements along the horizontal axis reflect cross-ethnic class solidarity. Diagonal movements are ambiguous, having both class and ethnic content. For instance, a negative diagonal could represent national and colonial oppression or movements for liberation from such oppression. Our main ocncern here is with the explanation of ethnic-type movements, i.e., positive vertical and negative horizontal.

Note that the figure should apply to inter-ethnic relations regardless of the territorial location of these groups. They can each occupy a discrete geographical territory, or a segment of one nation may have conquered and settled among another,[9] or a segment of one nation may have moved or been brought in as laborers to the territory of another, and so on. While there are important differences between these situations (Lieberson, 1961), they all juxtapose communalistic against class bases of affiliation.

Figure 2 presents very schematically several class approaches to the question of ethnic nationalism. They are intended not to represent a comprehensive coverage of all class theories of ethnicity but to illustrate the tremendous riches and diversity of ideas within a class orientation.

---

[9] This condition is itself quite variable depending on which classes move, i.e., a major distinction needs to be drawn between "white settler" colonies where members of the working class of the conquering nation settled in the colonized territory, and colonies where only foreign capitalists have been active. White settler colonies, such as the United States, Australia, and South Africa, have generally experienced much harsher ethnic problems, a fact that has raised considerable debate regarding competing explanations (Foner and Genovese, eds., 1969).

Figure 2. Five Types of Class Theory of Ethnicity.

A. *Nation-Building*

Ethnic Group 1 Ethnic Group 2

National Antagonism (1)

Bourgeoisie ⟷ Bourgeoisie

National Mobilization (2) National Mobilization (2)

Proletariat Proletariat

B. *Super-Exploitation*

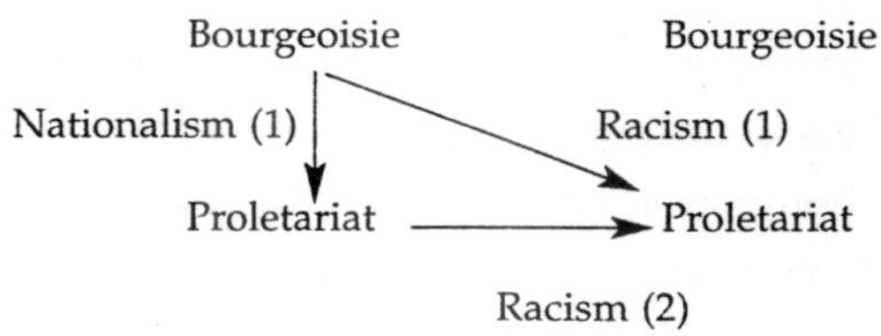


C. *Split Labor Market*

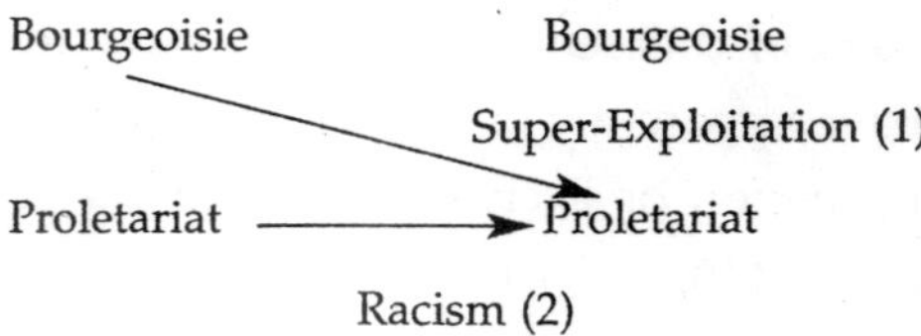


D. *Middleman Minorities*.

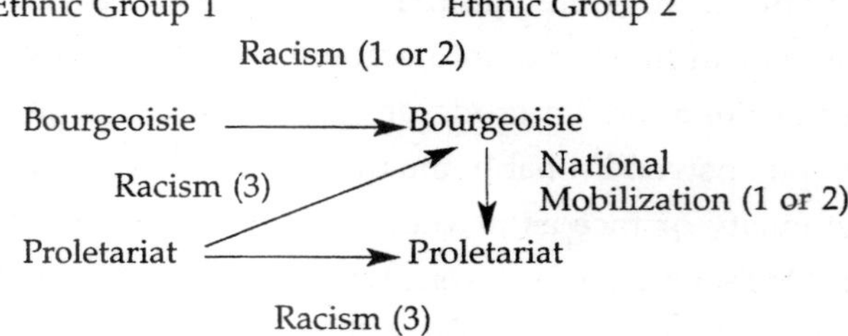


E. *National Liberation*

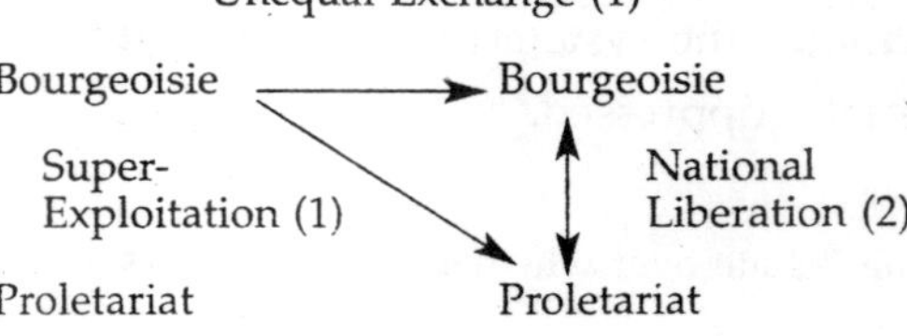

A. *Nation-building*

One of the simplest class theories of ethnicity or nationalism is that it is a movement reflecting an early stage of capitalist development in which capitalists seek to integrate a "national" market. This movement achieved its peak in Europe in the late nineteenth century (Hobsbawn, 1977). When capitalism became imperialistic, the national bourgeoisies of the various Western nations came into conflict with one another, leading ultimately to the two world wars (Lenin, 1939). The participants in these wars espoused nationalist ideologies as a mechanism by which the capitalist class could mobilize workers to support their cause. Exponents of this view hold that workers are not nationalistic since they are all exploited. Rather, they are internationalist, sharing a common interest in the overthrow of capitalism which transcends national boundaries. Nationalism is thus a movement representing the interest of the bourgeoisie. (This is illustrated in Figure 2A by showing that antagonism between national bourgeoisies leads to efforts at national mobilization by the bourgeoisies. The workers are objects, not generators, of this effort.)

B. *Super-exploitation*

The fact that workers of different nationalities have not easily joined with one another, and have apparently joined willingly with their "national bourgeoisie" in the oppression or exclusion of workers of other nationalities, revealed the limitation of this approach. Such cases as the U.S. South or South Africa, where white workers generally failed to join with blacks in a united working class movement, and instead identified with white capitalists and land-owners, led to some rethinking on the issue. An adequate explanation of communalism must take into account worker interests in it too.

"Super-exploitation," a crude designation for several schools of thought, provided an answer. Probably the most common class approach to ethnicity, it sees ethnicity or race as markers used by employers to divide the working class. One segment of workers, typically dark-skinned, are more oppressed than another, the latter typically of the same ethnicity as the exploiters. This enables the dominant bourgeoisie to make huge profits from the former segment, enough to pay off the more privileged sector of the working class, who then help to stabilize the system by supporting it and acting as the policemen of the specially oppressed.[10]

---

[10] There is some debate over whether ethnically or racially oppressed workers are

For several authors in this tradition (e.g. Cox, 1948), the super-exploitation of dark-skinned workers is rooted in the imperialistic expansion of Western European capitalism. Europe colonized the rest of the world in order to continue to accumulate capital more effectively. The ideology of racism grew as a justification for the exploitation of colonized peoples: they were "naturally" inferior and needed Europeans to "help" them move into the modern world. Racist ideology developed not only in relation to people living in the distant colonies, but also toward people living in "internal colonies," (Allen, 1970; Blauner, 1972) where either white settlers had become established or colonized workers had been brought under some degree of coercion. Even when separated in politically differentiated territories, the working class of the imperialist power could be used to keep the colonized in line. Thus, with imperialism, the major axis of exploitation shifted from capitalist versus workers to oppressor "nations" and oppressed "nations."

Within a multi-ethnic society, having an especially exploited, ethnically delineated class serves several "functions" for the capitalist class: it can be used as a reserve army of labor, permitting flexibility in the system to deal with business cycles (Baran and Sweezy, 1966); it allows employers to fill diverse labor needs, such as the "dual" requirements of a stable, skilled labor force in the monopoly and state sectors of the economy, and a flexibly, unskilled, low wage labor force in the competitive sector (Gordon, 1972; O'Connor, 1973); it helps get done the "dirty work" that other workers are unwilling to do by creating a class that is desperate for work (Oppenheimer, 1974); it helps in the accumulation of capital because wealth is extracted from the "underdeveloped" sector or ethnic group and passed on to the bourgeoisie of the dominant group (Blauner, 1972; Frank, 1967, 1969); and it helps to stabilize the system by keeping the working class fragmented and disorganized (Reich, 1972; Szymanski, 1976).

---

more exploited, in a technical sense, than dominant workers. The term "exploitation" refers to the amount of surplus value extracted from labor. Since ethnic minority workers are often employed in the most backward, unproductive sectors, the rate of surplus extracted from them may, in fact, be lower than for more privileged workers who work in the high-productivity, monopoly sector of the economy. Especially when minority workers suffer high rates of unemployment, it is difficult to see how surpluses are generated here (Willhelm, 1971). Still, there are other mechanisms by which surplus is extracted from minority workers, such as "unequal exchange." It seems undeniable that some form of wealth moves from ethnically oppressed labor to the dominant bourgeoisie, even if not via direct employment as wage labor. In any case this is a point of debate.

Within this broad perspective are found some major differences. One important issue of debate is whether white workers gain or lose from the racial oppression of minorities. The "internal colonialism" school supports the idea that white workers benefit, by being paid extra from the surplus taken from minorities, by being cushioned against unemployment, and by getting other psychological and political rewards. In other words, in this view, the racism of white workers is a "rational" response, rooted in their vested interest in imperialism.

In contrast, authors such as Reich and Szymanski contend that white workers lose from racism. Since workers of different ethnicity are pitted against one another, the working class movement is weakened, and all lose. Thus white worker racism is seen more as a product of manipulation by capital than a rational pursuit of self-interest by white labor.

Despite these differences, both schools of thought see ethnicity as created, or at least nurtured, by the bourgeoisie of the dominant ethnic group or nationality. It is used to mark off the super-exploited as inferior, through ideologies like racism. And it is used to bind the more advantaged workers to the ruling class through the ideology of ethnic solidarity, thereby masking conflicting class interests within that group. White workers, for example, are taught that their whiteness makes them superior to other workers and gives them a common lot with their employers. A possibility is even held out to them that they too may become part of the ruling class because they are white. By the mobilization of ethnic solidarity, then, the capitalist class can induce these workers to support the system and align themselves against other workers. As Figure 2B suggests, the racism of dominant group workers is secondary phenomenon, while that of the bourgeoisie is primary.

C. *Split Labor Market*

This approach places labor competition at the center of racist-nationalist movements, challenging the idea that they are the creation of the dominant bourgeoisie.[11] Uneven development of capitalism on a world scale, exacerbated by imperialist domination, generates "backwardness" or "under-development" for certain "nationalities." Workers of these nations, unable to defend themselves against exploitation of the severest kind, became "cheap labor"

[11] Bonacich, 1972; 1975; 1976; 1979. Some authors (Wilson, 1978) combine theories B and C, attributing them to different historical epochs.

(arrow 1 in Figure 2C). The availability of cheap labor leads dominant workers to be displaced or threatened with displacement, since employers would prefer to hire cheaper labor. The threat of displacement may be accompanied by other changes in production, such as deskilling. Dominant group workers react to the trheat of displacement by trying to prevent or limit capital's access to cheap labor, through efforts to exclude members of cheap labor groups from full participation in the labor market (arrow 2). That these exclusionary efforts have a "nationalist" or "racist" character is a product of historical accident which produced a correlation between ethnicity and the pride of labor.

In contrast to the "super-exploitation" school of thought, split labor market theory argues that dominant group workers do not share a "national" interest with capital in the exploitation of colonized people, nor are they even fooled into believing they share such an interest. Rather, dominant group capital and labor are engaged in struggle over this issue. Capital wants to exploit ethnic minorities while labor wants to prevent them from doing so. However, in attempting to exclude ethnic groups from certain jobs, labor's reactions may be just as devastating to minority workers as direct exploitation by capital. Where the dominant working class is successful, minority workers are kept out of the most advanced sectors of the economy, suffer high unemployment rates, and so on. In sum, this approach suggests that there are two distinct types of racial-national oppression, one stemming from capital, and the other from labor.

Split labor market theory sees the question of whether white workers gain or lose from racism as a false, or at least oversimplified, issue. It suggests that white workers are hurt by the existence of cordoned-off cheap labor sectors that can be utilized by capital to undercut them. White labor's efforts to protect itself may prevent undercutting, in the short run; however, in the long run, it is argued, a marked discrepancy in the price of labor is harmful to all workers, permitting capital to pit one group against another.

D. *Middleman Minorities*

Middleman minority theories deal with a particular class of ethnic phenomena, namely, groups which specialize in trade and concentrate in the petite bourgeoisie. Class explanations of this phenomenon vary. Some see these specialized minorities as creations of the dominant classes (not only bourgeoisies, since they arise in pre-capitalist societies as well) (Blalock, 1967; Hamilton,

1978; Rinder, 1958). By marking a group off as ethnically distinct, it can be forced to occupy a distinctive class position that is of special use to the ruling class, namely, to act as a go-between to the society's subordinate classes, while bearing the brunt of hostility towards the elite. The racist reactions of subordinate classes against the middleman group can thus be seen as secondary or tertiary phenomena, manipulated by ruling classes to protect themselves. (There are parallels in this tripartite system to the construction of ethnic divisions within the working class. In both cases, the creation of two ethnically distinct subordinate classes which are pitted against one another helps to keep the elite in power.)

Another interpretation of middleman minorities is to see them as internally generated by the minorities themselves. Bonds of ethnic loyalty are used by the dominant class within the minority to mobilize the group economically. The use of ethnic sentiments enables the group's leaders to mobilize resources cheaply and effectively. One of the most important of these cheap resources is ethnic labor. By emphasizing ethnic bonds, the ethnic elite is able to minimize class division within the ethnic group, thereby keeping labor effectively controlled (Benedict, 1968; Light, 1972). In this interpretation, the racist reactions of dominant group members in part derive from fears of competition. The dominant business class, as well as the potential business class among subordinated segments of society, has access to a less pliable work force and fears being undercut. The dominant working class resents the competition of cheap-labor-based firms. Anti-middleman minority movements are seen (Bonacich, 1973) to be rooted in these class antagonisms.

Several authors have pointed to a strong correlation between class position in the petty trader category, and ethnic solidarity. Not only does ethnic solidarity support trading, but the reverse holds true, namely, petty trading helps to hold the ethnic group together. Leon even coined the term "people-class" to express this coincidence. The argument follows that, when members of the ethnic group no longer occupy a unique class position, they will gradually lose their ties to the ethnic group and assimilate. Jews, according to Leon, who have ceased to be members of the petite bourgeoisie, have tended to disappear from the ranks of Judaism. If true, here is a clear example of the dominance of class over primordial roots of ethnic affiliation.

The people-class idea has also been used to describe groups that are not middleman minorities (or in the petite bourgeoisie). For instance, Leggett (1968) and Oppenheimer (1974) develop a similar conception of blacks in the

United States. Blackness represents not merely a racial category, but a class category as well: sub-proletarian, marginal working class, etc.[12] As blacks become less exclusively identified with a particular class position, the salience of "race" as a cetegory tends to decrease (Wilson, 1978). In other words, racial terminology and antagonism reflect, to some extent, the common and distinctive class position of blacks and reactions to that position. A similar approach is developed for U.S. white ethnic groups by Hechter (1978) and Yancey, et al. (1976), who see ethnic solidarity as linked to a concentration in particular occupations or subcategories of the working class.[13]

### E. *National Liberation*

Partly growing out of the notion that some national groups are particularly oppressed or occupy a unique class position in world capitalism, is a concern for movements of national liberation. While these movements are clearly reactions to external domination and underdevelopment, considerable debate has ensued over the conditions under which "nationalist" reactions are appropriate. On the one hand is the principle of the right of "nations" to self-determination (Lenin, 1968); on the other is the ambiguity of which groups actually constitute a viable nation and can therefore legitimately form separatist movements (Hobsbawm, 1977). For instance, a major debate ensued over whether or not U.S. blacks constituted a "nation" in the South which could reasonably aspire to statehood. More recently, the "internal colonialism" model of the black experience again suggests the legitimacy of a "nationalist" solution, this time for northern, urban, ghetto-dwellers, a position that has been challenged by those who feel that class solidarity should take precedence.[14]

---

[12] Geschwender, 1978, uses the concept "nation-class" more broadly to allow for class differentiation within oppressed ethnic groups. Thus blacks are differentiated by class, although disproportionately in the proletariat, but within each class they also experience "national oppression." Each case of coincidence between class and national categories is considered a "nation-class." Using a figure similar to Figure 1, Geschwender (1978, pp. 264–267), concludes that alliances and enmities can arise along both class and national axes.

[13] The concept "people-class" needs to be distinguished from Gordon's (1964) concept of "eth-class." For Gordon, class means status group rather than relations to the means of production. Gordon's eth-classes are social groupings which feel comfortable together because of similarity in style of life. They are not political-economic interest groups. Gordon's is not a class theory of ethnicity: it accepts ethnicity as a primordial tie.

[14] Harris, 1972; Geschwender, 1978, Chapters 4 and 5 review this debate.

An important aspect of this issue is the question of whether it is necessary to go through a capitalist (or at least not fully socialist) phase in order to develop economically. Most Third World "peoples," particularly those in separate states, but also some minorities within states, still live and work under systems with feudal or pre-capitalist remnants, such as peasant agriculture, or migrate between pre-capitalist and capitalist sectors.[15] It has been suggested that, under colonial conditions, a two-state revolution is necessary: first, workers and peasants must join their incipient national bourgeoisie in overthrowing the foreign oppressor. Once the national bourgeoisie is sufficiently liberated to begin to develop the "nation" economically, and a true proletariat is formed, then intra-national class struggle and true socialist revolution become possible. Note that, in a way, we have come full circle, back to Type A, though under very different historical circumstances. Nationalism in the Third World can represent the interests of the bourgeoisie or petite bourgeoisie (Saul, 1979) in establishing and consolidating modified forms of capitalism.

The necessity for a two-stage revolution has, of course, been challenged. On the one hand it is argued that the "national bourgeoisie" of oppressed nations is too linked to international capital to lead a liberation movement which will truly liberate. On the other, the ability of Third World peasants and other pre-capitalist classes as well as the incipient proletariat to engage in revolutionary movements has been proven. Indeed Third World peasant and proletarian movements have been far more successful on this score than the "developed" proletariat of Western Europe and the United States, though the degree to which these revolutions have produced truly socialist societies remains in question. Similarly, black workers in the United States, despite their sub-proletarian status (or perhaps more accurately, because of it) are undoubtedly more class conscious and ready for socialist revolution than the white working class (Leggett, 1968, Geschwender, 1977). Thus exclusively

[15] Focus on the national liberation movements of the colonized tends to lead to a disregard of class dynamics within the dominating nationalities. As stated earlier, national oppression is seen to have taken the place of class oppression as the major axis of world capitalist exploitation. This viewpoint again puts ethnicity at center stage, though it recognizes that national domination and colonialism are rooted in capitalism rather than in the "natural" tendencies of nations to despise one another. Still, by focusing on national oppression, writers in this school of thought tend to ignore the internal class dynamics of both national groups.

"nationalist" alliances are seen to be both undesirable and unnecessary, though colonized workers' movements against "white" capital still have a "national" component.

The debate is not so much concerned with explaining nationalist movements as prescribing when they are appropriate. However, implicit is an explanatory theme: movements for ethnic self-determination are likely to arise under conditions of colonial or neo-colonial rule; they repesent a temporary class alliance between the colonized bourgeoisie (or incipient bourgeoisie) and workers-peasants, in response to colonial domination.

As stated earlier, the five types of class theory are not intended to be definitive, but rather, illustrative of the multiplicity and complexity of ideas on this topic. Although I have presented them as if they were competing approaches, in fact they are not necessarily all incompatible. For instance, different kinds of communalistic movements may be appropriate to different stages of capitalist development. Thus the five approaches presented here may, to some extent, reflect sequential stages in the development of capitalism and imperialism. True, there are some genuine theoretical debates which need to be resolved one way or another, for example, whether or not most white workers have a vested interest in imperialist domination. I shall not, at this point, attempt to critically evaluate each of the various approaches since the criticisms will be inherent in the synthesis attempted in the next section.

Before moving on to the synthesis, however, one lesson from this review needs to be stressed: "Nationalism" is not a unitary phenomenon. Not only must we distinguish between the nationalisms of the exploiters and the exploited (Mandel, 1972), but also between nationalisms with different class roots, such as petit-bourgeois nationalism versus working-class nationalism. Indeed all four classes in our schema generate communalistic movements at times, and for quite different reasons. Some of the debates among class theorists may, in part, result from confusing different kinds of ethnic movements. To use the same example again, the debate over whether or not white workers have a vested interest in "racism" may confuse different kinds of racism: exploitation by the bourgeoisie versus exclusion by the working class. Any comprehensive class theory of ethnicity must take these differences into account.

## Towards an Integrated Class Approach

Since most of the important "ethnic relations" in the modern world have grown out of the rise of capitalism in Western Europe, and its resulting imperialist expansion, most of my analysis will concern this case. I assume that other capitalist imperialisms, notably that of Japan, produce a similar dynamic. Whether non-capitalist or state capitalist expansions, such as that of the Soviet Union, would fit the model, I do not know. The model will also not attempt to deal with pre-capitalist ethnic relations.

A promising new literature is developing which attempts to place ethnic phenomena within the context of the development of world capitalism.[16] The ideas which I am presenting here draw heavily upon their contributions.

A fully developed class analysis of ethnicity needs to consider all of the possible class relations between "ethnic groups" that result from imperialism. These are schematically presented in Figure 3, and again we must note that the figure is simplified along both dimensions. One ought to consider not only other classes, but also, perhaps, a semi-autonomous role for the state. And "ethnic" relations between imperialist powers (as in Figure 2A), let alone between colonized peoples, have been omitted. A total analysis would include all of these. Still, even this very simplified version enables us to begin to chart the relationships and demonstrates some of the complexities of the problem.

Before we start to examine each of the relationships, it is important to point out that I am using the term "colonized" loosely here to refer to any form of external domination by a capitalist power. It may range from a minimum of unequal trade relations, through foreign investment, to total political domination.[17] In addition, the geographical position of both nationalities may vary: they may each remain primarily in their homelands, or members of the imperialist nation may move into the territory of the colonized nation, or members of the colonized nation may move to the territory of the imperialist power (as in labor immigration or importation). While geographic location obviously affects the nature of the relations between national groups, there is, nevertheless, a fundamental similarity (or parallel) between these situations.

---

[16] A sample of this literature includes Amin, 1976; Bettelheim, 1970; Burawoy, 1976; Castells, 1975; Geschwender, 1978; Hechter, 1975; Petras, 1980; Portes, 1978; and many others. For an effort to develop a theoretical statement integrating some of this literature, see Bonacich and Hirata, 1979.

[17] The use of the term "colonized" should not be taken as an endorsement of all the assumptions of the "internal colonialism" model.

Figure 3. Class and Ethnic Relations Resulting from Imperialism.

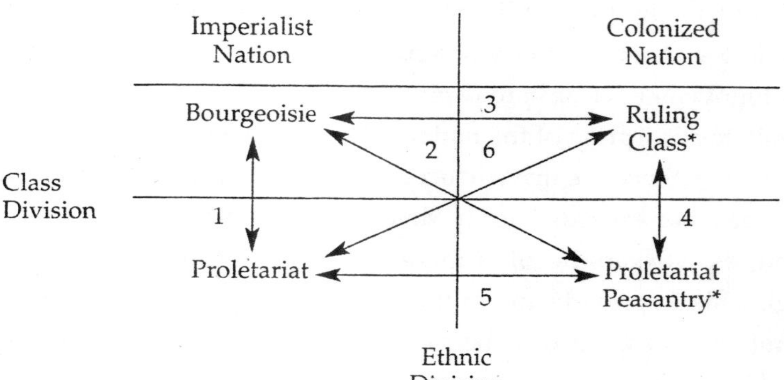


* The Classes here are left somewhat ambiguous to indicate the possibility that full-blown capitalism has not yet emerged.

A final preliminary caution: The following attempt has numerous problems. For one thing, it is very general and abstract, glossing over differences in historical period let alone location. For another, it suffers from the ignorance, both theoretical and factual, of its author. My goal is mainly to *suggest* a way of tying these things together, and to stress that all the class relations generated by imperialism, in all its forms, need to be considered as a system if we are fully to understand the emergence of "nationalist" movements.

1. *Class Relations Within Imperialist Nations*

Our analysis begins with class relations within imperialist nations. Needless to say, this encompasses the entire history of class struggle in the developed capitalist countries, a topic much too vast to cover here. I would like to examine one aspect of this topic, namely, the role of the "national" class struggle in the emergence of imperialism. While there is considerable debate over the roots of imperialism, it seems to me that one important push towards overseas expansion by capital comes from problems with its "national" working class. Put another way, as capitalism develops, the price of labor-power tends to rise, leading capital to seek cheaper labor-power (or commodities based upon cheaper labor-power) abroad.

The price of labor-power rises with the advance of capitalism for at least four reasons. First, increasing numbers of people are drawn from pre-capitalist modes of production into the proletariat until the potential national labor force is completely absorbed. We can see this process in the decline of independent farming and the rise of large cities, in the movement from self-employment to the predominance of wage and salary earners, and most recently, in the movement of women into the labor force. All of these shifts represent movements from pre-capitalist to capitalist relations of production. The complete absorption of the national labor force leads to a rise in the price of labor-power. Since the drive to accumulate capital continues unabated, the demand for labor exceeds supply, driving up the price.

Second, as workers become increasingly proletarianized, they are decreasingly able to provide any of the means of subsistence for themselves or their families. These need to be purchased from wages, which have to be increased in order to cover these new necessary expenses. In contrast, during transitional periods, when capitalism co-existed with pre-capitalist forms, part of the means of subsistence was provided by those forms. Women working in the home, processing food, making clothing, providing "free" childcare, and so on, meant that wages did not have to cover these items. But once the entire nation enters the proletariat, all goods and services become commodities, and they must be purchased with earnings.

A third factor in the rising cost of labor-power is that the social conditions of production become increasingly conducive to political organization among workers. In particular, large factories enable workers to compare their grievances and form organizations to protect their mutual interests. And their increasing divorce from their own means of subsistence, or any independent ownership of productive property, strengthens the motivation to organize. Thus, as capitalism advances, labor unionism develops and contributes to the rise in the price of labor-power.

Fourth, as capitalism develops, the rising demands of workers are likely to receive some state support. For example, under pressure from organized labor many advanced capitalist countries set minimum wages, regulate work conditions, provide old age pensions, and protect the rights of labor unions to provide independent representation for workers. In other words, the state helps to set national labor standards. In so doing, it provides a prop to the price of labor-power, helping both to maintain and raise it.

One important aspect of state intervention is protection against the use of the "army of the unemployed" to lower the price of labor-power in core industries. If left to their own devices, individual capitalists would respond to the rising cost of labor-power by introducing labor-saving machinery, throwing some people out of work, thereby putting competitive pressure on wages. Through "welfare" and unemployment insurance, the state cushions workers from the last aspect of this process, so that high levels of unemployment can, in fact, coexist with rising wages.

It is very important to recognize that a rise in the price of labor-power does not necessarily mean that workers are better off. The price goes up in part because the cost of living rises as people are increasingly dependent upon commodities. Many of these commodities are necessities (e.g., a car in Los Angeles), and in some cases their quality may be lower than when they were produced by unpaid family labor (e.g., homemade bread versus Wonder Bread). The rising price of labor-power may actually be associated with a decline in the quality of life.

Regardless of its impact on workers, the rising price of labor-power puts a squeeze on profits.[18] While there are various responses to this problem, including investment in labor-saving technology, one important response is to turn to new sources of labor-power. Having exhausted the national reserve army of the unemployed inaccessible because of welfare, capital looks overseas, especially to countries where capitalism is less fully developed, for "fresh troops." Essentially the process is one of continuing to absorb pre-capitalist modes of production and transformng their personnel into wage workers, except that now the process spills across national borders.

### 2. *Relations between Imperialist Capital and Colonized Workers*

Imperialist domination and exploitation of colonized workers is the fundamental root of "racism." Out of this exploitation grow efforts by imperialist capital to mobilize its "national" proletariat in support of colonial domination, utilizing racist, or nationalist, ideology. Also growing out of it are important divisions in the world's working class which lead to "nationalist" reactions on both sides.

As we have seen, capital tends to move overseas in search of cheaper labor-power. Labor is cheaper there for two reasons: first, the lower level of development decreases the price of labor-power; and second, imperialism itself distorts development, contributing to the perpetuation of a low price for labor-power beyond what might be expected under conditions of non-domination. Let us deal briefly with each of these in turn.

---

[18] An example of the "profit squeeze" argument is found in the work of Glyn and Sutcliffe (Glyn and Sutcliffe, 1971, 1972).

Early stages of development are associated with a lower price of labor-power. Essentially the reason lies in the participation in pre-capitalist modes of production. In pre-capitalist modes, people mainly work for their own subsistence. When confronted with capitalist employers, they are likely, at first, to work for capital only on a supplementary basis. Most of their subsistence is provided by pre-capitalist forms. As a result, the capitalist employer need not pay the worker his or her complete subsistence, but only that part of it which is necessary to sustain the worker at that moment. In other words, the subsistence of his family, including health care, education, and housing, can be left out of the wage calculation. This enables employers in transitional economies to "earn" extraordinary rates of surplus value and at the same time to undersell competitors who use fully proletarianized work-forces.

Other features of attachment to pre-capitalist modes of production also contribute to "cheap labor." For one thing, "new" workers are unfamiliar with trade unions. For another, because they are less dependent on the wage-earning job, they have less incentive to form or join organizations to further their long-term collective interests as workers. Stable labor organizing goes hand-in-hand with permanent proletarianization. In general, the more completely dependent upon wage labor, the more developed will be the labor organizations of a group of workers.

Another factor which lowers the price of labor-power in less developed societies is a lower standard of living. Such items as housing, furniture, even diet, and certainly gadgetry of all kinds, vary from society to society, but tend to be more "substantial" in advanced capitalist societies. This may partly reflect real differences in necessities (e.g., an urban worker must have a means of transportation to get to work, must have a radio to find out certain kinds of information, must have can-opener because much of his food comes in cans, etc.) but also seems to reflect different experiences and expectations, or what Marx terms an historical and moral element (Emmanuel, 1972). Housing standards are a case in point. In one society, straw huts or shacks are perfectly acceptable. In another they are not even permitted.

Undoubtedly, these differences reflect the different levels of productivity of the two types of economy. Advanced capitalism spews forth an endless stream of commodities which come to be defined as necessities (in part through capitalist efforts). In poor, undeveloped societies, these necessities are luxuries which people have lived without for time immemorial. Imperialists can capitalize on these low expectations by lowering wages accordingly.

Imperialist capital introduces a special coercive element into the relations with colonized labor. Colonial and neo-colonial labor systems take on a variety of forms, e.g., the retention of peasant agriculture and crafts, but with increasing exaction of surplus from these workers; the retention of peasant agriculture associated with the migration of labor between the subsistence sector and capitalist enterprises; and the creation of plantation-type enterprises which employ semi- or fully-coerced labor full time. They all share however, a coercive element which cannot be imposed upon the working class of the advanced capitalist nation.[19]

Imperialist-type exploitation can also arise with immigrant workers. If the immigrants are still attached to pre-capitalist modes of production in the homeland, some of the factors which cheapen labor-power there apply to them as well. More importantly, just as imperialist capital can utilize special coercion in its relations with labor in the colonies, so can it towards immigrant workers. Special legal constraints, justified by "national" differences, can be set up for immigrants, such as the denial of citizenship rights. The legal disabilities of immigrants permit capital to act in an unrestrained manner towards this special class of workers. As Castells states: "The utility of immigrant labour to capital derives primarily from the fact that it can act towards it as though the labour movement did not exist, thereby moving the class struggle back several decades."[20] The same could be said for all types of colonized labor.

In sum, imperialist capital is willing and eager to make use of all potential sources of labor-power. Capitalism is a system that seeks to proletarianize the world. Pre-capitalist remnants in colonized territories, combined with the ability of imperialist capital to introduce coercive elements into labor relations, serve to retard the ability of colonized workers to fully participate in, or develop, a labor movement. Thus capital can "exploit" these workers (in

[19] In some cases, the employees of foreign firms are among the most highly paid workers in a poor nation. They may be more fully proletarianized than other workers, and more likely to form unions. Foreign capital pays higher wages as a means of undercutting local manufactures. Still, despite higher wages relative to other workers in the same country, they are paid considerably less than workers in the imperialist country.

[20] Castells, 1972, p. 52. Some of the differences in experience between Eastern European and non-European immigrants in the United States may be accounted for by this. Eastern Europe was less thoroughly dominated by the advanced capitalist societies of Western Europe. Thus the immigrants came under a less coerced status and were more readily able to join the local labor movement.

the sense of extracting surplus from them, even if not always directly via the wage relationship) more thoroughly than it can exploit its own workers.

3. *Relations between Imperials Capital and Colonized Ruling Classes*

Imperialism has important consequences not only for the workers in colonized societies, but also for their ruling classes, including the incipient bourgeoisie. The relationship between these two classes can take two major forms: on the one hand, imperialist capital can retard and undermine the development of a colonized ruling class. On the other hand, it can utilize this class to help them dominate colonized workers more effectively.

Imperialist undermining of colonial ruling classes can take many forms, Perhaps the simplest is the exaction of tribute, or simple stripping of some of the wealth from the invaded area. This may be achieved by taxation, for instance. At another level, the imperialist power can impose unequal treaties, forcing colonies or neo-colonies to accept trade from the more advanced economy, thereby having their crafts and infant industries undermined by cheap imports. At still a "higher" level, when foreign capital is invested in colonial societies, their ruling classes lose control over the direction of development. Profits and interest are drained out of the territory, while technologies are monopolized by foreign capital. Since power is unevenly distributed, benefit and wealth tend to accrue to the imperialist bourgeoisie, often at the expense of the colonized bourgeoisie. This unequal relationship may also arise with ethnic minorities within the imperialist nation so that their petite bourgeoisie is kept in a "dependent" position.

The other face of this relationship concerns the utilization of colonial leaders as "middlemen" to help imperialist capital penetrate the territory more effectively. Again, this occurs at many levels, from using the local rulers to collect taxes, to having them conduct the trade in imperialist commodities and in the goods produced colonized workers. Perhaps the most important level is their role in helping to control colonized labor, the topic of our next section.

In sum, relationship 3 can be either competitive or cooperative. When the latter predominates, members of the colonial ruling class can become very wealthy, and develop a vested interest in the continuation of imperialism. Under such circumstances, there is little incentive to be "nationalist." When the relationship is competitive, however, nationalism is a likely response in the form of calling for the removal of "foreign domination." Both of these aspects may, of course, be present in the same territory, producing conflict within this class.

4. *Relationship between Colonial Ruling Classes and Workers*

The colonial ruling class can be used to make the "cheap labor" of colonial territories even cheaper, by the suppression and coercion of the workers. This suppression can take place at a variety of levels, from the individual entrepreneur or landholder, to the state, where oppressive "national" regimes can keep labor subdued for the benefit of foreign capital. The number of right-wing dictatorships propped up by foreign capital (aided by their states), which actively crush any movement that would improve the position of labor need scarcely be mentioned. These intermediary classes often play a critical role in keeping the relations of production partially pre-capitalist.

"Nationalism" may be an important ideological tool in this effort. In particular neo-colonial rulers may sometimes be able to persuade their workers to temper their demands, in the short run, in order to help the "nation" develop, and enable their exports to be competitive on the world market. While this effort may serve the interests of imperialist capital in its search for cheap labor, it also benefits colonial rulers and their bourgeoisies.

Ethnic minorities within capitalist societies may reveal both of these forms. The ethnic petite bourgeoisie can play a pivotal role in suppressing workers. Examples include labor contractors, padrones, and sweat shop owners. These people are able to take advantage of the vulnerable position of minority workers, while at the same time acting as intermediaries on behalf of big capital. They, too, can call upon "ethnic loyalty" as a technique of control. A garment sweatshop owner can appeal to his or her workers that it is in the "community interest" that the shop remain open, and provide jobs to community members. But this is conditional on their limiting their demands as workers, since the shop will only remain competitive if it can undersell others. Thus, ethnic solidarity can be used to retard the development of class consciousness as workers. Ultimately, this redounds to the benefit of big capital.

Since segments of the colonized ruling class are undermined by imperialist relations, another form of nationalism can emerge in this relationship, namely, an anti-imperialist alliance which calls for "national liberation." Although primordial symbolism may be invoked to bring the colonized ruling classes together with workers and peasants, the coalition is still essentially the product of "class" forces: the exploitation of colonized labor, and the unequal competition between imperialist and colonial bourgeoisies.

In sum, two quite different nationalisms can emerge in this relationship. In one case, nationalism is used as a tool of exploitation; in the other, as a tool of liberation. The difference between these two may not always be easy to disentangle.

5. *Relations within the Working Class*

National divisions in the working class arise, in part, out of the material differences in the situations of different national segments. The working class of the imperialist nation has been able to organize and wrest some concessions from capital. Colonized labor (including migrant labor), in contrast, is under a double layer of oppression, both from the imperialist bourgeoisie and from middlemen. They are frequently still tied to pre-capitalist economic forms, limiting their ability to participate fully in a working-class movement. And they can be placed under special legal statuses (such as "illegal aliens") which are much more coercive than the situation with which the rest of the proletariat has to deal.

Since colonized workers are especially exploitable by capital, they pose a threat to the proletariat of the imperialist nation, who fear that their hard-won labor standards will be undermined. Immigrant labor, or the runaway shop to cheap-labor countries or regions, is used by capital in the form both of threat and reality to constrain its national working class. The local working class can respond to this threat either by trying to limit capital's access to cheap labor (protectionism), or by fighting to raise the labor standards of cheap labor (inclusionism). The first of these is a "nationalist" response, the second, "internationalist."

Both nationalist and internationalist responses are found among the workers of advanced capitalist countries. The issue is usually a point of struggle within the working-class movement. Factors that affect which choice is made include: the extent to which capital controls colonized labor (making it difficult to coordinate transnational efforts), the immediacy of the competitive threat, the completeness of proletarianization of workers in the imperialist nation (or the degree to which there are petit-bourgeois remnants),[21] and so on.

[21] This theme is developed, with respect to the United States, and its long tradition of an "independent household mode of production" associated with the availability of land and concomitant ability to withstand complete proletarianization, in Bonacich,

Undoubtedly a very important factor is the ability of capital to manipulate "nationalist" sentiment by weeding out internationalist-oriented leaders from the working class movement.

Four quite different kinds of nationalism serve to divide the working class. First is imperialist capital's efforts to whip up nationalist sentiment among the workers to get them to support the oppression of the colonized. Second is the proletariat's own protectionist reactions (reinforced by segments of capital), which invoke nationalism (e.g., Buy American). Third is the nationalism generated by the colonial ruling class in an effort to keep colonized labor cheap for the benefit of international capital. And fourth is the nationalism promoted by colonized workers to overthrow the double and triple layers of oppression they face.

Neither set of workers has to respond in a nationalist manner, and segments of both frequently do not. But once nationalism is the dominant response, it tends to be mutually reinforcing such that each segment of the working class continues to distrust the other.

6. *Relations between the Proletariat of Imperialist Nations and the Colonized Ruling Class*

These two classes are often in a struggle for the affiliation of colonized workers, hence their relationship is typically conflictual. Colonized workers are either asked to join the working class movement and become aware of their class antagonism with their ruling class (or middlemen), or they are asked to cooperate with the ruling class, which uses a nationalist pitch, to develop the "nation" (or ethnic community), and set aside class antagonisms.

To the extent that the colonized ruling class exercises control over "its" workers, they will be inaccessible to the proletariat of the advanced capitalist nation. Labor contractors, or sweat shop owners, for example, may be able to use a combination of coercion, paternalism, and desperation on the part of the workers, to keep them in the "nationalist" fold. If accomplished, another wedge is driven between the segments of the working class, and the dominant nation's proletariat continues to be threatened with displacement and undermining.

---

1980. There I argue that this class, which oriented itself towards a pre-capitalist "golden age," contributed importantly to the generation of a powerful racist ideology. Since it often formed coalitions with the proletariat against the "monopolists," the working-class movement sometimes developed a racist cast.

This kind of conflict can occur both within states and between them. For instance, at the international level, the existence of a right-wing, dictatorial, "nationalist" regime which severely suppresses its workers, may preclude any efforts on the part of advanced capitalist workers to attempt to help raise labor standards in that country. The discrepancy in labor standards can be used by the ruling class to attract international capital, and as a basis for cheap exports. Within a single state, the leadership of a minority community may exercise a similar labor-control function, though on a much reduced scale, with the same effect of keeping labor standards low within the minority community, in part for the benefit of big capital.

Since both the ruling class and workers of colonized nations appear to conspire in maintaining the low level of labor standards, the advanced capitalist nation's proletariat is likely to have nationalist reactions. It sees all segments of the colonized nations as threatening its position, and may make crude generalizations about the nature of "those people." On the other side, protectionist reactions by labor in the imperialist nation may interfere with the plans of the colonized ruling class to penetrate international markets and may jeopardize the jobs of Third World workers in the affected industries.

In sum, there can be a major struggle between the workers of imperialist nations and colonial ruling classes over the affiliation of colonized workers to determine whether these workers will choose a nationalist or internationalist strategy emphasizing class or nationalist solidarity. Of course, such a struggle is only likely when the proletariat of the imperialist nation is not staunchly protectionist.

We have now briefly considered all six relationships represented in Figure 3. All interact with one another, creating "higher" levels of relationship. For example, if relationship 5 between the imperialistic proletariat and the colonized proletariat, becomes conflictual or nationalistic, imperialist capital can utilize the division to mute the class struggle of its national proletariat (relationship 1). This may lead workers in the imperialist nation to temper their demands and seek narrow concessions instead of revolutionary change. Thus nationalist divisions may be an important factor in the preservation of capitalism.[22] There are other such reverberations through the system: national-

[22] One may ask if nationalist movements are ever progressive. With important exceptions, I believe they are not. They always divide the working class movement. But sometimes they are necessary anyway, especially on the part of colonized workers who may have no other means to overthrow the double oppression that can stem

ism is one level tends to provoke counter-nationalism at other levels, while cross-national class alliances probably support one another.

Another point of elaboration, as suggested earlier, would be the addition of other classes and other ethnic groups. For instance, the imperialist nation's class structure includes important intermediary classes, such as managers and small business owners, which may foster nationalist reactions and make it more difficult for workers to support internationalist positions. Or, in the colonized nation, a special ethnic group may play the role of middleman, diluting the class struggle by turning it into an anti-ethnic (nationalist) movement against the middlemen.

In some cases, key classes may be absent, also with ramifications for nationalism. Thus, the fact that countries like Brazil and Mexico draw a less harsh "race line" than the United States and South Africa (both of which developed clear descent rules to protect the category "white") may in part be due to the absence of a large white working class in the former. There was, in other words, no sizable class to develop protectionist reactions against the absorption of colonized workers. Or in the absence of a large middleman element among immigrant workers may make cross-ethnic worker alliances easier to establish, thus blurring the lines of national difference.

Needless to say, there are numerous issues this model has not addressed, such as the effects of technological change, labor productivity, geography, natural resources and population density.[23] To understand the rise of nationalism, or its absence, in each particular case, such factors would have to be taken into consideration.

Despite its incompleteness, the model enables us to make four important points. First, nationalist movements are generated by each class, for different reasons, and with different content. Second, non-nationalist options are available to each class, and are often acted upon. The call upon "primordial attachments" frequently fails, indicating beyond doubt its lack of universality or inevitability. Third, the emergence of nationalist versus non-nationalist reactions depends upon the structure of the entire system of relationships. It is not simply an orientation that one group chooses to adopt in isolation. The

---

from imperialist capital's super-exploitation, combined with protectionist reactions by workers of the imperialist nation. Under such conditions, self-determination may be the only route to liberation. When this is the case, nationalism is progressive.

[23] An attempt is made to deal with some of these issues in Bonacich and Hirata, 1979, and Bonacich, 1980.

emergence of nationalism is contingent upon where a group fits within the entire world capitalist system, and how others react to it. And fourth, despite the fact that nationalism calls upon "primordial" bonds of affiliation, it both grows out of the class relations generated by the development of capitalism and imperialism, and represents efforts to create alliances across class lines, or, alternatively, to prevent alliances from developing within major classes across national lines. In other words, nationalist movements are, at root, the product of class forces.

Zillah Eisenstein

# Reflections on "Constructing a Theory of Capitalist Patriarchy and Socialist Feminism"

The following article, written over a quarter-century ago, remains at the core of my thinking *and* has also been revised and revisited over and over again. My understanding of capitalist patriarchy has evolved in and through the historical transformations that demand a progressive socialist feminist response. My more recent writings – *The Color of Gender* (University of California Press, 1994), *Hatreds, Racialized and Sexualized Conflicts in the 21st Century* (Routledge, 1996) *Global Obscenities* (New York University Press, 1998), and *Manmade Breast Cancers* (Cornell University Press, 2001) refocus capitalist patriarchy to its racialized and global formulations.

I look back at this early discussion and see the important beginnings of the theorization of sex/gender with its racial component. I look forward and see these ideas taking on new shape and new/old history. I now more fully recognize the intimate relationship between the racializing of gender and the engendering of race in the processes of exploitation and oppression. As a result the very notion of socialist feminism becomes opened and more inclusive giving explicit recognition to these complexities.

Zillah Eisenstein

# Constructing a Theory of Capitalist Patriarchy and Socialist Feminism

## I. Introduction

Radical feminists and male leftists, in confusing socialist women and socialist feminists, fail to recognize the political distinction between being a woman and being a feminist. But the difference between socialist women and socialist feminists needs to be articulated if the ties between radical feminism and socialist feminists are to be understood. The commitment of this paper is to make these important distinctions by articulating the growing efforts of socialist feminists to understand the mutual dependence of patriarchy and capitalism, an effort they are alone in making.

Although there are socialist women who are committed to understanding and changing the system of capitalism, socialist feminists are committed to understanding the system of power deriving from capitalist patriarchy. I choose this phrase, capitalist patriarchy, to emphasize the existing mutual dependence, of the capitalist class structure and male supremacy. Understanding this "interdependence" of patriarchy and capitalism is essential to the political analysis of socialist feminism. It becomes necessary to understand that patriarchy (as male supremacy)

The original version of this article appeared in *The Insurgent Sociologist* 7:3 (Summer, 1977), pp. 3-17.

existed before capitalism and continues in post-capitalist societies. And yet to say that, within the present system of power, either patriarchy or capitalism causes the other is to fail to understand their present mutually reinforcing system and dialectical relationship, a relationship which must be understood if the structure of oppression is to be changed. Socialist feminism in this sense moves beyond singular Marxist analysis and isolated radical feminist theory. The capitalist class structure and the hierarchical sexual structuring of society are the problem.

Power is dealt with in a dichotomous way by socialist women and radical feminists. In these analyses, they see power as deriving from either one's sex or one's economic class position. The critique of power as it is rooted in the male/female distinction focuses most often on patriarchy. The critique of power as it is rooted in the bourgeoisie/proletariat distinction focuses on capitalism. One studies *either* the social relations of production *or* the social relations of reproduction,[1] domestic *or* wage labor, the private *or* public realms, the family *or* the economy, ideology *or* material conditions, the sexual division of labor *or* capitalist class relations, as oppressive. Even though almost all women are implicated in both sides of these activities, "woman" is dealt with as though she were not. Such a conceptual picture of woman hampers one's understanding of the complexity of her oppression. Dichotomy wins out over reality. I will attempt here to replace this dichotomous thinking with a dialectical approach.[2]

The synthesis of radical feminism and Marxist analysis is a necessary first step in formulating a cohesive feminist political theory. This new formulation, Socialist Feminism, is not a mere adding together of these two theories

---

[1] Sheila Rowbotham, in *Women, Resistance and Revolution* (New York: Pantheon, 1972), makes clear that the social relations of production as well as reproduction need to be dealt with in any revolutionary theory.

[2] For our purposes here, dialectics helps us focus on the *processes* of power. Hence, in order to understand power, one needs to analyze the *relations* which define power father than treating it as a thing abstracted from the real conditions of society. Any "moment" embodies the relations of power which define it. The only way to understand what the "moment" is, is to understand it as a reflection of the processes involved in it. By definition, this requires one to see "moments" as part of other "moments" rather than as cut off from each other. Seeing things in separation from each other, as part of either/or options, reflects the dichotomous thinking of positivism. By trying to anderstand the elements defining the synthesis of power embodied in any moment, one is forced to come to terms with the conflict embodied within it, and hence the dialectical processes of power. See Karl Marx, *Grundrisse*, ed. by Martin Nicolaus (New York: Vintage, 1973), and Bertell Ollman, *Alienation: Marx's Conception of Man in Capitalist Society* (New York: Oxford University Press, 1971).

of power. It is rather a real mix of the interrelationships between capitalism and patriarchy as expressed through the sexual division of labor. To define capitalist patriarchy as the source of the problem is at the same time to suggest that socialist feminism is the answer. My discussion uses Marxist class analysis as the thesis, radical feminist patriarchal analysis as the antithesis, and from the two evolves the synthesis of socialist feminism. I will argue that the recognition of class analysis, patriarchal theory, and the dialectical method are supremely important in constructing socialist feminist theory.

## II. Thesis: Woman as Class

### a) *Marx: Revolutionary Ontology and Women's Liberation*

The importance of Marxist analysis to the study of women's oppression is two-fold. First, it provides a necessary class analysis for the study of power. Second, it provides a method of analysis which is historical and dialectical. Although the dialectic (as method) is most often connected to the study of class and class conflict, it can also be used to articulate the patriarchal relations of women's existence and hence their revolutionary potential.

One can use the dialectic to clarify this potential because Marxist analysis provides the tools for understanding all power relations, and there is nothing about the dialectical and historical method which limits it only to understanding class relations. What I do here is utilize Marx's analysis (class conflict), but also extract his method and apply it to dimensions of power relations to which he was not sensitive. In this sense I am using Marx's method to expand our present understanding of material relations in capitalism to include material relations in capitalist patriarchy.

These relations are illuminated by Marx's theories of exploitation and alienation. I am particularly interested here in the method of analysis rather than in the content of Marx's discussion of alienation. By not reducing the analysis to class and class conflict, we can extend the dialectical method present in the theory of alienation to the particular revolutionary potential of women. This means that although the theory of alienation is inclusive of exploitation it should not be reduced to it.[3]

[3] I do not think the Althusserian dichotomized view of the "early Hegelian Marx" and the later "materialist Marx" is a helpful distinction. Rather, I think the theories of alienation and exploitation are integrated throughout Marx's work although they

What is crucial for the application of Marx to the "woman question" is a way of thinking, which does not limit people's capacities to what society may force them to be. In his theory of alienation, expressed through his conception of "species being," Marx poses a revolutionary method of analysis. "Species beings" are those beings who ultimately reach their human potential for creative labor, social consciousness, and social living, through the struggle against capitalist society, and who fully internalize these capacities in communist society. This basic ontological structure defines one's existence alongside one's essence. Reality for Marx is thus more than mere existence. It embodies within it a movement toward human essence. This is not a totally abstract human essence, but rather an essence we can understand in historical contexts. "Species being" is the conception of what is possible for people in the unalienated society and which exists only as essence in capitalist society.

When extended to women, this revolutionary ontology suggests that the possibility of their freedom exists alongside their exploitation and oppression. This conflict between existence and essence lays the basis for revolutionary consciousness and activity. It allows an internally critical appraisal of any particular moment. Women's existence and essence have not merged in this society. But what she is today does not *determine* the outer limits of her capacities or potentialities. This analysis is the same for the alienated worker. While the worker is cut off from his/her creative abilities, s/he is still a creative being in terms of potential.

This contradiction of existence and essence lies both, therefore, at the base of the revolutionary proletariat, and the revolutionary woman. One's class position defines consciousness for Marx, but, if we utilize the revolutionary ontological method, it need not be limited to this. If we wish to say that women are defined in terms of their sex as well, patriarchal relations define their consciousness and have implications for their revolutionary potential as a result. The method – of posing revolutionary potential as it reflects conflicts between people's real conditions (existence) and their possibilities (essence) – can be extended to understand the patriarchal relations inhibiting the development of human essence. The reality of social relations involves both capitalist class *and* patriarchal relations. In this sense, the conception of

---

are given different priority in specific writings. The *Grundrisse* stands as persuasive proof of this position. See Marx, *Grundrisse, op. cit.*, and David McLellan's discussion of the importance of the *Grundrisse* in his *Karl Marx: His Life and Thought* (New York, Harper & Row, 1973).

species life points to the revolutionary potential of men and women for Marx.

However, the social relations defining the potential for woman's revolutionary consciousness are more complex than Marx understood them to be. A more complex set of relations made species life unavailable to women, and that hence its actualization could not come through dismantling the class system alone. As a result, Marx's statements on women are limited in depth, since he never questioned patriarchy as the hierarchical sexual ordering of society. But his writings on women are important because of his commitment to uncover the tensions between species life and capitalist alienated forms of social experience for all human beings.

b) *Women's Exploitation in History*

In *The German Ideology*, Marx and Engels discuss the division of labor in early pre-capitalist society in familial terms.

The division of labor "imposed by the family" is spoken of as natural; it is not reflective of the economic society which defines and surrounds it, but rather at this early historical stage it structures the society and its division of labor.

The first division of labor is the "natural" division of labor in the family through the sex act. The activity of procreation develops a division of labor, and it is through this act that the first appearance of property arises within the family. For Marx and Engels, this is when wife and child become the slaves of the husband.

There are here seeds of an early, albeit crude, insight into the sexual division of labor. What weakens and finally limits the insight is that, for Marx and Engels, this division of labor deriving from the sex act is coincidental and *identical* with the birth of private property, i.e., "division of labor and private property are moreover identical expressions. . . ."[4] There is no notion here that inequalities might arise from the sex act itself. The family has no existence outside of the series of property relations. *The German Ideology* presents, then, a skeletal analysis of women's condition as it changes through material conditions. Although reproduction is acknowledged as the first source of the division of labor, it never receives any specific, examination in terms of its relationship to the capitalist division of labor. Reproduction and pro-

---

[4] Marx, *German Ideology, op. cit.*, pp. 21, 22.

duction are seen as one, as they come to be analyzed in relation to the capitalist division of labor in society.

According to Engels in *The Origin of the Family, Private Property and the State,* the social organization of society is determined by production and the family.[5] He repeats here the theme developed in *The German Ideology*: the "first division of labor is that between man and woman for child breeding."[6] And the first social antagonism arises with the antagonism between man and woman in monogamous marriage.[7] This latter point is apparently obvious to Engels. But what this antagonism is based on is never made clear. His claim is that the first class antagonism *accompanies* (arises with) the antagonism between man and woman. Ultimately he speaks of the conflict between man and woman as class conflict; the man is the bourgeoisie within the family, the wife the proletariat.[8] But these (the bourgeoisie and the proletariat) are positions of power deriving from one's relation to the economic means of production, not the sex act of reproduction. The relations of reproduction are subsumed under the relations of production. It appears contradictory that Engels acknowledges male/female relations within the family as defining the

---

[5] Frederick Engels, *The Origin of the Family, Private Property and the State* (New York: International Publishers, 1942). Engels' analysis differentiates three historical periods – savagery, barbarism, and civilization – within which he traces the evolution of the family. The form of marriage coincident with savagery is group marriage. The family here is a group and the only limitation on it is the prohibition of sexual activity between parents and children, and between children. With such an arrangement one can be certain only who the mother is, and hence the line of inheritance is through the mother. This is termed the era of mother right. In the second period of barbarism the pairing marriage develops. The male line becomes more important and the defeat of mother right is imminent. With civilization comes monogamy; marriage and the family are based on private property.

The transition through these stages involved, according to Engels, catastrophic transformation in the lives of women. It saw the "overthrow of mother right which was the world historic defeat of the female sex" Engels, "Early Development," *op. cit.*, p. 75). Woman was relegated to the private household and the breeding of children. Parallel to this was the increase of wealth in society, which "made the man's position in the family more importart than the woman's and on the other hand created an impulse to exploit this strengthened position in order to overthrow in favor of his children, the traditional order of inheritance" Engels, *Origins, op. cit.*, p. 14. For Engels, history has been the retrogression of women's power from mother right in primitive communism to her subordination in the second stage of barbarism. However, for all that Engels explains *how* and *why* the switch from group sex to monogamous sex happens, it could be the structuring element of history as much as the relations of private property are. He really asserts rather than argues his position that private property relations necessitate monogamy.

[6] Engels, "Early Development," *op. cit.*, p. 65.

[7] *Ibid.*, p. 66.

[8] Marx, *Communist Manifesto, op. cit.*

division of labor in society, and yet completely subsumes them under categories of analysis related to production. He offers no explanation that could resolve this dilemma because it stands outside the terms of his analysis.

Thus the categories of analysis explaining the slavery of the woman in the family derive entirely from the relations of production. The family comes to be defined by the historical economic modes, rather than itself taking part in defining the economy as well as society. The flow has been reversed. The family is no longer spoken of as a source of the division of labor coincident with economic relations. Economic existence comes to determine the family.[9] Hence Engels assumes that the family will disintegrate with the elimination of capitalism, instead of analyzing how the family itself comes to support an economic mode.

Most of the time Engels works from his simple equation: oppression equals exploitation. Class existence defines powerlessness for Engels, although he has the core for understanding that woman's oppression is more complex than the system of exploitation. Even though Engels recognized that the family conceals domestic slavery, he believed at the same time that there were no differences (in kind) between domestic slavery and wage-slavery of the husband. They both were derived from capitalism.

> The emancipation of woman will only be possible when woman can take part in production of a large-social scale and domestic work no longer claims anything but an insignificant amount of her time.[10]

The real equality of women will come for Engels with the end of exploitation by capital and the transference of private housework to public industry. Given the lack of understanding of the sexual division of labor, however, even if domestic work were made public, it most probably would remain, for Engels, woman's work.

In conclusion, then, we can see that the analysis sketched by Marx and Engels reveals their belief that the family, at least historically, structured the division of labor in society, and that in some sense this reflects the division of labor in the sex act.

This analysis is lost however through the discussion of the family in capitalist society, where the family comes to be viewed as just another part of

---

[9] See Eli Zaretsky, "Capitalism, the Family and Personal Life," Parts I and II, *Socialist Revolution*, Nos. 13–14 (pp. 69–125) and 15 (pp. 19–70), January–April and May–June, 1973, for a discussion of the historical and economic changes in the family.

[10] Engels, *Origin of the Family, op. cit.*, p. 57.

the superstructure, totally reflective of class society. The relations of reproduction become subsumed under the relations of production. The point to be made is not that the family does not reflect society, but that through both its patriarchal structure and its patriarchal ideology the family, and the need for reproduction, structure society as well. This reciprocal relationship, between family and society, production and reproduction, defines the life of women. The study of women's oppression, then, must deal with both the sexual and economic material conditions if one is to understand oppression rather than merely understand economic exploitation.

While these criticisms are important in assessing the particular contribution of Marx and Engels, they by no means should prompt one to reject either their class analysis, or their ontological and historical method. The point rather is that the historical materialist method must be extended to incorporate women's relations to the sexual division of labor and society as producer and reproducer, as well as to incorporate the ideological[11] formulation of this relationship. Only then will her existence be understood in its true complexity and will species life be available to her too.

## III. Antithesis: Woman as Sex

### a) *Patriarchy and the Radical Feminists*

Although radical feminism is conventionally dated with the recent Women's Liberation Movement, around 1969–70, it has important historical ties to the liberal feminism[12] of Mary Wollstonecraft, Elizabeth Cady Stanton, and Harriet

---

[11] Ideology is used in this paper to refer to the ruling ideas of the society (see Marx, *German Ideology, op. cit.*). In this sense it is seen as a distortion of reality and as protective of existing power arrangements. More specifically, ideology is the ideas which protect both male and capitalist power arrangements. It is important to note here that although material conditions often do create the conditions for certain ideologies, I also see ideology and material conditions in a dialectical relationship. They are both involved in *partially* defining the other. For instance, the "idea" that women are weak and passive is both a distortion of women's capacities, and a partial description of reality – a reality *defined by* the ruling ideology.

[12] The definition of liberal feminism applies to the reformist understanding of the sexual division of labor. It is a theory which reflects a criticism of the limitations of sex roles but doos not comprehend the connection between sex roles and the sexual division of labor and capitalism. Limited by the historical boundaries of the time, early liberal feminists were unable to decipher the capitalist male power structure and instead applauded values which implicated them further within it. They were bound not only by the material conditions of the time (lack of birth control, etc.), but

Taylor Mill, who understood in their own fragmented way that men have power as men in a society organized into "sexual spheres." But while they spoke of power in caste terms, they were only beginning to understand the *structure of power* enforced upon them through the sexual division of labor and society. And the necessary connections between sexual oppression, the sexual division of labor and society, and the economic class structure were not made.

Radical feminism today has a much more sophisticated understanding of sexual power than its feminist forebears, one that has replaced the struggle for the vote and legal reforms with the revolutionary demand for the destruction of patriarchy. It is the biological family, the hierarchical sexual division of society, and sex roles themselves which must be fundamentally reorganized. The sexual division of labor and society expresses the most basic hierarchical division in our society between masculine and feminine roles. It is the basic mechanism of control for patriarchal culture. It designates the fact that roles, purposes, activity, one's labor, are *determined* sexually. It expresses the very notion that the biological distinction, male/female, is used to distinguish social functions and individual power.[13]

In much the same way that radical feminists have found the analysis of Wollstonecraft, Stanton, and Taylor incomplete, they have found the politics and theories of the left insufficient. The existing radical analyses of society failed, in their view, to relate the structure of the economic class system to its origins in the sexual class system. Economic class did not seem to be at the center of their lives. History was perceived as patriarchal, and its struggles have derived as such from sex conflict. The battle lines are drawn between men and women, rather than between bourgeoisie and proletariat. The determining relation is to reproduction, not to production.

Radical feminism offers a criticism of patriarchy through the analysis of sex roles themselves. Patriarchy is defined to mean a sexual system of power in which the male role is superior in possession of power and economic privilege. Patriarchy is the male hierarchical ordering of society. Although the legal institutional base of patriarchy used to be more explicit, the basic relations

---

also by the liberal ideology of the time, which presented segmented, individualistic conceptions of power.

[13] For classical versions of the sexual division of labor see J.S. Mill, *On the Subjection of Women* (New York: Fawcett, 1971), and J.J. Rousseau, *Emile* (London: J.J. Dent & Sons, 1911).

of power have remained intact. The patriarchal system is preserved, via marriage and the family, through the sexual division of labor and society. Sex roles themselves are understood to be units of power and oppression. Woman's position in this power structure is defined as derived, not from the economic class structure, but from the autonomous patriarchal organization of society. As a power structure, patriarchy is rooted in biological reality rather than in an economic or historical one. Manifested through male force and control, the roots of patriarchy are located in women's reproductive selves.

Through this analysis, radical feminists bridge the dichotomy of the personal/public. Sex, as the personal, is the political as well. Women share their position of oppression because of the very politics of the society. And this is a sexual politics which gives privileges to men and oppresses women. The structuring of society through the sexual division limits the realm of activity, work, desires, and aspirations of women. "Sex is a status category with political implications."[14]

## IV. Synthesis: Socialist Feminism

### a) *Exploitation and Oppression*

Marxist analysis seeks an historical explanation of existing power relationships in terms of economic class relations, and radical feminism deals with the biological reality of power. Socialist feminism, on the other hand, analyzes power in terms of its class origins as well as its patriarchal roots. In such an analysis, capitalism and patriarchy are not simply autonomous systems but neither are they one and the same thing. They are mutually dependent.

As a socialist feminist, my argument here is that oppression and exploitation are not equivalent concepts as they were for Marx and Engels. Exploitation speaks to the economic reality of capitalist class relations whereas oppression refers to power as it is defined within patriarchal and capitalist relations. Exploitation is a descriptive assessment of men and women workers in the labor force in capitalist society; women's oppression reflects her exploitation if she is a wage-laborer within capitalism but at the same time reflects the relations which define her existence in the patriarchal sexual hierarchy which

[14] Kate Millett, *Sexual Politics* (New York: Doubleday, 1970), p. 24.

defines her as mother, domestic laborer, consumer. Power, or the converse – oppression – derives from both sex and class, and this is manifested through both the material and ideological dimensions of patriarchy and capitalism. Oppression is inclusive of exploitation but reflects a more complex reality. It reflects the hierarchical relations of the sexual division of labor and society.

This system of oppression, which connotes the *mutual dependence* of capitalism and patriarchy as they are presently practiced, is what I have chosen to call capitalist patriarchy. It is the contemporary expression of the relationship between these two systems, although the historical development of capitalist patriarchy can be dated from the mid-18th century in England and the mid-19th century in America. Both of these periods reflect the developing relationship between patriarchy and the new industrial capitalism. Capitalist patriarchy, by definition, breaks through the dichotomies of class and sex, private and public, domestic and wage labor, family and economy, personal and political, ideology and material conditions.

Marx and Engels saw man's oppression existing in his exploited position as worker in capitalist society. They assumed that woman's existence was parallel to this. They equated the two when suggesting that domestic slavery was the same, in nature and essence, as wage-slavery.

Today, especially with the insights of radical feminism, we see not only that the equation of exploitation and oppression is problematic, but also that, if one uses Marx's own categories of productive labor as wage labor, domestic slaves are not "exploited" in the same way as wage-slaves. They would have to be paid a wage for this to be true. Women as domestic laborers have no direct relation to wages even if the basic stealing of one's labor (though this takes different forms) is parallel between the two.

The reduction of oppression to exploitation within Marxist analysis rests upon the equation between the economic class structure and the structure of power in society. I, however, differ with this assessment in that I believe that women's oppression is rooted in more than her class position (her exploitation), and that one must address as well her position within patriarchy – both structurally and ideologically – to fully understand woman's oppression. It is the particular relation and operation of the hierarchical sexual ordering of society within the class structure, or the understanding of the class structure within the sexual ordering of society, which focuses upon human activity in capitalist patriarchy. They exist together and cannot be understood when falsely isolated. It is important to note here that in dealing with these questions, one breaks down the division between material existence (economic or sexual) and ideology. This is because the sexual division of labor and society, which lays the basis for patriarchy as we know it, has both material form (sex roles themselves) and ideological reality (the stereotypes, myths, and ideas which define these roles). They exist in an internal web.

If women's existence is defined by capitalism and patriarchy through their ruling ideologies and institutions, then an understanding of capitalism alone (or patriarchy in isolation) will not deal with the problem of women's oppression. As Juliet Mitchell has written, "the overthrow of the capitalist economy and the political challenge that effects this do not in themselves mean a transformation of patriarchal ideology."[15] The overthrow does not necessitate the destruction of patriarchal institutions, either. Although practiced differently in each place, the sexual division of labor exists in the Soviet Union, in Cuba, in China. As we can see, patriarchy is cross-cultural by definition though it is actualized differently in different societies via the institutionalizing of sexual hierarchy. The contours of sex roles may differ societally but power has and does reside with the male.

Today patriarchy,[16] the power of the male through these sexual roles in capitalism, is institutionalized in the nuclear family. Juliet Mitchell ties this to the "law of the prehistoric murdered father."[17] In finding the certain root of patriarchy in this mythic crime among men at the dawn of our life as a social group, Mitchell risks discussing patriarchy more in terms of the ideology patriarchy produces, rather than in terms of its connection to its material for-

---

[15] Juliet Mitchell, *Psychoanalysis and Feminism* (New York: Pantheon, 1974), p. 414. Within the women's movement today there is a varied dialogue in progress on the dimensions and meaning of Socialist Feminism. In some sense, the appropriate questions are still being formulated. Juliet Mitchell spoke to this issue in *Woman's Estate* (New York: Pantheon, 1971) when she said, "we should ask the feminist questions, but try to come up with some Marxist answers" (p. 99), in *Psychoanalysis and Feminism, op. cit.*, she still is trying to define the "important" questions. "It seems to me that 'why did it happen' and 'historically when?' are both false questions. The questions that should, I think, be asked in place of these are: how does it happen and when does it take place in our society?" (pp. 364–365). In other words, we can start by asking how does it happen now?

[16] Sheila Rowbotham, in *Woman's Consciousness, Man's World* (Baltimore: Penguin, 1973), defines patriarchal authority as "based on control over the woman's productive capacity and over her person" (p. 17). Juliet Mitchell sees patriarchy as defining women as exchange objects based on the exploitation of their role as propagators (*Psychoanalysis and Feminism, op. cit.*, pp. 407–408). Hence, she states, "it is not a question of changing (or ending) who has or how one has babies. It is a question of overthrowing patriarchy" (*ibid.*, p. 416).

[17] See Mitchell, *Psychoanalysis and Feminism, op. cit.*

mulation in the confrontation between man and woman. She roots the Oedipus complex in the universal patriarchal culture. Culture however is defined for her in terms of an exchange system which primarily exists in ideological form today. For Mitchell, patriarchy precedes capitalism through the universal existence of the Oedipus complex.

I contend, however, that patriarchy precedes capitalism through the existence of the sexual ordering of society which derives from ideological and political interpretations of biological difference. In other words, men have chosen to interpret and politically use the fact that women are the reproducers of humanity. And arising from both this fact of reproduction and the political control of it, we have the relations of reproduction arising in a particular formulation of woman's oppression. Although there is a patriarchal culture which is carried over from one historical period to another to protect the sexual hierarchy of society, I question whether the Oedipus complex is the tool by which really to understand this culture. Today the sexual division of society is based on real differences that accrue from years of ideological pressure. Material conditions define necessary ideologies and ideologies in their turn have impact on reality and alter reality. There is a two-way flow here. Women are products of their social history, and yet women can shape their own lives as well.

In socialist feminism, historical materialism is not defined in terms of the relations of production without understanding its connection to the series of relations that arise from woman's sexuality which are tied to the relations of reproduction.[18] And the ideological formulations of these relations are key here. An understanding of feminist materialism must direct us to an understanding of the particular existence of women in capitalist patriarchy. The general approaches of both Marxists, in terms of class, and radical feminists, in terms of sex, obfuscate the reality of power relations in women's lives.

### b) *Pioneers in Feminist Materialism: de Beauvoir and Mitchell*

Simone de Beauvoir confronts the interrelationship between sexuality and history in *The Second Sex*. She states that "the division of the sexes is a biological fact, not an event in human history."[19] And yet she goes on to say

---

[18] See Rowbotham, *Women, Resistance and Revolution, op. cit.*, for the usage of this model of historical materialism in the study of history.

[19] Simone de Beauvoir, *The Second Sex* (New York: Bantam, 1952), p. xix.

"that we must view the facts of biology in the light of an ontological, economic, social, and psychological context."[20] She understood that women were defined by men and as such cast in the role of the "other", but she also realized that the sexual monism of Freud and the economic monism of Engels[21] were inappropriate for the full analysis of women's oppression.

De Beauvoir's initial insights were further developed by Juliet Mitchell in her *Woman's Estate*. In this important book Mitchell[22] offered a rigorous criticism of classical socialist theory, criticizing it for locating woman's oppression too narrowly in the family and in an undifferentiated manner. She rejects the reduction of woman's problem to her incapacity to work,[23] which stresses her simple subordination to the institutions of private property.[24]

What Mitchell does instead is to define four basic structures in which woman's powerlessness is rooted. These "structures" of (a) production, (b) reproduction, (c) sexuality, and (d) socialization of children define the four-dimensional existence of women in capitalist society. To be able to cope with the series of oppressions women experience, Mitchell thinks it first necessary to differentiate among them. Reproduction is the "natural" role in producing children. The biological function of maternity is a universal, atemporal fact[25] which has come to define woman's existence. Woman is socializer in that "woman's biological destiny as mother becomes a cultural vocation in her role as a socializer of children."[26] The causal flow which Mitchell constructs of woman's oppressive existence derives from woman's capacity as reproducer and its connected consequences for her social and economic activity. Woman's biological capacity defines her social and economic purpose. Maternity has set up the family as an historical necessity, and the family has become woman's world. Hence woman is excluded from production and public life, which results in sexual inequality and in woman's resulting powerlessness.

The four structures are meant to be inclusive of women's activity. Produc-

[20] *Ibid.*, p. 33.

[21] *Ibid.*, p. 54.

[22] Juliet Mitchell, "Women: The Longest Revolution," Free Press pamphlet, and *Woman's Estate, op. cit.*

[23] Mitchell, "Women: The Longest Revolution," *op. cit.*, p. 4. It has been pointed out that Mitchell herself did not fully understand women's essential role in society as workers. She termed them a marginal or reserve labor force rather than viewing them as necessary to the economy, both as domestic laborers and as wage laborers.

[24] *Ibid.*, p. 6.

[25] *Ibid.*, p. 10.

[26] *Ibid.*, p. 16.

tion or work is activity which exists both within and outside the family. Reproduction most often takes place within the family structure, whereas the structure of sexuality affects women in all areas of life. The socialization of children which is done by mothers is located within the family, although socialization takes place at all times. Mitchell locates woman's oppression through structures which, though not limited to the family, do not exclude it. Both the family and society in general are implicated in woman's oppression. Thus Mitchell is led to conclude that, by focusing on the destruction of the family, one does not necessarily substantially alter woman's situation. For Mitchell, "socialism would properly mean not the abolition of the family but the diversification of the socially acknowledged relationships which are forcibly and rigidly compressed into it."[27]

Mitchell analyzes the family in capitalism as a supportive pillar to woman's oppressive condition, in terms of its support both of capitalism and of the sexual division of labor and society. According to her, capitalism sees conflict and disruption as very much a part of people's lives. The family provides the affection bonds and a medium of calm for life to be maintained amidst the disruption. The family supports capitalism economically in that it provides a productive labor force at the same time that it supplies the market with an arena for massive consumption.[28] The family also performs an ideological role in that it cultivates the notions of individualism, freedom, and equality basic to the belief structure of society, albeit they are at odds with social and economic reality.[29]

The importance of Mitchell's analysis consists in her picturing of the different dimensions of woman's activity without denying her sexuality or her class oppression. She focuses on the very powerlessness that women experience because they are reproductive beings, sexual beings, working individuals, and socializers of children. She makes it clear that woman's oppression

[27] *Ibid.*, p. 28. It is interesting to note that Juliet Mitchell in *Psychoanalysis and Feminism, op. cit.*, focuses on the relationship *between* families as key to understanding women in patriarchal culture. It is the relationship between families which distinguishes human society from other primate groups (p. 374). "The legally controlled exchange of women is the primary factor that distinguishes mankind from all other primates, from a cultural standpoint" (p. 372). It is hence socially necessary for the kinship structure to have exogamous exchange. The psychology of patriarchy that Mitchell constructs is based on the relations of the kinship structure.

[28] Mitchell, *Woman's Estate, op. cit.*, p. 155.

[29] *Ibid.*, p. 156.

is based in part on the support the family gives the capitalist system in trapping woman in sexual and class oppression via these different structures. In this analysis, power is seen in its more complex reality. We are still left, however, with the basic problem of clarifying the relationship of the family and the political economy in capitalist patriarchal society.

c) *The Sexual Division of Labor and Society in Capitalist Patriarchy: Towards a New Feminist Theory*

One of the critical problems in trying to construct a persuasive argument about the interconnections of patriarchy and capitalism is that the language at hand (the family vs. the economy) treats them as separate systems. In order to avoid this false separation I will discuss how patriarchy and capitalism operate within the sexual division of labor and society, rather than within the family. As the most basic definition of people's activity, purposes, goals, desires, and dreams, according to their biological sex, the sexual division of labor and society is at the structural and ideological base of patriarchy and capitalism. It divides men and women into their respective hierarchical sex roles and structures their related duties in the family domain and within the economy.

This statement of the mutual dependence of patriarchy and capitalism not only assumes the malleability of patriarchy to the needs of capital but assumes the malleability of capital to the needs of patriarchy. In other words, when one states that capitalism needs patriarchy in order to operate efficiently one is really noting the way in which male supremacy, as a system of sexual hierarchy, supplies capitalism (and systems previous to it) with the necessary order and control. As such, this patriarchal system of control is necessary to the smooth functioning of society and of the economic system, and hence should not be undermined. This argument is to underscore the importance of the system of cultural, social, economic, and political control that emanates from the system of male supremacy. To the extent that the concern with profit and the concern with societal control are inextricably connected (but cannot be reduced to each other), patriarchy and capitalism become an *integral process*, with specific elements of their own system necessitated by the other.

Capitalism uses patriarchy . . . and patriarchy is defined by the needs of capital. This statement does not undermine the above claim that, at the same time that one system uses the other, it must organize around the needs of the other in order to protect the specific quality of the other. Otherwise the other system will lose its specific character and with it its unique value. If I were to state this as simply as possible I could say that patriarchy (as male supremacy) provides the sexual hierarchical ordering of society for political control, and as a political system cannot be reduced to its economic structure; while capitalism, as an economic class system driven by the pursuit of profit, feeds off the patriarchal ordering. Together they form the political economy of the society; not merely one or another, but a particular blend of the two.

There are problems with this oversimplified statement. Mainly it severs relations which exist within both spheres. For instance, capitalism has a set of controls which emanate directly from the economic class relations of society and their organization in the work place. Moreover, this example it seems to assume a harmony between the two systems at all points, whereas an uneasy relation between the two systems seems to be appearing as we move further into advanced capitalism. This conflict appears in some sense in the conflicting pulls on women between their employers and their husbands. The role of women in the labor force does seem to undermine some of the control of patriarchal relations, as the double day becomes more obvious. The ghettoization of women in the labor force, however, does maintain a system of hierarchical control of women, both sexually and economically, which leaves the sexual hierarchy of society intact. And deference to patriarchal hierarchy and control is shown in the very fact that the search for cheap labor has not led to a full integration of women into all parts of the labor force. Although women's labor is cheaper, the system of control which maintains both the necessary order of the society and, with it, the cheapness of women's labor must be protected by segregating women in the labor force. The *justification*, however, for women's double day and unequal wages is less well protected today.

Although the sexual division of labor and society antedates capitalism, it has come to be further institutionalized and specifically defined through the nuclear family in terms of the needs of advanced capitalism. It now has much more form and structure than it did in pre-capitalist societies.[30] In pre-capitalist

[30] See Linda Gordon, "Families," Free Press pamphlet; A. Gordon, M.J. Buhle, and N. Schrom, "Women in American Society," *Radical America* 5:4, July–August 1971; Mitchell, *Psychoanalysis and Feminism, op. cit.*; Mary Ryan, *Womanhood in America* (New

society, the home was defined as the producing economic unit. Men, women, and children worked together in the home, the farm, or the land to produce the goods necessary for their lives. Women still were procreators and child raisers, but the necessities and organization of work *limited the impact* of this sexual role distinction. This is not to say that sexual equality existed, but rather to point to the importance of understanding the specific structure and use of the sexual division of labor today.

With the rise of industrial capitalism, men were brought out of the home into the wage-labor economy, disrupting the earlier organization of labor. Women became relegated to the home and viewed as non-productive. They were now viewed *solely* in terms of the previous loosely defined sex roles. Although women were "mothers" before industrial capitalism, this was not an exclusive role, whereas with industrial capitalism women became "housewives." "The housewife emerged, alongside the proletariat – the two characteristic laborers of developed capitalist society."[31] The work that women continued to perform in the home was not conceived of as work. Productive labor was now defined as wage-labor. It was labor which produces surplus profit – capital.

> In sheer quantity, household labor, including child care, constitutes a huge amount of socially necessary production. Nevertheless, in a society based on commodity production, it is not usually considered "real work" since it is outside of trade and the market place.[32]

The conditions of production in society, then, define and shape production, reproduction, and consumption in the family. So, too, the family mode of production, reproduction, and consumption affects commodity production. They work together to define the political economy. Within a capitalist patriarchal economy – where profit, which necessitates a system of political order and control, is the basic priority of the ruling class – the sexual division of labor and society serves a specific purpose. It stabilizes the society through the family while it organizes a realm of work, as domestic labor, for which

York: Viewpoints, 1975); R. Baxandall, L. Gordon, and S. Reverby, *America's Working Women* (New York: Vintage Books, 1976); and Zaretsky *op. cit*.

[31] Zaretsky, *op. cit.*, p. 114.

[32] Margaret Benston, "The Political Economy of Women's Liberation," New England Free Press pamphlet, p. 15.

there is either no pay (housewives), or limited pay (paid houseworkers), or unequal pay (in the paid labor force). This last category shows the ultimate connection of women as affected by the sexual division of labor within the class structure. Her position as a paid worker is defined in terms of being a "woman," which is a direct reflection of the hierarchical sexual divisions in a society organized around the profit motive.

All of the processes involved in domestic work help in the perpetuation of the existing society. (1) Women stabilize patriarchal structures (the family, housewife, mother, etc.) by fulfilling their very roles. (2) Simultaneously, women are reproducing new workers, for both the paid and unpaid labor force. They "care" for the men and children of the society. (3) They work as well in the labor force, for lesser wages. (4) They stabilize the economy through their role as consumers. And this role is perpetuated very specifically through patriarchal institutions and ideology. If the other side of production is consumption, the other side of capitalism is patriarchy.

It is important to note the discrepancy between patriarchal ideology and the material reality of women's lives. Although all women are defined as mothers (and non-workers) as a group, close to 45% of the women in the United States work in the paid labor force, and almost all labor in the home. Today 38.6 million women hold jobs in the labor force.

Because women, however, are not defined as workers within the ruling ideology, women are not paid for their labor, or are paid less than men. The sexual definition of woman as mother keeps her in the home doing unpaid labor, and/or enables her to be hired at a lower wage because of her sexual definition of inferiority. Given high unemployment rates, they either do not find jobs or are paid at even a lower rate. The sexual division of labor and society remains intact even with women in the paid economy. Ideology adjusts to this by defining women as working mothers. And the two jobs get done for less than the price of one.

The bourgeoisie profits from the basic arrangement of women's work, as do all individual men, who benefit in terms of labor done for them in the home. All men, regardless of class, benefit, although differentially, from the system of privileges they acquire within patriarchal society. This could not be organized as such if the ideology and structures of sex roles were not basic to the society. It is this which largely protects the sexual division of labor and society along with the artificial needs that have been created through the class system.

When the ruling class desires the preservation of the family, this reflects its commitment to a division of labor which not only secures the greatest profit, but which also hierarchically orders the society culturally and politically. Once the sexual division of labor is challenged, particularly in terms of its connection to the capitalist order, one of the basic forms of the organization of work will be challenged. This challenge endangers a free labor pool (which infiltrates almost all aspects of living) and a cheap labor pool, and also endangers the fundamental social and political organization of the society, which is sexual hierarchy itself. The very order and control which derive from the arrangements of power implied in the sexual organization of society will be destroyed.

If we realize that there are basically two kinds of work in capitalist society, wage labor and domestic labor, we realize we must alter the way we think-about workers. What is really needed at this point is further work on what class analysis specifically means for women. What does it mean to say that a middle class woman's life is different and easier than a working class woman's life when her status is significantly different from her middle class male "equivalent"? What of the woman who earns no money at all (as houseworker) and is termed middle class because her husband is? Does she have the same freedom, autonomy, or control over her life as one attributes to the middle class man who earns his own way? How does her position compare to a single woman with a poorly paying job?

I do not mean by these questions to imply that class labels are meaningless, or that class privilege does not exist among women, or that housewives (houseworkers) are a class in themselves. What I am suggesting is that we must develop a vocabulary and conceptual tools which deal with the question of differential power among women in terms of their relation to men *and* the class structure. Only then will we see what effect this has on our understanding of organizing women.

A feminist class analysis must begin with distinctions drawn among women in terms of the work they do within the political economy as a whole (the family and the paid labor force). This would involve making distinctions among (1) working women outside the home, distinguishing professional from nonprofessional; (2) houseworkers, distinguishing housewives from wealthy women who do not work; (3) women who are houseworkers (housewives) and also work outside the home; (4) welfare women; and (5) unemployed women. Whether a woman is (a) married, (b) single, or (c) divorced

Categories for Feminist Class Analysis.

| | Reproduction | Child rearing | Mainte-nance of home | Sexuality | Consumption |
|---|---|---|---|---|---|
| Unemployed women<br>Welfare women | | | | | |
| Housekeepers (housewives) | | | | | |
| Working women outside of home – non-professional | | | | | |
| Working women outside of home – professional | | | | | |
| Wealthy women who do not work (even in their own home) | | | | | |

also is important in analyzing how her work defines her class position. These class distinctions need to be further defined in terms of the issue of race.[33]

We then need to study how women within these categories relate to the major activities of women in terms of the shared experience of women (rather than in terms of the class differentiations among them) – reproduction, child rearing, sexuality, consumption, maintenance of home. What we will discover in this exploratory feminist class analysis, then, is a complicated and varied pattern, whose multi-gridded conceptualization mirrors the complexity of sex and class differentials in the reality of women's life and experience (see chart).

The model with which we would be working would direct attention to class differences within the context of the basic relationship between the sexual

[33] Although I have not dealt specifically with the issue of race in this paper, it is in integral part of the analysis of socialist feminism. The question of race has fallen outside the scope of this particular paper, in its examination of the relationship between sex and class, but I think that the question of race is absolutely fundamental to an anderstanding of woman's class and sexual identity. To the extent that this paper does not include the discussion of race, it is an incomplete study of the specificity of women's oppression.

hierarchy of society and capitalism. Hopefully, the analysis of socialist feminism can continue to explore the relationships between these systems, which in essence are not separate systems, and hence need to be dealt with in their internal web. Hopefully, also, such an examination should serve one overriding objective of the liberation of woman. It should seek to realize her potential for living in social community, rather than in isolated homes; her potential for creative work, rather than alienating or mindless work; her potential for critical consciousness as opposed to false consciousness; and her potential for uninhibited sexuality arising from new conceptions of sexuality.

d) *Some Notes on Strategy*

What does all of the preceding imply about a strategy for revolution? It implies that the existing conceptions of revolutionary strategy are inadequate and need rethinking. First, the existing conceptions of a potentially revolutionary proletariat are inadequate for the goals of socialist feminism. Second, there are severe problems with this potential, as defined in classical Marxian terms, ever becoming real in the United States. And although I think the development of theory and strategy should be interrelated, I see them as somewhat separate activities. Theory allows you to think about new possibilities. Strategy grows out of the possibilities.

This paper has been devoted to developing socialist feminist theory and I am hesitant to develop statements of strategy from it. Strategy will rather have to be fully articulated from the political attempts at using the theory. When one tries abstractly to define strategy from new and developing statements of theory, the tendency to impose existing revolutionary strategies on reality is too great. Existing formulations of strategy tend to limit and distort new possibilities for organizing for revolutionary change.

The importance of socialist feminist strategy, to the extent that it exists, is that it grows out of women struggling with their daily existence – production, reproduction, children, consumption, jobs. The potential for revolutionary consciousness derives from the fact that women's lives under capitalist patriarchy are being squeezed from the most intimate levels, such as how they feed their children, to the more public levels of their monotonous, tiring, low-skill, sex-defined, low-wage jobs. Women are working in the labor force, and for less, and they are maintaining the family system, having less to make do with. This is the base from which consciousness can develop. Women need to try organizing political action and developing political consciousness about our oppression within the hierarchical sexual division of society and from an understanding of how this connects to the capitalist division of labor. Or consciousness will develop then from our everyday lives. I agree with Nancy Hartsock when she states:

> Thus the power of feminism grows out of contact with everyday life. The significance of contemporary feminism is in the reinvention of a mode of analysis which has the power to comprehend and thereby transform everyday life.[34]

One has to ask whose everyday life we are speaking about. Although there are real and severing differences among women's everyday lives, there are also points of contact that lay a basis for cross-class organizing. These differences must be acknowledged and struggled with for a sense of political *priority*. The commonality among women derives from the particular roles women share in patriarchy. From this commonality begins the feminist struggle.

Many of the socialist feminist women I have worked with in the women's movement were radical feminists first. They first felt their oppression and women and then, as they came to understand that capitalism was fully implicated in this system of oppression, became committed to socialism as well. Similarly, there are more and more women as housewives who are coming to understand their daily lives as part of a much larger system. Women working outside the home, both professional and unprofessional, who bear the pressures and anxieties about being competent mothers, and caretakers of the home, are becoming conscious of their "double day" of work.

Male leftists and socialist women often say that women, as women, cannot be organized because of their isolation in the home, the privatization of their lives, their commitments to their husbands' class. But a strategy to reach all women, regardless of class, has never been tried in a self-conscious manner. That its implementation will be difficult goes without saying. But a beginning is already in process as women try to take some control over their lives.

---

[34] Nancy Hartsock, "Feminist Theory and the Development of Revolutionary Strategy," unpublished manuscript, Johns Hopkins University, 1976, p. 19. Portions of this paper appeared as "Fundamental Feminism, Process and Perspective," *Quest* 2, Fall 1975, pp. 67–79.

# V. Capitalism and the World Economy

Erik Olin Wright

# Introductory Comments to "Alternative Perspectives in Marxist Theory of Accumulation and Crisis"

It has been over a quarter of a century since "Alternative Perspectives in the Marxist Theory of Accumulation and Crisis" was published in *The Insurgent Sociologist*. It was written in the midst of the vibrant renaissance Marxist thinking in the academy that emerged in the aftermath of the student movements of the 1960s. When I wrote the paper I was a member of a circle of mainly young Marxist-inspired intellectuals who worked on the journal *Kapitalistate* in the San Francisco Bay Area. We enthusiastically read and debated the newest Marxist work coming out of Europe, especially Althusserian structuralist Marxism from France and capital logic and critical theory from Germany; we had study groups on the classics of the Marxist tradition, particularly on *Capital;* and we rediscovered political economy through Sweezey, Dobb and others. It was a period in which for many left intellectuals Marxism was, if not the only game in town, the game where most of the action took place.

In this general intellectual context, there were a number of more or less taken for granted assumptions that I brought to the paper and which shaped important features of its argument:

1) *The labor theory of value.* Throughout the paper it is assumed that the labor theory of value provided adequate concepts for analyzing the inner workings

and dynamics of capitalism. While there were specific problems within the labor theory of value with which I took issue in the paper – in particular the technical debates over how to define the "organic composition of capital" – I did not entertain the possibility that this was a flawed framework for understanding capitalist economies in general and capitalist crisis tendencies in particular. The only issue was how to creatively deploy the labor theory of value in the contemporary context, not its relevance.

2) *Socialism.* Underlying the vision of the historical trajectory of capitalism in the paper is the view that socialism was on the historical horizon of capitalism's future, even if it was not on the immediate historical agenda. I accepted the view not simply that democratic socialism was normatively desirable (which I still believe), nor that there are feasible institutional designs in which it could be economically efficient (which I also believe), but that socialism was immanently and actively posed by the internal contradictions of capitalism. There was certainly no skepticism about the idea of socialism, nor a feeling of a need to give it a defense.

3) *Crisis*. The intellectual work that went into the paper took place in 1973 and 1974. This was the period of the first oil shock, of emerging stagflation, of the end of the post-WWII boom. There was a general sense both in the popular media and even more on the left that capitalism was entering a period of severe and sustained crisis. Along with this came a belief that underlying this crisis were such severe contradictions that the outcome would have to be some large developmental transformation in capitalist institutional forms. Of course there was little clarity on precisely what capitalism would look like at the end of the crisis period, but there was a strong belief that the crisis would augur in massive transformations for better or worse.

4) *Statism*. One of the tacit assumptions in much Marxist work of the early 1970s was the conviction that the statist turn in capitalism could not be dramatically reversed. In the course of the long post-WWII boom capitalism had become increasingly state-centered in various ways. The welfare state had expanded, forms of state regulation had deepened, Keynesian macro-economic policies involved considerable state steering of the market. While it was broadly recognized that the economic crisis tendencies of the 1970s put considerable strain on such statist forms of capitalism – as argued forcefully in James O'Connor's very influential book of the period, *The Fiscal Crisis of the State* – no one seriously envisioned the wholesale dismantling of the welfare state, the deregulation of markets, the partial reversal of statist capital-

ism as a way of coping with the crisis tendencies of the period. Most forecasts envisioned an extension and deepening of state involvement in accumulation; neoliberalism was not broadly viewed as an option.

If I were to write this paper today, there would be significant changes in each of these assumptions.

First, I no longer believe that the labor theory of value is a satisfactory way of grounding a theory of capitalism and capitalist dynamics. While I still hold that class relations and class exploitation are fundamental to capitalism, I no longer think that the technical apparatus of the labor theory of value provides an adequate framework of political economy. This would not negate all of the analyses of crisis tendencies and their potential resolution in the paper, but the specific analysis of the organic composition of capital would no longer be on firm foundations.

Second, it would be impossible for me to write a paper today in which I invoked socialism as the normatively desirable way of transcending capitalist crisis tendencies without providing some more explicit discussion of what I meant by socialism and how it would actually solve various problems. Above all, some account of how markets and socialism could be articulated would be needed. The easy assumption that simply by radically democratizing statist socialism it would function effectively is no longer tenable.

Third, while I do not for a moment believe that capitalism has finally resolved its inherent tendencies towards crisis and disruption, the sense of crisis in the year 2004 is very different from 1975. While global forces played an important role in 1975 as well as the present, the central axis of crisis tendencies as many people understood them in the early 1970s still centered on the articulation of national institutions with national class struggles and national capitalism. Ideas such as the profit squeeze, underconsumption, overproduction, the fiscal crisis of the state, and so on, all were rooted in an understanding of capitalism as a national system of production and exchange. Global forces (including imperialism as a global expression of capitalism) could intensify or attenuate these domestic crisis mechanisms, but the primary mechanisms were themselves national. No analysis of capitalist dynamics and contradictions would root the analysis so heavily in strictly national conditions today.

Finally, the problem of the state and the capitalist economy seems very different today than in the early 1970s. In the paper I imagined that some new form of state-directed monopoly capitalism might be a way of resolving the specific crisis tendencies I saw in the early 1970s. Rather than consider a neoliberal retreat of the affirmative state I envisioned a further extension and deepening of the state's direct involvement in capital accumulation. Now, particularly in the context of globalization of markets and the significant reduction of many aspects of state regulations, this statist assumption would no longer make sense. Once again, capitalism has proved a much more robust and flexible social order than Marxists anticipated, capable of new developmental leaps and institutional reorganizations.

In the face of the acknowledgment of these faulty assumptions and their implications for the analysis of the paper, one might wonder what, if anything, remains worthwhile in it. I think the main value of the paper is in the second part where I attempted to chart an historical trajectory of the forms of capitalist crisis, the emergent structural solutions to each of those crisis tendencies, and ways in which new crisis tendencies were generated by such solutions. While some of the specific crisis mechanisms postulated in this historical mapping may be problematic, this general way of thinking about the contradictions of accumulation and the ways in which attempts at resolving those contradiction push the system to new configurations, remains fruitful.

Erik Olin Wright

# Alternative Perspectives in Marxist Theory of Accumulation and Crisis*

There is not one Marxist theory of economic crisis, but several competing theories. While all Marxist perspectives on economic crisis tend to see crisis as growing out of the contradictions inherent in the process of capital accumulation, there is very little general consensus on which contradictions are most central to understanding crisis, or even on how the contradictions in accumulation should be conceptualized in the first place.

This paper will attempt to lay bare the logical structure of each of the general Marxist perspectives on economic crisis and to provide a preliminary synthesis. I will argue that there is no intrinsic incompatibility in these diverse conceptions of the contradictions in accumulation if they are viewed as part of a historical process. Specifically, I will make the following argument:

1. At different stages of capitalist development the accumulation process faces different dominant

---

* Original version of this article appeared in *The Insurgent Sociologist*, 6:1 (Fall, 1975), pp. 5–39.

Because of space limitations, some sections of the original version of this paper had to be cut. In particular, throughout the paper, discussions that mainly engaged technical issues in the labor theory of value or extended reviews of debates on particular concepts, have been cut. One section of the original paper, "the meaning of accumulation," in which the foundations of the labor theory of value and its relation to crisis theory, has been entirely eliminated. Readers interested in this specific discussion can find a version of it in Erik Olin Wright, *Class, Crisis and the State* (London: Verso, 1978), pp. 113–124.

constraints or impediments. These impediments are not exogenous factors which interfere with the accumulation process but are generated by the accumulation process itself.

2. In order for capitalist production to continue, these constraints must be overcome. In a fundamental sense capitalists do not have the choice of passively accepting the impediments to accumulation. As individuals, capitalists must attempt to overcome these impediments in order to survive in a competitive world; as a class, capitalists must strive to remove the impediments to accumulation in order to contain the class struggle.
3. The systemic solutions to the dominant impediments at a given stage of capitalist development generate the new impediments which constrain the accumulation process in the subsequent stage. It is in this sense that the impediments to accumulation can be considered *contradictions* in accumulation rather than merely obstacles to accumulation. They are contradictions because the "solutions" to a particular impediment become themselves impediments to accumulation.
4. The current world-wide capitalist economic crisis can be (tentatively) understood as part of a transition from one pattern of constraints on accumulation, characterized by Keynesian solutions, to a new set of emergent constraints which were in part caused by those very Keynesian strategies in earlier crises and which are no longer amenable to Keynesian solutions.

We will begin, in the next section of this paper, by examining how different traditions of Marxist crisis theory identify different potential constraints on the process of capital accumulation. This will be followed by an analysis of how these potential constraints on accumulation assume different importance in different periods of capitalist development. The paper will conclude with a more speculative discussion of likely developments in the immediate future.

## I. Impediments and Contradictions in the Accumulation Process[1]

Contemporary Marxist literature on contradictions in the accumulation process generally focuses on one of four critical impediments to accumulation: 1) the

[1] This discussion presupposes basically familiarity with the basic concepts of the labor theory of value as it was traditionally deployed within Marxism. In the original published version of this paper, the relvant elements in Marxist political economy were presented on pp. 6–13. See also Wright (1978: 113–125).

rising organic composition of capital (Mattick 1969, Yaffe 1973a, Cogoy 1973, Mage 1963); 2) the problem of realizing surplus value, and in particular problems of underconsumption in capitalist society (Sweezy 1942, Baran and Sweezy 1966, Gillman 1965); 3) a low or falling rate of exploitation resulting from rises in wages (Glyn and Sutcliffe 1972); and 4) the contradictory role of the state in accumulation (Cogoy 1972, Yaffe 1973a, O'Connor 1973, Offe 1973 and 1974). Most of our discussion of these four impediments to accumulation will be based on the value categories discussed in part I. It is important to stress that such a value analysis does not exhaust the Marxist work on economic crisis. A complete understanding of crisis would also involve an analysis of monetary instability, credit imbalances, and other problems strictly in the sphere of circulation. These issues will not be discussed in the present paper, since, while such problems are important, there is a theoretical priority to analyzing the impediments to accumulation in terms of contradictions in the sphere of production. It is on these contradictions that my analysis will be focused. (For a collection of papers on economic crisis which is not restricted to value analysis, see Mermelstein 1975.)

1. *The organic composition of capital and the falling rate of profit*

It is a fundamental premise of Marxist political economy that only living labor can produce surplus value, and thus profits. The rate of profit, however, is based not merely on labor costs of the capitalist (v) but on all capital costs (c + v). Therefore, the reasoning goes, if it should happen in the course of capitalist development that the value of the dead labor used in production should grow much more rapidly than the living labor, there will be a tendency all other things being equal, for the rate of profit to decline. This constitutes the basic logic for studying the relationship between changes in the productive forces of capitalist society – the technology broadly conceived – and the rate of profit. The "organic composition of capital" is a ratio that is designed to reflect the salient aspects of technology that impinge on the rate of profit. The most useful simple expression for this is the ratio of dead labor (constant capital) to living labor in production:[2]

[2] This expression is not the traditional way that Marxists have defined the organic composition of capital. The usual practice has been to regard the ratio c/v as the organic composition of capital. This has been the usage by economists such as Sweezy, Dobb, Mattick, and Gillman. This expression constitutes the ratio of dead to living capital and is generally treated by these writers as reflecting in value terms what in bourgeois economics is called the capital-intensity of the technology.

$$Q = \frac{c}{v + s}$$

One other expression, the rate of exploitation (also called the rate of surplus value), will be important in the discussion of the falling rate of profit. The rate of exploitation is defined as the ratio of the unpaid to the paid portions of the working day, or, alternatively, the ratio of surplus value to variable capital:

$$e = \frac{s}{v}$$

We can then write the rate of profit as:

$$r = \frac{s}{c + v} = \frac{e}{Q(1 + e) + 1} \qquad (1)$$

Equation (1) will help us to explain the theory of the falling tendency of the rate of profit. There are six propositions in the argument:

1) There are forces intrinsic to the process of capital accumulation which tend to raise the level of the organic composition of capital.

2) As the organic composition of capital rises, there is a tendency for the rate of profit to fall *unless* the rate of exploitation increases sufficiently to counter-balance the rise in the organic composition of capital (or unless some other counteracting force intervenes).

3) In the long run, rises in the rate of exploitation cannot completely counteract the rising organic composition of capital, and thus there will be a definite tendency for the rate of profit to decline.

4) When the decline in the rate of profit becomes sufficiently serious and can no longer be compensated for by the existing rate of exploitation, an economic crisis occurs: the least profitable capitals disappear as businesses go bankrupt; and capitalists increasingly withhold investments because there are no profitable outlets. Aggregate demand, which is fundamentally derived from the rate of accumulation, therefore declines with the result that the crisis takes on the *appearance* of a crisis of overproduction of commodities.

---

In a number of recent works (Cogoy 1973, Mage 1963, Laibman 1974) it has been argued that the ratio c/v is not an adequate measure of capital intensity since, the level of v depends in part upon the rate of exploitation and not merely on the relative amounts of constant capital and human labor in production. The ratio of dead labor to living labor in production, c/v + s, has therefore been substituted for the ratio of constant capital to variable capital.

Whereas underconsumptionists (see below, subsection 2) argue that crisis is caused by an overproduction of commodities, by an overproduction of surplus value, the theory of the falling rate of profit argues the exact opposite.

> Because *not enough* [surplus value] has been produced, capital cannot expand at a rate which would allow for the full realization of *what has been* produced. The relative scarcity of surplus-labor in the production process appears as an absolute abundance of commodities in circulation. (Mattick 1969: 79)

5) These conditions of crisis, however, serve the function of restoring conditions favorable for subsequent profitable accumulation. Several mechanisms accomplish this: a) unproductive capital is eliminated from the market, thus leaving the remaining capital at a higher level of productivity; b) in addition, when individual capitals go bankrupt they are forced to sell their existing constant capital at prices below real exchange values. This devaluation of capital means that in the aggregate the numerator in the organic composition of capital declines, thus raising the rate of profit; c) finally, workers are thrown out of work, the reserve army of the unemployed swells, and capitalists can push the wage below its value, thus increasing the rate of exploitation. Once these processes have advanced sufficiently to restore an acceptable rate of profit, accumulation resumes and the crisis ends.

6) While the crisis tendency of capitalist society takes the form of periodic business cycles, there is also an over-arching tendency for cycles to become progressively more severe. Each successive crisis occurs at a higher level of accumulation and thus a higher level of the organic composition of capital. The problems of restoring conditions for renewed profitable accumulation thus tend to become more difficult in each successive crisis (Mattick 1969: 69).

With slight variations, these six propositions are all held by proponents of the theory of the falling tendency of the rate of profit. The first three constitute the heart of the theory, for if it can be demonstrated that there is a tendency for the rate of profit to fall, the particular conception of how this in turn produces economic crisis and how economic crisis itself restores conditions of renewed accumulation follows fairly naturally. We will therefore concentrate our attention on the first three propositions.

The second and third of these can be dealt with purely formally in terms of equation (1). It is immediately obvious from equation (1) that for any fixed value of the rate of exploitation, the rate of profit becomes simply a function of the inverse of the organic composition of capital. Thus, if Q rises and e remains constant, the rate of profit will necessarily fall. The second proposition in the argument therefore follows immediately from the definitions of r, Q, and e.

The validity of the third proposition is less obvious. While it is clear that if the organic composition were to rise to infinity even an infinite rate of exploitation could not counteract the fall in the rate of profit, this limiting case is not very helpful for understanding the movements of the rate of profit in the real world. What we would like to know is the extent to which a rise in the organic composition of capital will constrain in the accumulation process at *any* arbitrary level of Q, and not just in the limiting case where Q is infinite. One way of examining this problem is to ask if the extent to which the rate of exploitation can function as a counteracting force is itself affected by rises in the organic composition of capital. It is easy to show using elementary calculus that as the organic composition of capital rises, the rate of profit becomes progressively less sensitive to changes in the rate of exploitation. Thus, not only does a high organic composition of capital produce a lower possible profit, but it also makes changes in the rate of exploitation less useful as a strategy for bolstering the rate of profit. Furthermore, the higher the rate of exploitation already is, the less sensitive will the rate of profit be to subsequent changes in the rate of exploitation. Thus, *if* in fact there is a secular rise in the organic composition of capital, then, even if the rate of exploitation also rises, it becomes progressively less and less likely that it will be able to counteract completely the rising organic composition of capital. It is therefore quite reasonable to regard rises in the organic composition of capital as a significant impediment to the accumulation process, and equally reasonable to assume that if it does tend to rise, complementary rises in the rate of exploitation will not be able to counteract the fall in the rate of profit in the long run.

The first proposition in the argument is the most problematic. Neither the empirical demonstrations of a general tendency for the organic composition of capital to rise over time, nor the theoretical arguments marshalled in its support, have been particularly convincing. It is unquestionably true that in *physical* terms the amount of machines, raw materials, buildings, etc., per worker has vastly increased with capitalist development. But the organic composition of capital is a *value* concept, and it is far from obvious that the value of constant capital per worker has risen or has tendency to rise, especially in the later stages of capitalist development.

For the value of constant capital per worker to rise there must be a net excess of labor-saving technological innovations (inovations which substitute machinery for labor power) over *capital-saving* innovations (innovations which substitute cheap machines – machines that require relatively little socially necessary labor time to produce – for expensive machines). When Marx wrote *Capital*, this was a fairly plausible assumption to make. Although Marx did recognize the possibility that increasing productivity in the capital goods sector of the economy might result in a "cheapening of the elements of constant capital" (Marx 1967: 236), he regarded this as at most a transient countertendency to a generally rising organic composition of capital. In Marx's view, progressive introduction of labor-saving technologies was an intrinsic part of the accumulation process.

There are several plausible arguments which suggest that in advanced capitalist economies there should be some tendency for a relative increase to occur in the selective pressures for capital-saving over labor-saving innovations. In earlier periods of capitalist development, when mechanization was first occuring, the introduction of machines necessarily implied the substitution of machines for workers. Once an industry is fully mechanized, however, all innovations tend to take the form of machines replacing machines. Even if such machines do in fact still replace workers, there is no reason why they should not also be cheaper machines. In the competitive struggle among the producers of machines, after all, there will be attempts to expand markets by producing less expensive machines as well as more productive machines (i.e., machines which produce more output per total labor input). Furthermore, it might also be expected that as constant capital increases as a proportion of total costs (i.e., as the *value* composition of capital, c/v, rises), individual capitalists will tend to be more concerned about saving on constant capital. A plausible model for the rate of increase in the organic composition of capital could postulate that, all other things being equal, the net *rate* of labor-saving innovations over capital-saving innovations is inversely related to the proportion of labor costs in production. Thus as the organic composition of capital rose, it would tend to rise at a slower and slower rate, perhaps even asymptotically approaching some high relatively stable level.

Furthermore, even if it should happen that in highly mechanized industries the organic composition of capital continues to rise, the aggregate social level of the organic composition might remain constant if there were a relatively faster rate of growth in unmechanized sectors of the economy. The enormous growth of "service sector" employment, which is typically highly labor-intensive, could counterbalance the continuing growth in capital intensity in the industrial sector. The tendency for the competitive labor-intensive sector of the economy to grow in a symbiotic relation with the monopoly sector would also tend to counter to some degree the rise in the *aggregate* organic composition (see O'Connor 1973, chap. 2). All of these pieces of suggestive reasoning indicate that, while a thorough model predicting the relative proportions of labor-saving and capital-saving innovations has yet to be worked out, there is no a priori reason to assume a general preponderance of labor-saving innovations in a developed capitalist economy.

The empirical evidence is at best indecisive on the question of whether or not the organic composition of capital has risen, done nothing, or even fallen. Since national income accounts are not figured in terms of embodied labor times, and since data on capital invested includes many entries that Marxists would not even consider capital, it is of course highly problematic how data on the organic composition could be reliably gathered. Even as strong a proponent of the rising organic composition thesis as Cogoy has to admit that the meager data which support his views are as equivocal as the data which oppose them (Cogoy 1973: 63).

If the theoretical basis is weak, for assuming there is a tendency for the organic composition to rise, and if the empirical evidence is non- existent, why bother with the theory at all? There are several reasons. First, while there is considerable dispute about the relevance of the theory of the rising organic composition of capital to late-20th-century capitalism, there is general agreement among Marxists that it was a significant characteristic of 19th-century capitalism. As we will see in section III of this paper, the theory of the rising organic composition of capital is essential for a historical understanding of the development of capitalist accumulation.

Second, even if it is true that there is no consistent long term tendency for the organic composition of capital to rise, it (the organic composition) still acts as a real constraint on the accumulation process. The results we discussed above indicate that when an economy is in a situation of relatively high organic composititon of capital, the rate of profit becomes less sensitive to increases in the rate of exploitation. This means that if the rate of profit were to decline because of some factor other than the organic composition of capital (for example, the growth of unproductive expenditures), the system would be more rigid because of the high organic composition. No one has argued that the organic composition of capital has fallen to any great extent in the past several decades, and thus one can say that it still acts as an impediment to accumulation, even though it may not be the great dynamic source of crisis that its defenders claim.

Finally, even if a secular rise in the organic composition of capital is not the general cause of capitalist crisis, a destruction of values and a corresponding temporary fall in the organic composition of capital may be a crucial part of the solution to crises. If sometime during the first quarter of the 20*th* century, a relatively stable, fairly high level of organic composition of capital was reached, it could still be the case that the organic composition of capital has dropped considerably during periods of crisis, and then returned to this stable level during periods of prosperity as post-crisis un-devaluated constant capital replaced the cheap, devaluated capital acquired during the crisis. A fall in the organic composition of capital can be a solution to crisis without a rise in the organic composition being the fundamental cause of crisis. Under these assumptions, if it should happen that institutional changes in the economy – in particular, growth of government subsidies of inefficient monopolistic firms – should block the fall in capital values during a crisis, then it would be expected that a serious "crisis of crisis management" might occur. This issue will be more fully discussed in section II below.

2. *Underconsumptionist theories of economic crisis*

Marx very explicitly states in the Grundrisse that the inherent tendency for the rate of profit to fall is

> the most important law of modern political economy and the most essential one for understanding the most complicated relationships. It is the most important law from an historical standpoint. (Quoted in Yaffe 1972a: 200.)

But he also makes a number of statements which some Marxists have taken to indicate that Marx supported an underconsumptionist view of crisis. "The last cause of all real crisis," Marx writes in *Capital*, Vol. III:

> always remains the poverty and restricted consumption of the masses as compared to the tendency of capitalist production to develop the productive forces in such a way, that only the absolute power of consumption of the entire society would be their limit. (Marx 1967)

As often happens in debates among Marxists, the dispute between the two positions has frequently taken the form of competiting exegeses of passages from *Capital.* On that score it seems to me that the proponents of the falling rate of profit probably have the upper hand. While Marx did see the underconsumption of the masses as a chronic state in capitalist society, it only became a factor in crisis given the dynamics of accumulation and the problem of the rising organic composition of capital. Engels states this position very clearly:

> The underconsumption of the masses, the restriction of the consumption of the masses to what is necessary for their maintenance and reproduction, is not a new phenomenon. It has existed as long as there have been exploiting and exploited classes. . . . The underconsumption of the masses is a necessary condition of all forms of society based on exploitation, consequently also of the capitalist form; but it is the capitalist form of production which first gives rise to crises. The underconsumption of the masses is therefore also a prerequisite condition for crises, and plays in them a role which has long been recognized. But it tells us just as little why crises exist today as why they did not exist before. (Quoted in Yaffe 1973a: 216.)

A correct exegesis of Marx, however, doth not a correct interpretation of the world make. The cogency of underconsumptionist views must be assessed on the strength of their logical status, not on their formal agreement or disagreement with Marx's own work.

One of the initial problems in assessing the underconsumptionist logic is that most writings from the underconsumptionist perspective fail to lay out the assumptions and structure of the argument in as coherent a way as the falling-rate-of-profit theorists. The following acccount of underconsumptionist theory is thus not taken directly from any one defender of the perspective. It is rather my own construction of what I feel a coherent Marxist underconsumptionist theory would be.

A Marxist theory of underconsumption contains four basic propositions:

1) There is a general tendency in capitalist society for absolute level of surplus value to rise. In addition, with increases in productivity, there is a tendency for the rate of surplus value to increase as well.

2) There is an intrinsic contradiction in capitalist society between the conditions of production of surplus value and the conditions of the realization of surplus value. For realization *not* to be a problem, the growth in aggre-

gate demand must occur at the same rate as the growth in productivity and surplus value. This is always problematic in capitalist society since individual capitalists always try to minimize their wage bills. There is an intrinsic tendency for demand to lag behind growth in surplus value and thus for part of the surplus value to remain unrealized.

3) The inability of the capitalist to realize the full value of the produced surplus value is experienced by capitalists as a fall in the actual rate of profit. This leads to a reduction of investment, bankruptcies, unemployment, etc. Such crisis conditions are resolved when some exogenous source of new demand – such as the state – steps in and restores conditions of profitable realization of surplus.

4) While underconsumptionist tendencies are present at all stages of capitalist development, they become especially acute, and become the source of serious economic crisis, only in the monopoly stage of capitalism. Monopoly power greatly augments the tendency for surplus value to rise, and thus the tendency for underconsumption to occur.

There is relatively little disagreement over the first of these propositions. With some exceptions most Marxists feel that with increasing productivity, the value of wage goods tends to fall and that thus, although the standard of living of workers might even rise in real terms, the value of labor power will also tend to decline. This results in an increase in the rate of surplus value and, with expanded reproduction of capital, an increase in the mass of surplus value as well. While the underconsumptionists and the falling-rate-of-profit theorists disagree vehemently on the relationship of monopoly to a rising rate of surplus value, they agree on the general proposition that it tends to rise.

On the second proposition there is no such agreement. The falling-rate-of-profit theorists insist that realization problems are a consequence rather than a cause of the fall in the rate of profit (see Cogoy, 1973: 64).

If all aggregate demand is derived from accumulation, and if capitalists are constantly striving to maximize the rate of accumulation, then clearly the only reason there can ever be an effective demand inadequate for absorbing all of the produced surplus value would be if something happened to the rate of accumulation. This is precisely what the theory of the rising organic composition of capital attempts to provide.

The problem with this reasoning, and that of similar critics of underconsumption theories, is that aggregate demand in capitalist society is not simply derived from accumulation. Especially under monopoly conditions, a sizable part of total demand does not come directly from accumulation but from such nonaccumulating sources as capitalist personal consumption, much of state expenses, and so on.

To analyze the underconsumption problem it is useful to introduce a distinction between potential profits and actual profits. Potential profits are those that would occur in the absence of any realization problems. Actual profits will always be less than or equal to such potential profits. The underconsumption argument is an analysis of why there are *tendencies* for a portion of the surplus to remain unrealized, and thus for actual profits to fall short of potential profits.

If the organic composition of capital is more or less constant and the rate of exploitation is rising, there will necessarily occur a rise in the rate of potential profits in value terms. The question then becomes, what are the equilibrium conditions such that all of this increasing surplus will be realized? That is, what total demand must be forthcoming so that the entire surplus product in value terms will be sold?

The tendency toward underconsumption in capitalist society stems fundamentally from the fact that there are no automatic mechanisms which guarantee that the rate of unproductive demand will grow sufficiently fast to fill the gap between the rate of accumulation and the rate of potential profit.[3] The demand for unproductive, wasteful consumption does not grow spontaneously in the same way that demand directly derived from accumulation grows automatically with economic growth. Waste is a social invention, and the maintenance of high levels of wasteful consumption requires conscious planning and intervention. The growth on a massive scale of consumer credit, and built-in obsolescence of many consumer durables, the wide range of state interventions in the economy of the Keynesian variety, and so on and so forth, all represent conscious strategies to increase the rate of unproductive demand and thus avoid realization/underconsumption crises. As we will see in section III, these solutions themselves create new problems which the capitalist economy is only beginning to face.

---

[3] It must be stressed that the expression "unproductive" is being used in a non-normative sense. An expenditure is unproductive in capitalist society if it does not contribute directly or indirectly to the production of value and surplus value. Some of these expenditures might in fact be "productive" in terms of meeting human needs, but they are not productive in terms of the functioning of a capitalist economy.

While underconsumptionist tendencies are present at all stages of capitalist development, they have remained largely latent until the monopoly stage. As long as the organic composition of capital did have a tendency to rise, much of the rising surplus was in fact automatically absorbed by the accelerating rate of investment (of accumulation). With the emergence of monopoly capital, however, the situation decisively changes, both because, as already argued, there appears top be a tendency for the organic composition of capital to become relatively stable in this stage of capitalism (or at least to rise at a much slower rate), and because in monopoly capitalism surplus value is extracted from workers not only in the labor process but also through monopoly pricing in the sphere of circulation.

Two general social processes have evolved which at least partially counteract this tendency toward underconsumption in monopoly capitalist society. The first has already been mentioned: the invention and growth of Keynesian policies designed to stimulate aggregate demand through the expansion of unproductive spending, primarily by the state. Such spending has the secondary consequence of bolstering the confidence of investors in the stability of the economy, and thus fosters a higher rate of accumulation.

Second, the growth of collective bargaining may have the effect of reducing the rate of increase in the rate of surplus value itself. Especially in monopoly sector industries, where wages since the war have been fairly closely tied to productivity increases, the gradual rise in the wage has undoubtedly lessened to some extent underconsumption tendencies. The continued growth of monopoly power, however, has at least partially neutralized this counteracting process, since much of the productivity wage increases have in turn been passed on to the working class as a whole in the form of monopoly pricing. This has the effect of further increasing the rate of surplus value for capital as a whole.

The most serious weakness in the underconsumptionist position is that it lacks any theory of the determinants of the actual rate of accumulation. The falling-rate-of-profit theorists have a specific theory of the determinants of the rate of accumulation. In equating the rate of profit with the rate of accumulation, they see a combination of the organic composition of capital and the rate of exploitation as the basic determinant of the actual rate of accumulation. Since they view the organic composition of capital as rising and thus constantly pushing down the rate of profit, the assumption that the rate of profit and the rate of accumulation are equivalent does no damage to their general argument. If anything, the impact of the rising organic composition of capital would be even greater if not all profits were accumulated.

In the underconsumption argument, however, the rate of profit and the rate of accumulation cannot be equated. If they were, there would not be a tendency for underconsumption (i.e., there would be no need for the rate of unproductive spending to increase). Much underconsumptionist writing has, at least implicitly, opted for Keynes' solution to this problem by focusing on the subjective anticipations of profit on the part of capitalists as the key determinant of the rate of accumulation. From a Marxist point of view, this is an inadequate solution. I have not yet seen an elaborated theory of investment and the rate of accumulation by a Marxist underconsumptionist theorist, and thus for the time being the theory remains incomplete.

3. *Theories of the profit squeeze*

Both underconsumptionists and organic-composition-of-capital theorists maintain that with capitalist development there tends to be a rising rate of surplus value. Where they differ is in their view of the relationship between this rising rate of surplus value and the movements of the rate of profit. The organic-composition theorists insist that changes in technology within the production process itself tend to negate rise in the rate of surplus value and thus produce a fall in profits; underconsumptionists argue that the forces for a rising surplus tend to be stronger than any counterforces, especially under conditions of monopoly capital.

The proponents of the profit squeeze view of crisis agree with the organic-composition theorists that the rate of profit tends to fall, but they do not agree that this has anything to do with changes in technology, and they disagree with both the organic-composition theorists' and the underconsumptionists' belief that there is any tendency for the rate of surplus value to rise.

The essential argument of the profit squeeze is very simple: the relative share of the national income going to workers and to capitalists is almost entirely a consequence of their relative strengths in the class struggle. There is therefore no intrinsic reason for wage struggles to be limited, even in the long run, to demands that real wages rise as rapidly as productivity. To the extent that the working class develops a strong enough labor movement to win wage increases in excess of productivity increases, there will be a tendency for the rate of profits to fall (to be "squeezed" by rising wage bills). Such a decline in profits results in a corresponding decline in investments and thus in even slower increases in productivity. The end result is economic crisis. Conditions for profitability are restored to the extent that – because of the growth of the reserve army of the unemployed during the crisis – the bargaining strength of the working class is lessened relative to capitalists and thus the profit squeeze is relaxed. This position has been most thoroughly argued by Andrew Glyn and Bob Sutcliffe in a recent analysis of the current stagnation of British capitalism (1971, 1972). (For a similar analysis dealing with American business cycles, see Body and Crotty, 1975.)

4. *State expenditure and accumulation*

Marxist theories of accumulation and crisis have generally conceptualized state expenditures as unproductive (again: unproductive in the sense of not producing surplus value).

In the underconsumptionist model of crisis this unproductive quality of state expenditures constitutes the central mechanism by which crisis is averted or at least minimized; in rising-organic-composition models, the expansion of such unproductive expenditures is seen as a critical factor which exacerbates the inherent crisis tendencies in the system. In both theories, however, state activity is seen as largely unproductive and as absorbing an increasing share of the surplus value produced in the economy.

This traditional conception can be criticized both in terms of its view of the *sources* of state revenue and of its view of the *impact* of state spending.

The view that all taxes constitute a tax on the *existing* pool of surplus value is based on a mechanistic and static interpretation of the meaning of the value of labor power. Since it is obviously the case that taxation reduces the real wages of workers, the view that all taxes come from surplus value implicitly assumes that prior to taxation the real wages were above the true value of labor power. Taxation then merely appropriates that part of the surplus value which had previously been in the disguised form of an inflated money wage. The implicit logic is that if taxation did not occur, wages would be reduced to the present after-tax level anyway. In other words, if the state did not tax this surplus value it would be available to the capitalist for accumulation. These assumptions are at best dubious, if real wages and taxation are seen as at least partially the outcome of class struggle. Because of the enormous weight of the state's power of legitimation, it is reasonable to assume that many workers are willing to accept a level of taxation on their money incomes greater than a corresponding wage cut that might occur in the absence of such taxes. Taxation can thus be seen as, in part, a weapon in the class struggle by which the state appropriates a certain amount of surplus labor that is *unavailable* to private capitalists. From a total social point of view, therefore, taxation, like monopoly pricing, has the capacity to increase the aggregate rate of surplus value. This is not to say that there are no limits on the extent to which taxes can have this effect; and certainly not that all or even most taxation in fact expands surplus value, but merely that the assumption that all taxation constitutes a drain on the existing pool of surplus value is incorrect.

Quite apart from the problem of the relationship of taxation to existing surplus value, there is the question of the impact of taxation on the subsequent production of surplus value. It is certainly true that, with very few exceptions, state production itself is not production for the market and the state does not accumulate capital out of any realized profits from its own production. Most state expenditures therefore do not *directly* produce surplus value. But as O'Connor (1973) has thoroughly argued, this does not keep the state from playing an important role in *indirectly* expanding surplus value and accumulation. Many state expenditures have the effect of reducing the reproduction costs of labor power by socializing many expenses that would otherwise have to be paid for by individual capitalists (medical care, training and education, social security, etc.). Furthermore, a great deal of state spending on research and development, transportation infrastructures, communications, etc., has the effect of increasing the level of productivity of capital as a whole and thus contributing to accumulation. Even in terms of classical, wasteful, Keynesian demand-maintenance state interventions, such state spending may have the side effect of increasing capacity utilization and thus increasing productivity. Again, this is not to say that such indirectly-productive expenditures are necessarily the dominant mode of state activity, but rather that it is incorrect to see the state's role in the accumulation process as being simply a drag on accumulation.

Given that to some extent taxes themselves can expand surplus value and that to some extent state spending can expand accumulation, the crucial thing to analyze becomes not merely the forces which produce a general expansion of state activity, but also the extent to which those forces selectively expand the unproductive or indirectly-productive activities of the state, and the extent to which either surplus-expanding or surplus-absorbing taxation tends to grow more rapidly.

Little can be said about the latter issue. The current growth of the so-called taxpayers' revolt might indicate that the growth of surplus-expanding taxation has reached some sort of limit. Certainly the general battering that the legitimacy of the state has taken in the last several years would tend to reduce the state's capacity to use taxes to extract extra surplus value from the working class. At any rate, for the rest of this discussion we will assume that there has not been any major trend one way or the other in the balance between surplus-expanding and surplus-absorbing taxation.

More can be said about the relationship between unproductive state expenditures and indirectly-productive state expenditures. Given the underconsumptionist tendencies inherent in monopoly capital, it is obviously necessary for unproductive expenditures to grow more rapidly than productive expenditures. The growth of classical Keynesian madework and waste programs, most notably in military spending, reflects this requirement. There are several critical contradictions contained within this role of the state, however, which disrupt the smooth adjustment of unproductive state spending to the needs of monopoly capital.

a) *Contradiction of legitimation and accumulation*

The state does not serve the function merely of facilitating accumulation through demand maintenance; the state also serves a vital legitimation function in capitalist society which helps to stabilize and reproduce the class structure as a whole. The legitimation function directs much state activity toward co-opting potential sources of popular discontent by attempting to transform political demands into economic demands. The expansion of Keynesian programs beginning in the 1930's created a perfect political climate for dramatically expanding such legitimating state expenditures. For a long time it appeared that the state could kill two functional birds with one economic-policy stone.

The difficulty, however, is that once a demand on the state to provide some social service or to meet some social need is granted and becomes institutionalized, it becomes viewed as a right. There is a certain logic to legitimation which decrees that the political apparatus gets progressively diminishing returns in added legitimation for a given program over time. Once a program becomes seen as a right the continuation of that program adds little to the legitimacy of the state, whereas a cutback in the program would constitute a source of delegitimation. There is thus not only a tendency for programs once established to continue, but also a constant pressure for programs to expand, regardless of the requirements of the accumulation process. The hypothesis can therefore be advanced that, once Keynesian demand maintenance programs become bound up with the legitimation functions of the state, there is a tendency for unproductive spending to rise more rapidly than the systemic requirements for realization of surplus value might dictate.

b) *Military Keynesianism and productivity*

The particular institutional form that much Keynesian spending takes – specifically the system of state contracting known as the military-industrial complex – tends not only to absorb surplus but also to put a considerable damper on the subsequent development of productivity (except for occasional technological "spin-offs" from military research and development). Corporations who are major suppliers of military hardware are guaranteed a given profit rate by the state (especially in cost-plus contracts) and are thus under relatively little pressure to introduce inexpensive, efficient innovations into their production processes. Since for most military production there are only one or two potential suppliers, and since the criterion for awarding contracts generally has little to do with the efficiency of the corporation, military Keynesianism tends generally to reduce the average level of productivity in the economy.

c) *The weakening of mechanisms of crisis management*

The usual scenario for crisis and recovery is for the least productive capitals to be wiped out, capital to be devaluated, and conditions for profitable accumulation to be restored. The growth of monopoly capital, and especially of the dominant role of the state in regulating the economy, tends to weaken seriously this restorative mechanism. This is most obvious in the case of corporations which become locked into production for the state. In part because of the personal ties between the corporate elite and the state apparatus (especially in the military-industrial nexus), and in part because of the social dislocation that would result from the bankruptcy of a major monopoly corporation, the state finds it very difficult to abandon a corporation, even as that corporation's productivity declines. But the state is also forced to underwrite the low productivity of many other sectors of the economy, simply in order to avoid major disruptions of the economy (the railroads are a good example).

The upshot of these contradictions in the role of the state is as follows: although Keynesian policies originally emerged in an effort to cope with the problem of excessive surplus – as portrayed in the underconsumptionist model –, the policies in the end recreated the image of crisis held by the organic-composition-of-capital model – inadequate levels of surplus value – while simultaneously undermining the restorative mechanisms in the economy. That is, in spite of the necessity for waste in a period of monopoly capital, there is a tendency for the level of waste (i.e., unproductive spending) to expand more rapidly than the capacity of the system to produce waste (i.e., the rate of increase in productivity). Because the crisis-solving mechanisms are partially blocked, the result is chronic inflation combined with relatively high levels of unemployment, or what has come to be called "stagflation."[4]

The obvious solution to these dilemmas is, of course, for the state to shift the balance of its activities from unproductive to indirectly-productive spending. Indirectly-productive expenditures have certainly been steadily growing over the past several decades, although generally at a slower rate than unproductive expenditures. The state is increasingly involved not merely in what Offe (1974) calls "allocative" policies (policies which basically redistribute resources already produced or which mobilize the production of resources strictly for Keynesian purposes), but in "productive" policies as well (policies which directly impinge on the production process and which contribute to the productivity of the economy). As the productive forces in advanced capitalism have developed (i.e., highly sophisticated techonologies, increasingly interdependent productive processes, increasing requirement for highly specialized technical labor, etc.), it has become more and more difficult for individual capitals to provide all of the requirements for their own expanded reproduction, and they have turned to the state for various forms of socialized investments. It might well be thought, therefore, that the solution to the contradictions of Keynesian policies can be found in a dramatic expansion

[4] The implications of the internationalization of capital are that a given amount of effort by the state to reduce inflation will result in greater increases in unemployment than would otherwise be the case, since such state policies will tend to increase the movements of capital across national boarders (see Martinelli 1973). Internationalization will thus tend to push the Phillips curve away from the origin. It is probably impossible to disaggregate empirically the relative effects of (a) increasing internationalization of capital, and (b) increasing unproductive state spending, on the deterioration of the trade-off of inflation and unemployment, since empirically the two tend to move together.

of these emergent forms of indirectly-productive socialized investments. The problem is that the fundamentally Keynesian politics of the contemporary capitalist state – a politics rooted in pluralist interest-group demands, special interest subsidies, military production, etc. – act as a serious constraint on the potential growth of these newer productivity-enhancing forms of state intervention. This is the heart of the "fiscal crisis of the state": the constant pressures from the growth of unproductive spending, which are exceedingly difficult to curtail (for the reasons spelled out above), make it highly problematic for the state to finance the new forms of state policy which would help reverse the problem of declining productivity itself. Until such time as new political forces can be mobilized successfully to generate what O'Connor (1973) has aptly called a new "social industrial complex," it is difficult to see how this impasse can be overcome.

## II. The Historical Development of Capitalism and the Impediments to Accumulation

It should be obvious by now what the punch line of this paper is: At each stage of capitalist development there is a characteristic pattern of impediments to the accumulation process. Through a combination of class strategies by the capitalist state and individual strategies by individual capitalists attempting to maximize their profits, these impediments are overcome and the accumulation process continues in new forms. The solutions to the dominant impediments at each level of capitalist development, however, contain within themselves new contradictions which gradually emerge in the subsequent stages. This dialectic of the accumulation process is summarized in Chart 1.[5]

The chart is, of course, highly oversimplified. The structural "solutions" to a particular impediment to accumulation do not generally eliminate the problem altogether, but merely help it recede into the back-ground. Every period of capitalist development contains, if only in a residual form, the contradic-

[5] This chart draws heavily from a number of sources. The first three stages come fairly directly from Marx's discussion of primitive accumulation in Part VIII of Vol. I of *Capital*; the shift from stage 3 to stage 4 is quite similar to the analysis by David Levine (1973), especially Part III of his analysis, "The Theory of the Growth of the Capitalist Economy"; the analysis of stage 5 is based largely on that of James O'Connor (1973); and the analysis of the emergent problems of stage 6 has grown out of the analysis of Offe (1974).

tions characteristic of earlier periods. The purpose of the chart is not to present a rigid "stage theory" of capitalism, but rather to capture the overarching problems and movements of the capitalist system.[6]

Let us briefly examine each of the stages in the chart.

### 1. *Transition from simple commodity production to expanded reproduction*

The two crucial constraints on the accumulation process in the early period of primitive accumulation were, on the one hand, the existence of institutional forms of production which made close supervision and control of the workforce difficult, and, on the other, the relatively small size of the proletariat and thus the limited amount of exploitable labor. The lack of supervision of workers under conditions of cottage industry meant that the capitalist had little control over exactly how much the worker worked per day; it was also often exceedingly easy for the worker to embezzle considerable amounts of raw materials from the capitalist (see Marglin 1974 for an excellent discussion of these issues). The result was that the rate of exploitation tended

[6] The chart may give the impression that the particular path of capitalist development, and the particular pattern of contradictions which emerges at each stage in the process, are rigidly determined. This raises some extremely important questions about the underlying logic of the concept of "contradiction." In what exact sense are the contradictions schematically laid out in the chart "inevitable"? Do the solutions to impediments to accumulation in one period necessarily lead to future impediments? While it is obvious that each of the "solutions" outlined in the chart have certain inherent limits, it is less obvious that each of the "solutions" outlined in the chart have certain inherent limits, it is less obvious that the social forces in capitalist society necessarily push the system toward the limits, and thus transform a structural solution into a contradiction. Why, in other words, does each adaptive strategy of the capitalist system tend to exhaust itself in time?

A simple answer is that none of these adaptive strategies can eliminate the inherent class antagonisms of capitalism. Class antagonisms make a simple, homeostatic reproduction of the system impossible. A more complex answer is that the forms that class struggle takes are themselves molded by the dominant adaptive strategies of the system. The working class is not merely a passive force, even in its most integrated and contained periods. It adapts its strategies to the "structural solutions" which emerge in the course of capitalist development. In their most class-conscious form, these working class strategies are explicitly focused on exploiting the structural solutions and pushing them to their limits.

A similar argument can be made about the effects of struggle among capitalists (competition): as solutions to the impediments of accumulation emerge, individual capitalists adopt new forms of competition, new strategies for maximizing their individual accumulation. Since there is no overall planning in capitalist society to coordinate these individual strategies, there is an inherent tendency for these strategies gradually to push toward the limits of the existing structure within which accumulation takes place. There is thus a dialectic between the structural solutions to earlier constraints on accumulation and the forms of class struggle and competition which develop in response to those structural solutions.

to be low because the effective unpaid portion of the work day was low. In combination with the restricted size of the proletariat, this meant that the mass of surplus value available for accumulation tended to be quite low.

As Stephen Marglin has argued, in the English Industrial Revolution the creation of the factory provided the structural solution to the first of these constraints. Workers were brought together under a single roof and closely supervised in their work. They were forced to work as many hours as the capitalist dictated, and thus the amount of surplus labor increased considerably. The creation of factories, however, only heightened the problem of the shortage of free exploitable labor. A variety of state policies, such as open immigration, rural depopulation, closing of the poor houses, etc., contributed to the solution of the labor shortage.

2. *Transition from primitive accumulation to manufacture*

The continual expansion of the proletariat and of the factory system characterizes the transition from primitive accumulation to the period of manufacture. In the early period of this transition the major way of increasing the rate of exploitation was through the expansion of "absolute surplus value" (i.e., increases in surplus value resulting from the expansion of the working day and the intensity of work). Very quickly, the working day was increased virtually to its biological maximum. In spite of this, however, the actual rate of exploitation remained relatively low because of the generally low productivity of technology and the accompanying high value of labor power. Even when the standard of living of the worker was pushed down to bare subsistence, it still took a relatively high proportion of the working day for the worker to reproduce the value of his/her labor power.

The solution to the problem of the relatively low rate of surplus value came through the proliferation of technical innovations, which drastically cheapened the goods consumed by wage labor and thus lowered the value of labor power. Since many of these innovations were labor saving, they also had the effect of expanding the reserve army of the unemployed, thus further alleviating the general problem of the shortage of labor that characterized the period.

3. *Transition from manufacture to machinofacture*

The progressive introduction of machines into the production process defines the transition from simple manufacture to machinofacture. The earlier tendencies – expansion of factories, expansion of the proletariat, and so on – continue, but there is added a constant stream of new innovations. In addition, in this period the first effective forms of proletarian class organizations emerge. Demands are made both for a shortening of the working day and for raises in real wages. The increasing intensity of class struggle creates considerable additional pressure on capital to introduce labor-saving innovations. The result is that in the period of transition from manufacture to machinofacture there is a very rapidly growing organic composition of capital. Thus, in spite of an increasing rate of surplus value, there was a definite tendency for the rate of profit to fall.

The solution to this impediment to accumulation was contained within the impediment itself. The classic pattern of unproductive capitals, and increasing concentration and centralization of capital, provided the social mechanisms for periodically restructuring capital in ways which restored conditions favorable to accumulation.[7]

4. *Rise of monopoly capital*

As the organic composition of capital continued to rise in the 19th century and into the 20th century, two things occurred: capital tended to become ever more concentrated and centralized, and the rate of increase in the organic composition of capital tended to slow down. By some time in the first quarter of this century, it appears, the organic composition of capital more or less stabilized. The rate of exploitation, however, continued to rise, both because of general increases in productivity (both capital-saving and labor-saving) and because of monopoly power itself. The result was that a strong tendency toward realization and underconsumption problems emerged.

Simultaneous with these developments, the labor movement began to gather considerable strength, especially in the monopolized sectors of the economy. While demands tended to center on issues of wages and immediate working conditions, the growth of socialist and communist forces within the labor

[7] In addition to these structural solutions, many Marxists have argued, classical 19th-century European colonialism provided a (temporary) structural solution to the problem of the falling rate of profit. By bringing technologically backward, labor-intensive economies into the world capitalist system, colonialism in effect lowered the organic composition of capital on a world scale. Furthermore, colonialism involved the transfer of vast amounts of surplus value from the third world to the developed capitalist countries. This further reduced the tendency for the rate of profit to fall. For a discussion of this perspective on imperialism, see Mattick 1969, chap. 19.

Historical Pattern of Constraints on Accumulation and Emergent Structural Solutions

| *Stage of Capitalist Development* | *Central Constraints on Accumulation* | *Structural Solutions to Constraints* |
|---|---|---|
| 1. Early period of Primitive Accumulation: transition from simple commodity production to expanded reproduction. | Limits on the *mass* of surplus value due to the restricted size of the working class; limits on the unpaid portion of the working day caused by the lack of close supervision of the working class in the labor process (low rate of "absolute surplus value"). | Various institutional changes designed to expand the size of the proletariat (immigration, enclosures, etc.); creation of factories by the capitalist class to increase the control of the work process and the length of the work day. |
| 2. Transition from primitive accumulation to Manufacture. | Relatively low *rate* of surplus value because of the low level of productivity of the technology and the accompanying (relatively) high value of labor power; continuation of general shortage of labor. | Technical innovations, especially in the production of consumer goods which result in the cheapening of labor power; especiallyimportant are labor-saving innovations which increase the reserve army of the unemployed. |
| 3. Transition from manufacture to machinofacture. | Tendency for the organic composition of capital to rise with an accompanying tendency for the rate of profit to fall; early forms of the labor movement demanding a shorter work day. | Business cycles which devaluate capital and lead to an increasing concentration of capital; continuing pressure for labor-saving innovations to expand the reserve army and undermine the labor movement. |
| 4. Rise of Monopoly Capital | | |

| | | |
|---|---|---|
| | Tendency for the surplus to rise more rapidly than consumption demand, with a resulting tendency toward underconsumption/realization crises; growth of a more militant labor movement with socialist and communist currents. | → Keynesian forms of state intervention designed to expand aggregate demand, especially military spending; creation of complex promotion structures, job hierarchies, etc., general acceptance of collective bargaining. |
| 5. Advanced Monopoly Capital | Ever-increasing reproductive costs of the system as a whole stemming from the contradictions of the accumulation and legitimation functions of the state, resulting in stagnation with chronic inflation. These tendencies are considerably exacerbated by the continued growth of monopoly capital and the internationalization of capital. | → Extension of state intervention from simple Keynesian manipulations of effective demand to active involvement in the production process itself: state policies geared directly to increasing productivity ("post-industrial" state policies). |
| 6. State Directed Monopoly Capitalism | Ever-deepening politicization of the accumulation process itself: heightened contradiction between the socialization of production and the continuing private appropriation and control of the surplus product. Commodity production itself requires an increasingly decommodified sphere of production. | ?→ The emergence of a full-fledged, repressive "state capitalism." |

movement made the potential for a more genuinely revolutionary labor movement seem likely.

The great social invention of state-sponsored waste, academically legitimated as Keynesianism, constituted the major solution to the impediment of underconsumption. The discovery of collective bargaining and the creation of complex systems of job hierarchies and promotion structures (see Stone 1974 and Braverman 1974) helped to contain the labor movement in bounds compatible with such Keynesian solutions.

5. *Advanced monopoly capital*

The Keynesian solutions to underconsumption tended at least initially to dovetail with the political requirements for legitimation. But the initial harmony was shattered as the growth of unproductive state expenditures tended to expand faster than the surplus-absorbing requirements of the system. The continuing growth of monopoly on both a national and international scale has further contributed to the deterioration of the trade-off between inflation and unemployment. The internationalization of capital in particular has confounded the situation by undermining the capacity of national governments in the advanced capitalist countries to regulate effectively their own national economies.

The emergent solution to these problems of the ever-expanding reproductive costs of monopoly capitalism relative to the growth in productivity, is to move from simply Keynesian interventions in the economy to active state involvement in the production process itself. This is the juncture at which American monopoly capital finds itself in the mid-1970's. Qualitatively new forms of state intervention are called for, but the state apparatus seems prepared only to try once more the old Keynesian solutions. After this final attempt flounders, as it almost surely will, it is reasonable to expect that some tentative steps toward these new forms of state intervention and control of the economy will be taken.

---

[8] This expression should not be confused with the theory of "State Monopoly Capital" (commonly referred to as StaMoCap theory), in which the state is seen as manipulated by the dominant financial interest groups of monopoly capita. The implicit theory of the state underlying the present discussion is much closer to O'Conner's (1973) and Offe's (1973, 1974) than to StaMoCap theory. See Gold, Lo, and Wright (1975) for a general discussion of the theory of the state.

It is dangerous to make predictions about history, and especially dangerous to make predictions about the new forms of contradiction that are likely to emerge in the future. Nevertheless, some things seem fairly safe to say. As monopoly capitalism moves toward qualitatively new forms of state involvement in production, toward State Directed Monopoly Capital, there will be an ever-deepening politicization of the accumulation process itself. It will become increasingly difficult to apply a "neutral" market rationality to production; political criteria will become more and more central to production itself. Although it is almost certain that in the United States few major corporations would be formally nationalized, a greater and greater proportion of production will be *de facto* organized by the state. This does not mean, of course, that commodity production (production for exchange) would disappear, but rather that an increasingly important part of total production would be organ-ized by a logic other than commodity logic.

All of this would occur within the continuing context of capitalist social relations and a capitalist state which serves the function of reproducing the class structure of capitalist society. The expanded decommodified sphere of production would be strictly constrained by the requirements of reproducing commodity production itself. The new forms of impediments to accumulation would therefore center on the heightened contradiction between the progressive socialization (and politicization) of the process of production and the continuing private appropriation (through commodity production) of the surplus product.

While in a sense socialism is always an immanent potentiality in advanced capitalist society, the ever-increasing role of the state in accumulation is likely to move the socialist alternative more into the center of working class politics. This however in no sense implies that socialism is the only solution to these emergent contradictions. It is quite possible to imagine the development of a full-fledged state capitalism in the United States (although dressed in the symbols of private capitalism) which would deal with the glaring contradictions between legitimation and accumulation by means of considerable repression and centralized planning. There is, however, no automatic reason for the "solution" which is functional for capitalism to be the solution which emerges. Whether or not such a structural reordering of monopoly capital occurs depends, on the one hand, on the cohesiveness of the capitalist class and its capacity to generate a class politics in the interests of capital as a whole, and, on the other, on the strength of socialist movements in the working class and its capacity to organize a class politics capable of transforming decommodified production in the service of capital into socialist production controlled by the working class.

Fred Block

# Introduction to "Contradictions of Capitalism as a World System"

Returning to an article published almost thirty years ago is like exhuming a deceased relative; there is considerable dread as to how badly the body will have decomposed. With an article, the passage of time can be destructive in several distinct ways. First, the author's subsequent intellectual and political development can make earlier writings appear hopelessly naive. Second, historical change can reveal one's arguments and analysis to have been simply wrong or utterly irrelevant. Finally, changes in intellectual fashion or scholarly concern can enormously accelerate the process of decay by invalidating the basic premises of earlier scholarship.

It is only relative to this last process, that "Contradictions of Capitalism as a World System" can be said to have aged well.[1] The question of "globalization" and debates over the organization of the global economy have more currency in academia and actual politics than ever before in the U.S. Hence, the core question that the article asks – how will global capitalism organize itself? – is a more urgent question than ever. The article has stood up less well against subsequent historical developments. The article provides

[1] Even the term "capitalism" which was still the province largely of left wing academics in the mid-70's has aged well. It is now the term that the business press uses to describe the global market economy. The irony, of course, is that the term's critical valence has completely disappeared.

a useful account of the critical period of transition in the 1970's when the old Bretton Woods system was giving way to a new era of more disorganized global capitalism, but it failed to anticipate three key patterns. The first has been the extraordinary expansion of global financial flows, currency trading, and speculation in derivatives and other complex instruments that has occurred over the past twenty-five years. In a word, I imagined back then that the very small steps towards liberalization of financial flows in the global economy that had occurred in the early 1970's had already created an open world economy in which capital was free to move across national boundaries in response to market signals. The reality was that most nations still had a variety of capital controls in place and the process of liberalization had only just begun. What appeared to me then as a dangerous level of global financial anarchy looks in retrospect like a highly organized and stable system when compared to the results of two decades of financial liberalization.

The second and more humbling failure is my exaggeration of the instability of this newly liberalized global financial order. The article assumes that without movement towards substantially greater international economic coordination, the global economy would be vulnerable to escalating financial crises that could lead to a replay of the crisis of the 1930's. There has been a succession of international crises and severe economic problems, including the Third World debt crisis, the long term rise of European unemployment levels, the Japanese economic downturn in the 1990's, and the East Asian financial crisis at the end of the 1990's. But the dominant story has been the amazing resilience of the global economy and the ability of U.S. and other international policymakers to manage successfully a series of global crises. These successes in turn, helped to facilitate the dramatic economic booms in the U.S. in the 1980's and again in the 1990's. Writing in the 1970's, I simply could not imagine that an increasingly liberalized and fragile global financial system would be able to limp through thirty years without a disastrous crisis or escalating economic warfare among the major powers.

I also completely failed to anticipate the successful management of inflation in the U.S. and other developed capitalist societies in the 1980's and 1990's. In the 1970's, powerful inflationary pressures seemed to be part of the very nature of capitalism, and it was difficult to imagine that a series of shocks between 1978 and 1983 would bring inflation under control. The assumption that inflation would remain a central economic problem was, in turn, linked to my exaggeration of the fragility of global economic arrangements. With inflation under control, some of the problems of global economic coordination became more manageable than they had been in the 1970's.

Several aspects of my own subsequent intellectual development also make it unsettling to reopen this particular coffin. For one thing, I find the prose of the piece overly wordy and marked by too many passive constructions, so I am glad that the editor has cut the paper to its intellectual essentials. For another, the article was written with certain New Left Marxist assumptions that I have since discarded. Foremost among these is the idea that capitalism is a form of social organization characterized by a set of fixed internal contradictions that can be managed but never fully overcome. Hence, the fundamental economic contradiction at the heart of capitalism means that either it will be marked by periodic and deep economic downturns *or* it will face ongoing and intensifying inflationary pressures. Moreover, as this contradiction is displaced into the global arena, it will make global capitalism extremely vulnerable to either inter-imperialist conflicts or economic collapse. In short, those parts of the article that have aged the worst can be traced to these particular Marxist underpinnings.

"Contradictions of Capitalism as a World System" was written against the backdrop of the U.S. war in Southeast Asia. The article grew out of my dissertation – completed in 1974 – that examined the rise and fall of the Bretton Woods system (It was published after revisions as Block 1977), and even at the time, it was obvious that the growing strains in the global financial system were a direct consequence of the Vietnam War. Since I am revisiting this essay, as United States troops continue to wage military operations in Iraq and as theorists of the right now talk openly of an "American Empire", it is useful to also revisit the connection between capitalism and U.S. military interventions.

Let me begin by contrasting the way I thought about the Vietnam War at the time and the way that I think about the Iraq War now. In the movement against the Vietnam War, there was a critical fault line between liberals and radicals. For those of us on the radical side, liberals were the misguided people who believed that the Vietnam War was the result of a series of accidents or bad decisions. While we welcomed their participation in demonstrations to swell the numbers, we insisted to them that the war was not an accident. U.S. capitalism needed to expand abroad to extract resources and profits from the developing world. When this expansion encountered resistance, as it did in Vietnam, the United States had little choice but to confront that resistance militarily.

During the wave of demonstrations leading up to the U.S. invasion of Iraq, a similar division emerged. Some in the antiwar movement insisted that this was a war for oil and that it followed inevitably from the nature of U.S. capitalism and particularly the political power of the petroleum industry. Others insisted, however, that this was clearly a war of choice and that the main impetus came from the peculiar and particular political strategies of the Bush Administration. The irony was that in this second debate, I found myself on the "liberal" side of this divide.

My view is that the war decision grew out of the Bush Administration's struggle to resolve two deeply conflicting sets of influences. The first are the interests of internationally oriented U.S. businesses that push the United States to project its power internationally and engage with other nations to organize effective governance institutions for the world economy. The second are the preferences of the President's Christian conservative political base that are deeply hostile to multilateral institutions as indicated by the platform of the Republican Party of Texas that urges the U.S. to leave the United Nations, the International Monetary Fund, and the World Trade Organization. The Administration's "solution" has been to develop a unilateralist, preemptive, and heavily military foreign policy as a way to continue to project U.S. power internationally while retaining the support of its right wing and anti-internationalist political base (Block forthcoming).

The invasion of Iraq was a demonstration project for this new militarized foreign policy. In my view, oil and control of the Middle East were decidedly secondary to the primary objective of demonstrating the power of U.S. weaponry and the willingness of the U.S. to initiate war at a time and a place of its own choosing. To be sure, different interest groups within the Administration had somewhat different agendas, but what held them together was a belief that the United States needed to have a war in early 2003. But it follows from this analysis that this particular war by no means was inevitable or even the best way to protect the global interest of U.S. businesses.

The shift in my views from the Vietnam era to Iraq could be a simple product of aging and absorption into the academic mainstream. Just as my generation of radical sociologists rebelled against many of our teachers who had come to the discipline as radicals in the 1930's and 1940's, so it is probably our turn to be seen as apologists for the *status quo*. But I want to offer a different, more substantive, explanation that has to do with the history of Marxist theory.

Both in the 1960's and today, the identification of the "war as inevitable" position as the more radical is linked to the continuing influence and authority of Marxist theory. For more than 150 years, Marxist critics have insisted that poverty, class exploitation, and foreign wars are rooted in the capitalist mode of production and can only be eliminated through a radical transformation that breaks with private ownership of the means of production. And through to the end of the 1960's, Marxism helped inspire extraordinary upsurges of protest activity by workers, farmers, students, and others against poverty, war, and exploitation.

Since the end of the 1960's, however, Marxism has been in retreat as a political movement. While it continues to command the loyalty of pockets of militants in different parts of the world who sometimes are able to play a central role in mass movements, Marxism has ceased to be the central idiom even of those protest movements who target the institutions of global capitalism. For example, the World Social Forum in Porte Allegre, Brazil gathers militants from around the world to oppose neoliberal globalization, but its debates are not framed within a Marxist vocabulary.

There are a variety of reasons for this most recent "crisis of Marxism". The most obvious is the failure and ultimate collapse of many of the regimes that claimed to be realizing Marx's dream of building socialism. But while the failure of the Soviet Union helped to discredit the idea of socialism, this cannot be the only factor. After all, hope springs eternal and the belief that "another world is possible" continues to inspire resistance to capitalist globalization. A second less recognized problem is that particularly with the intensification of globalization in the 1970's, Marxist theory has had the ironic effect of making radical change seem too difficult to achieve. Precisely because capitalism is a global system, radical change in even two or three major nations would not be enough. Moreover, traditional Marxist doctrine tends to be highly suspicious of any forms of gradualism, so it is difficult to envision a series of changes that would cumulate over time in a break with capitalism. The result is that at a certain point, the radical argument that we need a worldwide revolution to establish a new type of society sounds to many to be a counsel of despair and defeatism (Gibson-Graham 1996; Block 2000).

Instinctively, many activists and theorists have begun to search for alternative theories that would still be as radical as Marxism in challenging the existing order but which envision the possibility of a series of partial and incomplete victories that would produce both meaningful reforms *and* establish conditions for even stronger movements to realize a vision of global social justice (For an interesting case study of one of the more important anti-globalization movements, see Ancelovici 2002). My view is that the framework of this alternative theory is beginning to emerge out of an extended conversation among theorists drawing on a range of different intellectual traditions (See, for example, Unger 1998; Domhoff 2003; Burawoy 2003).

This new framework results, in part, from turning Marx's own critique on Marxism. One strand of this derives from the way that Marx critiques bourgeois ideology. He argues that bourgeois ideology takes that which currently exists and naturalizes it by providing powerful arguments that there is simply no other way to organize a social order. So, for example, if poverty and misery were widespread in early industrial England that was because, as Ricardo and Malthus insisted, the iron law of wages dictated that the working class could only be paid wages sufficient for bare survival. Marx's point was that such arguments had no scientific value; they were simply devices designed to justify the status quo and discourage rebellion against it.

But what then of Marx's own claims that certain aspects of capitalism cannot really be changed without a root and branch destruction of the existing social order? How can we be certain that such claims are accurate? Perhaps, they are the mirror image of the arguments by bourgeois ideologists that the current order of things is a seamless web and any small change is likely to set off a chain of perverse consequences. Taking this critique seriously leads to the idea that there is far more contingency – far more that is up for grabs – in a given social order – even a capitalist social order – than both Marxism and conservative apologetics suggest. For example, the fact that the number of children who grow up in poverty in France or Germany is far lower than in the United States indicates that market societies have considerable leeway in constructing social policies that shape the extent and severity of poverty.

This point is reinforced by a second strand of argument that goes back to Marx – the idea that "Men [sic] make their own history, but not in conditions of their own choosing." Social constructionists have elaborated this epigram to argue that it is simply wrong to imagine that any given society has the coherence and internal unity of a living organism. On the contrary, actually existing societies are full of tensions and conflicts among different groups, different institutions and different ideas and there needs to be ongoing efforts to construct a sense that the ensemble of institutions can even hold together. In fact, ongoing political struggles can be understood as the efforts of competing groups to make this uneasy mixture fit together more coherently.

In this emergent approach, the exercise of class power by those who own the means of production continues to be an important factor in shaping market societies, but there are many more factors at work in determining the shape of social institutions. One must take account, for example, of the structure of the global system of political and economic power, the unique historical trajectories of national societies, and the particular institutional infrastructure of these societies – the shape and forms of their civil societies (See, particularly Burawoy 2003).

One can see this emergent radical social theory as resulting directly from the engagement of theorists from the Marxist tradition with a variety of non-Marxist intellectual currents including Weberian analysis, symbolic interactionism, and legal realism In my own intellectual development, the work of Karl Polanyi, especially *The Great Transformation* (2001 [1944]) has been extremely important. Significantly, Polanyi himself was struggling to synthesize Marxism with other theoretical elements in the 1930's and 1940's (Block 2003; Burawoy 2003).

Through this process of engagement, the distance between radical sociology and the mainstream of the discipline has narrowed considerably. To be sure, there are still many sociologists with a strong preference for work that is largely quantitative and apolitical, but it is now far easier within the discipline to do scholarly work that seeks not just to understand the world but to change it. Correspondingly, the distance between mainstream sociologists and the current Administration in Washington has never been greater. Whether it is foreign policy, energy policy, welfare policy, tax policy, science policy, or civil liberties, the disagreements seem to grow wider every day.

An explanation for this growing divergence is that the United States now faces one of those great historical turning points – comparable to the historical break that occurred in the 1930's. As at that time, the standard option for the society of simply muddling through the crisis with only a few minor course corrections is not a real alternative. There are only two possible options. The first is the kind of sharp rightward turn that the current Administration favors – a militaristic foreign policy abroad and a shredding of public services at home that will further deepen inequality and the marginalization of significant sectors of the society. The second is a renewal of progressive reforms that would challenge entrenched corporate power, reshape the United States' relations with the rest of the world, shift our energy policy to conservation and renewable sources, reduce social and economic inequalities, and rebuild and renew the public sector.

Despite the right wing's current domination over Congress, the Executive Branch, and much of the Federal Judiciary, the direction that the United States takes over the next decade is still very much up for grabs. Strange as it might sound, the emergence of an alternative radical social theory and the narrowing gap between radical and mainstream sociologists could be harbingers of a new era of social transformation in the United States on a scale comparable to the New Deal.

Fred Block

# Contradictions of Capitalism as a World System*

Some social institutions are only recognized and analyzed during the period of their decline. During normal times, their workings are perceived as part of the natural order of things. But as the institution begins to break down its existence becomes more obvious and subject to analysis. This is the way it has been with the organization of the post-World War II capitalist world economy.

Study of the international monetary system – the set of rules and institutions for organizing international economic transactions – follows this pattern. During and after World War II, the United States struggled, with eventual success, to impose on the rest of the world an international monetary system with both a high degree of openness (that is, a system in which goods and capital are free to cross national boundaries in response to market forces) and a large measure of special rights and responsibilities for the United States. During much of the post-War period the existence of an international monetary system with a specific structure was barely recognized in the U.S. However, beginning in the late fifties and continuing through the sixties, the United States experienced serious balance of payments deficits that had a devastating impact on the existing international monetary structures.

---

* The original version of this article appeared in *The Insurgent Sociologist*, 5:2 (Winter 1975), pp. 3–21.

The purpose of this essay is to develop a critique of the post-War international monetary system. My argument is that many of the problems of the world economy – particularly global inflation – are rooted in the high level of openness that has been institutionalized in the post-War international monetary system. It is my argument that this level of openness can only be sustained if some type of strong international economic coordination emerges. However, I will attempt to show that the obstacles to such coordination are enormous because of the reluctance of the U.S. to sacrifice its imperial interests for the sake of international economic order. In the final section, I argue that the probable direction of the world economy is toward increased regional organization and a further breakdown of the international monetary system.

Part of the purpose of this argument is to establish that the international monetary system faced a fundamental crisis even before the four-fold increase in the price of oil created huge new international payments problems. The problem of financing oil imports sharpens previously existing strains in the international monetary system and it is problematic whether the international monetary system will survive this new burden. But even if a solution to the immediate problem of financing the greatly increased petroleum bills is devised, the underlying problems described in this essay will still remain.

## Inflation and Post-War Capitalism

The tendency towards permanent inflation is rooted in the various techniques that post-World War II capitalism has used to avert the periodic crises that characterized the classical business cycle. But a particular country's rate of inflation at a particular time depends on a variety of factors – including the combativitiveness of its working class, the degree of monopoly power in pricing decisions, the level of economic maturity, the politically tolerable level of unemployment, and the political capital of the government in power.[1]

[1] I view inflation as the visible manifestation of the contradictions of advanced capitalism, in the same way that periodic economic crises were the indication of contradiction in classical capitalism. This means that there is no single cause of inflation, but it can be traced in a variety of ways to the fundamental contradictions of a system of production for private profit. The view of inflation presented here has drawn on a variety of writings: Andrew Glyn and Bob Sutcliffe, *Capitalism in Crisis* (New York, 1972); Paul Mattick, *Marx and Keynes* (Boston, 1968); James O'Connor, *The Fiscal Crisis of the State* (New York, 1973); David Bazelon, *The Paper Economy* (New York, 1963); Jacob Morris, "The Crisis of Inflation," *Monthly Review*, September, 1973. The discussion here is somewhat U.S.-centered, but much of the analysis applies to other developed capitalist economies.

The use of anti-deflationary devices to protect governments from the political consequences of deflation has contributed further to inflationary pressures. Maintenance of high levels of employment improves the bargaining power of labor. The response of the employers is to grant higher wages, but the employers raise the prices of their products to prevent redistribution of income away from profits. This results in general price rises which make the workers' wage gains illusory. In the classical business cycle, this process was brought to a halt by a severe deflation that reduced wage levels by massive unemployment and lowered price levels through the drying up of purchasing power. However, the successful prevention of deflation means that this kind of reduction of wages and prices never occurs. Instead, wages and prices continue moving upward at varying rates of speed.

As the government runs budget deficits to sustain high levels of aggregate demand, the expanded government debt serves as the foundation for an expansion of bank credit. This growth in available credit – necessary for the circulation of commodities at higher prices – means an expansion in consumer and business debt, including the accumulation of much debt of a speculative kind.

Expansion in government spending can also come to exert an inflationary pressure on the economy. The Keynesian-inspired increase in government spending originally served to absorb the social surplus that could not find profitable investment outlets. During the postwar years, the quantity of government spending grew parallel with the growth of the entire social product. However, only a part of the government spending serves to increase productivity in the private sector, while the state faces increasing demands on its resources from capitalists, government contractors and the public.

Government spending can therefore grow significantly faster than the total social product. This creates a situation in which the state is not only sustaining aggregate demand, but is competing with the private sector for resources. When the government attempts to finance its expanded budget by higher taxes or increased borrowing, the result is inflationary pressure. If taxes are raised, then business attempts to pass on the taxes through higher prices, while workers attempt to offset tax increases through larger wage gains.

Although Keynesian measures are not directly responsible, the development of post-World War II capitalism has seen increased domination of key industries by oligopolies – a further source of upward pressure on prices. The oligopolistic firms avoid price reductions which could set off costly price wars.

As inflation continues over a period of time, an "inflationary psychology" emerges that places further upward pressure on wages and prices. Labor unions come to understand the money illusion through which paper wage gains can go hand in hand with reductions in real wage levels. Unions respond with attempts to link wage levels to the rate of inflation through escalator provisions or they fight for wage gains greater than the annual rise in the cost of living. But because of the resistance by employers to a reduction in their profit levels, the higher wage increases are generally met with even larger price increases.

The difficulty of controlling this inflationary dynamic rests on the political impossibility of tolerating a deflation severe enough to reduce wages, prices, and interest rates dramatically. And increasingly, mild deflations are ineffective in even slowing inflation.

The major alternative to deflation as an anti-inflationary strategy has been the development of an incomes policy – a government imposed system of wage and price controls. The idea of such controls is to maintain a constant relationship between profits and wages through administrative measures, rather than market forces and inflation. While controls of this sort appear to have some initial success in halting inflation, they tend to break down over time. As individual capitalist enterprises experience government interference with their decision-making processes, they begin to agitate for a return to earlier freedom through the elimination of the controls. As long as the controls continue to exist, firms will attempt to subvert them through downgrading product quality, by tolerating the rise of black markets, and by the creation of artificial shortages.

## Inflation in an Open World Economy

The problem of controlling inflation on the national level is greatly complicated in a world economy in which goods and capital move across national boundaries in response to market forces. The most dramatic illustration of this complexity is the ironic consequences of domestic monetary policies. The normal use of monetary policy to prevent an overheating of the domestic economy involves pushing interest rates up. However, higher interest rates can attract capital from abroad which will act as a stimulus to the domestic economy.

Inflationary pressures in one national economy can also spill over into other economies through spreading shortages of commodities. Agricultural shortfalls, production bottlenecks, sharply increased speculative purchases, and even sudden growth in consumer demand can lead one country to rapidly increase its imports of certain products, resulting in parallel shortages in other countries. Inflation is exported by bidding up the price of certain commodities, and the increased price of those goods sets off price rises on related products.

If the various processes through which inflationary pressures are transmitted internationally worked to equalize the rate of inflation in all countries, then the problem of balance of payments adjustment would be greatly reduced. However, that equalization does not occur. National rates of inflation vary according to specific national conditions and the vulnerability of economies to imported inflations also differs dramatically. Sharp differences in inflation levels most often lead to balance of payments problems for high inflation countries.

Overcoming this kind of inflation-induced balance of payments deficit is the heart of the adjustment problem in post-war capitalism. And it is the ineffectiveness and unreliability of the major anti-inflationary tools that makes this kind of adjustment so difficult. The process is further complicated by the reluctance of low inflation countries with balance of payments surpluses to share the burden of adjustment. If low inflation countries allowed their rates of inflation to rise by a portion of the difference between the low and high rates, then the task of high inflation countries would be more manageable. However, there is no institutional mechanism for forcing the low inflation countries in this direction, and they are extremely reluctant to increase their rates of inflation through deliberate action.

This rationale against deliberately increasing the rate of inflation fits with the clear advantages of running limited balance of payments surpluses. It has frequently been noted that there is a lack of symmetry in the way that balance of payments deficits and surpluses are treated in the international monetary system. While countries with deficits are under strong pressure to restore equilibrium to prevent the depletion of currency reserves, there is no parallel pressure on surplus countries. In fact, there are good reasons for surplus countries to protect their surplus position. Since the international balance of payments is a zero-sum game, every balance of payments deficit is matched by surpluses somewhere else. So that if most governments shape their economic policies to maintain surpluses instead of aiming for equilibrium, then some countries within the system are bound to end up in deficit. This bias towards surplus makes it far more difficult for deficit countries to restore equilibrium.

## Exchange Rate Adjustments

The orthodox economic solution to balance of payments deficits caused by high rates of inflation is a downward shift in the deficit country's exchange rate. The problem is that this mechanism often fails to work in the way that economic theory indicates it should. Devaluations are designed to restore international equilibrium by reducing domestic expenditures through a market device. However, if a country's labor movement is anxious to preserve the existing level of real income, it will fight for wage increases to compensate for the losses due to devaluation. If successful, this could set off new inflationary dynamics that would easily eliminate the potential trade gain from devaluation. Even when devaluations are combined with efforts to control inflation through monetary or fiscal restraint, the strength of unions in key sectors can still prevent the reduction in real incomes that devaluations are intended to produce.

Since exchange rate changes do not automatically restore balance of payments equilibrium and sometimes even have adverse effects, floating exchange rates are not the universal panacea that they have been alleged to be. An international monetary order in which exchange rates are free to find their "correct" level in the free market could only work if real wage levels could be readily lowered. For real incomes to be successfully reduced without inflation in contemporary society requires, at the very least, a concerted and conscious policy by business and government.

## Solutions to the Adjustment Problem

The absence of any clear-cut technique for high inflation-deficit countries to restore balance of payments equilibrium means that countries must rely on a mix of policies that include direct controls over trade and capital, monetary and fiscal restraints, and exchange rate changes. However, if a particular mix of policies is to be successful, some cooperation from low inflation-surplus countries must be forthcoming. If surplus countries respond to the policies of deficit countries with parallel measures – for example, matching interest rate increases with increases of their own – then there is little likelihood that adjustment measures will work.[2]

---

[2] Eric Chalmers, *International Interest Rate War* (London, 1972), documents the way in which countries raised their interest rates competitively during the 60's, a competition in which both deficit and surplus countries participated.

The occasional resort to capital and trade controls as part of the balance of payments mix highlights the importance of cooperation among surplus and deficit countries. The resort to import quotas or an import surcharge always creates the risk of retaliation and a possible trade war. In addition, at the existing level of international economic interdependence controls over capital movements create certain dangers.

While much progress was made during the 1960's developing international forums for discussion and exchange of information about international economic policies, little progress has been made in actually coordinating policies.[3] When national governments face serious balance of payments crises, they still tend to develop their responses independently. While international consultations occur, they generally take the form of explanations of the governments' decisions, rather than international formulation of those decisions.

### The Need for Coordination

The problem of balance of payments adjustment in an inflation-prone world economy is not the only reason that there is an increasing need for a high level of international coordination in the management of the international monetary system. The failure to control closely the annual changes in the supply of international liquidity can have disastrous deflationary or inflationary consequences.

The point is simple: the greater the openness of the world economy, the greater the extent of international economic interdependence and the greater the need for institutions to manage the international economy in the same way central banks and national governments manage domestic economies. The problem, of course, is how one establishes such an international institutional structure in a world of competing nation states. Three basic solutions to the problem exist: the exercise of this coordinating and managing role by one dominant and responsible power, the development of supranational institutions to which national governments cede important elements of economic sovereignty, and the development of an effective joint partnership among a number of major nations that would coordinate the world economy in their common interest.

---

[3] The principal forums for economic policy discussions have been the working parties of the OECD, the Group of Ten, and the central bankers who meet monthly at Basle for meetings of the Bank for International Settlements.

The international monetary system has worked best in those periods when one nation had the economic and political power to assure general acceptance of a code of international economic behavior and could provide by itself adequate quantities of international credit and liquidity. But the continuing U.S. balance of payments deficit indicate that the U.S. no longer has the absolute economic superiority to fulfill that coordinating role. And if the U.S. lacks that power, certainly no other country or region can even pretend that it could play that role. This leaves only the second and third solutions as possible means towards international economic coordination today. The critical question is whether those solutions can be reconciled with the defense of U.S. imperial interests and the aspirations of Western European and Japanese capitalists.

### The Supranational Solution

The idea of creating an international central bank with broad powers to intervene in national economies has existed since before Bretton Woods. But significantly, national governments have shown little willingness to cede economic sovereignty to supranational agencies and those supranational institutions that have been created have had little independent power. In consequence, the advocates of such supranational structures have generally been dismissed as unrealistic visionaries.

But in recent years, the idea of an international central bank surrounded by a whole network of other supranational economic agencies has gained support from a new quarter – the spokesmen and defenders of the multinational corporations. These business internationalists argue that the nation state is no longer a viable economic unit. In their view, the nation state acts as a fetter on economic progress in the same way that principalities and duchies slowed the rise of capitalism before the creation of national markets.

The multinational corporate utopia is a recreation of the 19th century utopia of a self-regulating international market.[4] Both derive their intellectual legitimation from an economic theory that systematically obscures the differential benefits for different countries and different classes of such an open

[4] For a description of the 19th century utopia, see Karl Polanyi, *The Great Transformation* (Boston, 1957).

world economy. The reality is that the 19th century self-regulating market was a product of Britain's economic and military hegemony, and it lasted only as long as Britain's international dominance. The contemporary utopia, and the rapid expansion of multinational enterprises that has generated the utopia, similarly is a product of U.S. hegemony. It has been U.S. political, economic, and military power that have made the world safe for multinational enterprises, and it is no mere coincidence that the vast majority of these multinational enterprises are U.S.-based firms.

The real question is what will happen as U.S. multinational firms face increasing competition from multinational firms based in Japan and Western Europe. It hardly seems likely that U.S. multinational firms would be willing to give up the diplomatic support that they presently get from their home government in exchange for the support of some new international institution. Nor is it probable that the United States or any other government would be willing to abandon the right to back its corporations in the struggle for scarce raw materials, for scientific and technological innovations, and for access to important foreign markets.

Another reason why this kind of internationalization of key economic functions seems unlikely has to do with the growth of the national state's domestic economic responsibilities. The rapid growth in levels of international trade and investment has occurred simultaneously with an expansion of the state's role in the coordination and stabilization of the domestic economy. The successful completion of a range of tasks by the state – maintenance of high levels of employment, of reasonable price levels, of satisfactory quantities of key commodities, of adequate expenditures for social welfare and social infrastructure – are necessary for the economy to work effectively enough to preserve social peace.

This does not mean that any form of internationalization of economic functions is impossible. International conventions and even effective international regulations can be developed in areas such as patents where the common interest is strong and national practices are similar. It is also possible that some limited form of international central banking could evolve as long as it concentrated on reserve creation and the management of international capital markets, while leaving governments free to determine their own policies.

## Coordination Through Joint Management

If the emergence of a supranational structure for the coordination of the capitalist world economy is not in the cards, then some form of joint management is necessary to assure coordination and the smooth growth of international credit and liquidity.

But joint management would require the United States to abide by a definite set of rules in its international economic behavior including, particularly, the management of its balance of payments. Over time, it seems likely that tensions would develop between adherence to those rules and the pursuit of U.S. global political, military and economic goals.

One risk is that a policy of retrenchment in a period of intensifying international competition could further worsen the U.S. international economic position, forcing ever more serious retreat. A cutback in the U.S. overseas political and military presence could cause U.S.-based firms to lose economic opportunities to foreign based firms. The loss of major construction contracts and the loss of control or access to lucrative raw materials could hurt the profits of U.S.-based firms and lead to higher prices for U.S. raw material imports.

In addition to strengthening the relative position of Western European and Japanese capitalists, American retrenchment might also mean a strengthened position for the Socialist bloc and for revolutionary and nationalist forces in the underdeveloped world. If U.S. retrenchment is not matched by a complementary extension of political and military efforts by Western Europe and Japan, there would be increased opportunities for countries to opt out of the capitalist world economy.

The risks involved in retrenchment compound the difficulties facing a state apparatus that must design a strategy for imperial retreat combining maximum balance of payments savings with minimum damage to the international position. If the state were free to pursue the most rational strategy, the job would be merely difficult, but the state must formulate its policies in the context of pressures by a variety of powerful interest groups, many of which are strongly represented in the state apparatus itself.

Joint management would also have consequences for U.S. domestic economic policies. Particularly if only a limited retrenchment could be organized, the domestic economy would bear most of the burden of restoring balance of payments equilibrium. The United States would no longer have the relative freedom to inflate that it has enjoyed in the past. This would dictate increasing economy in government expenditures, a higher modal unemployment rate and a firmer wages policy.

## Western Europe and Japan

The position of Western and Japan towards joint management is complex. While their governments and strongest firms have much to gain from a coordinated management of the world economy and the consequent American retrenchment, there is likely to be strong domestic resistance to an expanded international role.

The most immediate gain for Western Europe and Japan from joint partnership will be greater ease in domestic economic management. Limits on the U.S. ability to export its deficits and its inflation would help reduce the inflationary pressure elsewhere. Agreement with the United States on new rules for adjustment would probably depoliticize the adjustment process and make it simpler to manage the entire economy.

For Western Europe the pursuit of a coherent international policy depends either on the further development of a supranational authority or on the emergence of a cohesive alliance among its most powerful countries – West Germany and France. The first development is problematic for the near future for many of the same reasons that make the emergence of international economic management unlikely – most fundamentally, the reluctance of states to cede sovereignty over crucial economic policy decisions. The latter development is more likely, but there is the continuing possibility that an alliance can be shattered by international conflicts of interest or by domestic pressures that block agreement on critical issues. But without a reasonably stable alliance at the center, the European nations would be left to formulate independent foreign policies.

Japan also would find it difficult to make a claim to global joint partnership if Western Europe as a region did not participate in the effort. But even under the most ideal circumstances, it is uncertain whether domestic resistance to a greatly expanded international role for Japan could be overcome. The rapid pace of Japan's post-World War II industrial growth has left a huge backlog of social demands that might interfere with an expanded international role.

Western Europe and Japan can also be dissuaded by the United States from pressing too hard for an effective global partnership. As long as joint management is seen by the United States as an undesirable alternative, the U.S. can attempt to play on internal divisions in and between Western Europe and Japan to block an effective challenge.

## Past Patterns and Prospects

The evolution of the international monetary system since the early Sixties has been characterized by two critical patterns. The first is the gradual abandonment of the formal and informal rules for managing the system, usually at the initiative of the United States. The second is the slow but steady expansion in the economic influence of Western Europe and Japan over a larger regional area, generally outside of any formal international framework. The continuation of these two patterns points to an international economy without a coherent international structure – held together by a series of *ad hoc* measures and understandings among countries that are increasingly organized on a regional rather than an international level. While this could provide a high degree of flexibility and adaptability for the world economy, it could leave the international monetary system with little institutional structure or with few resources for handling a serious international political-economic crisis.

The most dramatic example of the abandonment of previously existing rules has been the changing relationship between the dollar and gold. Another modification of the rules has been the use by the United States of capital controls. While these are allowed under the IMF articles, it is one of the unwritten rules that an international reserve center must maintain free access to its capital markets for those countries that deposit their currency reserves in the center country. The use of the 10% import surcharge by the United States in 1971 is another illustration of rule breaking. U.S. actions are also largely responsible for the final significant rule violation – the end of a regime of fixed exchange rates.

The abandonment of the old rules has occurred without their replacement by new rules. Rule abandonment has generally been an adaptive device designed to allow the system to continue to work, usually on U.S. terms, but with less definite structure. Agreement on new rules is problematic because it raises all of the issues of joint management. But without new rules, more and more aspects of the system become variable – the price of gold, the price of currencies, day to day management of exchange rates, and the trade policies that are internationally tolerated. With fewer certainties, it is more difficult to anticipate the reaction of others and to make rational calculations. The formulation of national adjustment policies becomes even more complex. The result is an international system that is subject to high levels of speculative activity as economic actors attempt to defend themselves against uncertainty. And speculation itself becomes another source of uncertainty and instability.

The second pattern – the gradual growth in the regional economic influence of Western Europe and Japan – does not contradict the earlier argument that these countries will find it difficult to assume the responsibilities of joint management of the international economy. While it would require greater domestic consensus and more extensive resources for the EEC or Japan to play the role of global powers, they have been able with existing political and economic resources to extend their power along regional lines. Within an international structure that is guaranteed by U.S. power, the EEC and Japan have consolidated close economic and political ties to a number of countries in their part of the world. Although the nature of these ties varies enormously, the point is that for many of these countries, their political and economic future is defined in relation to the EEC or Japan. The increasingly elaborate ties these countries have to the EEC or Japan provide the major structure for their international economic relations.[5]

Particularly in the case of the Common Market countries, the close economic ties to other European countries or to former colonies in Africa are of long historical standing. However, the formation and development of the Common Market has altered the relationship because of the enormous size of the unified market and the increased resources available for aid and investment. There might have been, for example, a strong tendency for France's former African colonies to drift out of the French orbit after independence in order to maximize their economic opportunities. However, the advantages of association with the Common Market as a whole are sufficiently great to discourage that kind of drift.

In a somewhat similar fashion, European countries who are outside of the EEC face a strong pressure to link their economies even closer to the Common Market. The sheer size of their trade with the EEC makes it imperative that

[5] The tendency towards regionalization is addressed in William Diebold, *The U.S. and the Industrial World* (New York, 1972). The emergence of a Japanese-dominated region is explored in Jon Halliday and Gavan McCormack, *Japanese Imperialism Today* (New York, 1973).

they do everything possible to assure that trade will continue uninterruptedly despite shifts in EEC policy. For some of the countries of Southeast Asia as well as for Taiwan and South Korea, increasing dependence on Japan for markets and for steady flows of aid and credit also dictates an effort to coordinate their economies with Japan's.

While the precise significance of this kind of incipient regional organization is difficult to evaluate, one way of understanding the possibilities is in terms of potential currency areas. As close economic and political ties develop around a strong central country, there is a tendency for the weaker countries to hold their currency reserves in the stronger country and to maintain their currencies in a relatively fixed relation to that central currency. While the EEC is still far from the full economic integration that would make possible a common currency, the EEC's strongest currency, the German mark, is increasingly being used as a reserve currency. The German authorities had resisted this tendency because of a fear that they would lose control over domestic economic conditions, but their opposition appears to have softened. Increasingly, European countries outside of the EEC and underdeveloped countries with close ties to the EEC are holding mark assets in their reserves.

The actual and potential pattern of regional organization tends to create more stable and predictable conditions within the regional areas, but the relations between regional areas become problematic. Despite strong patterns of trade and investment within regional groupings, there is also a great quantity of trade and investment across regional groupings. It is this increasingly internationalized character of the world economy that creates the need for structures that effectively coordinate the international economy as a whole.

There is a possibility that something close to joint management of the world economy could evolve out of cooperation among increasingly consolidated regional blocs. However, there are a number of reasons for doubting this outcome. First, with each region focusing on its own internal health, the health of the international economy as a whole would be no one's special concern. It is hard to see how the complex tasks of managing the international economy as a whole could be carried out in those conditions. Second, the very strength of regional blocs could lead them to engage in aggressive economic behavior that would make cooperation extremely difficult. Finally, in the event of some kind of major political-economic crisis in the world economy, there would be a powerful temptation to seek solutions at the regional level that would be inimical to the health of the world economy as a whole.

While drawing out predictions about the future from these patterns is hazardous, it is necessary to highlight the precarious position of the international monetary system. The gradual dissolution of the post-war international monetary order means that international economic relations occur in a context of few shared rules and increasing uncertainty. To be sure, the international economy can probably continue for a long time just on the basis of a shared interest in avoiding chaos. But the absence of a real international monetary order heightens the possibility that the normal competition among capitalist powers can escalate into economic warfare, especially as the world economy is faced with new and unexpected strains such as the oil price rise and global food shortages.

# VI. The Future for a Critical Sociology

Michael Burawoy

# The Critical Turn to Public Sociology[1]

> The standpoint of the old materialism is civil society; the standpoint of the new is human society, or social humanity.
>
> The philosophers have only interpreted the world, in various ways; the point is to change it.
>
> – Karl Marx

Revisiting "radical sociology" of the 1970s one cannot but be struck by its unrepentant academic character, both in its analytic style and its substantive remoteness. It mirrored the world it sought to conquer. For all its radicalism its immediate object was the transformation of sociology not of society. Like those Young Hegelians of whom Marx and Engels spoke so contemptuously we were fighting phrases with phrases, making revolutions with words. Our theoretical obsessions came not from the lived experience or common sense of subaltern classes, but from the contradictions and anomalies of our abstract research programs. The audiences for our reinventions of marxism, and our earnest diatribes against bourgeois sociology were not agents of history – workers, peasants, minorities – but a narrow body of intellectuals, largely cut off from the world they claimed to represent. The grand exception was feminism of which Catharine MacKinnon (1989: 83) wrote

[1] Thanks to Rhonda Levine, Eddie Webster, and Erik Wright for their comments on an earlier draft.

that it was the "first theory to emerge from those whose interests it affirms," although it too could enter flights of abstract theorizing, even as it demanded connection with experience.

To be sure some radical sociologists pursued political work in the trenches of civil society, but only for a chasm to separate it from academic work – an ironic endorsement of Max Weber's division between politics and science. Such political activity might have been a hidden impetus behind critical sociology, but it rarely gave the latter content or direction. The purpose of this essay is to bring this hidden impetus into the limelight, name it, validate it, cultivate it and expand it into public sociologies. My thesis here is that critical sociology is, and should be, ever more concerned with promoting public sociologies, albeit of a special kind.

## Fifty Years of Sociology: From Ideology to Utopia

If the collection reproduced here is typical then the task of "radical sociology" was not to produce a concrete vision that would seize the imagination and galvanize the will of some subordinate class, but rather it was to convince intellectuals, and especially academics, of the power of Marxist thinking. Reversing the prevailing wisdom, we tried to demonstrate that Marxism was the true science while sociology was but ideology. In appealing to fellow academics, we sometimes even believed that we were the class, or a fraction thereof, that was about to make history – whether Ehrenreich and Ehrenreich's (1977) "professional-managerial class" or the ubiquitous "new class" as it was so often called. This is rather ironic since for the most part, we behaved like run-of-the-mill scholars, scavenging the writings of Marx and Engels (and their successors) for material that would help us comprehend the limits and possibilities of contemporary capitalism.

With *Capital* and other iconic texts, as our exemplars, we interrogated capitalism's tendency toward self-destruction. Was overproduction or the falling rate of profit the root cause of capitalism's deepening crises? How precarious was the international capitalist system? How did the capitalist state – or was it the state in capitalist society? – contain those crises, and how, at the same time, did it regulate class struggle? What was the relation of the state to the ruling class? Did the ruling class even rule? And further, what after all were classes? Are they observable? How does one know one when one sees one? Or more concretely, how could one move beyond Marx's bipolar conception of class structure? What was middle about the middle class? And, moving into the realm of the superstructures, how were classes reproduced? Who produced the ruling ideas – ideology – and how were those ideas accepted by the ruled? What was the function of education – an instrument of mobility or the preparation of class subordination? And what of gender? Could Marxists accommodate patriarchy in their class analysis? Or was the marriage of Marxism and Feminism doomed from the beginning? And race? Was race merely a way of dividing the working class, or the reproduction of cheap labor power? What chance for a class coalition of white and black? Could race be reduced to class or did it require a framework of its own? These were some of the issues, reproduced in the articles of this volume, that consumed our passion for a new world.

There is no doubt that we were writing first and foremost for ourselves – we were aspiring to produce, in Dick Flacks's (1972) words, a "*socialist sociology*." We staged a two pronged attack to replace sociology with Marxism – trenchant criticisms of the former and creative reinvention of the latter. Our efforts were largely geared to what Louis Althusser enthroned as "theoretical practice" – his attempt to liberate Marxism-Leninism from the Stalinist vice of the French Communist Party. Was it not strange, however, that Marxists should think ideas to be so important? Was it not strange that we made so little effort to persuade people beyond the academy of the validity and power of our ideas! What were we up to?

We were not as absurd as I am implying. A little context might help. The world had just been in flames – student movements had made vigorous and often violent assaults on the citadels of power from Mexico to Beijing (remember Victor Nee's (1969) *The Cultural Revolution at Peking University*!) from Berlin to Tokyo, from Manila to Seoul, from Berkeley to Paris. This was an era of civil rights protests across the United States, the anti-Vietnam War solidarity movement across advanced capitalism and beyond. This was the period of the Prague Spring, of the Third World revolution of Regis Debray, Frantz Fanon and Che Guevara. And there was the women's movement battering against so many institutions. The American Sociological Association did not escape: militant Blacks, Hispanics, women, liberation sociologists all demanded access to and representation in their association. A new order was being born which initially faced fierce resistance from mainstream sociology. The radical sociologists of the 1970s were trying to carve into theory what was happening in practice, trying to catch up with a world pregnant with its opposite. We were merely (!) taking the revolution to the university – bastion of power in the knowledge society.

Sociology, after all, was still in the hands of a messianic professoriate, who, when the ghettos were in flames and the napalm bombs were falling, were celebrating the undying virtues of "America" – its liberal democracy, its openness, its economic dynamism, its affluence, exalting its model as "the first new nation." Schooled in structural functionalism, these missionary – sociologists saw themselves as the guardians of value consensus, inventors of stratification theory, the debunkers of collective behavior as pure irrationality, celebrants of racial accommodation and complementary sex roles and, of course, apostles of the end of ideology. As disinterred by Alvin Gouldner (1970) – critical sociologist par excellence – sociology was in deep crisis because its domain assumptions, its guiding theories were out of keeping with the society they sought to comprehend. Gouldner claimed that structural functionalism's days were numbered, and he was right.

The radical assault on postwar sociology was surprisingly successful. From the early 70s on, trench after trench succumbed to invading forces: stratification gave way to class analysis and later more broadly to the study of inequality, conditions of liberal democracy gave way to studies of state and revolution, social psychological adaptation to work gave way to theories of alienation and the transformation of work, sex roles gave way to gender domination, value consensus turned into the diffusion of ruling ideologies through school and media, irrational collective behavior became the politics of social movements. Fortresses fell as old classics went into abeyance and new ones appeared. Marx and Engels became part of the canon while Durkheim and Weber were given radical reinterpretations. Feminism and then Foucault were soon knocking at the door.

It seemed to many as though sociology was suffering defeat after defeat, but it was actually reorganizing itself, albeit with our help. In a barely-conscious war of position sociology-in-crisis had reinvented itself by selective appropriation of radical sociology. The result, therefore, was a far cry from our imagined socialist sociology. Indeed, the very notion of socialism was now expunged from sociological vocabulary, even before the fall of the Berlin Wall. To be sure mainstream sociology had imbibed a near fatal dose of marxism and feminism. But it didn't die, it only choked, vomiting up much of the critical ingredient. We had been warned. From the beginning Frankfurt-influenced critical theorists had been skeptical of competing with bourgeois science on its own terrain, the danger of losing sight of critique, of subjugating what could be to what is. Science was the problem not the solution. By sidestepping debate over goals and values, the new Marxism was in danger of reproducing the very domination it criticized. Foucault would claim to put the final nail in the coffin of science with his adumbration of the iron embrace of knowledge and power. This put radical sociology on the defensive, trapped in a black hole – remote from its historic agents and absorbed into disciplinary practices.

The critical theorists and poststructuralists were not entirely off the mark but they did miss what was gained. Even if marxism and feminism proved to be the saviors rather than the grave-diggers of sociology, still the new discipline had displaced the old guard of structural functionalism together with their anointed successors. They, in turn, confirmed their displacement with displays of displeasure at the state of the discipline. Through the 1980s and into the 1990s we heard about the dissolution of sociology, its incoherence, its fragmentation, its lack of center. We heard lament after lament about the sorry state of our discipline in, for example, Stephen Turner and Jonathan Turner's (1990) *The Impossible Science*, Irving Louis Horowitz's (1993) *The Decomposition of Sociology*, Stephen Cole's (2001) edited collection of mainly the old guard, *What's Wrong with Sociology?* In that volume Seymour Martin Lipset complained of politicization – when he was young he learned to separate politics from science, but not the new generation. James Coleman (1990–1) penned various articles about the invasion of "norms" (always potentially dangerous in a rational choice world) to disrupt the free play of ideas in the university. The Turners (1990) rewrote the history of sociology – now an impossible science. From its inception it was too weak to stand on its own two feet, bereft of resources and sponsors, overrun by public controversies. What a departure from the earlier triumphalism of the 1950s' and 60s' when Merton, Lazarsfeld, Stouffer, Parsons and Shils saw sociology as the science of the new age!

Nor was the displaced generation completely wrong, sociology had lost its singular program, that amalgam of grand theory and abstracted empiricism, with "middle range theory" holding both to the fire, all controlled by an old boy network that spanned a few elite departments. Since then the American Sociological Association has undergone democratic decentralization with the proliferation of journals, sections, and awards. For those who lost control this was anarchy, disrupting the consensus necessary for the growth of science, and therefore prefiguring the decline of sociology. Those of the old guard with a political will sought to turn the clock back. During the 1980s and 1990s, they tried to engineer an authoritarian recentralization, to reassert their control over journals or create new ones, bolster the command of elite institutions, destroy democratic committee representation in the ASA, terminate the careers of infidels, design new hegemonic projects based on the supremacy of quantification or rational choice theory. All to little avail. The old guard could not outlive its defeat. The successor generation, weaned on critical sociology, held sway, embraced democratic decentralization, widened the doors to minority groups, deepened participation, and set about creating alternative sociologies.

If the impulse behind the "radical sociology" of the 1970s was to catch up with a turbulent world that we thought harbored revolutionary change, today the situation is moving in reverse. The world lags behind sociology. Now, the point is not to transform sociology but to transform the world. Invoking Karl Mannheim (1936), we may say that over the last 50 years sociology has moved from an "ideology" affirming the status quo to become something more akin to a "utopia" threatening "the bonds of the existing order." It is not only that sociology has become more "radical," but the world has become more reactionary (and more insidious and astute in normalizing its appalling deeds). To put it crudely, market tyrannies and state despotisms have deepened inequalities and abrogated freedoms both within and among nations – both tendencies unleashed by the Fall of Communism and consolidated in the aftermath of September 11th. If there are fortifications holding up the advance of these two forces, they lie, broadly speaking, within civil society, the breeding ground of movements for the defense of human rights, environmental justice, labor conditions, etc. This is sociology's home ground. It has an important role to play in these struggles, both in sustaining civil society itself and in nurturing organizations and movements on its terrain.

Why should such a burden fall on the shoulders of sociology? If political science can be distinguished by its object and value, namely the state and the defense of order, and if economics can be distinguished by its object and value, the market and its expansion, then sociology's object and value are civil society and its resilience. To be sure, these are sweeping generalizations that overlook the internal heterogeneity of these disciplines, that ignore, for example, the perestroika movement in political science and the prominent dissidents within economics – Joseph Stiglitz, Amatya Sen, and Paul Krugman to name but three. Indeed, all disciplines are contested fields, but, that having been said, they all have their defining projects, their central tendencies which set the terms of opposition. Thus, sociology too, is no unitary vanguard party, fanning the flames of civil society. It too has its oppositions – radical and conservative – that borrow from economics and political science as well as more thinly from anthropology, the humanities, and even biology. Indeed, disciplines are not watertight compartments. Just as sociology borrows from its neighbors, so the perestroika opposition and the dissident economists draw from sociology. But again this transplanting takes place within the framework of the overall disciplinary project. Thus, states and markets are of great interest to sociologists but from the standpoint of their connection to civil society or their embeddedness in the social.

Let me be clear, our disciplinary project cannot and should not be reduced to *critical sociology*, which makes no sense without a *professional sociology* to criticize or even without a *public sociology* to infuse with its commitments, just as all three find their complement in a *policy sociology* with its more instrumental deployment of knowledge. It would take me far afield here to elaborate this quadripartite division of our discipline, suffice to say that its health depends upon the interdependence and interconnection among the four sociologies even while recognizing their unequal power. (See Burawoy et al. 2004.) Professional sociology, in particular, by which I mean the development of our research programs primarily within an academic context, gives legitimacy and expertise to the other three sociologies, but it also defines our overall project as one inextricably connected to civil society.

Sociology's connection to civil society is as immediate as the connection of economics to the economy, and both connections are the product of history.[2] Sociology grew up in the 19th. century with the birth of civil society – in the United States it was born in the reform movements, amelioration associations, religious communities, in Europe it came of age in the late 19th. century with mass education, political parties, trade unions, organs of public opinion, and a panoply of voluntary associations. Where civil society died, as in Stalinist Russia, Fascist Italy, or Pinochet's Chile, sociology also disappeared. Where civil society was resurgent, as in the perestroika twilight of the Soviet Union, in the proliferation of community-labor organizations in

[2] As Marion Fourcade-Gourinchas (2003) has shown, the relation between economists and the economy is far more self-conscious and transparent, which is, of course, in part, the secret of its success.

South Africa or civil rights in the United States – then sociology too was resurgent. Sociology's fate today depends on its connection to a vibrant civil society, and therefore the interest of sociology coincides with the universal interest – humanity's interest – in containing if not repelling the terrorist state and the commodification of everything, that ruinous combination we call neoliberalism.

## The 21st Century: Prospects for a Public Sociology

My thesis, then, is that critical sociologists should focus less on radicalizing professional sociology, although there is *always* room for that, and more on fostering public sociologies to bolster the organs of civil society. So much for the critical need for public sociology, but what are its prospects? There is much evidence that such an outward looking project is supported by a growing sentiment among United States sociologists themselves.[3]

The initiatives span a spectrum of political stances. We can begin with the least radical, which must include the new magazine *Contexts*, that broadcasts the best and most publicly relevant of sociological research. It has been enthusiastically received by sociologists even if it has not yet found a wider audience. Another index of outward engagement is the activities of the executive office of the ASA. Acting at the insistence of its members, it has campaigned to defend research interests around human subjects protocols and in specific areas such as sexual behavior that have come under attack from within Congress and the Department of Health and Human Services. Further afield it has defended sociologists imprisoned for human rights activism such as the Egyptian, Saad Ibrahim. And it has supported sociology departments threatened with closure, both at home and abroad.

In 2003 the ASA went beyond its own corporate interests on a number of issues. It submitted an Amicus Curiae brief to the Supreme Court in defense of affirmative action in the Michigan Law School case, and later in the year it opposed California's Racial Privacy initiative. More controversially but no less decisively a two-thirds majority supported a member resolution to oppose the war in Iraq. Members voted in full cognizance of possible adverse effects

[3] Needless to say in many third world countries sociology *is* public sociology. Only in the United States, where professional sociology is so strong do we have to coin the very notion of "public sociology." I am, in this essay, only concerned with the United States. But see, for example, Burawoy (2003a).

for sociology. In 1968, at the height of the anti-Vietnam-War protests, a similar resolution was *defeated* by a two-thirds majority. While in a personal opinion poll just over half (54%) were opposed to the Vietnam War, 35 years later a full 75% of voters were opposed to the Iraq War. All of which suggests that sociologists have become more critical of the state and more prepared to voice that criticism.[4]

It's not only that collective sentiments predispose sociology to take a public turn, the decentralized structure of the discipline has become better equipped to address multiple publics. If the proliferation of sections, journals, prestige hierarchies, etc. heralds the dissolution of sociology for some, for others it harbors and advances public dialogue. The division into overlapping but coherent subfields – sex and gender, medical, work and occupations, labor and labor movements, race and ethnicity, crime and deviance, immigration, etc. – map the terrain of actual publics for sociologists to address. It is important to give some underlying coherence to these diverse fields and hence the larger sections – culture, political sociology, theory – also have a role to play. Underpinning these larger visions are the broadest understandings of our discipline, visions that are nurtured, sustained, channeled, reconstructed by critical sociologies – the reflexive heart of our discipline, its collective conscience if you will.

The dissolutionists – the hegemons of yesteryear – would prefer a very different discipline, more akin to that of economics where precepts and presuppositions do not form a diffuse collective conscience but a singular set of assumptions, models, exemplars that all have to accept as the price of admission. Economics is organized along the lines of the communist party with a politburo that directs the profession at home and spreads market doctrine abroad – all under the banner of freedom of choice. Such a centralized despotism is conducive to effective interventions in the policy arena where definitive

[4] This, of course, did not go unopposed. 102 sociologists signed a petition addressed to the ethics committee of the ASA to declare the resolution as being in violation of its code of conduct. There was a fear that the ASA was becoming a political pressure group rather than a body concerned with the pursuit of science. The ethics committee rejected the petition as being beyond its purview and there the matter rested. Again the democratic structure of the ASA stands out, requiring any member resolution that garners support from 3% of the membership to be endorsed by the Executive Council or, if it is not endorsed, it then goes to the vote of the membership at large. The American Political Science Association and American Economics Association by contrast are constitutionally barred from resolutions that go beyond their immediate professional interests.

answers are at a premium. This is so different from sociology's array of overlapping research programs. Its decentered universe encourages reflexivity, and multiple conversations with diverse publics. We are less effective as servants of power but more effective as facilitators, educators, raising consciousness, turning private problems into public issues. Our heterogeneity is better suited to a public rather than a policy role.

Of course, it may not be simply the structure of our discipline that handicaps us in the policy field, but also the messages we carry. The United States government is ever less interested in assuring social and economic rights – guaranteeing minimum welfare, protecting civil liberties, reducing racism, improving medical benefits for all, creating a more secure world for all. Perhaps at the local level where municipal administration is more sensitive to the needs of its citizens there is more scope for sociological intervention. Indeed, as the national state becomes more socially irresponsible, as it becomes less concerned with its public mission and more with the private interest, so more and more of the welfare, caring, education, security burden is downloaded onto the locality. Here is a more likely terrain for a policy sociology.[5] Leaving the question of policy sociology aside, however, we must ask whether our message is also too left of publics let alone states? Can we produce the ignition to spark the conversation?

It would be a mistake to underestimate the gap but it would be equally foolish to ignore our accomplishments. I note, for example, the excitement around the creation of the new labor and labor movements section in the ASA, and the University of California's Institute of Labor and Employment which in its short life has fostered a rare collaborative engagement between labor and sociology around a myriad of issues, including substandard working conditions, strategies for organizing campaigns, the changing face of the labor market, family leave, not to mention the educative role of its labor centers.[6]

[5] The possibility of a public sociology, therefore, varies by state. In the New Deal or Civil Rights Era sociology made deeper inroads into federal agencies than in the era of the neoliberal state. Equally, we note that in some countries, such as Norway, Finland and Sweden, sociology enjoys a much stronger presence in government. Still, I would argue that sociology's comparative advantage and spontaneous object lies with civil society and that the autonomy of policy sociology will depend upon the strength of public sociology.

[6] Thus, Edna Bonacich, author of articles on the split labor market, one of which is reproduced in this collection, has followed the road to public sociology by researching the apparel industry in close collaboration with the union (UNITE) and the anti-sweatshop campaign (Bonacich and Appelbaum, 2000).

Its vitality and success is underlined by the hostile attention it has received from right wing think tanks, and the conservative press. Despite an earnest battle it could be one of the first victims of the Schwarzenegger Regime. Moving to other terrains sociologists have for a long time been engaged in a dialogue with communities of faith, prison communities, neighborhood associations, and immigrant groups. Thus, one should be careful not to reduce public sociology to its "traditional" form as opinion pieces in national newspapers. Although these national interventions are important they obscure the vast swathe of grass roots or "organic" public sociologies, less visible but no less important. We need to recognize what has hitherto been marginalized and privatized, to validate public sociology – in all its varieties – by bringing it into the company of professional sociology. It is truism that students are our first public and, moreover, they take sociology to other publics, what we might call secondary publics, but we could think more broadly of public sociology as an extension of our educative role, bringing sociology directly to diverse publics. Just as students may initially resist our messages only later to be gripped by them, so the same can be true beyond the academy.

Still, we have not finished with the doom and gloom school. Political scientists, such as Robert Putnam (2000) and Theda Skocpol (2003), aided and abetted by some sociologists, have been sounding the alarm about the decline of civil society, gobbled up by the state, by bureaucratization, by the media. Their results are far from unequivocal, but leaving that issue aside, if social capital is indeed diminishing then surely we should be in the business of shoring it up. Here we would do well to think of the success of feminists, sociologists among them, in turning women from an inert social category into an active public, ready to march for its interests. As sociologists we not only invent new categories but also give them normative and political valence. To fail to do so is to give carte blanche to state and market to fill the vacuum with their own needs. We are in the business of fostering such publics as the poor, the delinquent, the incarcerated, women with breast cancer, people with AIDS, single women, gays and so on not to control them but to expand their powers of self-determination. We should not abandon them to the regulatory state but engage them directly. When we study social movements we simultaneously endorse their presence as a public. We should be more self-conscious about our relation to the people we study, and the effects we produce in the act of research.

If skeptics remain – those who believe that the terrain of civil society is too arid, too infertile for us to cultivate publics – then to them I say, we have always recourse to our own organizations. One of the peculiar features of US civil society is the presence of strong and independent professional associations. To be sure they have generally fought for their own corporate interests but not always. Lawyers, for example, have led the way in civic professionalism, concerned themselves with the defense of human and civic rights. It may amount to no more than a public relations face that camouflages enormous power, but it is nonetheless important for all that. As a discipline sociology was born in close proximity to moral reform just as individual sociologists are often born in moral combat. Professionalism has tried to smother the moral impetus in a cloak of science, just as it has forced us into careers that disparage moral commitment. The moral moment, however, may be repressed or marginalized, it may be suspended or put into remission, but it never disappears. It springs back to life when and where it is least expected. As we saw above the sentiments behind civic professionalism within sociology are strong and growing. Still, it is ironic, but also hopeful, that when publics were strong critical sociology turned inward, whereas now, when publics are weaker, critical sociology turns outwards.

In rebutting the nay-sayers I do not want to sound an overly triumphant note. We should not forget that we are still critical sociologists, trained to see the negative as well as the positive! In underscoring the opportunities as well as the urgency of the issues at stake, we should not lose sight of the continuing professional opposition to public sociology. It's not just a matter of one recalcitrant generation, but, as Andrew Abbott (1988) has noted, of the inbuilt tendencies of professions to establish their status by distancing themselves from publics, by fetishizing the inaccessibility of their knowledge. There will always be a tension, a symbiotic opposition if you will, between professional and public sociology that critical sociology will have to navigate.

## Real Utopias: An Agenda for a Critical Public Sociology

The "critical turn" to public sociology has two very different meanings. So far we have only focused on one meaning, namely the *necessity and possibility* of public sociology, the necessity and possibility of moving from interpretation to engagement, from theory to practice, from the academy to its publics. Thus, the *necessity* for public sociology comes from the "scissors" movement – the disciplinary field of sociology drifting leftwards as broader politics and economics moves rightwards. The *possibility* for public sociology comes from sociology's spontaneous connection to – its reflexive relation with – civil society.

There is, however, a second meaning to the "critical turn," namely a turn to *critique*, that is a public sociology that is *"critical of"* as well as *"critical to"* the world it engages, a public sociology that seeks to transcend rather than uphold what exists. To put it another way, a critical sociology cannot endorse every turning outwards, every strengthening of civil society. We should be wary of the communitarian tendency, seeing civil society and the publics that traverse it as inherently virtuous, always repelling the evil forces of state despotism and market tyranny. Civil society can be the arm of authoritarian and fascist regimes just as easily as it can defend humanity against dictatorship. Its expansion and resilience are necessary but not sufficient conditions for defensive struggles against the terrorist state. More generally, civil society is the collaborative arm of all capitalist states, to which it is connected by a thousand threads, reproducing consent to capitalist domination. Furthermore, increasingly, states themselves promote civil society in order to make it the overburdened recipient of civic responsibilities – offloading responsibility for welfare, medical care, care for the elderly, education, unemployment, poverty, environmental degradation and the like onto social markets and voluntary associations. Finally, civil society originates its own forms of domination – racial divides, scattered hegemonies of gender and sexuality, capillary powers – that call for their own war of position. Still, if civil society is no panacea it is nonetheless the best possible, indeed the only, terrain for sociologists to organize their public initiatives.

Given the Janus faced character of civil society – simultaneously an instrument of domination and a launching pad for enhanced self-determination – we need to develop normative and institutional criteria for progressive intervention. We need to foster a civil society that is not only strong and autonomous but also democratically self-governing, responsive to multiple interests, and moreover one that penetrates the state itself. We need to make the state responsive to civil society, facilitating, promoting and protecting the conditions of participatory democracy. This is the vision that lies behind Archon Fung and Erik Wright's (2003) empowered participatory governance (EPG) – a model of an active, self-governing civil society that they derive from the interrogation of participatory budgeting in Porto Alegre, Panchayat Reform in Kerala, neighborhood governance of public schools in Chicago, and habitat conservation planning in the United States. From these experiments Fung and Wright have developed a set of political principles, design characteristics and background conditions for EPG that have been debated in many venues around the world.

This sets out an agenda for a critical approach to public sociology. It begins from the common sense of different communities; it interrogates that common sense for generalizable principles; it draws up a design that is accessible to and thereby an object for discussion by other communities. In other words, it becomes a *real utopia,* that is a utopia based in the existing world. But the analysis doesn't stop here. It draws on sociology's wealth of knowledge, its scientific heritage, to ask of any such real utopia three further questions: What are the conditions of its genesis – can it be transplanted? What are the conditions of its existence – how can it be reproduced over time? What are its internal and external contradictions – what is its long term trajectory? Here once again there are possibilities for an exciting convergence of professional, public and policy sociologies on terms defined by critical sociology.

We might say that critical engagement with real utopias is today an integral part of the project of *sociological socialism.* It is a vision of socialism that places *human society, or social humanity* at its organizing center, a vision that was central to Marx but that was too often lost before it was again picked up by Gramsci and Polanyi (Burawoy, 2003b). If public sociology is to have a progressive impact it will have to hold itself continuously accountable to some such vision of democratic socialism.

# Notes on Contributors

**Fred Block** is Professor of Sociology at the University of California at Davis. His recent work has centered on developing a Polanyian understanding of the interaction of states and markets in contemporary societies. His essay, "Karl Polanyi and the Writing of *The Great Transformation*," appeared in *Theory and Society*, June 2003 and his essay on "The State and The Economy" (with Peter Evans) will appear in the second edition of *The Handbook of Economic Sociology* in 2004.

**Edna Bonacich** is Professor of Sociology and Ethnic Studies at the University of California, Riverside. Her major research interest is the study of class and race, with special emphasis on racial divisions in the working class. She has studied the garment industry, co-authoring *Behind the Label: Inequality in the Los Angeles Apparel Industry*. She is currently pursuing research on the ports of Los Angeles/Long Beach and the surrounding logistics systems.

**Samuel Bowles** is Director of the Behavioral Sciences Program at the Santa Fe Institute and Emeritus Professor of Economics at the University of Massachusetts at Amherst. His recent scholarly papers have appeared in *Nature, American Economic Review, Journal of Theoretical Biology, Philosophy and Public Affairs, Quarterly Journal of Economics, Journal of Economic Literature, Journal of Economic Perspectives, Behavioral and Brain Science, Theoretical Population Biology,* and the *Economic Journal.*

**Michael Burawoy** is Professor of Sociology at the University of California, Berkeley. He has brought his experiences of industrial work in Zambia, United States, Hungary and Russia to an academic Marxism. He has written and edited numerous books, the most recent of which is *Global Ethnography: Forces, Connections and Imaginations in a Postmodern World* (University of California Press, 2000). He is now studying the work of academe to reverse the flow of knowledge.

**Val Burris** is Professor of Sociology at the University of Oregon. His major research interests are in the areas of power structure research and economic and political elites. His recent articles have appeared in *American Sociological Review, Critical Sociology, Social Problems, and Sociological Focus.*

**G. William Domhoff** is Research Professor in the Department of Sociology at the University of California, Santa Cruz. He is the author of numerous books on power in America, the most recent of which are *Who Rules America? Fourth Edition* (McGraw-Hill, 2002) and *Changing The Powers That Be: How The Left Can Stop Losing and Win* (Rowman and Littlefield, 2003).

**Zillah Eisenstein** is Professor of Politics at Ithaca College. Her recent publications include *Hatreds, Sexualized and Racialized Conflicts of the 21st Century* (Routledge, 1996),

*Global Obscenities (*NYU Press, 1998*), Manmade Breast Cancers* (Cornell University Press, 2001) and *Against Empire* (Zed Press, forthcoming 2005).

**Richard Flacks** is Professor of Sociology at the University of California at Santa Barbara. He is the author of *"Making History" The American Left and the American Mind* (1968), co-author (with Jack Whelan) of *Beyond the Barricade: the Sixties Generation Grows Up* (1989), and coeditor (with Barbara Epstein and Marcie Darnovsky) of *Cultural Politics and Social Movements* (1995).

**Martha E. Gimenez** is Professor of Sociology at the University of Colorado at Boulder. She has published numerous articles and book chapters on Marxist theory, Marxist feminism, U.S. politics of racial and ethnic enumeration, and social inequality. Her recent publications have appeared in *Race, Gender & Class, Organization & Environment*, and *Radical Philosophy*.

**Herbert Gintis** is Emeritus Professor of Economics and the University of Massachusetts and External Faculty at the Santa Fe Institute. His recent books include *Moral Sentiments and Material Interests: On the Foundations of Cooperation in Economic Life* (MIT Press, 2004), *Foundations of Human Sociality: Ethnography and Experiments in Fifteen Small-scale Societies* (Oxford University Press, 2004), and *Game Theory Evolving* (Princeton University Press, 2000).

**Rhonda F. Levine** is Professor of Sociology at Colgate University. Her most recent books include *Class, Networks, and Identity: Replanting Jewish Lives from Nazi Germany to Rural New York* (Rowman and Littlefield, 2001) and *Social Class and Stratification: Classic Statements and Theoretical Debates*, ed. (Rowman & Littlefield, 1998) She is currently doing research on the hopes, fears, and educational experiences of African American teenagers in a diverse small-city high school in the northeast.

**Harvey Molotch** is Professor of Sociology and Metropolitan Studies at New York University. His most recent book is *Where Stuff Comes From* which analyzes the worlds of consumption and product development. His prior works have earned numerous awards, including Distinguished Contribution to the Discipline of Sociology, Award for Lifetime Achievement in Urban and Community Studies (Lynd Award), and Outstanding Scholarly Publication in Urban and Community Studies (Park Award).

**Goran Therborn** is Director of the Swedish Collegium for Advanced Study in the Social Sciences and University Professor of Sociology at Uppsala University. In 2004 he published *Between Sex and Power: Family in the World 1900–2000* (Routledge), (as editor and co-author) *Inequalities of the World* (Verso), and (as co-editor and co-author) *Asia and Europe under Globalization* (Brill).

**Erik Wright** is Vilas Distinguished Professor of Sociology at the University of Wisconsin. His academic work has been centrally concerned with reconstructing the Marxist tradition of social theory and research in ways that attempt to make it more relevant to contemporary concerns and more cogent as a scientific framework of analysis. His recent books include *Class Counts: Comparative Studies in Class Analysis* (1997, 2000), and *Deepening Democracy: Innovations in Empowered Participatory Governance* (with Archon Fung, 2003).

# Bibliography

Abbott, Andrew. 1988. *The System of Professions*. Chicago: University of Chicago Press.

Allen, Robert. 1970. *Black Awakening in Capitalist America*. Garden City, N.Y.: Doubleday.

Alliances Against Women's Oppression. 1983. *Poverty: Not for Women Only – A Critique of the Feminization of Poverty*. AAWO Discussion Paper No. 3, September.

Alston, L.J., & Ferrie, J.P. 1999. *Southern Paternalism and the American Welfare State*. New York: Cambridge University Press.

Amenta, E. 1998. *Bold Relief: Institutional Politics and the Origins of Modern American Social Policy*. Princeton: Princeton University Press.

Amin, Samir. 1976. *Unequal Development*. New York: Monthly Review Press.

Amin, Samir. 1975. "Toward a Structural Crisis of World Capitalism," *Socialist Revolution*, No. 23.

Ancelovici, Marcos. 2002. "Organizing against Globalization: The Case of ATTAC in France," *Politics & Society* 30:3 (September): 427–463.

Banfield, Edward. 1962. *Political Influence*. New York: Free Press.

Banton, Michael. 1974. "1960: A Turning Point in the Study of Race Relations," *Daedalus* 103:40–41.

Baran, Paul and Sweezy, Paul. 1966. *Monopoly Capital*. New York: Monthly Review Press.

Barth, Fredrick, ed. 1969. *Ethnic Groups and Boundaries*. Boston: Little, Brown.

Beamish, Tom. 2002. *Silent Spill*. Cambridge, MA: MIT Press.

Benedict, Barton. 1968. "Family Firms and Economic Development," *Southwest Journal of Anthropology* 24:19–24.

Benston, Margaret. 1969. "The Political Economy of Women's Liberation," *Monthly Review*, September.

Berg, Ivan. 1971. *Education and Jobs: The Great Training Robbery*. Boston: Beacon Press.

Berger, Peter L., and Thomas Luckman. 1966. *The Social Construction of Reality: A Treatise in the Sociology of Knowledge*. Garden City, N.J.: Doubleday.

Berman, Daniel M. 1978. *Death on A Job – Occupational Health and Safety Struggles in the United States*. New York: Monthly Review Press.

Berry, J. 1999. *The New Liberalism*. Washington: Brookings Institution Press.

Bettelheim, Charles. 1970. "Economic Inequalities Between Nations and International Solidarity," *Monthly Review* 22:19–24.

Binstock, Jean. 1970. "Survival in the American College Industry," unpublished Ph.D. dissertation for Brandeis University.

Birkelund, Gunn Elisabeth. 2002. "A Class Analysis for the Future," *Acta Sociologica* 45: 217–221.

Blackburn, Robin. 1997. *The Making of New World Slavery: From the Baroque to the Modern, 1492–1800*. London: Verso.

Blalock, Hubert M., Jr. 1967. *Toward a Theory of Minority Group Relations.* New York: John Wiley.

Blauner, Robert (n.d.). "Marxist Theory, Nationality, and Colonialism," unpublished manuscript.

Blauner, Robert. 1972. *Racial Oppression in America.* New York: Harper and Row.

Block, Fred. Forthcoming. "The Global Economy in the Bush Era," *Socio-Economic Review.*

Block, Fred. 2003. "Karl Polanyi and the Writing of *The Great Transformation,*" *Theory and Society* 32:3 (June): 275–306.

Block, Fred. 2000. "Deconstructing Capitalism as a System," *Rethinking Marxism* 12:3 (Fall): 83–98.

Block, Fred. 1977. *The Origins of International Economic Disorder.* Berkeley: University of California Press.

Bluestone, Barry and B. Harrison. 1986. "Most Jobs in the U.S. Low-Paying," *Boulder Daily Camera,* December 10.

Blumer, Herbert. 1965. "Industrialization and Race Relations," in *Industrialism and Race Relations,* edited by Guy Hunter. London: Oxford University Press.

Body, Raford, and James Crotty. 1975. "Class Conflict and Macro-Policy: The Political Business Cycle," *Review of Radical Political Economics,* Vol. 7, No. 1.

Bonacich, Edna. 1980. "The Development of U.S. Capitalism and its Influence on Asian Immigration," unpublished manuscript.

Bonacich, Edna. 1979. "The Past, Present, and Future of Split Labor Market Theory," in *Research and Ethnic Relations,* edited by Cora B. Marrett and Cheryl Leggon. Greenwich, Conn.: JAI Press.

Bonacich, Edna. 1976. "Advanced Capitalism and Black/White Relations in the United States: A Split Labor Market Interpretation," *American Sociological Review* 41:34–51.

Bonacich, Edna. 1975. "Abolition, the Extent of Slavery and the Position of Free Blacks: A Study of Split Labor Markets in the United States, 1830–1863," *American Journal of Sociology* 81:601–628.

Bonacich, Edna. 1973. "A Theory of Middleman Minorities," *American Sociological Review* 38:583–594.

Bonacich, Edna. 1972. "A Theory of Ethnic Antagonism: The Split Labor Market," *American Sociological Review* 37:547–559.

Bonacich, Edna and Hirata, Lucie Cheng. 1979. "International Labor Migration: A Theoretical Orientation," unpublished manuscript.

Bonacich, Edna and Richard Appelbaum. 2000. *Behind the Label.* Berkeley and Los Angeles: University of California Press.

Bonjean, Charles M., Richard J. Hill, and S. Dale McLemore. 1967. *Sociological Measurement: An Inventory of Scales and Indices.* San Francisco: Chaldler.

Boorstin, Daniel. 1961. *The Image: A Guide to Pseudo Events in America.* New York: Harper.

Bowles, Samuel, and Herbert Gintis. 1975. *Schooling in Capitalist America: Reform and the Contradictions of Economic Life.* Basic Books, forthcoming.

Braverman, Harry. 1974. *Labor and Monopoly Capital*. New York: Monthly Review.

Brenner, Marshall H. 1968. "The Use of High School Data to Predict Work Performance," *Journal of Applied Psychology*, Vol. 52, No. 1, January.

Brown, J. Larry. 1987. "Hunger in the U.S.," *Scientific American* 256(2): 37–41.

Burawoy, Michael. 1976. "The Functions and Reproduction of Migrant Labor," *American Journal of Sociology* 81:1050–1087.

Burawoy, Michael, William Gamson, Charlotte Ryan, Stephen Pfohl, Diane Vaughan, Charles Derber, and Juliet Schor. 2004. "Public Sociologies: A Symposium from Boston College," *Social Problems*, 51(1): 103–130.

Burawoy, Michael. 2003a. "Public Sociology: South African Dilemmas in a Global Context," Address to the South African Sociological Association, June 29th.

Burawoy, Michael. 2003b. "For a Sociological Marxism: The Complementary Convergence of Antonio Gramsci and Karl Polanyi," *Politics and Society* 31: 193–261.

Bureau of the Census. 1987. *Current Population Reports, Series P-60, No. 157, Money Income and Poverty Status of Families and Persons in the United States: 1986*. No. 2 (February): 37–41. Washington, D.C.: U.S. Government Printing Office.

Bureau of the Census. 1986a. *Current Population Reports, Series P-60, No. 152, Characteristics of the Population Below the Poverty Level: 1984*. Washington, D.C.: U.S. Government Printing Office.

Bureau of the Census. 1986b. *Current Population Reports, Series P-60, No. 157, Money Income and Poverty Status of Families and Persons in the United States: 1986*. Washington, D.C.: U.S. Government Printing Office.

Bureau of the Census. 1986c. *Statistical Abstracts of the United States: 1987* (107th Edition). Washington, D.C.: U.S. Government Printing Office.

Burris, Val. 1987. "The Neo-Marxist Synthesis of Marx and Weber on Class," pp. 67–90 in N. Wiley, ed., *The Marx-Weber Debate*. Newbury Park, CA: Sage.

Burris, Val. 1986. "The Discovery of the New Middle Class," *Theory and Society* 15: 317–349.

Burris, Val. 1980. "Capital accumulation and the rise of the new middle class," *Review of Radical Political Economics* 12(1).

Carchedi, Guglielmo. 1986. "Two Models of Class Analysis," *Capital and Class* 29: 195–215.

Carchedi, Guglielmo. 1977. *On the Economic Identification of Social Classes*. London: Routledge and Kegan Paul.

Carnoy, Martin and Derek Shearer. 1980. *Economic Democracy*. New York: Random House.

Castells, Manuel. 1975. "Immigrant Workers and Class Struggles in Advanced Capitalism: The Western European Experience," *Politics and Society* 5, 1:33–66.

Center for the Study of Social Policy. 1985. "The Flip Side of Black Families Headed by Women: the Economic Status of Black Men," pp. 232–238 in R. Staples, ed., *The Black Family*. Belmont, Ca.: Wadsworth.

Chavkin, Wend, ed. 1984. *Double Exposure: Women's Health Hazards on the Job and at Home*. New York: Monthly Review Press.

Clark, Terry and Seymour M. Lipset. 1991. "Are Social Classes Dying?" *International Sociology* 6: 397–410.

Cogoy, Mario. 1973. "The Fall in the Rate of Profit and the Theory of Accumulation," *BSCE*, Winter, pp. 52–67.

Cogoy, Mario. 1972. "Les Theories Neo-Marxistes, Marx et l'Accumulation du Capital," *Les Temps Modernes*, September–October, pp. 396–427.

Cohen, Abner. 1969. *Custom and Politics in Urban Africa: A Study of Hausa Migrants in Yoruba Towns*. Berkeley: University of California Press.

Cole, Stephen. 2001. *What's Wrong with Sociology?* New Brunswick, NJ: Transaction Publishers.

Coleman, James. 1990–91. "The Sydney Hook Memorial Award Address: On the Self-Suppression of Academic Freedom," *Academic Questions* 4(1): 17–22.

Collins, Randall. 1979. *The Credential Society*. New York: Academic Press.

Congressional Quarterly. 1983. "Problems of the Unemployed," pp. 129–155 in *Employment in America*. Washington, D.C.

Cox, Oliver. 1948. *Caste, Class, and Race*. New York: Modern Reader.

Dollars & Sense. 1987a. "Even Young Men Feel the Pinch," no. 131 (November): 10–11.

Domhoff, G.W. 2003. *Changing The Powers That Be: How The Left Can Stop Losing And Win*. Lanham, Maryland: Rowman and Littlefield.

Domhoff, G.W. 2002a. "The power elite, public policy, and public opinion," in J. Manza, F. Cook, & B. Page (eds.), *Navigating public opinion: Polls, policy, and the future of American democracy* (pp. 124–137). New York: Oxford University Press.

Domhoff, G.W. 2002b. *Who Rules America?* (Fourth ed.). New York: McGraw-Hill.

Domhoff, G.W. 1996. *State Autonomy or Class Dominance? Case Studies on Policy Making in America*. Hawthorne, NY: Aldine de Gruyter.

Domhoff, G.W. 1990. *The Power Elite and the State: How Policy Is Made in America*. Hawthorne, NY: Aldine de Gruyter.

Domhoff, G.W. 1979. *The Powers That Be*. New York: Random House.

Domhoff, G.W. 1972. *Fat Cats and Democrats: The Role of the Big Rich in the Party of the Common Man*. Englewood Cliffs, NJ: Prentice-Hall.

Edelman, Murry. 1964. *The Symbolic Uses of Politics*. Urbana: University of Illinois Press.

Edwards, Richard C. 1975. "Personal Traits and 'Success' in Schooling and Work," *Journal of Applied Psychology*, forthcoming.

Ehrenreich, Barbara. 1987. "Making Poverty A Women's Issue," *Dollars & Sense*, Special Issue on Women and Work.

Ehrenreich, Barbara and John Ehrenreich. 1977. "The Professional-Middle Class," *Radical America* 11(2).

Emmanuel, Arghiri. 1972. *Unequal Exchange: A Study of the Imperialism of Trade*. New York: Monthly Review Press.

Erikson, Robert and John Goldthorpe. 1992. *The Constant Flux: A Study of Class Mobility in Industrial Societies*. New York: Clarendon Press.

Finegold, K., & Skocpol, T. 1995. *State and Party in America's New Deal*. Madison: University of Wisconsin Press.

Flacks, Richard. 1995. "The Party's Over So What Is To Be Done?" in Larana, Johnston and Gusfield, eds., *New Social Movements: From Ideology to Identity*. Philadelphia: Temple University Press.

Flacks, Richard. 1988. *Making History: The American Left and the American Mind*. New York: Columbia University Press.

Flacks, Richard. 1972. "Toward a Socialist Sociology," *Insurgent Sociologist* 2(2): 18–27.

Foner, Laura, and Genovese, Eugene, eds. 1969. *Slavery in the New World*. Englewood Cliffs, N.J.: Prentice-Hall.

Fourcade-Gourinchas, Marion. 2003. "The Construction of a Global Profession: The Case of Economics," unpublished manuscript, Department of Sociology, University of California, Berkeley.

Frank, Andre Gunder 1969. *Latin America: Underdevelopment or Revolution*. New York: Monthly Review Press.

Frank, Andre Gunder. 1967. *Capitalism and Underdevelopment in Latin America*. New York: Monthly Review Press.

Freudenburg, William R. and Robert Gramling. 1994. *Oil in Troubled Waters: Perceptions, Politics, and the Battle over Offshore Drilling*. Albany NY: State University of New York Press.

Fung, Archon and Erik Wright. 2003. *Deepening Democracy*. London: Verso Books.

Gans, H. 1997. "Best-sellers by sociologists: An exploratory study," *Contemporary Sociology*, 26, 131–135.

Garfinkel, Harold. 1967. *Studies in Ethnomethodology*. Englewood Cliffs: Prentice-Hall

Geertz, Clifford. 1963. "The Integrative Revolution: Primordial Sentiments and Civil Politics in New States," in *Old Societies and New States*, edited by Clifford Geertz. New York: Free Press of Glencoe.

Geschwender, James. 1978. *Racial Stratification in America*. Dubuque, Iowa: William C. Brown.

Gibson-Graham, J.K. 1996. *The End of Capitalism (as we knew it)*. Oxford: Blackwell.

Giddens, Anthony. 1973. *The Class Structure of the Advanced Societies*. New York: Harper & Row.

Gillman, J. 1965. *Prosperity in Crisis*. New York: Marzani and Munsell.

Gintis, Herbert. 1974. "Welfare Criteria with Endogenous Preferences. The Economics of Education," *International Economic Review*, June.

Gintis, Herbert. 1972. "Alienation and Power," in James Weaver (ed.), *Readings in Political Economy*, Rockleigh, N.J.: Allyn and Bacon.

Gintis, Herbert. 1971. "Education, Technology and the Characteristics of Worker Productivity," *American Economic Review*, May.

Glazer, Nathan, and Moynihan, Daniel P., eds. 1975. *Ethnicity: Theory and Experience*. Cambridge, Mass.: Harvard University Press.

Glyn, Andrew and Sutcliffe, Bob. 1972. *British Capitalism, Workers and the Profit Squeeze*. Hammondsworth: Penguin.

Glyn, Andrew and Sutcliffe, Bob. 1971. "The Critical Condition of British Capital," *New Left Review* 66:3–33.

Gold, David, Clarence Lo, and Erik Olin Wright. 1975. "Some Recent Developments in Marxist Theories of the State," *Monthly Review*.

Goldberg, Marilyn P. 1971. "The Economic Exploitation of Women," in David M. Gordon (ed.), *Problems in Political Economy*. Lexington, Mass.: D.C. Heath and Co.

Goldthorpe, John. 2002. "Occupational Sociology, Yes: Class Analysis, No," *Acta Sociologica* 45: 211–217.

Goldthorpe, John. 2000. "Rent, Class Conflict, and Class Structure," *American Journal of Sociology* 105: 1572–1582.

Goldthorpe, John. 1996. "Class Analysis and the Reorientation of Class Theory," *British Journal of Sociology* 45: 481–506.

Goldthorpe, John. 1987. *Social Mobility and Class Structure in Modern Britain*. 2nd ed. Oxford: Clarendon Press.

Goldthorpe, John. 1982. "On the Service Class, its Formation and Future," pp. 162–185 in A. Giddens and G. Mackenzie, eds., *Social Classes and the Division of Labor*. New York: Cambridge University Press.

Goldthorpe, John and Gordon Marshall. 1992. "The Promising Future of Class Analysis," *Sociology* 26: 381–400.

Goldthorpe, John, David Lockwood, David Beckhoffer, and Jennifer Platt. 1969. *The Affluent Worker in the Class Structure*. Cambridge: Cambridge University Press.

Gordon, David M. 1972. *Theories of Poverty and Unemployment*. Lexington, Mass.: D.C. Heath.

Gordon, Linda. 1970. *Families*. Cambridge, Mass.: A Bread and Roses Publication.

Gordon, Milton M. 1978. *Human Nature, Class and Ethnicity*. New York: Oxford University Press.

Gordon, Milton M. 1964. *Assimilation in American Life*. New York: Oxford University Press.

Gorz, Andre. 1982. *Farewell to the Working Class*. London: Pluto Press.

Gouldner, Alvin. 1970. *The Coming Crisis of Western Sociology*. New York: Basic Books.

Greely, Andrew M. 1978. "Group Formation and the Cultural Division of Labor," *American Journal of Sociology* 84:293–318.

Greely, Andrew M. 1974. *Ethnicity in the United States*. New York: John A. Wiley.

Grusky, David and Jesper Sørensen. 1998. "Can Class Analysis Be Salvaged," *American Journal of Sociology* 103: 1187–1234.

Grusky, David and Kim Weeden. 2001. "Decomposition without Death: A Research Agenda for a New Class Analysis," *Acta Sociologica* 44: 203–218.

Hamilton, Gary. 1978. "Pariah Capitalism: A Paradox of Power and Dependence," *Ethnic Groups* 2:1–15.

Harrington, Michael. 1984. *The American Poverty*. New York: Penguin.

Harris, Donald J. 1972. "The Black Ghetto as a Colony: A Theoretical Critique and Alternative Formulation," *Review of Black Political Economy*, 2:3–33.

Harris, Marvin. 1964. *Patterns of Race in the Americas*. New York: Walker.

Hechter, Michael. 1975. *Internal Colonialism: The Celtic Fringe in British National Development, 1536–1966*. Berkeley: University of California Press.

Herndon, James. 1968. *The Way It Spozed to Be*. New York: Simon and Schuster.

Hirsch, Seymour, "On Uncovering the Great Nerve Gas Cover-Up," *Ramparts* (3 July) 12–18.

Hobsbawm, Eric. 1977. "Some Reflections of 'The Break-up of Britain,'" *New Left Review* 105:3–23.

Hodgson, G. 1974. "The Falling Rate of Profit," *New Left Review*, No. 84.

Hoetnik, H. 1967. *Caribbean Race Relations*. London: Oxford University Press.

Hooks, G. 1991. *Forging the Military-Industrial Complex*. Urbana: University of Illinois Press.

Horowitz, Irving Louis. 1993. *The Decomposition of Sociology*. New York: Oxford University Press.

Howe, Florance, and Paul Lauter. 1970. "The Schools Are Rigged for Failure," *New York Review of Books*, June 20.

Hunt, Allen. 1977. "Theory And Politics In The Identification Of The Working Class," in Alan Hunt, ed., *Class and Class Structure*. London: Lawrence and Wishart.

Hunter, F. 1959. *Top leadership, U.S.A.* Chapel Hill: University of North Carolina Press.

Isaacs, Harold R. 1975. "Basic Group Identity: the Idols of the Tribe," in *Ethnicity: Theory and Experience*, edited by Nathan Glazer and Daniel P. Moynihan. Cambridge, Mass.: Harvard University Press.

Karier, Clarence; Joel Spring; and Paul C. Violas. 1973. *Roots of Crisis*. Chicago: University of Illinois Press.

Kingston, Paul. 1994. "Are There Classes in the United States?" *Research in Social Stratification and Mobility* 13:3–41.

Klinenberg, Eric. 2003. *Heat Wave*. Chicago: University of Chicago Press.

Kohn, Melvin. 1969. *Class and Conformity: A Study of Values*. Homewood, Illinois: Dorsey.

Krasner, S. 1978. *Defending the National Interest*. Princeton: Princeton University Press.

Kuper, Leo, and Smith, M.G., eds. 1969. *Pluralism in Africa*. Berkeley: University of California Press.

Laclau, Ernesto and Chantal Mouffe. 1985. *Hegemony and Socialist Strategy*. London: Verso.

Laibman, David. 1974. "The Organic Composition of Capital: A Fresh Look at Marxian Accumulation Theory," unpublished Ms.

Larson, Magali Sarfatti. 1977. *The Rite of Professionalism*. Berkeley: University of California Press.

Leggett, John C. 1968. *Class, Race, and Labor: Working Class Consciousness in Detroit*. New York: Oxford University Press.

Lenin, V.I. 1968. *National Liberation, Socialism, and Imperialism: Selected Writings*. New York: International Publishers.

Lenin, V.I. 1939. *Imperialism: The Highest State of Capitalism*. New York: International Publishers.

Leon, Abram. 1970. *The Jewish Question: A Marxist Interpretation*. New York: Pathfinder.

Levine, David. 1973. *Accumulation and Technical Change in Marxian Economics*. Unpublished Ph.D. dissertation, Yale University.

Lieberson, Stanley. 1961. "A Societal Theory of Race and Ethnic Relations," *American Sociological Review* 26:902–910.

Light, Ivan. 1972. *Ethnic Enterprises in America*. Berkeley: University of California Press.

Lipset, Seymour Martin. 2001. "The State of American Sociology," pp. 247–270 in Stephen Cole (ed.), *What's Wrong with Sociology?* New Brunswick, NJ: Transaction Publishers.

Lockwood, David. 1958. *The Blackcoated Worker*. London: Allen & Unwin.

Lundberg, Ferdinand. 1969. *The Rich and the Super-Rich*. New York: Bantam.

MacKinnon, Catharine. 1989. *Toward a Feminist Theory of the State*. Cambridge, Mass.: Harvard University Press.

Mage, S.H. 1963. *The Law of the Falling Tendency of the Rate of Profit*. Unpublished Ph.D. dissertation, Columbia University.

Mandel, Ernest. 1972. "Nationalism and the Class Struggle," *International Socialist Review* 33:19–23, 38–39.

Manela, Roger. 1971. "The Classification of Events in Formal Organizations," Ann Arbor: Institute of Labor and Industrial Relations, mimeo.

Maney, A. and Bykerk, L.G. 1994. *Consumer Politics: Protecting Public Interests On Capitol Hill*. Westport, CT: Greenwood Press.

Mann, M. 1986. *The Sources Of Social Power* (Vol. 1). New York: Cambridge University Press.

Mann, M. 1975. "The ideology of intellectuals and other people in the development of capitalism," in L. Lindberg & R. Alford (eds.), *Stress and Contradiction in Modern Capitalism*. Lexington, MA: Lexington Books.

Mannheim, Karl. 1936. *Ideology and Utopia: An Introduction to the Sociology of Knowledge*. New York: Harcourt, Brace and World.

Marglin, Stephen A. 1974. "What do Bosses Do?" *Review of Radical Political Economics*, Vol. 6, No. 2, Summer.

Martinelli, Alberto. 1973. "Nation States and Multinational Corporations," *Kapitalistate*, No. 1.

Marx, Karl. 1967. *Capital*, Vol. III. New York: New World Paperbacks.

Marx, Karl. 1963. *The Economic and Philosophical Manuscripts of 1844*, in Dirk Struick (ed.), New York: International Publishers.

Marx, Karl. 1962. *Wages, Price and Profit*, in *Selected Works*, Vol. I. Moscow: Foreign Languages Publishing House.

Marx, Karl. 1906. *Capital*, Vol. I (Charles H. Kerr & Company edition). New York: The Modern Library.

Marx, Karl and F. Engels. 1969. *The German Ideology*. New York: International Publishers.

Mattick, Paul. 1969. *Marx and Keynes*. Boston: Porter Sargent.

Mermelstein, David. 1975. *The Economics Crisis Reader*. New York: Random House.

Meyer, Peter J. 1972. "Schooling and the Reproduction of the Social Division of Labor," unpublished honors thesis, Harvard University, March.

Mills, C. Wright. 1959. *The Sociological Imagination*. New York: Oxford University Press.

Mills, C. Wright. 1956. *The Power Elite*. New York: Oxford University Press.

Mills, C. Wright. 1951. *White Collar*. New York: Oxford University Press.

Mitchell, Juliet. 1972. *Woman's Estate*. New York: Pantheon.

Molotch, Harvey. 1976. "The City as a Growth Machine," *American Journal of Sociology*, 82, 309–330.

Molotch, Harvey. 1970. "Oil in Santa Barbara and Power in America," *Sociological Inquiry* 40 (Winter): 131–144.

Molotch, Harvey and Marilyn Lester. 1975. "Accidental News: The Great Oil Spill as Local Occurrence and National Event," *American Journal of Sociology* 81: 235–260.

Molotch, Harvey and Marilyn Lester. 1974. "News as Purposive Behavior: On the Strategic Use of Routine Events, Accidents and Scandals," *American Sociological Review* 39: 101–113.

Naim, Tom. 1975. "The Modern Janus," *New Left Review* 94:3–29.

Nee, Victor. 1969. *Cultural Revolution at Peking University*. New York: Monthly Review Press.

Nicolaus, Martin. 1970. "Proletariat and Middle Class in Marx," in J. Weinstein and D. Eakins, eds., *For a New America*. New York: Random House.

Nisbet, Robert. 1959. "The Decline and Fall of Social Class," *Pacific Sociological Review* 2:11–17.

Noble, C. 1986. *Liberalism at Work: The Rise and Fall of OSHA*. Philadelphia: Temple University Press.

Noble, David. 1979. "The PMC: a Critique," in Pat Walker, ed., *Between Labor and Capital*. Boston: South End Press.

Novak, Michael. 1971. *The Rise of the Unmeltable Ethnics*. New York: Macmillan.

O'Connor, James. 1973. *The Fiscal Crisis of the State*. New York: St. Martin's Press.

Offe, Claus. 1974. "The Theory of the State and the Problem of Policy Formation," unpublished manuscript.

Offe, Claus. 1973. "The Structural Problem of the State," unpublished manuscript.

Offe, Claus. 1970. *Leistungsprinzip und Industrielle Arbeit*. Frankfort: Europaische Verlaganstalt.

O'Hare, William P. 1985. "Poverty in America: Trends and New Patterns," *Population Bulletin*, Vol. 40, No. 3 (June). Washington, D.C.: Population Reference Bureau.

Omi, Michael and Howard Winant. 1986. *Racial Formation in the United States: From the 1960s to the 1980s*. New York: Routledge and Kegan Paul.

Oppenheimer, Martin. 1974. "The Sub-Proletariat: Dark Skins and Dirty Work," *Insurgent Sociologist* 4:7–20.

Oppenheimer, Martin, Martin J. Murray, and Rhonda F. Levine. 1991. "Introduction: the Movement and the Academy," pp. 3–14 in Martin Oppenheimer, Martin J. Murray, and Rhonda F. Levine (eds.), *Radical Sociologists and the Movement: Experiences, Lessons, and Legacies*. Philadelphia: Temple University Press.

Orloff, A.S. 1993. *The Politics of Pensions: a Comparative Analysis of Britain, Canada, and the United States, 1880–1940*. Madison: University of Wisconsin Press.

Ossowski, Stanislav. 1963. *Class Structure in the Social Consciousness*. New York: Free Press.

Page, B. 2002. "The Semi-Sovereign Public," in J. Manza, F. Cook, & B. Page (eds.), *Navigating public opinion: Polls, policy, and the future of American democracy* (pp. 325–344). New York: Oxford University Press.

Page, B. and Shapiro, R.Y. 1992. *The Rational Public: Fifty Years of Trends in Americans' policy preferences*. Chicago: University of Chicago Press.

Paluski, Jan and Malcolm Waters. 1996. "The Death of Class," *Theory and Society* 25:667–691.

Parker, Richard. 1972. *The Myth of the Middle Class*. New York: Liveright.

Patterson, Orlando. 1977. *Ethnic Chauvinism: The Reactionary Impulse*. New York: Stein and Day.

Petras, Elisabeth M. 1980. "Toward a Theory of International Migration: The New Division of Labor," in *Sourcebook on the New Immigration*, edited by R.S. Bryce-Laporte. New Brunswick, N.J.: Transaction Books.

Piven, Frances and R.A. Cloward. 1985. *The New Class War*. New York: Pantheon.

Portes, Alejandro. 1978. "Migration and Underdevelopment," *Politics and Society* 8, 1:1–48.

Poulantzas, Nicos. 1975. *Classes in Contemporary Capitalism*. London: New Left Books.

Poulantzas, Nicos. 1973. *Political Power and Social Classes*. London: NLB.

Przeworski, Adam. 1977. "The Proletariat Into a Class: the Process of Class Formation From Karl Kautsky's the Class Struggle to Recent Controversies," *Politics and Society* 7(4).

Putnam, Robert. 2000. *Bowling Alone*. New York: Simon and Schuster.

Reich, Michael. 1972. "The Economics of Racism," in *The Capitalist System*, edited by Richard C. Edwards, Michael Reich, and Thomas Weisskopf. Englewood Cliffs, N.J.: Prentice-Hall.

Rex, John. 1970. *Race Relations in Sociological Theory*. New York: Schocken.

Rinder, Irwin. 1958–1959. "Strangers in the Land: Social Relations in the Status Gap," *Social Problems* 6:253–260.

Rist, Ray C. 1970. "Student Social Class and Teacher Expectations: The Self-Fulfilling Prophesy in Ghetto Education," *Harvard Educational Review*, August.

Rodgers Jr. and Harrell, R. 1986. *Poor Women, Poor Families*. New York: M.E. Sharpe.

Roediger, David R. 1991. *The Wages of Whiteness: Race and the Making of the American Working Class*. London: Verso.

Rose, Stephen J. 1986. *The American Profile Poster*. New York: Pantheon.

Rosenthal, Burton E. 1972. "Educational Investments in Human Capital: The Significance of Stratification in the Labor Market," unpublished thesis for Harvard University.

Roszak, Theodore. 1995. *The Making of a Counter Culture: Reflections on the Technocratic Society and Its Youthful Opposition*. Berkeley: University of California Press.

Rowthorn, Bob. 1974. "Skilled Labor in the Marxist System," *BCSE*, September, pp. 25–45.

Rueschemeyer, Dietrich and James Mahoney. 2000. "A Neo-Utilitarian Theory of Class?" *American Journal of Sociology* 105: 1583–1591.

Saul, John S. 1979. "The Dialectic of Class and Tribe," *Race and Class* 20:347–372.

Saxton, Alexander. 1990. *The Rise and Fall of the White Republic*. London: Verso.

Schutz, Alfred, and Themas Luckman. 1973. *The Structures of the Life-World*. Evanston, Illinois: Northwestern University Press.

Shelley, M.C. 1983. *The Permanent Majority: The Conservative Coalition in the United States Congress*. University, Ala.: University of Alabama Press.

Shoup, L. 1977. "The Council on Foreign Relations and American Policy in Southeast Asia, 1940–1973," *Insurgent Sociologist*, 7:19–30.

Shoup, L. 1975. "Shaping the Postwar World: The Council on Foreign Relations and United States War Aims," *Insurgent Sociologist*, 5:9–52.

Sidel, Ruth. 1986. *Women and Children Last – The Plight of Poor Women in Affluent America*. New York: Viking.

Simpson, George C., and Yinger, J. Milton. 1972. *Racial and Cultural Minorities: An Analysis of Prejudice and Discrimination*. New York: Harper and Row.

Skocpol, Theda. 2003. *Diminished Democracy*. Norman: University of Oklahoma Press.

Skocpol, T. 1980. "Political responses to capitalist crisis: Neo-Marxist theories of the state and the case of the New Deal," *Politics and Society*, 10:155–202.

Skotnes, Andor. 1979. "Structural Determination of the Proletariat and the Petty Bourgeoisie: a Critique of Poulantzas," *Insurgent Sociologist* 9(1).

Smith, Gene M. 1970. "Non-intelligence Correlates of Academic Performance," mimeo.

Smith, Gene M. 1967a. "Usefulness of Peer Ratings of Personality in Educational Research," *Educational and Psychological Measurements*.

Smith, Gene M. 1967b. "Personality Correlates of Academic Performance in Three Dissimilar Populations," Proceedings of the 77th Annual Convention, *American Psychological Association*.

Smith, M.G. 1965. *The Plural Society in the West Indies*. Berkeley: University of California Press.

Sørensen, Aage. 2000. "Toward a Sounder Basis for Class Analysis," *American Journal of Sociology* 105:1523–1558.

Sparr, Pamela. 1987. "Re-Evaluating Feminist Economics: Feminization of Poverty Ignores Key Issues," *Dollars & Sense*, Special Issue on Women and Work.

Stallard, Karin et al. 1983. *Poverty in the American Dream: Women and Children First*. Boston: South End Press.

Staples, Robert. 1985. "Beyond the Black Family: The Trend Toward Singlehood," pp. 99–105 in R. Staples, ed., *The Black Family*. Belmont, Ca.: Wadsworth.

Stone, Katherine. 1974. "The Origins of Job Structures in the Steel Industry," *Review of Radical Political Economics*, Vol. 6, No. 2, Summer.

Sweezy, Paul. 1942. *The Theory of Capitalist Development*. New York: MR Press.

Sweezy, Paul. 1974. "Some Problems in the Theory of Capital Accumulation," *Monthly Review*, Vol. 26, No. 1.

Szasz, A. 1984. "Industrial Resistance to Occupational Safety and Health Regulation: 1971–1981," *Social Problems*, 32, 103–116.

Szymanski, Albert. 1976. "Racial Discrimination and White Gain," *American Sociological Review* 41:403–414.

Taubman, Paul, and Terance Wales. 1972. "Earnings: Higher Education, Mental Ability, and Screening," unpublished paper for the University of Pennsylvania, May.

Therborn, Göran. 2002. "Class Perspectives: Shrink or Widen?" *Acta Sociologica* 45: 221–225.

Thorton Dill, Bonnie. 1987. "Race, Class, and Gender: Prospects for All-Inclusive Sisterhood," pp. 204–213 in R. Takaki, ed., *From Different Shores – Perspectives on Race and Ethnicity in America*. New York: Oxford University Press.

Tuchman, Gaye. 1972. "Objectivity as Strategic Ritual," *American Journal of Sociology*.

Turner, Stephen and Jonathan Turner. 1990. *The Impossible Science*. Newbury Park, Ca.: Sage Publications.

Unger, Roberto. 1998. *Democracy Realized: the Progressive Alternative*. London: Verso.

Vanneman, Reeve. 1977. "The occupational composition of American classes," *American Journal of Sociology* 44(1).

Vogel, D. 1989. *Fluctuating fortunes: The political power of business in America*. New York: Basic Books.

Wallerstein, Immanuel. 1985. "The Construction of Peoplehood: Racism, Nationalism, Ethnicity," mimeograph paper, Fernand Braudel Center for the Study of Economies, Historical Systems and Civilization, SUNY Binghamton, New York.

Wallerstein, Immanuel. 1983. *Historical Capitalism*. London: Verso.

Warner, W. Lloyd, and Srole, Leo. 1945. *The Social System of American Ethnic Groups*. New Haven: Yale University Press.

Weber, Max. 1982. "Determination of Class Situation by Market Situation," pp. 60–61 in A. Giddens and D. Held, eds., *Class, Power and Conflict*. Berkeley: University of California Press.

Willheim, Sidney. 1971. *Who Needs the Negro?* New York: Doubleday Anchor.

Williams, Eric. 1944. *Capitalism and Slavery*. Chapel Hill: University of North Carolina Press.

Williams, Robin M., Jr. 1964. *Strangers Next Door: Ethnic Relations in American Communities*. Englewood Cliffs, N.J.: Prentice-Hall.

Williamson, Thad, David Imbroscio, and Gar Alperovitz. 2003. *Making a Place for Community: Local Democracy in a Global Era*. New York: Routledge.

Wilson, William J. 1978. *The Declining Significance of Race*. Chicago: University of Chicago Press.

Wolpe, Harold. 1970. "Industrialism and Race in South Africa," in *Race and Racialism*, edited by Sami Zubaida. London: Tavistock.

Wright, Erik Olin. 2000. "Class, Exploitation, and Economic Rents," *American Journal of Sociology* 105:1559–1571.

Wright, Erik Olin. 1997. *Class Counts*. Cambridge: Cambridge University Press.

Wright, Erik Olin. 1985. *Classes*. London: New Left Books.

Wright, Erik Olin. 1982. "The Status of the Political in the Concept of Class Structure," *Politics and Society* 11(3).

Wright, Erik Olin. 1980. "Varieties of Marxist Conceptions of Class Structure," *Politics and Society* 9(3).

Wright, Erik Olin. 1979. *Class Structure and Income Determination*. New York: Academic Press.

Wright, Erik Olin. 1978. *Class, Crisis and the State*. London: New Left Books.

Wright, Erik Olin. 1976. "Class Boundaries in Advanced Capitalist Societies," *New Left Review* 98.

Yaffe, David. 1973a. "The Marxian Theory of Crisis, Capital and the State," *Economy and Society*, Vol. 2, pp. 186–232.

Yaffe, David. 1973b. "The Crisis of Profitability, A Critique of the Glyn-Sutcliffe Thesis," *New Left Review*, No. 80, pp. 45–62.

Yancey, William L., Erikson, Eugene P., and Juliani, Richard N. 1976. "Emergent Ethnicity. A Review and Reformulation," *American Sociological Review* 41:391–403.

Young, T.R. and Timothy Lehman. 1972. "Conflict Methodology," paper presented at meetings of the American Sociological Association, August, New Orleans.

Zaretsky, Eli. 1973. "Capitalism and Personal Life," in *Socialist Revolution*, January–April.

# Index